D0498336

FAIR GREECE, SAD RELIC

TERENCE SPENCER

FAIR GREECE
SAD RELIC

Literary Philhellenism from
Shakespeare to
Byron

Fair Greece! sad relic of departed worth!
Immortal, though no more; though fallen, great!
Who now shall lead thy scattered children forth,
And long-accustomed bondage uncreate?

Childe Harold's Pilgrimage

OCTAGON BOOKS

A DIVISION OF FARRAR, STRAUS AND GIROUX

New York   1973

First published in 1954

Reprinted 1973
by special arrangement with Weidenfeld & Nicholson, Ltd.

OCTAGON BOOKS
A DIVISION OF FARRAR, STRAUS & GIROUX, INC.
19 Union Square West
New York, N. Y. 10003

Library of Congress Catalog Card Number: 73-5940
ISBN 0-374-97557-4

Printed in U.S.A. by
NOBLE OFFSET PRINTERS, INC.
New York, N.Y. 10003

CONTENTS

LIST OF ILLUSTRATIONS

INTRODUCTION

THIS is a survey of the literary contacts between England and the modern country of Greece during the three centuries preceding the romantic enthusiasm which greeted the Greek national revival in the early nineteenth century. To examine these relations provides a supplement to the classical background of English literature, and one which is, I think, generally and unjustly ignored. The country of Greece and the people of Greece, as much as the monuments and the literature, were among the remarkable ruins which had survived from Antiquity; and as such, before the Revolution, they received the attention of the erudite, the literary, and the sentimental.

"Philhellenism" is the name which, from the ancient Greek usage of *philhellên*, has been accepted in most European languages to describe that devotion to the welfare of Greece, and that faith in her future, which was widespread among foreigners in the early nineteenth century. The enthusiasm was derived from a classical partiality in favour of the supposed descendants of the ancient pagan Hellenes; and it inspired the notion that there existed an urgent moral obligation for Europe to restore liberty to Greece as a kind of payment for the civilization which Hellas had once given to the world. The Philhellenes, particularly so named, were those who, from many countries in Europe and America, dutifully and Byronically set out for Greece on the outbreak of the national revolution in 1821, with high hopes, if not of re-creating the republics of Pericles and Lycurgus, at any rate of releasing an important, interesting and classical people from the cruel oppression of the infidel, and of restoring them to the comity of Christian nations.

The philhellenism of the early nineteenth century deserves detailed investigation because it is one of the very clear instances of a meeting-point between literature and action. Impressions derived from literature (which we can easily study) provoked certain sentiments and opinions (which can be clearly defined), and these sentiments and opinions prompted actions (which can be a matter of direct historical investigation).

In England philhellenism found its best-known expression in the poems of Byron and in Shelley's *Hellas*. I show that (contrary to what is commonly supposed) this attitude to Greece had a long history. By the time Byron arrived in Greece in 1809, the reading public had for many generations been prepared to accept a responsible and prophetic vision of modern Greece, and was willing to regard the contemporary inhabitants of the country as the descendants and representatives of that nation of antiquity whose literature and art had for long been regarded as the foundations of education and taste.

It was in Athens in 1940, as I was spending my leisure hours among the books of George Finlay the philhellene and historian (his library is now in the possession of the British School of Archaeology), while Greece was steeling itself to resist and to endure the tramplings of yet another conquest, that the idea of writing the rise and culmination of philhellenic sentiment first started to my mind. But my original plan was circumscribed to the part played by Byron and his contemporaries in the few decades preceding the Revolution; and though my reading and reflections began to point towards that object, some years have elapsed and several avocations intervened, before I was seriously engaged in the execution of the task. I soon discovered that the opinions of Byron upon Greece had deeper roots than his personal experience during residence and journeys in 1809-1811; that philhellenic opinion was something which existed before the nineteenth century and before the French Revolution; and that he who would chronicle the part played by contemporary Greece in English literature would be compelled to begin not in the eighteenth century, nor yet in the seventeenth, but in the sixteenth century when the curtain, which had fallen with the Ottoman conquest of the Greek lands, became a little less impenetrable. This has expanded my book; but at least I have the satisfaction of having begun at the beginning and of having concluded with the work of the English poet whose writings are the culmination of the sentiments, hopes, and actions I describe.

He who studies Opinion as a background to literature must give his evidence, so far as possible, in the very language of his witnesses. Opinion is not information; and it is very difficult to turn it into information; for Opinion is of too subtle a nature, and often too contradictory, to be translated into general terms without reference to the characteristic ways of expression in each age. This reference can be provided only by authentic quotation. Therefore, in bringing together estimable opinions and in chronicling the habits of thinking and feeling about Greece during some three centuries (from the later fifteenth to the early nineteenth), I have tried to allow my witnesses to speak for themselves, in their own words; and I have generally refrained from composing paraphrases of what was thought and said. The kind of narrative I am here giving can only be written by means of samples. Of course, I hope that I have not omitted anything which the major English writers have said about Greece during the period I have explored; and I believe that I have come across a fair proportion of what is relevant among minor writers. Yet from those authors

uncharitably described by Carlyle as "wooden"—who provide the
background of opinion against which the more interesting authors
expressed themselves—I can merely give occasional specimens. Only
a small number of the opinions and observations which I have collected are here recorded. But I hope that I have selected the most
appropriate. That does not always mean the most amusing, stimulating, and original. On the contrary, it is often among the writers whom
we can least suspect of originality that we obtain the best witnesses of
the ordinary state of opinion in their time. The lively notions of the
eccentric may be interesting and may help to brighten the narrative;
it is foolish to construct from them generalizations about the state of
mind in each period. I have sometimes permitted myself to quote
from French writers, for the comparison between the attitudes of the
French and English to Greece is instructive; and occasionally allusions
to other literatures appear, when they seem appropriate and when
foreign opinion was likely to be influential in England. Thus, the
English attitude to the Turkish menace and to the fate of the Greeks
in the sixteenth century was something based upon European opinion;
and it would be misleading to limit oneself to English statements. The
poetic reactions to the achievements of John Sobieski in 1683, as seen
in Edmund Waller and Vincenzo da Filicaia, show more than the
difference between a minor poet and an important poet; they put
Waller into his European context. Similarly, the group of sentimental
books on Greece by French writers in the later eighteenth century
was known throughout Europe, and provoked rapture or (especially
in England) ridicule; they provide important evidence about the
growth of philhellenism.

A few paragraphs in this book, on Milton and on the legendary
Trojan origin of the Turks, have already appeared, in a slightly
different form, in two articles in *Modern Language Review*. I have to
thank the Editor (Professor C. J. Sisson) for permission to re-use the
material here.

I am not aware that much attention has hitherto been paid to this
subject as a whole, although, of course, in several parts of my book I
find myself treading in well-worn paths; and French scholars have
not neglected the interest which French writers have shown in contemporary Greece. Probably my nearest rival is the late Stanley
Casson's *Greece and Britain* (1943). This was, however, a war-time
picture book, issued with a propagandist intention, and doubtless
written *currente calamo*; for there are innumerable minor mistakes,
confusions, and illogical arrangements of material; and the narrative is
deliberately and intolerably biased. Yet, like almost all that Casson
wrote, it is urbane, intelligent, and delightful; and the writer of a

laborious book which marches along on its footnotes may perhaps be pardoned a glance of envy at Casson's readable little volume, casually illustrated with amusing old engravings and with pretty peeps by modern artists. To the writings of my friend the late William Miller (on whom fell the mantle of Finlay as the historian of medieval and modern Greece) I owe something,[1] as well as to Athenian discussions with him. It is to me a matter of regret that he died before I could send him this book. W. G. Rice's paper on "Early English Travellers in Greece and the Levant"[2] is a valuable piece of work in a narrower field than mine, but the author, recording some of the facts of Levantine travel in the sixteenth and early seventeenth centuries, does not concern himself, as I do, with the consequences of this movement. Some of the writers who have studied romantic Hellenism have a little to say on Philhellenism. B. H. Stern's *The Rise of Romantic Hellenism in English Literature, 1732–1786* (Menasha, 1940), has a merely incidental relation to my subject, although we have read several of the same poets and travellers of the half-century with which his book is concerned. I have read with profit M. L. Clarke's *Greek Studies in England, 1700–1830* (Cambridge, 1945), which has two interesting chapters on eighteenth-century and early nineteenth-century archaeology in Greece; I find myself differing from Professor Clarke's estimates of some of those who wrote about Greece; but his book has provided a valuable background to my study, and praise would be impertinent. W. A. Borst's *Lord Byron's First Pilgrimage*[3] contains two chapters of detailed investigation into Byron's activities in Greece; unfortunately these are mostly outside the limits of my study, but I have found the book accurate and useful. S. A. Larrabee's *English Bards and Grecian Marbles* (New York, 1943) drew my attention to several minor works on Greece which otherwise I might perhaps have overlooked. Three papers by W. C. Brown on "The Popularity of English Travel Books about the Near East, 1775–1825", "English Travel Books, 1775–1825", and "Byron and English Interest in the Near East"[4] have given me very little help; the author does not separate Greece from the rest of the world as the object of sentiment and attention. He takes with too much solemnity the ironic or platitudinous remarks of reviewers and travellers; and he finds significance in the feeble statements of magazine-writers. The same

[1] *Essays in the Latin Orient* (Cambridge, 1921), *The English in Athens before 1821* (a lecture to the Anglo-Hellenic League) (1926).
[2] *Essays and Studies in English and Comparative Literature*, University of Michigan, X (1933).
[3] Yale Studies in English, No. 109 (New Haven, 1948).
[4] *Philological Quarterly*, XV (1936), 70–80 and XVI (1937), 249–71; *Studies in Philology*, XXXIV (1937), 55–64.

defect in the method of collecting relevant evidence of opinion is to
me apparent in two papers (which I may mention although they
strictly speaking do not concern my study) by Virginia Penn on
"Philhellenism in England (1821–1827)".[1] In endeavouring to describe the emotional and cultural background to Philhellenism at the
time of the outbreak of the Revolution in 1821, the author quotes
newspaper articles describing the Greek-Turkish situation in terms
that had been current for centuries, as if they were important and
original contributions to opinion in those years.

These are the principal studies which have, at various points, cut
across mine. But a scholar's deepest debt of gratitude is often due,
not to those who have written books related in subject to his own, but
rather to those who have written books in the same spirit. And so I
would acknowledge what I owe to two scholars who were writing a
century ago, to George Finlay and to the Comte de Laborde. They
knew Greece, ancient and modern, and they knew its literature and its
art; they knew the Greeks and their tormented history. Their
writings do not always, perhaps, possess the tranquil disinterestedness
of some erudite or whimsical studies of recent years. It was to the
company of Finlay and Laborde that this book once aspired; and it is
their company that it has failed to reach.

---

[1] *The Slavonic Review*, XIV (1935–6), 363–71, 647–60.

CHAPTER I

THE DISAPPEARANCE OF GREECE

That famous *Greece*, where learning flourish'd most,
Hath of her Muses long since left to boast;
Th'unlettered *Turk* and rude *Barbarian* trades
Where HOMER sang his lofty *Iliads*.
> Michael Drayton, *To Master George Sandys.*

But mourn (fair Greece) mourn that that sacred band
Which made thee once so famous by their songs,
Forced by outrageous fate, have left thy land,
And left thee scarce a voice to plain thy wrongs.
> William Drummond of Hawthornden, *Sonnet before a poem of Irene.*

. . . These desire nothing but arms & captains, & they would rise against the Turks for their liberty, & would furnish men, money & horses sufficient. This I have learned of divers wise & wealthy Greeks that do wish for this help with tears.
> Sir Thomas Sherley, in Constantinople 1603–5.

AFTER the fall of Constantinople in 1453 and the completion of the Turkish conquest of the Greek mainland in 1460, Greece disappeared as a political entity in Christendom. Western Europe, preoccupied with its own national struggles, paid little attention to the Greek people. The study of the language and literature of the Ancients became part of every educated man's experience after the Renaissance; and it was not doubted that the contemporary inhabitants of the southern part of the Balkan peninsula and the fringe of Asia Minor were the descendants of the contemporaries of Socrates and Dionysius the Areopagite. But the venerable past seemed to bear little relation to the contemptible present. To many, Greece must have then seemed (as perhaps it seems to some classical scholars even nowadays) to be a corner of Europe whose existence almost, along with its language, belonged to a former epoch in the history of the world.

There were several reasons, however, why Englishmen were gradually reminded of the continued existence of Greece as a country and as the home of a nation, and why they were attracted to it. Trade took them there. Religious interests and classical erudition brought them experience of persons and places. From 1500 to 1800 a steadily developing knowledge of contemporary Greece and of its affinities with the past can be traced. But while the Turk was strong, the lands he occupied were difficult of access; and therefore the interest in Greece really begins from the time that the Turks ceased to be a menace to Christendom. The first phase followed the Battle of Lepanto (1571), which, however fruitless in reality, delighted Europe as the first great defeat of the invincible Turk. The second phase began nearly a century later, when the Battle of St. Gotthard in 1664 showed that the Turks were no longer invincible even on land. By the end of the next decade and before the Venetian invasion of the Morea in 1685, energetic travellers and topographers in Greece had laid the foundations of a re-interpretation of ancient literature and art by means of increasing knowledge of the country in which that culture was created. Observation of the manners and customs of the contemporary Greeks led to political speculation about the future of this interesting enslaved nation. Merchants and chaplains, each in their own way, became more deeply concerned with the present condition of the Greek peoples. By the eighteenth century men of sensibility and men of scholarship made the contemporary situation in Greece familiar even to magazine-readers. Both poets and peers swell the procession; until the arrival of Byron in Athens in 1809 brought an English poetical personality of the first rank to a country stirring itself for the second national uprising. It is difficult to find anything that Byron said about modern Greece which had not been familiar in England, in prose and verse, for a long time. Moreover, Byron was only one of a number of English poets (the rest are now obscure names) who, towards the end of the eighteenth and the beginning of the nineteenth century were finding modern Greece an attractive subject for their poetic sensibility. When Byron went to Greece Philhellenism was already "in the air"; it had been breathed into the spirit of the age by poets and periodical-writers, by political pamphleteers and by sentimental scholars. Byron found a reading public sympathetic to his themes. The Maid of Athens had a genealogy; the Mood of Marathon was an inheritance.

Nearly a hundred English and American Philhellenes set out for Greece when the Revolution began in 1821. These were not merely military adventurers. They belonged mostly to the educated classes. They were inspired by a complicated sentiment for Greece which had taken several centuries to develop. What this sentiment was and how it grew up, what nourished it and what weakened it, I now record.

The number of Greek exiles who came to Italy during the first half of the fifteenth century, when the Ottoman attack on Constantinople became imminent, was considerable. Many of them were men of distinction. A rebirth of Hellenism had already begun in Greece during the first half of the fifteenth century, especially during the wonderful years at Mistra when Gemisthos Pletho was teaching his system of neoplatonism. It was this initial Greek renaissance which made more speedy that secondary renaissance which took place in Italy while Greek culture was being annihilated in its own country. It was the scholarship and the intellectual excitement of the circle at Mistra that Pletho and Bessarion brought to Florence.

Some of the exiled Grecians came to England;[1] and more of them were met by the English humanists who journeyed to Italy. At Florence William Grocyn (who for long had the reputation of being the first Englishman to teach Greek at Oxford and was certainly one of the pioneers) shared the instruction given to the young princes Piero and Giovanni dei Medici, not only by Poliziano but also by Demetrius Chalcocondylas. But William Lily went farther afield. He had actually learnt his Greek *en famille* in Rhodes about 1490, before the island was taken from the Knights of St. John by the Turks.[2] A contemporary (Beatus Rhenanus) describes him as a man of very wide learning who knows not only the Greek writers but also the home life of the people, having dwelt for some years in the island of Rhodes.[3] But even before Lily went there to learn his Greek, Rhodes was of particular interest to the English; and early news was received of the great siege by Mahomet II in 1480. An account which had been written in Latin by Gulielmus Caorsin was translated into English by John Kay, the first recorded English poet-laureate, and dedicated to Edward IV (who died in 1483).[4] We are there told that in 1480 Rhodes was stoutly defended by the Order of St. John, "of which the most manliest men were born in England and in France, and in other countries of the west".[5] The Turcopolier (commander of the light-armed soldiers) at the time of the siege, although not necessarily then present, was an Englishman; the features of John

[1] Roberto Weiss, *Humanism in England during the Fifteenth Century* (Blackwell, Oxford, 1941), pp. 144–8.
[2] For Lily's life see J. H. Lupton, *Life of John Colet* (1887).
[3] Gulielmus Lilius, Mori sodalis, . . . Britannus est, vir omnifariam doctus, non modo Graecos autores, sed & eius nationis mores vernaculos domestice notos habens, ut qui in insula Rhodo fuerit aliquot annos commoratus: is nunc ludum literarium, quem Londoni Coletus instituit, magna cum laude exercet.
The Epistle of Beatus Rhenanus printed as an introduction to the first edition (1518) of More's *Epigrammata* by Froben of Basel.
[4] Kay's work was printed about 1482; cf. Duff, *Fifteenth Century English Books* (1917), p. 75.
[5] Reprint of 1870 by Alexander Murray, p. 150.

Kendall have been preserved for us in an Italian medal which was struck in his honour.[1] Similarly in the siege of 1522, when Suleiman at last succeeded in wresting Rhodes from the Knights under the famous Villiers de l'Isle Adam, the English formed a considerable part of the garrison and were commanded by the Grand Master himself.[2]

Although the English men of arts and arms thus had some acquaintance with Greeks, and even had experience of Greek lands, yet during the hundred years following the fall of Constantinople Western Europe had little sentiment to expend on the descendants of the Hellenes. The danger from the Turk was too close. It is probable that only the death of the great conqueror Mahomet II prevented an extensive Turkish invasion of Italy. The Venetian and the Genoese were constantly anxious on account of their trading rights in the Levant. The Eastern Church was heretical in the eyes of the Church of Rome; and the theological conflicts, accompanied by the bitterness of mutual denunciations as schismatics, were things of recent, or obstinately preserved, memory. A disunited Europe, increasingly nationalistic, was in no mood to entertain the old Crusading spirit. The humanist Aeneas Sylvius Piccolomini, who became Pope Pius II (1458–64), fruitlessly spent his short pontificate in endeavouring to arouse the princes of Europe to understand their peril and to safeguard themselves by speedy action against the infidel.[3] Before he died in 1464 he was compelled to witness the dispersal of much of the meagre force he had accumulated at Ancona. The visit of the papal legate, Lorenzo Campeggio, to Henry VIII of England in 1518 to gain support for a crusade against the Turk was a waste of time.

Moreover, the claims of the Byzantine Empire for reinstatement soon became insignificant. In 1494 Andreas Palaeologus, the nephew of the Emperor Constantine who had fallen in the defence of Constantinople in 1453, made over his rights, as heir to the Byzantine throne, to Charles VIII of France. Charles dreamed of conquering the Turkish Empire. From Otranto to Valona was but sixty miles of sea; from Valona to Constantinople was but eighteen days' journey by land; and were there not thousands of Greek Christians, in the heart of the Turkish Empire, who would be ready to take up arms as

[1] Reproduced in G. F. Hill, *Select Italian Medals of the Renaissance in the British Museum* (1915), plate 27, No. 3. Hill says that the medal was probably made in Rome or Florence about 1484–5 (*op. cit.*, p. 11). The legend is: 10. KENDAL. RHODI. TVRCVPELLERIVS. TEMPORE. OBSIDIONIS. TVRCHORVM. M.CCCCLXXX.

[2] Richard Knolles, *Generall Historie of the Turkes* (1603), p. 581. This distinction was long remembered. Davenant in his introductory note to his play, *The Siege of Rhodes* (1656), wrote: "The renown of the English valor made the Grand Master *Villerius* to select their station to be most frequently commanded by himself" (ed. Tupper (1909), p. 191).

[3] See his *Bulla de profectione in Turcos* (*Epist.* ccccxii in *Opera quae extant omnia*, Basel, 1551, p. 914).

soon as their deliverer appeared?[1] However, the failure of Charles's
expedition into Italy, and the prompt intelligence which the Venetians
supplied to the Porte, soon ended this fantasy. And before Andreas
Palaeologus died, childless, in 1502 he had bequeathed his hereditary
rights in the Greek Empire to Ferdinand and Isabella of Spain. It
was not a valuable legacy.

The story is well known how one of the alleged descendants of the
Palaeologi had emigrated to England by 1615 with his daughter and
son-in-law; then married an English wife named Balls, and was buried
in the churchyard of Landulph, on the River Tamar, near Plymouth,
where a monumental inscription, engraved with the imperial arms,
still survives:

> Here lyeth the body of Theodoro Paleologus
> Of Pesaro in Italye descended from ye Imperyail
> Lyne of ye last Christian Emperors of Greece
> Being the sonne of Camilio ye sonne of Prosper
> the sonne of Theodoro the sonne of John ye sonne
> of Thomas second brother to Constantine
> Paleologus the 8th of that name and last of
> yt lyne yt raygned in Constantinople untill sub-
> dewed by the Turkes who married with Mary
> Ye daughter of William Balls of Hadlye in
> Suffolke Gent & had issue 5 children . . . and de-
> parted this life at Clyfton ye 21th of January 1636.[2]

One of his sons is alleged to have fallen at the battle of Naseby, and
a grandson to have died in 1694 in the service of the British Navy.[3]
But the evidence for this is uncertain. Many Greeks assumed high-
sounding names in order to impose themselves upon Western Europe,
and these Palaeologi who settled in Cornwall may have been of any
origin. There are certainly families of the name still in England who
lay claim to a long ancestry. One member of them was a pretender to
the throne of Greece in the nineteenth century. An important

[1] Philippe de Commines, *Memoires*, vii, 17.

[2] *Archaeologia*, XVIII (1817), p. 83 sqq. "Some Observations on a Monumental
Inscription in the Parish Church of Landulph, Cornwall", by Fr. V. Jago. The
inscription is more accurately printed in *Notes and Queries*, VIII (1853), 408.

[3] A correspondence regarding these Palaeologi began in *Notes and Queries* in
1852 (V, 173) and continued for many years. It had a second phase in *The Times
Literary Supplement* in 1943-4 regarding one Ferdinando Palaeologus who was
buried on Barbados in 1678; the tombstone reads:

Here Lyeth ye Body of Ferdinando Palaeologus descended from ye Imperial
Lyne of ye Last Christian Emperors of Greece, Churchwarden of this Parish,
1655-1656, Vestryman, Twentye Years. Died Oct. 3. 1678.

result of the incursion of the Palaeologi into England in the early seventeenth century was to provide some of the material for Quiller-Couch's admirable romance *Sir John Constantine*. It was into such trivialities as the Cornish Palaeologi that the interests of the Byzantine Empire had sunk.

The war between the Christian world and the Moslem world (which was the medieval phase of the age-long conflict between Europe and Asia in the eastern Mediterranean) had changed its character from what it had been in the Middle Ages. As the first example of printing with an ascertained date (Mainz, 1454), a certain amount of notoriety has been awarded the indulgence granted by Nicholas V to those who were prepared to contribute their offerings towards the expenses of the war in defence of Cyprus against the Turks. But these international appeals were rapidly becoming anachronistic. The war had, in fact, ceased to be European; it was no longer a war of Christendom against the infidel for the purpose of recovering the Holy Places of religion. It soon degenerated into a recurrent local conflict between the Venetians and the Turks for the control of a few islands and trading stations in the Greek lands.

It is not altogether surprising, therefore, that a sympathetic concern with the fate of contemporary Greece was not often expressed between the fall of Constantinople and the battle of Lepanto. An occasional lament for the absorbing of Christian Greece into the empire of the infidel, emphasizing the transitoriness of human glories, is what we generally find. The humanist Aeneas Sylvius Piccolomini should perhaps be regarded as an exception, for he wrote to Nicholas V, as soon as the news of the fall of Constantinople reached him, deploring the loss that literature would suffer from the Turkish advance.[1] How many names of famous men will perish! he exclaims. It is a second death to Homer and Pindar and Menander. The whole of Aeneas Sylvius's public career proves how sincerely and how deeply he was moved by the fate of Greece. In another letter he wrote eloquently: "O noble Greece, behold now your end, now you are at last really dead. Alas, how many cities which once enjoyed fame and prosperity are now destroyed! Where is now Thebes, where Athens, where Mycenae, where Larissa, where Sparta, where Corinth, where those other memorable cities of old! If you seek for their walls, you will find not even ruins."[2] With equal feeling Girolamo Vida

---

[1] 12 July 1453. *Epist.* clxii.
[2] O nobilis Graecia, ecce nunc tuum finem, nunc demum mortua es. Heu quot olim urbes fama rebusque potentes sunt extinctae. Vbi nunc Thebae, ubi Athenae, ubi Mycenae, ubi Larissa, ubi Lacedaemon, ubi Corinthiorum ciuitas, ubi alia memoranda oppida, quorum si muros quaeras, nec ruinas inuenias. . . . *Epist.* cxxxi (*Opera quae extant omnia*, Basel, 1551, p. 681).

inserted some lines into his *Poetica* of 1527. We point to the Greeks as having given the models of literary excellence; but what of the Greeks now? "The glory of their language is almost lost; their rulers are removed from their ancestral thrones and driven out; their citizens are forced into exile, seek a refuge in foreign lands, and in poverty wander hither and thither. The victorious Barbarian has taken possession of all they once enjoyed; and Greece now deplores her ruined fortunes."[1] Ariosto jeers at the papal disregard for the plight of hapless Greece. The second of the *Satire* (printed in 1534, the year following his death) is in the form of an epistle to his brother Galasso Ariosti, dissuading him from entering the Church as a profession. What good would it do, the poet asks, even supposing that the aspirant were to become Pope? He would only be concerned with advancing his family to important positions, and would neglect the duty of recovering the lost Greek lands for Christendom. Ariosto suggests that if the Pope must give high rank and office to his relatives, he ought to make them rulers of Arta or the Morea; to drive out the Ottoman would be a task worthy of his high station.[2]

The general silence of the humanists regarding the fate of Greece needs an explanation, however, other than the preoccupation of the princes of Europe with other cares. The date 1453, when the Ottomans captured Constantinople, has become one of the best known of historical landmarks. That it was hardly regarded as such a landmark by contemporaries may not be considered relevant by the modern historian; but in the history of opinion about Greece its apparent unimportance is of some significance. The event was, I believe, ignored by the English chroniclers of the period, who were busy with the wars of York and Lancaster. This was not mere provinciality. The fall of Constantinople was only the last and most important of the Turkish conquests in Europe and the concluding phase of the subjugation of the Greeks, which had been progressing for a century

[1] Jamque fere Inachiae restincta est gloria linguae
Omnis, et Argolici jussi concedere avitis
Sunt pulsi reges soliis, civesque coacti
Diversa exilia, atque alienas quaerere terras.
Huc illuc inopes errant: habet omnia victor
Barbarus, et versis nunc luget Graecia fatis. (i, 143–8.)

[2] Che fia s'avrà la cattedra beata?
  Tosto vorrà li figli o li nepoti
  Levar da la civil vita privata.
Non penserà d'Achivi o d'Epiroti
  Dar lor dominio; non avrà disegno
  In l'Arta o in la Morea farli despoti;
Non cacciarne Ottoman, per dar lor regno,
  Ove da tutta Europa avria soccorso,
  E faria del suo ufficio ufficio degno. (ii, 208–216.)

and a half. Before his death in 1326 Othman had made himself master of nearly all the lands of the Asiatic Greeks; and in 1399 his great-grandson Bayezid I (subsequently to be familiar to Shakespeare's contemporaries as Tamburlaine's caged victim) had conquered northern and central Greece; so that in the fifteenth century the Emperor at Constantinople could claim suzerainty over only Salonica, Athens, and the Morea. Moreover, the disjointed condition of the Greek lands hardly deserved the name of a "Greek" empire. They were ruled by a miscellaneous group of tyrants—the Greek emperors of the family of Palaeologus and their relations in the Morea, Frankish princes and dukes, Venetian and Genoese signiors. The coming of the Ottomans was merely the substitution of one tyranny for another. A lament for the servile condition of the Greeks could have begun long before 1453; and when in 1456 Athens passed from the last Frankish Duke into the hands of the Moslems without a blow being struck in her defence, Europe spared not a tear, not a thought, for the city of Pallas Athene in her hard necessity.[1]

Thus, although the siege and conquest of Constantinople were a stirring episode, and threw down a challenge to Western Europe to unite in defence of Christendom, the truth is that few of the events connected with the conquest of Morea, Athens, the Peloponnesus, and the Islands, were of a nature to arouse any sentiments in the rest of Europe. The Greeks, as a nation, temporarily disappeared from history. No instances of patriotic despair (observed the historian George Finlay) ennobled the records of their subjection.[2] This perhaps is exaggerated, for there were stories of Greek patriotism in circulation. Bandello in one of his *Novelle* tells of the damsel Marulla, daughter of one Demetrius, who distinguished herself at the siege of Lemnos by the Turks[3] and was congratulated and rewarded by the Venetians for her conduct. Bandello declares that this Grecian heroine deserved to be compared with the happiest instances of feminine excellence and accomplishments recorded in the annals of either Greece or Rome.[4] But broadly speaking, Finlay was right. The lack of organized resistance by the inhabitants of Greece was interpreted as national apathy. For us to remark on the absence of any philhellenic sentiment abroad would be anachronistic.

Furthermore, the sixteenth-century view of the Greek cause was marred by a curious notion regarding the origin of the Turks. In narrating the Tale of Troy divine, medieval sentiment was generally

---

[1] Laborde, *Athènes*, i, 4.
[2] *The History of Greece under Othoman and Venetian Domination* (1856), p. 6.
[3] Presumably in the wars which led to the ceding of Lemnos to the Turks in 1478.
[4] meritava essere aguagliata a qualunque altra donna di quelle che piu famose furono, così de le greche come latine. (IV, xviii.)

favourable to the Trojans and hostile to the Greeks. This bias was, of course, mostly due to the legendary descent of many of the nations of Europe from Trojan exiles. But in the fifteenth and sixteenth centuries the contemporary situation in the Greek lands gave a new turn to this pro-Trojan feeling. It was apparently widely believed that the Turkish conquest of Greece was in some way a revenge for the Grecian conquest of Troy about two and a half thousand years before.[1] The identification of the Turks with the Trojans was inviting. In the first place, the Trojans had been a powerful nation in Asia Minor; and the Turks had been ruling in that part of the world for a long time. Moreover, the name for the Trojans which had been made widely familiar by Virgil (although it was not found in Homer) was *Teucri*; to associate this with the *Turci* or *Turcae* (Latin) or *Turchi* (Italian) was easy.[2] Cardinal Isidore, who was present at the siege of Constantinople in 1453 and whose eye-witness account is preserved in a letter printed in Bernard von Breydenbach's *Peregrinatio in terram sanctam* (1486), actually named the Sultan Mahomet II as prince of the Trojans (*Teucrorum princeps et dominus*).[3]

It is possible that the Greeks themselves (speculating in the manner of Herodotus) assisted in spreading this unfortunate interpretation of historical events. Laonicus Chalcocondylas in his account of the siege of Constantinople, written a few years after the event, compared it with the siege of Troy; it was commonly believed, he said, that "the barbarians" wrought this calamity upon Constantinople in revenge for the destruction of Troy by the Greeks; and by the "Romans" (that is, in the West) it was firmly believed that this was so.[4]

On the assumption that the Turks were the representatives of the

[1] See T. Spencer, "Turks and Trojans in the Renaissance" (*Modern Language Review*, XLVII (1952), pp. 330–3). There is also a discussion of this idea, from rather a different point of view, by A. Eckhardt in the Hungarian periodical *Körösi Csoma Archivum*, II (Budapest, 1926–32), pp. 422–33 ("La légende de l'origine troyenne des Turcs"). I have to thank Professor Bernard Lewis for drawing my attention to this paper.

[2] Gibbon condescended, in a derisive note, to mention that this idea had been current. (*Decline and Fall*, chapter lxviii; ed. J. B. Bury, 1900, vii, 193.)

[3] Audite et notum sit vobis quod praecursor veri Antichristi, Teucrorum princeps et dominus, servus autem tot dominorum quot vicinorum, cujus nomen est Mahumet, inimicus crucis Christi, haeres rei et nominis illius primi pseudo-prophetae, *etc.* Thirteenth folio from end, verso (Latin normalized). The letter was subsequently reprinted in several histories and collections of Turkish tracts; also in Migne, *Patrologia*, Series Graeca, vol. clix, col. 953.

[4] viii, 214. (Migne, *Patrologia*, Series Graeca, vol. clix, col. 397 C). This was available in western Europe in a French translation printed at Paris in 1584 (*L'histoire de la decadence de l'empire grec, et establissement de celuy des Turcs ... De la traduction de Blaise de Vigenere Bourbonnois*), where the relevant passage appears on p. 532. See likewise Leonardus of Chios in his *Epistola de expugnatione Constantinopolitanae urbis* (Migne, vol. clix, col. 927 B), and others.

Trojans, some of the medieval pro-Trojan sentiment survived in considering the conflict between the Turks and Greeks, although this was entirely at variance, one would have supposed, with natural Christian sympathies. The continuators of the Chronicles of Enguerran de Monstrelet printed a letter which was alleged to have been written, in Latin and in French, by Mahomet II to Pope Nicholas V (1447–55) complaining of the crusade which was being preached in Europe: "We are surprised that the Italians are against us, and we can hardly believe it. For we have a natural inclination to love them. They draw their origin from the blood of Troy and have thence their original nobility and power. Now, we are the ancient heirs of that same blood and power, and our ancestors, who were the issue of the great king Priam and his line, have increased and improved them. We therefore have the intention of extending our empire into parts of Europe, in accordance with the promises made to our ancestors by our gods. We have also the intention of rebuilding Troy and of avenging the blood of Hector by reducing to subjection the empire of Greece and uniting it to the realm of our god Pallas [sic]; and we shall punish the heirs of the wicked men who destroyed Troy."[1]

This was repeated with no hint of incredulity in the serious treatise of Innocent Gentillet (d. 1595) against Machiavelli, *Discours sur les moyens de bien gouverner et maintenir en bonne paix un Royaume ou autre Principauté* (Geneva, 1576), where we are told that the Sultan, writing in 1453, declared "that it was the Jews who had wickedly crucified Christ. And as for himself, he was not descended from the Jews but from the blood of the Trojans, from whom the Italians say that they also are descended. Their duty should be, both of them, rather to restore Troy and to avenge the blood of their ancestor Hector upon the Greeks, than to make war against each other."[2]

[1] Nous esmerueillons aussi et doutons que les Ytaliens se sont mys contre nous. Comme il soit ainsi que nous auons inclination naturelle a les aymer. Car ilz sont ains yssus du sang de Troye & en ont leur primitiue noblesse & seigneurie. Duquel sang & seigneurie nous sommes anciens hoirs & les nostres auoir este augmentateurs & acroisseurs lesquelz estoient yssus du grant roy Priamus & de sa ligne. En laquelle nous sommes nez & auons intention de mener nostre seigneurie et empire es parties d'Europe selon les promesses que noz peres ont ouyes de noz dieux. Nous auons aussi intention de reparer Troye la grant & de venger le sang de Hector / de la royne Yxion (*lege* Ylion, *i.e.* Ilione, *cf.* Virgil, *Aen.* i, 653) en subiugant a nous l'empire de Grece & en l'unissant a l'estat de nostre dieu Palas / & pugnirons les hoirs des transgresseurs. Paris, 1512, 3 vols. (vol. iii, folio ccxxiii, verso); apostrophes and capitals have been added.

[2] que c'estoyent les Iuifs qui auoyent à tort crucifié Iesus Christ. Et quant à luy, qu'il n'estoit point descendu des Iuifs, mais du sang des Troyens, duquel les Italiens se disent aussi estre descendus. Et que leur deuoir seroit des vns & des autres de restaurer plustost Troye la grand', & venger la mort de Hector leur ancestre sur les Grecs, que de se faire la guerre, comme de sa part il estoit apres à le faire, ayant desia subiugué la pluspart de la Grece. III, i. (p. 262). This work

The sceptical Montaigne was in this matter as credulous as the rest; at least, he does not doubt the existence of the correspondence. In his essay "of the worthiest and most excellent men" he declares that no glory can compare with Homer's; indeed, most nations seek to derive themselves from his inventions. "For Mahomet II wrote to our Pope Pius II" [by now it is the humanist Pope, Aeneas Sylvius Piccolomini, who is the recipient of the Sultan's letter]: "I am amazed", said he, "that the Italians should band against me, seeing that we have our common origin from the Trojans, and that I have, as they have, an interest in avenging the blood of Hector upon the Greeks, whom they take upon themselves to favour against me."[1]

Of course, the learned might cast doubt on this genealogy of the Turks. For example, Aeneas Sylvius Piccolomini, unwilling that any false sentiment about the Turks should interfere with his intended European crusade, did what he could to stamp out the error. In his historical work *Europa*, written about 1458, he declared: "I notice that many writers in our time, not only story-tellers and poets but also historians, fall into the error of calling the Turks by the name of the *Teucri*. I suppose that they are influenced by the fact that the Turks are now in possession of Troy, which the *Teucri* once inhabited."[2] Likewise, Andrea Cambini, whose little *Libro . . . della origine de Turchi* was published at Florence in 1529 and soon translated into English, scornfully alluded to the notion that the *Turchi* were the same as the *Teucri*. This was held by some people, he said, "for that they have seen them rule in those parts where the city of Troy once was".[3] On the whole, a Scythian origin was thought to be more likely,[4] especially if the present conduct of the Turks was

was translated by Simon Patericke as *A Discourse upon the meanes of well governing and maintaining in good peace, a kingdome* (London, 1602), in which the relevant passage appears on p. 148.

[1] Mahumet, second de ce nom, Empereur des Turcs, escriuant à nostre Pape Pie second: Ie m'estonne, dit-il, comment les Italiens se bandent contre moy, attendu que nous auons nostre origine commune des Troyens, & que i'ay comme eux interest de venger le sang d'Hector sur les Grecs, lesquels ils vont fauorisant contre moy. Livre II, chapitre xxvi (ed. F. Strowski, Bordeaux, 1906, tom. II, p. 569). Pierre Bayle remembered this passage and quoted it in his *Dictionnaire Historique et Critique* (1696), s.v. "Acarnanie", Note B (5th ed., 1740, I, 40), with the comment "Voiez comment des maux chimériques, forgés par des Poëtes, ont servi d'apologie à des maux réels".

[2] Video complures aetatis nostrae non autores aut poëtas duntaxat, uerum etiam historicos eo errore teneri, ut Teucrorum nomine Turcas appellent. Credo eos idcirco motos, quoniam Turcae Troiam possident, quam Teucri coluere. Cap. iv (*Opera quae extant omnia*, Basel, 1551, p. 394). Cf. his *Cosmographia*, cap. c, and *Epist.* cxxxi (*Opera*, pp. 383, 681).

[3] John Shute's translation of this pamphlet in his *Two very notable Commentaries*, folio I (London, 1562).

[4] See, for example, Paolo Giovio, *Commentario dele cose de Turchi* (Venice?, 1538); Raffe Carr's compilation, *The Mahumetane or Turkish Historie* (London, 1600); and others.

compared with the abominations of the Scythians as related by the ancients.

Yet the Trojan ancestry of the Turks made a strong appeal to the imagination.[1] In 1506 the chaplain who accompanied Sir Richard Guildford on his pilgrimage to Jerusalem and wrote an account of it, printed in 1511, gave his opinion that "all the country of Troya is the Turk's own country by inheritance, and that country is properly called now Turkey, and none other. Nevertheless he hath lately usurped Greece, with many other countries, and calleth them all Turkey."[2] Julius Caesar Scaliger in one of his poems precisely parallels the Turkish conquest of Greece with the Roman conquest, both of them apparently of Trojan origin, and both of them a kind of revenge for the sacking of Troy: "Twice has old Ilion been overthrown by Grecian arms; twice has new Greece lamented her ancestors' victories. The first time was when mighty Rome brought back to Troy the descendants of the ancient Trojans; and the second time since the Turks now hold sway there."[3]

Thus the national apathy of the Greeks and the belief that their subjection was a just revenge for the Trojan War provided some salve to the conscience of Western Europe in abandoning a not inconsiderable Christian nation to the oppression of the infidel. It was fairly easy, too, to find explanations for the failure of the Greeks to defend themselves in their treachery to the West. Felix Fabri, the great traveller in the Near East in the fifteenth century, who in 1484

[1] We need not take seriously Pistol's indignant description of Falstaff as "Base Phrygian Turk!" (*The Merry Wives of Windsor*, I, iii, 97).
[2] *The Pylgrymage of Sir Richard Guylforde to the Holy Land*, A.D. *1506*, ed. by Sir Henry Ellis for the Camden Society, 1851, p. 13. The statement was repeated by Richard Torkington who made his journey in 1517; *Ye Oldest Diarie of Englysshe Travell*, ed. by W. J. Loftie (1884), p. 19.
[3]   Bis uetus euersum est Argiuis Ilion armis:
              Bis noua uictores Graecia luget auos:
            Maxima Troianos retulit cum Roma nepotes:
              Atque iterum, imperium cum modo Turcus habet.

Poematia (Lugduni, 1546), p. 382. Of course, this idea had almost completely disappeared by the seventeenth century, and I have only very rarely come across it later. But, as a curiosity, I may note how Lord Macaulay imposed a "Phrygian" nationality on the Turks in his translation (1828) of Vincenzo da Filicaia's canzone on the deliverance of Vienna in 1683:

            And soon, they [the Ottomans] cried, shall Austria bow
              To the dust her lofty brow,
              The princedoms of Almayne
              Shall wear the Phrygian chain;
            In humbler waves shall vassal Tiber roll.

(*Miscellaneous Writings*, 2 vols., 1860, ii, 422). Here Filicaia merely writes:

              E disser: l'Austria doma,
              Domerem poi l'ampia Germania; e all'Ebro
              Fatto vassallo il Tebro. (22–4.)

returned from Palestine for the second time, with Bernard von Breydenbach's party, says that the Greeks "have an exceeding fiery hatred for the Church of Rome; wherefore they have surrendered almost the whole of Greece to the Turks, thus casting away both themselves and their country out of hatred to the Latin Church".[1] Such bitter language can perhaps be regarded as excusable so soon after the ominous advance of the Ottoman to the shores of Italy. But later the Greeks themselves were characteristically ingenious (or to the Europeans they seemed to be so) in explaining their speedy conquest by the Turks and their present utter subjection. That agreeable and doubtless plausible Greek, Christophoros Angelos, who arrived at Yarmouth in 1608 and published his tracts at Oxford and Cambridge, displays some subtlety. The Greeks (he would have us believe) remembered St. John's prophecy (*Rev.* xiii) about the beast rising out of the sea with seven heads and ten crowns, and

> when they saw the Turks come, said, This is the Beast, that Saint John speaketh of, and would not fight with the Turk. They fought a little in the beginning, and afterward yielded; and for this were not carried away captives. In like manner they carried all their goods with them, and bought all of the King of the Turks. This thing also did the Monks, and redeemed their Monasteries, and fields, and houses, and whatsoever they possessed before. Therefore to this day, they retain all their old Books, and observe their Country Laws, and live as the Christians and Monks in former ages.[2]

Purchas, of course, displays indignation at this example of Greek fabulosity, and writes in the margin: "Simple silliness either of this Monk or of this Nation! Or rather base courages palliated with Scripture misapplied. The true cause is, that they, weakened by divisions amongst themselves and from the Latins, and not assisted from Princes abroad, were not able to hold out." What Purchas said was the simple truth. The Greeks were submerged by a powerful foreign invader because they were politically disorganized; because they hated the Italians; because there was no philhellenic sentiment abroad to encourage them; and because Western Europe lacked both the unity and the prudence to make Greece a bulwark against the aggression of the Ottoman against Christendom.

[1] *The Wanderings of Felix Fabri*, translated by Aubrey Stewart (Palestine Pilgrims' Text Society, vol. X, 1892–7), vol. II, pt. ii, p. 387.
[2] Reprinted in *Purchas his Pilgrims*, Glasgow edition, 1905, i, 422.

It was easier, however, to say that the Greeks had so far degenerated from their glorious ancestors that they were not worth troubling about. They fully deserved their fate. Tasso was particularly offensive. In Goffredo's army are two hundred Greeks under their leader Tatino—a mere two hundred says the poet; and these were the only Greeks who accompanied the Latin arms. What a shame, what a disgrace! were not these wars, o Greece, in your neighbourhood? and all you could do was sit as an onlooker, awaiting the end of these mighty happenings! Now that you are in vile servitude, do not complain. It is what you deserve. It is justice upon you, not an outrage.[1] It was in this spirit that Fynes Moryson recorded that "the Greeks are more despised by the Turks than any other Christians, because they lost their liberty and Kingdom basely and Cowardly, making small or no resistance against the Turks' Conquest".[2]

How Europe felt, or how her best minds thought Europe ought to have felt, in the face of the danger in the sixteenth century we can see from many tracts that were in circulation. A vigorous specimen is the treatise of Andrea Cambini on the origin and history of the Turks (Florence, 1529), which was translated into English in 1562 by John Shute in his *Two very notable Commentaries*. With his translation Shute gave a long "Epistle dedicatory" on military discipline, to which, the world was assured, the Turks owed their remarkable success; Cambini's book, the translator asserts, would reveal "the whole means whereby they attained to that mighty seat in the which they now sit and command, to the great dishonour of the Christian princes". In one of his poems Julius Caesar Scaliger reproves his fellow-Christians for their negligence regarding Rhodes, the capture of which (1522) was one of the first events of the reign of Suleiman the Magnificent: "Glorious Rhodes—but glorious *once*, not now. A terrible storm has obscured her radiant head. Is Christendom indifferent to her fate? Does the shepherd snore while the cruel wolf

[1]   e sol fu questi
Che Greco accompagnò l'armi latine.
Oh vergogna, oh misfatto! or non avesti
Tu, Grecia, quelle guerre a te vicine?
E pur quasi a spettacolo sedesti,
Lenta aspettando de' grand' atti il fine.
Or, se tu se' vil serva, è il tuo servaggio
(Non ti lagnar) giustizia, e non oltraggio.

La Gerusalemme Liberata, I, stanza 51. After this introduction it is not surprising that eventually Tatino deserts the Christian army, together with his men (XIII, stanza 68).

[2] His account as printed by Charles Hughes with the title *Shakespeare's Europe* (1903), p. 496.

has seized the best of the flock?"[1] The Turkish conquest of most of the remaining Greek islands—Rhodes (1522) was followed by Patmos, Scyros, and Paros (1537), Chios (1566), and Cyprus (1571)— through the sixteenth century had a progressively powerful effect on men's minds. As William Malim, who was at Constantinople in 1564, later wrote in his dedication (dated 23 March, 1572/3) of his translation of a pamphlet on the siege of Famagusta (1571) to the Earl of Leicester: "Certainly it moveth me much to remember the loss of those three notable Islands, to the great discomfort of all Christendom, to those hellish Turks, horseleeches of Christian Blood."[2] The conquest of Cyprus from the Venetians by the Turks took place when Shakespeare was a boy of seven; but *Othello* is full of the excitement of war "against the general enemy Ottoman". England was regarded as out of danger of Turkish invasion, of course; but the Elizabethans often felt anxiety, or at least curiosity, about the progress and intentions of the infidel. Among common topics of speculation was the question:

> Whether the Turkish new Moon minded be,
> To fill his horns this year on Christian coast.[3]

The Turk was acknowledged to be, as Bacon wrote, the most potent and most dangerous enemy of the faith, and there always existed, argued the casuists of international law, justification for war between Turks and Christians.[4] It is not for nothing that in our Prayer Book, inherited from the sixteenth century, we are instructed, in the third collect on Good Friday morning, to pray for the conversion of the Turks: "take from them all ignorance, hardness of heart, and contempt of thy Word, and so fetch them home, blessed Lord, to thy flock".

Shakespeare makes King Henry V say to his Princess Katherine:

[1] Clara Rhodos, sed clara olim: nunc horrida nimbis
    Obnubit nitidum dira procella caput.
Ah dolor, ah mors, ah siquid morte atque dolore
    Durius, aut etiam tetrius esse potest.
Stertitis? & ferus armenti Lupus optima carpit?
    O iam sit iam aliquis uelle perire pudor.
                Poematia, Lugduni, 1546, p. 380.

[2] Reprinted in Hakluyt (v, p. 122), *The true Report of all the successe of Famagosta, a Citie of Cyprus.* (*L'assedio e presa di Famagosta*, by Nestore Martinengo, Verona, 1572.)

[3] Sidney, *Astrophel and Stella*, sonnet xxx (quarto 2); *Works*, ed. Feuillerat (Cambridge, 1922), ii, 254, 374.

[4] *Turcae, gens licet et stirpe et disciplina crudelis et sanguinaria* and *Turcis praesto est semper, et ad nutum, belli causa*, Bacon writes in the *De Augmentis Scientiarum* VIII, ii, 14 and iii, 7; *Works*, ed. Spedding (1858), i, 758, 800.

"Shall not thou and I, between Saint *Denis* and Saint *George*, compound a Boy, half French, half English, that shall go to Constantinople, and take the Turk by the Beard. Shall we not?"[1] This is, of course, an "anachronism". In the reign of Henry V (1413–22) the Turk was not yet at Constantinople. But Shakespeare is thinking of his own times, and there is evidence that schemes of this nature against the Turks were not unknown to the military braggarts of his day. At any rate, in *The Time's Whistle; or a new Daunce of Seven Satires . . . compiled by [R. C.] Gent.*, which is dated about 1614, the braggart does not only boast that

> He hath made to fly
> The potent Turk, & got the victory
> By his own valour.

But he also proposes to liberate Greece:

> He'll chase the Turk out of Hungaria,
> And force him leave his seat in Grecia;
> Europe he'll free from his vexation.[2]

The great naval victory of Lepanto on October 1st 1571, where the young Cervantes fought gallantly and lost the use of his left hand, stirred the whole of Europe. When the news reached London on November 9th, "the people for joy made bonfires and other pleasant signs of rejoicing . . . and gave almighty God humble and hearty thanks, for if in this fight by Sea the Turks had prevailed, it would have bred great woe and great danger to all Christendom".[3] Yet it seems not to have been remembered that the battle was fought in Greek waters, near Naupactus, where in earlier times other great naval encounters had been as bitterly contested.[4] Nevertheless, in their interest in the situation in the Levant and in the memorable victory of Lepanto, the English and the Scots were given a royal lead; the curious poem, *The Lepanto*, written by James VI of Scotland, later James I of England, is of interest in this respect. It was printed in *His Maiesties Poeticall Exercises at vacant houres*, Edinburgh (1591); and in his preface ("The Author to the Reader") James says that he "composed these things in my very young and tender years". James

---

[1] V, ii, 19–23.
[2] Satira 2, 683–5, 697–9; ed. J. M. Cowper, E.E.T.S. (1871), p. 25.
[3] John Stowe, *The Annales, or Generall Chronicle of England* (1614), p. 670.
[4] Somewhat later, however, Peter Heylyn (*Microcosmus*, Oxford, 1621, p. 214) curiously connects the battle of Lepanto with the battle of Actium, suggesting that "this place seemeth to be marked for a stage of great designs, & that this latter naval battle, was but the second part of the first".

was 25 in 1591, when they were published; so *The Lepanto* may have been composed within about ten years of the battle. He carefully exculpates himself from the suggestion that such a subject for poetical excitement is unbecoming his station as a Protestant Monarch; and declares he is unwilling that he "should seem far contrary to my degree and Religion, like a Mercenary Poet, to pen a work, *ex professo*, in praise of a foreign Papist bastard", namely Don John of Austria. James sees the battle of Lepanto simply as a conflict between Christians and Mohammedans; he expresses the grief of the Christian peoples who groan under the Turkish yoke, and the anger of the Venetians who were losing Levantine possessions:

> The Turk had conquered Cyprus Isle,
> And all their lands that lay
> Without the bounds of Italy.

But there is no trace of any sentiment that the battle has special significance as taking place in or near a land once hallowed by courage, virtue, and civilization. The only Greek mentioned is a bloodthirsty brute:

> A MACEDONIAN soldier then
> Great honour for to win,
> Before the rest in earnest hope
> To BASHA bold did rin,
> And with a Cutlass sharp and fine
> Did whip me off his head,
> Who lacked not his reward of him
> That did the Navy lead.[1]

But the Latin translator, besides calling the poem, significantly, *Naupactiados, sive Lepantiados*, embellishes this episode by the "antique parallel". Like Macedon and Monmouth, "the situations, look you, is both alike".

> Cum Macedo, Macedum decus immortale, suoque
> Dignus Alexandro, viva spe raptus honorum
> Involat . . .[2]

When Richard Knolles in 1603 came to dedicate to the king his great work, *The Generall Historie of the Turkes from the first beginning of*

---

[1] II, 144–6, 864–71.
[2] "When a Macedonian—the immortal glory of Macedonia and a hero worthy of his own Alexander—prompted by an eager hope of glory rushes on. . . ." Thomas Moravius in Arthur Johnston's *Delitiae Poetarum Scotorum* (Amsterdam, 1637), ii, 196.

that Nation, he reminded him that the author of *The Lepanto* was a very appropriate patron for such a history. After James's death his panegyrists did not forget this poem, and regarded it as a sign that the king was at heart a Crusader;

> for as his Pen he wreathed
> With endless bays, his sword he would have sheathed,
> Within those bowels, that in part have eaten
> Thine Heritage, o *Christ*, and all do threaten.
> Of Christendom though he abhorred the cumbers,
> A battle yet he sung in haughty numbers:
> That all may gather how the Heavenly poem,
> Was of his great intentions but the proem.[1]

It was not supposed that the English were entirely indifferent to the fate of the unfortunate Greeks, at least as early as the beginning of the sixteenth century. There is in existence an English printed version of a letter of indulgence dated 1518, sent out by Leo X in favour of an inhabitant of Athens who had been captured by pirates and enslaved. This indulgence informs the faithful that "our said holy father hath understand that his well beloved child John Sargy of Corfu, Layman of the diocese of Athens, being born of a noble progeny, with his two brethren passing by ship upon the sea of Egey towards the isle of Creta was taken by certain Turks, robbers upon the sea, and brought by them unto miserable servitude and bondage."[2] Three hundred ducats had been paid for his ransom, and his brothers were still enslaved. The letter of indulgence had been given him to help him raise money as alms. This presumably means that John Sargis had come to England as a likely place to raise the money to ransom his brothers.

The pamphlets about the Turks, exhorting Europe to unity and to action, were mostly soon made available in several European languages. One of the most famous was the narrative of Bartholomaeus Georgevitz, who published two tracts, at Antwerp in 1544.[3] These appeared in English about 1570 as *The ofspring of the house of Ottomanno,* translated by Hugh Goughe. Bartholomaeus had spent

---

[1] Hugh Holland, *A Cypres Garland* (1625), Sig. C2. Holland had travelled as far as Jerusalem. He was a fellow of Trinity College, Cambridge, and a member of the Mermaid Club; and he wrote a sonnet prefixed to the first folio of Shakespeare's plays. I could wish there were evidence that this far-travelled minor poet was an acquaintance of Shakespeare (Holland was about ten years younger).

[2] Pollard and Redgrave, *Short-Title Catalogue of Books printed 1475–1640,* No. 15476; reprinted by Laborde, *Athènes,* i, 45, from which I quote.

[3] *De afflictione tam captiuorum quàm etiam sub Turcae tributo viuentium Christianorum* and *De Turcarum ritu et caeremoniis.*

many years in bondage and at length escaped. He tells a horrific story of the perils and afflictions of Christian captives. But he speaks with approbation of "the favourable affection of Grecians and Armenians towards fugitives". Although the punishment for harbouring escaped slaves is death and forfeiture of all goods, "notwithstanding the *Armenians* and *Grecians* do not cease daily to hide the Christian captives in their houses, and bring them disfigured with their apparel unto the ships of the *Venetians*, or other *Christians*, and give provision requisite for their journey, with all other things necessary, neither by them are there omitted any tokens of godly love. . . ."[1]

The dangers and miseries of falling into captivity are well illustrated by *The Rare and most wonderful thinges which Edward Webbe an Englishman borne hath seen and passed in his troublesome travailes* (printed in 1590).[2] Webbe was a master-gunner of a ship in the Levant trade, and in 1572 he was captured and made a galley-slave. Afterwards, "constrained for want of victuals" he revealed his skill in gunnery, and served in many campaigns throughout the Ottoman Empire. Eventually, in 1588, he was among twenty Englishmen who were ransomed by the English ambassador at the Porte. "Myself and others were released by means of her Majesty's favourable Letters, sent to the great Turk, brought by the foresaid Master Harborne: some by the Ransom money gathered at sundry times by the Merchants in the City of London, for the Godly purpose."[3] Through all this plucky narrative by a completely unlettered man is disclosed the indignation of the Englishman at the manners and customs of the great Mohammedan world ruled by the Ottoman Turk. A somewhat similar and equally horrifying story of an Englishman's experiences as a slave in the Levant is given by Richard Hasleton in a curious pamphlet of 1595, *Strange and Wonderful things happened to Rd. Hasleton, borne at Braintree in Essex, in his ten years travailes in many forraine countries. Penned as he delivered it from his owne mouth.*[4] But not all the stranded Englishmen displayed such fortitude in clinging to their Christian faith as Edward Webbe and Richard Hasleton. Thomas Dallam tells a curious story of an adventure which befell him and his party as they were travelling over the Parnassan range in December 1599; "we were dogged, or followed, by four stout villains that were Turks. They would have persuaded our dragoman, which was our guide, to have given his consent unto

[1] Sig. H.v verso and vi.
[2] Reprinted in Arber's *English Reprints* (1868).
[3] Arber's reprint, pp. 20, 29.
[4] Reprinted in 1600. It was included by Arber in *An English Garner* (1877), vol. 8, and reappears in the 1903 edition of the same collection in vol. 2 of 'Voyages and Travels".

the Cutting of our throats in the night, and he did very wisely Conceal it from us, and delayed the time with them, not daring to deny their suit." For four days they were followed "over Parnassus"; and each night the faithful dragoman hinted that the Englishmen should keep good watch, especially on the fourth night because the Turks were purposed to go no farther, and the dragoman had been compelled to agree to the murder. However, he made the Turks very drunk and drugged their liquor, so that they could do nothing. When the party reached Lepanto, the worthy dragoman told Dallam and his friends of the danger they had been in, and then (most surprising of all) revealed himself: "This man that was sent with us to be our dragoman, or interpreter, was an English man, born in Chorlay in Lancashire; his name Finche. He was also in religion a perfect Turk, but he was our trusty friend."[1]

It is necessary to understand the sixteenth-century attitude to the Turk in order to appreciate the sixteenth-century attitude to the Greek. In explaining and condoning Europe's indifference to the plight of the Greeks, it must be taken into account that the Ottoman Empire was nearer to Shakespeare's contemporaries than we sometimes remember. It was a great exotic civilization, strange, infidel and anti-Christian, inexorable and almost invincible, menacing and unpredictable. It made a fearsome appeal to the imagination; and a good deal of Ottoman history appeared on the Elizabethan stage. Marlowe had told the story of the downfall of Bayezid I at the hands of Tamburlaine; "T. G.", an imitator of Marlowe, wrote *The Tragicall Raigne of Selimus* (printed 1594), relating the terrible exploits of Selim the Grim; another dramatist, probably Kyd, produced Suleiman the Magnificent upon the stage in *The Tragedye of Solyman and Perseda* (printed 1599). Shakespeare seems to write assuming that his allusions to the Turkish Empire, its organization, and its manners and customs, will be readily understood by his audience. His casual use of the word "Turk" as a term of opprobrium he probably merely takes over from everyday speech. References to eunuchs of the seraglio and the fantastic concubinage of the Sultans show typical hearsay knowledge. But when Henry V, newly acceded to the throne, addresses his brothers:

> This is the English, not the Turkish Court;
> Not Amurath an Amurath succeeds,
> But Harry Harry,[2]

[1] *Early Voyages and Travels in the Levant*, 1. The Diary of Master Thomas Dallam, 1559–1600 ... edited by J. T. Bent for the Hakluyt Society (1893), pp. 83–4.
[2] *2 Henry IV*, V, ii, 47–9.

it is clear that the strangling of his nineteen brothers by Mahomet III at his accession to the Sultanate in 1595, on the death of their father Amurath (or Murad) III, was an event well known in England.

The Turk, therefore, rather than the Greek, dominated the imagination of the Elizabethan when he thought of events and conditions in the Levant. Learned Greeks who might have spoken for their nation, rarely travelled as far as England in the sixteenth century; and some of those who did come to England were imposters or mere beggars. But it should be remembered that Greek mercenary soldiers (called "estradiots", from the Greek *stratiôtai*) were employed in many countries in Europe at this time. Nicander Nucius of Corfu, who came to England in 1546 and wrote an entertaining account[1] of the country and his experiences here, reports that among the mercenaries[2] being employed by Henry VIII in an expedition against Scotland that year (1546), he found Argives from the Peloponnesus, who had their own commander, one Thomas of Argos. Nucius of Corcyra, like Odysseus of Ithaca, was ready for any interesting experience of men's cities and their minds; and so (he tells us) having joined his fellow-countrymen, he set off for the war against the Scots. It is difficult to believe that any of these Greeks, once having reached Western Europe, would have returned to their own country under the oppression of the Turks (although they might, I suppose, in spite of the heavy taxation, have in some cases gone back to islands that were under Venetian rule). The presence of such Greek mercenaries in England should perhaps be remembered when we try to interpret that curious personage "old John Naps of Greece" who is mentioned a generation or so later in *The Taming of the Shrew* among the cronies of Christopher Sly the tinker.[3] Was he a mercenary who had retired and settled down? "Naps" might be an Anglicized detrimentum of some Greek name, such as Yannopoulos or Papayannopoulos.[4]

The attitude towards the Greeks in sixteenth-century Europe, then, was merged into the attitude towards the Ottoman peril. Sympathy for the contemporary Greek was weakened by religious hostilities and by credulous calumniation. It is not until the letters of the great Busbecq, who twice went as ambassador from the Emperor Ferdinand to Suleiman the Magnificent shortly after the middle of the sixteenth

[1] Edited for the Camden Society (vol. xvii) as *The Second Book of the Travels of Nicander Nucius of Corcyra*, by J. A. Cramer (1841), from a MS. in the Bodleian Library which once belonged to Archbishop Laud; p. 90.

[2] Fortescue does not mention Greeks; but he declares (and deplores the fact) that there were many foreign mercenaries employed in the British army in the sixteenth century. *A History of the British Army* (1899), i, 114.

[3] Induction, ii, 95.

[4] See the discussion of "old John Naps of Greece" by T. Spencer in *Modern Language Review*, XLIX (1954).

century, that we find knowledge and sympathy, combined with a
sense of Europe's debt and duty towards the hapless Greeks. "Our
respect for religion and our sense of duty", he wrote, "ought to have
impelled us to succour our afflicted brethren. But even if a love of
glory and a sense of honour has not warmed our dull minds, yet at
any rate self-interest, the first principle of our conduct nowadays,
ought to stir us to recover those places which, so fair and full of such
great resources and advantages, have been seized by the barbarians,
and ourselves to possess them in their stead."[1] Busbecq declared
that he saw descendants of the imperial families of the Cantacuzeni
and Palaeologi passing their lives among the Turks in positions more
contemptible than that of Dionysius at Corinth, who (Busbecq's
original readers had no need to be informed), when he was banished
from Syracuse, became a schoolmaster.[2] But it is more deeply
afflicting that Greece, the home of the nymphs, the land of the muses,
should be crushed into servitude. She longs for Christian care and
culture. Once she was glorious and flourishing, now she is unde-
servedly wretched. She was once the creator of all the ennobling
arts of life, all liberal culture; and now she seems to be begging back
from the Europe she has civilized something of the humanity which
she has bequeathed to us. She appeals to all those things which in
common we hold sacred, and implores our help against the Scythian
barbarism which oppresses her. But it is all in vain (sadly adds the
experienced diplomat); the Princes of Christendom have their minds
set on quite different things.[3]

[1] Debuerat quidem nos pietas & officium impellere vt afflictis sociorum rebus
succurreremus. sed si nec laudis nec honesti pulchritudo animos torpentes
inflammauit; certè vtilitas, cuius hodie prima ratio ducitur, mouere potuit, vt loca
tam praeclara tantísque commoditatibus & opportunitatibus plena, Barbaris
erepta à nobis potius quàm ab illis vellemus possideri. Epistle 1 (1554) in *Legationis
Turcicae Epistolae Quattuor* (Paris, 1589), 28. Epistle 1 was first published at
Amsterdam in 1581 as *Itinera Constantinopolitanum et Amasianum*.
[2] Vidi item posteà aliis locis Cantacuzenorum & Palaeologorum, imperatorij
generis, reliquias, contemptius inter Turcas degentes, quàm vixit Dionysius
Corinthi (*op. cit.*, 16 verso). This piece of dubious information became traditional
and was often borrowed by later writers without acknowledgement: ". . . you shall
find the Daughters of ancient Greek Houses espoused to Shepherds and Carters,
and the ancient Reliques of the noble Families *Cantacuzeno* and *Paleologi*, living
more contemptuously at *Constantinople*, than ever *Dionysius* did at *Corinth*".
(Paul Ricaut, *The History of the Present State of the Ottoman Empire* (1668),
5th ed. 1682, p. 131.) See, likewise, the anecdote of "Constantine Paleologus",
the stable-groom of an English merchant, in Aaron Hill, *A Full Account of the
Present State of the Ottoman Empire* (1709), 2nd ed. (1710), p. 174, quoted on
p. 143 below.
[3] ô Nympharum domos! ô sedes Musarum! ô loca litteratis apta secessibus!
ea me herclè, . . . lugere nunc videntur & operam cultúmque Christianorum
requirere. sed multò magis ipsa Constantinopolis, vel tota potius Graecia: quae
quondam florentissima, nunc indigna premitur seruitute; bonarum olim artium

These were noble words. They were spoken to Europe. They were the birth of Philhellenism; and it is appropriate that they should have come from the admirable Busbecq. The English, however, soon learnt the lesson; and before the end of the sixteenth century, at any rate one Englishman saw that, as the Turk weakened, all the Greeks required was leadership and arms for them to regain their liberty. Sir Anthony Sherley left Venice for Aleppo in May 1599 and visited some of the Greek lands on his route. In his account of this journey he writes:

> to *Cyprus*, and *Paphos*, where we found nothing to answer the famous relations given by ancient Histories of the excellency of that Island, but the name only (the barbarousness of the *Turk*, and time, having defaced all the Monuments of Antiquity), no shew of splendour, no habitation of men in a fashion, nor possessors of the ground in a Principality; but rather Slaves to cruel Masters, or prisoners shut up in divers prisons: so grievous is the burthen of that miserable people, and so deformed is the state of that Noble Realm.

But this sort of lament, with which we are now familiar, is not enough; he continues with some shrewd observations on the possibility of a revival of the Greek nation:

> . . . if the little remnant of people, which is left there had courage; or if they have courage, had also armes; or if the Princes Christian had but a compassionate eye turned upon the miserable calamity of a place so near them . . . I do not see . . . but the redemption of that place and people were most facile . . . and the glory would be immortal to the Actor.[1]

This was not the only voice raised in favour of the oppressed Greeks during Shakespeare's lifetime. Sir Thomas Sherley, the brother of Sir Anthony, was in Constantinople from August 1603 until February 1606/7, and suffered imprisonment, but found time to write his very acute and interesting *Discours of the Turks*.[2] Sherley draws attention to the significance of the fact that the Turk is in a small minority in all the countries he occupies; and if his military power at any time relaxes, intervention by the Christian powers would be sure of success.

omnísque liberalioris doctrinae inuentrix humanitatem, quam nobis tradidit, reposcere videtur, & opem pro iure communium sacrorum aduersus Scythicam barbariem implorare: sed frustra, euntibus in alia omnia Principum Christianorum animis. *Op. cit.*, folio 28.

[1] *Sir Anthony Sherley: His Relation of his Travels* (1613), pp. 6, 7.
[2] Camden Miscellany, vol. xvi (1936), ed. E. Denison Ross; see p. 9.

The Great Turk has reason, he says, to fear

> the great number of Christians that are in all his countries that
> have been formerly baptized, which do far exceed the Turks in
> number, yea even in Constantinople itself; & these desire nothing
> but arms & captains, and they would rise against the Turks for
> their liberty, & would furnish men, money, & horses sufficient.
> This I have learned of divers wise and wealthy Greeks that do wish
> for this help with tears.

Thus, at about the time that Shakespeare was writing *Othello* and
more than two hundred years before Byron arrived in Greece, an
Englishman was discussing with divers wise and wealthy Greeks the
necessity for the provision of arms and officers if the Greeks were to
rise against the Turks and regain their liberty.

CHAPTER II

TRADE AND CALUMNY

... the *Phoenix*, and her fraught from *Candy* ...

Twelfth Night, V, i, 64.

I am a Greek, of noble speech and blood,
Yet the Romans with me be marvellous wood;
For their woodness and cursing I do not care;
The more that I am cursed, the better I do fare.

Andrew Boorde, *The Fyrst Boke of the Introduction of Knowledge*
(1542).

... lett'red *Greece*, the Lottery of Arts,
Since *Mars* forsook her, subtle, never wise.

Fulke Greville, Lord Brooke, *Mustapha* (1609).

Greeks have condemned all the world but themselves of barbarism,
the world as much vilifies them now.

Robert Burton, *The Anatomy of Melancholy* (1621).

THE pilgrims to the Holy Land in the fifteenth and in the early sixteenth century had, to a certain extent, come into contact with the Greeks. William Wey, who made pilgrimages to Jerusalem in 1458 and 1462, thought it useful to include in his book a vocabulary and phrase-list of the contemporary Greek tongue.[1] Bernard von Breydenbach of Mainz, whose party made the journey to the Holy Land in 1483 and who brought out the magnificent travel-book of 1486, describes their journey by way of the Ionian Islands, Modon (then still Venetian), Rhodes, and Crete. The famous illustrations to the book, by Erhard Reuwich, include views of Corfu, Modon, Candia, and Rhodes, and representations of contemporary costumes. But the great days of the pilgrimages in the Levant were soon to be over. Pilgrims gave place to traders.

There is evidence that, before the end of the fifteenth century,[2] English ships were visiting Crete and Chios, especially for malmsey wine. The English appear surprisingly early in the Levant. By 1513

---

[1] *The Itineraries of William Wey*, translated by A. Way, Roxburghe Club, 1857.
[2] The Byzantine historian Michael Ducas (quoted by Gibbon, *Decline and Fall*, chapter lxv), writing shortly after the middle of the fifteenth century, reckons the *Inglênoi* among the nations who traded to a port on the Ionian Coast.

there was a consul for the English at Chios, appointed by Henry VIII;
he was an Italian named Baptista Justiniano. In 1522 Censius son of
Balthazari, a resident in Crete was appointed, for life, as governor,
protector, and consul of the English nation in that island. This shows
that English merchant ships were fairly numerous there by that date.
In 1530 one Dionysius Harrys, an Englishman from London was
appointed consul for life in Crete.[1] These early consulships seem to
have been confined to the parts of Greece which had not yet been
occupied by the Turk. It is uncertain whether Sir Richard Shelley,
who lived from about 1513 to about 1589, was, as he himself supposed, the first Englishman to visit Constantinople since the city fell
into the hands of the Ottoman; but he was probably the first who went
there for the fun of the thing. He travelled in the train of the
Venetian ambassador, setting out from Venice in May 1539.[2]

It is clear from the evidence of the consulships that England was
beginning to share with the Venetians some of the lucrative carrying-
trade in the eastern Mediterranean and to find new markets for
English goods. Hakluyt prints several accounts of voyages by
British seamen, who, amid the danger from Barbary pirates, soon
gained by their daring an advantage over most of their competitors.
The fine cloth, too, which was produced by English weavers,
made them welcome traders everywhere. In his chapter on "The
antiquity of the trade with English ships into the Levant", Hakluyt
says that

> In the years of our Lord 1511, 1512, &c. till the year 1534, divers
> tall ships of London . . . had an ordinary and usual trade to Sicilia,
> Candy, Chio, and somewhiles to Cyprus, as also to Tripolis and
> Barutti in Syria. The commodities which they carried thither were
> fine Kersies of divers colours, coarse Kersies, white Western
> dozens, Cottons, certain cloths called Statutes, and others called
> Cardinal-whites, and Calveskins, which were well sold in Sicily,
> &c. The commodities which they returned back were Silks,
> Chamlets, Rhubarb, Malmesies, Muskadels and other wines,
> sweet oils, cotton wool, Turkey carpets, Galls, Pepper, Cinnamon,
> and some other spices, &c. . . .[3]

A few of these voyages Hakluyt describes. He tells of "A voyage
made with the ships called the Holy Cross, and the Mathew Gonson,

[1] Rymer, *Foedera*, xiii, 353, 766; xiv, 389.
[2] Two of his letters are in Gairdner, *Letters and Papers of Henry VIII*, XIV, i,
No. 910 and ii, No. 273; the latter is dated from Constantinople, October 2nd 1539.
[3] *The Principal Navigations Voyages Traffiques & Discoveries of the English
Nation* (Glasgow edition, 1903, v, 62–3).

to the Isles of Candia and Chio, about the year 1534"; of this he got
an account from the mouth of one John Williamson, citizen and
cooper of London, who was still living in 1592. The "voyage of M.
Roger Bodenham with the great Bark Aucher to Candia and Chio in
the year 1550" is a fine record of daring escapades in the Aegean Sea.
When Bodenham got to Crete he found that there was danger of a
Turkish invasion; and the author picturesquely describes the typical
outlaw population amongst the Cretans, who came down from the
mountains during such an emergency:

> There be in that Island of Candia many banished men, that live
> continually in the mountains; they came down to serve, to the
> number of four or five thousand; they are good archers, every one
> with his bow and arrows, a sword and a dagger, with long hair, and
> boots that reach up to their groin, and a shirt of mail, hanging the
> one half before, and the other half behind. . . . They would drink
> wine out of all measure.[1]

By the middle of the sixteenth century this trade had developed
to such an extent that there was need for official protection and
support, if Englishmen were not to be at a disadvantage in competition for Levant commerce. In 1553 Anthony Jenkinson was given
trading privileges throughout the Turkish Empire by Suleiman the
Magnificent. Hakluyt likewise prints "A discourse of the trade to
Chio, in the year 1569, made by Gaspar Campion . . .", where it is
said that "English men do buy more commodities of Chio than any
other nation". Campion adds: "I have traded in the country above
this 30 years, and have been married in the town of Chio full 24 years,
so that you may assure yourself that I will write nothing but truth."[2]
It was for long a favourite scheme of Queen Elizabeth to effect an
alliance with the Sultan Amurath III. It had come to be realized,
of course, that the Turks could be made to play no insignificant part
in the balance of power in Europe. Earlier in the century, the French
had already been successful in concluding alliances and effecting
commercial treaties. For Francis I had abandoned his early Crusader
boastings (he is supposed to have declared that, if elected to the
Empire, he would be, within three years, either in Constantinople
or in his coffin); and after his defeat at Pavia in 1525 he saw that it
would be useful to play off the Turks against his bitter enemies, the

---

[1] v, 67, 71–6.
[2] v, 109–10, 111 sqq. But after the Turks took Chios from the Genoese this
English trade had almost ceased. (A. C. Wood, *A History of the Levant Company*
(1935), p. 3, quoting from a memorandum by William Harborne, the first ambassador to the Porte.)

Hapsburgs. He obtained the grant of certain privileges to French subjects in the dominions of the Sultan; and in 1535 a treaty of commerce was concluded. A French company was formed to take advantage of the newly conferred rights. By the terms of this treaty the French were to be regarded as a favoured nation in all the dominions of the Ottoman. Not only was freedom of trade and of navigation ensured, but the French were also granted capitulations by which their nationals were to be under the jurisdiction of their own consuls. The only foreign vessels to be permitted to enter Turkish waters were those flying the French flag. For some years, in fact, English adventurers had to trade in the Levant under French protection, or not at all. That the English were well known to the Porte at that time is proved by a clause in this treaty of 1535 for the admission of the King of England to the agreement if his ratification was sent within a specified time.

No political alliance between England and the Ottoman Empire developed from Elizabeth's efforts to rival the French influence at the Porte. But in 1578 William Harborne went to Constantinople and procured the first of the "Heroical Letters", dated March 15th 1579,[1] from the Sultan to the Queen. In 1580 Amurath issued a charter of privileges to English traders, granting them the same rights as other European traders in the Ottoman Empire. In the following year Elizabeth gave her charter to the Turkey Company; and in 1583 Harborne returned to Constantinople as the first English ambassador to the Sublime Porte. All this was in spite of vigorous opposition from the Venetians and the French, who were jealous of their commercial privileges; and as a result of their antagonism, calumnies were in Europe spread against the Queen, alleging that she had become confederate with the Turk. She was accused of having incited the Turk to make war against Christendom. But she boasted, on the contrary, that her reputation at the Porte had influenced the Turk to refrain from invading Poland in 1590. If England had a representative at the Porte (wrote Bacon in 1592), he was only a commercial agent, maintained at the merchants' expense; whereas several other Christian powers had for long had ambassadors liegers.[2]

The staple of the English trade with the Levant was currants— a luxury which was vigorously condemned by many Englishmen. The Greeks, wrote one traveller in 1599, "wonder what we use to do with so many Currants, and ask sometimes whether we use to dye with them, or feed Hogs with them. They were a very poor kind of

[1] Printed in Hakluyt, v, 169 sqq.
[2] James Spedding, *The Letters and the Life of Francis Bacon* (1861), i, 135, 204; *Works*, ed. James Spedding (1858), vi, 356–7.

people, when our English Merchants used traffic there first; but now they are grown rich and proud."[1] The same story is told by William Lithgow, who speaks of there being "here in England of late . . . some Liquorous lips, who forsooth can hardly digest Bread, Pasties, Broth, and (*verbi gratia*) bag-puddings without these currants: And . . . these Rascal Greeks, becoming proud of late with this lavish expense, contemn justly this sensual prodigality."[2] The best currants came from Zante and Cephalonia, which were parts of Greece under the Venetians, who took advantage of the English taste for these berries to impose heavy duties on their export. This was a cause of bitter complaint against Venetian policy.

We can judge the vigorous development of this trade in the Levant, during the half-century following the foundation of the Company, from the descriptions in Lewes Roberts's two books, *The Marchants Mappe of Commerce* (1638) and *The Treasure of Traffike* (1641). He tells us that the Levant Company

> for its height and eminency, is now second to none other of this land, for not yearly, but monthly, nay almost weekly their ships are observed to go to and fro, exporting hence the *cloths* of *Suffolk*, *Gloucester*, *Worcester* and *Coventry*, dyed and dressed, *Kersies* of *Hampshire* and *York*, Lead, Tin, and a great quantity of . . . *India spices*, *Indico* and *Calicoes*, and in return thereof import from *Turkey* the raw *silks* of *Persia*, *Damasco*, *Tripoly*, &c . . . *Cottons*, and *Cotton yarn* of *Cyprus* and *Smyrna*, and sometimes the *Gems* of *India*, the *drugs* of *Egypt*, and *Arabia*, the *Muscadins* of *Candia*, the *Currants* and *Oils* of *Zante*, *Cephalonia*, and *Morea*.[3]

Speaking of the people of Manchester he says:

> They buy Cotton wool, in *London*, that comes first from *Cyprus* and *Smyrna*, and at home work the same, and perfect it into Fustians, Vermilions, Dymities, and other such Stuffs, and then return it to *London*, where the same is vended and sold, and not seldom sent into foreign parts.[4]

It is clear that Manchester had already begun the manufacture of cotton goods from the raw material brought from Greek lands by the merchants of London.

[1] William Biddulph, *The Travels of certaine Englishmen* (1609), p. 5.
[2] *The Totall Discourse of the Rare Adventures and Painefull Peregrinations* (1632), ii, 65 (Glasgow edition, 1906, pp. 58–9).
[3] *Mappe*, p. 259.   [4] *Treasure*, p. 33.

The foundation of the Levant Company was very important for extending the knowledge of Greece amongst English people. The grant of charters did not merely mean that trade was developed and regularized in the Levant. It also solved, for ordinary people, the practical problem of visiting Greece, although the risks of travel, owing to dangers from sea, disease, and pirates, remained, of course, very great. The rates of insurance were normally between three-to-one and five-to-one *against* return. Henry Moryson went with his brother Fynes on the latter's journey in 1595 to Jerusalem and Constantinople, and "put out some four hundred pounds, to be repaid twelve hundred pounds upon his return from these two Cities, and to lose it if he died in the journey".[1] The phrase "putter-out of five for one" has become familiar to us from Shakespeare's use of it as a periphrasis for "a traveller from a far country".[2] But probably a voyage to the Levant was not quite so perilous as seems to be implied by these fearful odds, if we may judge from Ben Jonson's joke in *Every Man out of his Humour*; there Sir Puntarvolo declares,

> I do intend, this year of *Jubilee* coming on [i.e. 1600], to travel: and (because I will not altogether go upon expense) I am determined to put forth some five thousand pound, to be paid me, five for one, upon the return of my self, my wife, and my dog, from the *Turk's* court in *Constantinople*.[3]

But travel or residence in any land under Turkish rule was a humiliating and often a dangerous experience. It was forbidden to a giaour to carry arms. It was even forbidden to look a Turk straight in the face. The traveller was compelled patiently to endure affronts and to submit to injuries. To deliver a blow to, or to draw a weapon upon, a Moslem was a capital offence. That is why Othello boasts of the bravest action of his career, almost as suicidal as the blow with which he is about to end his own life:

> in *Aleppo* once,
> Where a *Malignant* and a *Turban'd Turk*,
> Beat a *Venetian*, and traduc'd the State;
> I took bi'th' throat the circumcised dog
> And smote him thus . . .[4]

Difficulties and humiliations were long to be the lot of any traveller

[1] *Itinerary*, I, iii, 198 (Glasgow edition (1907), i, 425).
[2] *The Tempest*, III, iii, 48.
[3] II, iii, 243–8; *Works*, ed. Herford and Simpson, iii, 477.   [4] V, ii, 352–6.

in Turkish Greece. But from the year 1583 an English ambassador was maintained at Constantinople. Consuls and vice-consuls were established in the chief cities of the Levant.[1] Other Englishmen were needed as officials—chaplains and treasurers for the colonies of British people, just as they are needed today. From the time of Sir Thomas Glover, who went to Constantinople in 1606, the ambassadors were generally accompanied by their wives, among whom Lady Mary Wortley Montagu was to be famous. The ambassadors' wives were, so far as I have been able to discover, the only English women to visit the Turco-Greek lands until towards the end of the eighteenth century.[2]

The Levant Company's chaplains were an important sequence of men, whose writings, investigations, and opinions will be frequently mentioned in these pages. They included many scholars of ability. The appointments were unlikely to be sought for, except by men of an adventurous temperament. But to those who were interested in antiquities, whether classical, biblical or ecclesiastical, a Levant chaplaincy was an excellent opportunity for study and experience. Many of these young clergy who had spent a few years in the Levant rose to important positions in the Church, in the universities, and in the world of scholarship.[3] For more than two and a half centuries, that is, until its dissolution by Act of Parliament in 1825, the Levant Company was the most important organization which brought England into contact with Greece.

The consequence was that to become a "Turkey merchant" was the lot of many an adventurous younger son of good family in England.[4] Travel became possible, first of all for the adventurer, and soon it became possible for the adventurous scholar and man of letters. English people began to hear something about Greece.

[1] There was a consul at Patras by about 1585 as we learn from Hakluyt, v, 285–6. His name was Guines and he was met by Laurence Aldersey on his second voyage into the Levant in 1586 (Hakluyt, vi, 40).

[2] Virginia Woolf's Orlando, during the reign of Charles II, was sent to Constantinople as Ambassador Extraordinary; and in order to celebrate his elevation to a Dukedom, which took place while he was there, gave a magnificent reception, at which many English ladies were present. Some of these ladies co-operated in performing an elegant masque, and one of them, Miss Penelope Hartopp, in a letter to a female friend at Tunbridge Wells, gave an account of the ladies' hairdresses, etc. (chapter iii). I am afraid that the historical possibility here is rather similar to that exemplified by the author's allowing Orlando to mingle with the crowd on Galata Bridge (built 1837), and (as a woman) along with the gypsies, including women, to keep her sheep on Mount Athos.

[3] A considerable amount of curious information about these men was collected by John B. Pearson in *A Biographical Sketch of the Chaplains to the Levant Company*, Cambridge, 1883.

[4] See George Wheler's account, p. 127 below.

What they heard was far from favourable. The principal reason for this fact is rather a curious one; it was because the modern Greeks were seen as the representatives of the ancient Greeks, that they endured such disparagement in Europe. If this seems paradoxical, it should be remembered that the romantic view of ancient Hellenic civilization, which inevitably determines the way we think of ancient Greece and which influenced the way the nineteenth-century Philhellenes nursed hopes for modern Greece, was not to be found in the minds of the Renaissance enthusiasts for the classics. It was, in fact, necessary to idealize ancient Greece before it became possible to romanticize modern Greece. Our emotional approval of the Grecians and their civilization is a comparatively recent attitude; and to build up this mood of admiration (and sometimes of nostalgia) many influences have been at work: Winckelmann, the Elgin marbles, the *Ode on a Grecian Urn*, Matthew Arnold's "Hellenism", the works of Victorian anecdotal painters, the sharp focus on the culture of fifth-century Athens in nineteenth-century educational institutions; these, and many other things, have played their part. On the whole, in spite of all that modern cynics, anthropologists and economic historians have said, a distinctly favourable impression persists regarding the glory that was Greece, "land of lost gods and godlike men"; and that this vision of Grecian life is shared by the unliterary is occasionally revealed by modern advertisements.

It is quite misleading to expect to find something resembling our admiring attitude towards the ancient Greeks in the literature of the Renaissance. This was written with an entirely different background. It is true, of course, that Greek literature then had a great reputation (being fairly well known in Latin translations) and that certain Greek sages were regarded with admiration and awe. But this respect was by no means transferred to the ancient Greeks as a whole, to their national character, to their way of living. The reason was simple. Latin literature was much more familiar than was Greek literature; and the opinion about the ancient Greeks which prevailed in the sixteenth century, and for some time afterwards, was, broadly speaking, that of the Romans of the Republic and the Empire. It was derived from a reading of the favourite Latin writers; and the prejudices thus acquired were, in most cases, far from favourable. Of course, the Greeks were the great inventors of the arts and the sciences, the civilizers of the human race. But, as *men?* . . . Such being the attitude to the glorious ancient Greeks, we cannot expect the usual estimate of the hapless modern Greeks to be very high.

We learn from Plutarch, in a passage in his life of Cicero that, as terms of contempt, "*Grecian* and scholar . . . are the two words, the which the artificers (and such base mechanical people at Rome) have ever ready at their tongues' end."[1] One Roman opinion, perhaps plebeian, of the Greeks was clearly revealed in Roman comedy, and was therefore well known in the Renaissance. In Plautus the verb *pergraecari* had come to mean "to spend the hours in mirth, luxurious drinking and eating, and general dissipation."[2] Likewise, *congraecare* meant "to squander one's money in luxury and fast living".[3] To drink "in the Greek fashion" (*graeco more*) was interpreted as referring to the continued drinking of healths.[4] "To play the Greek" (*graecari*) meant to live luxuriously and effeminately; and Horace's rustic sage, Ofellus, sneers at those who, having become accustomed to the loose ways of living of the Greeks, find Roman field-sports to be too exhausting and therefore prefer ball-games.[5]

The convivial, dissipated Greek might be pardoned or tolerated; but the perfidious Greek was not to be endured. To the Romans, "Greek faith" was proverbial, like the Greek Calends, and meant no faith at all. When in Plautus's *Asinaria* the bawd Cleareta informs the eager young lover, "We carry on our commercial dealings with Greek faith" (*Graeca mercamur fide*),[6] she is referring to purchases for ready cash, no credit being allowed. We must also take into account the strongly anti-Greek bias of the *Aeneid*, probably the most widely read and highly esteemed work of Latin literature during the Renaissance. There, the hostile comments on Greek conduct, although of course dramatically appropriate in the poem, were capable of being given a wider application. "Listen now to my story of the underhand dealings of the Greeks", says Aeneas in relating the trick by which Troy was eventually taken, "and from this one example of their treachery learn what they are all like."

> accipe nunc Danaum insidias et crimine ab uno
> disce omnes.[7]

Most famous of all were the proverbial "Greek gifts" (*timeo Danaos*

---

[1] North's *Plutarch*, Nonesuch ed. (1930), iv, 198.
[2] dies noctesque bibite, pergraecaminei,
    amicas emite, liberate: pascite
    parasitos: opsonate pollucibiliter.

Mostellaria, 21; similarly 64, 960; cf. also *Bacchides*, 813, *Poenulus*, 603, and *Truculentus*, 88. Festus gave the simple definition: *pergraecari est epulis et potationibus inservire.*

[3] *Bacchides*, 742–3.
[4] cf. Cicero *in Verrem*, II, i, 26, para. 66. Discumbitur; fit sermo inter eos et invitatio, ut Graeco more biberetur; hortatur hospes; poscunt majoribus poculis; celebratur omnium sermone laetitiaque convivium.
[5] Romana fatigat militia assuetum graecari. *Satires* II, ii, 10–11.
[6] *Asinaria*, 199.   [7] ii, 65–6.

et dona ferentes[1]), which could be construed as a general condemnation of Greek double-dealing.

Cicero, who brought so much Greek culture to Latin literature and philosophy, wrote disparagingly of the *graeculus* on many occasions;[2] and the Romans of the Empire declared their contempt, dislike, or derision of the Greeks, often in highly vituperative terms, which made a deep impression upon the habits of thought of the men of the Renaissance. Everybody knows Juvenal's superb and scathing passage of indignation at the insinuating Greek in Rome; "I cannot endure, O ye venerable citizens of Rome, a city that has gone Greek" (*non possum ferre, Quirites, Graecam urbem*), the poet exclaims. Pushing, versatile, quick-witted, and utterly unscrupulous, the Greek worms his way into the confidence of great men. He is ready to play any part, physician or professor, acrobat or soothsayer, what you will; he knows everything, the hungry Greekling (*omnia novit Graeculus esuriens*).[3] The brilliant phrase stuck. Other Roman writers were equally emphatic. The elder Pliny wrote of the portentous mendacity and fabulosity of Greece;[4] and likewise Livy, Seneca, Quintilian and others, sneered at the failings of the Greeks, their impudence, venality, mendacity, vanity, and servility. There were very few good Greeks; and *they* were all dead. Tacitus records the rebuke of the proud Roman Piso to Germanicus the romantic Hellenist, for his honouring not the genuine Athenians, who were long since extinct, but those dregs of nations.[5]

Even stronger and more convincing testimony to the bad qualities of the Greeks (ancient, and therefore modern equally) was provided by St. Paul. Writing to Titus, whom he had left in Crete as the first bishop there, he warns his friend that he is likely to run into difficulties, owing to the evil disposition of the Cretans. For, did not one of their own sages[6] declare that his countrymen were always liars, vile beasts, and idle gluttons?[7] As regards the lying propensities of the Cretans, St. Paul thus corroborated Ovid's opinion (*mendax Creta*) in his *Ars Amatoria* (i, 298). Furthermore, in his first epistle to the

---

[1] ii, 49. During the recent war, I heard a British major-general utter these words (to the bewilderment of his colleagues) at a conference which discussed a proposal to incorporate certain Greek military units into the British Army.

[2] *Tusc. Disp.*, i, 35 (86) (*ineptum sane negotium et Graeculum*); *in Pis.*, xxix (70); etc.

[3] iii, 60–1, 77–8.

[4] portentosa Graeciae mendacia (v, 1, 4); Graeciae fabulositas (xii, 5, 11).

[5] non Athenienses, tot cladibus exstinctos, sed conluviem illam nationum. *Annales*, ii, 55, 1.

[6] St. Paul is stated by Jerome to be here quoting from the half-fabulous poet and sage of Crete, Epimenides.

[7] *Titus*, i, 12–13.

Corinthians (vi, 9 sqq.) St. Paul gives a lengthy catalogue of Greek vices and depravities, which will keep them out of the Kingdom of Heaven.

Here then was weighty testimony against the Greek character; and it was this Roman and Scriptural point of view that, on the whole, dominated the writers of the Renaissance. Erasmus clearly understood the situation and with his accustomed simplicity explained how the reputation of the Greeks was due to the attitude of the Roman writers.[1]

But Erasmus himself in his *Adagia* incorporated all these Roman prejudices; and so words and phrases such as *pergraecari, fide graeca,* etc.[2] were given authority in the numerous editions, epitomes, adaptations and translations of Erasmus's great garnering of flowers of speech, elegant aphorisms, and figurative and proverbial expressions in the Latin tongue. Every schoolboy could learn to sneer at the Greeks.

This explains why the very word "greek" appeared in sixteenth-century English as a common noun in derogatory senses.[3] There were two usages, both based upon Roman precedent.

First, the word "greek", generally preceded by an epithet like "gay", "mad", or "merry", became an ordinary conversational expression meaning a person of loose and lively habits, a boon companion, a fast liver. The name of the well-known character Mathewe Merygreeke in *Roister Doister* (about 1540) is obviously related to Plautus's use of *pergraecari*. Nashe mentions "one *Dick Litchfield,* the Barber of *Trinity College*, a rare ingenuous odd merry Greek, who (as I have heard) hath translated my *Piers Penniless* into the *Macaronical* tongue".[4] The phrase is common in Ben Jonson,[5] who, for example, in his prefatory contribution to *Coryats Crudities* in 1611 ("the Character of the famous *Odcombian*"), gave his testimony of the author; "He is a mad *Greek*, no less than a merry".[6] There are

---

[1] Graecorum gens mala audit passim apud poëtas Latinos, et item apud Ciceronem, non solum quasi voluptatibus addicta, et effoeminata delitiis, verum etiam quasi lubrica fide (*Adagia*, IV, i, 64).

[2] IV, i, 64; I, viii, 27; I, ii, 29. I use the folio edition (*Adagiorum Opus*) printed at Lyons in 1541. Some evidence for the currency of provebrs based upon these is given in M. P. Tilley's *Dictionary of the Proverbs in England in the Sixteenth and Seventeenth Centuries* (Ann Arbor, University of Michigan Press, 1950), C. 822, F. 31, M. 901.

[3] It had a parallel development in French; see E. Huguet, *Dictionnaire de la Langue Française du Seizième Siècle* (Paris, 1949), tom. iv, 366–7, s.v. "grec".

[4] *Have with you to Saffron-Walden* (1596), *Works*, ed. McKerrow (1905), iii, 33.

[5] *A Tale of a Tub*, The scene interloping, 23; *The Case is Altered*, IV, ix, 17; *The New Inn*, II, v, 42. (*Works*, ed. Herford and Simpson, iii. 63; iii, 164; vi, 432.)

[6] *Works*, ed. Herford and Simpson, viii, 377.

In *The Civil Conversation of M. Steeven Guazzo*, as translated by George Pettie (1581), Annibal declares "touching conditions, you know that the Greeks, though singular in learning and eloquence, yet are they disloyal and faithless, and therefore it is proverbially said, The Greekish faith".[1] In Lyly's *Euphues, The Anatomy of Wit* (1578) and its continuations and imitations, this attitude to the Greeks is a commonplace. When Philautus fears that his friend Euphues has robbed him of his love Lucilla, he soliloquizes:

> Is this the courtesy of *Athens*, the cavilling of scholars, the craft of *Grecians*? Couldst thou not remember *Philautus* that Greece is never without some wily *Ulysses*, never void of some *Sinon*, never to seek of some deceitful shifter? Is it not commonly said of *Grecians* that craft cometh to them by kind, that they learn to deceive in their cradle?[2]

In lists of national characteristics, it is this derogatory view of the Greeks that is introduced as a matter of course. Euphues, "being demanded of one what countryman he was, he answered, what countryman am I not? if I be in *Crete*, I can lie; if in *Greece*, I can shift; if in *Italy*, I can court it".[3] Almost the same words are used in *Euphues and his England* (1580), where one of the characters says: "If I met with one of *Crete*, I was ready to lie with him for the whetstone. If with a *Grecian*, I could dissemble with *Synon*. . . ."[4] And in *Euphues and his Ephoebus*, the Elizabethan reader was told that "of old it was said to a *Lacedemonian*, that all the *Grecians* knew honesty, but not one practised it".[5] In like manner, in *Greene's Mourning Garment* (1590) the Greeks are notorious:

> In *Crete* thou must learn to lie, in *Paphos* to be a lover, in *Greece* a dissembler, thou must bring home pride from *Spain*, lasciviousness from *Italy*,[6]

and so on. In the anonymous play, *The Statelie Tragedie of Claudius Tiberius Nero* (printed 1607), the ambitious Sejanus declares that "He that will climb, and aim at honours white" must be able to accommodate himself to all temperaments,

---

[1] Reprinted in the "Tudor Translations" (2 vols., 1925), i, 64. In Italian the phrases *vivere alla greca* (i.e. *nel lusso molle*) and *feda greca* were proverbial, as elsewhere in Europe.

[2] *Works*, ed. Bond, i, 232.

[3] *Op. cit.*, i, 186. This is an addition in the second edition (1579).

[4] *Op. cit.*, ii, 24.

[5] *Op. cit.*, i, 275. This is a conflation of two Plutarchan anecdotes; *Apophthegmata Laconica*, Varia, 52 and 62.

[6] *Works*, ed. Grosart (1881–6), ix, 136 (where the 1616 edition is reprinted).

Drink with the German, with the Spaniard brave:
Brag with the French, with the Egyptian lie,
Flatter in Crete, and fawn in Graecia.[1]

Donne in one of his epigrams jeers at the *Mercurius Gallo-Belgicus*, a periodical publication of the early seventeenth century which gave news of events in Europe, some of it apparently untrustworthy:

Change they name: thou art like
Mercury in stealing, but liest like a *Greek*.[2]

With this background, it is easy to see how, from the early sixteenth century onwards, a "greek" had the meaning of "a crook". It was widespread for three centuries.[3] A favourite use of the word was for a sharper at cards, but it could be applied to any kind of cheat. For example, in *The Defence of Cony-Catching* (1592) we are told "A pleasant Tale how a holy Brother Cony-catched for a Wife". A sly rogue hears of a young lady who has an ample portion in her own right; so "to this girl goeth this proper Greek a-wooing, naming himself to be a Gentleman of *Cheshire* . . .".[4]

Although "Greek" meaning "a dissipated person" hardly survived after the seventeenth century (I know only of one example of its use in the eighteenth century), "Greek" meaning "a sharper" continued in use, as a cant term, far into the nineteenth century. In *The Spirit of the Public Journals for the Year MDCCCXXIII* (London, 1824) is an essay "On Gambling. Rules for Greeking", which begins:

The "*Modern Greek*", if he does not possess *all* the attributes of the ancient one, at least lays claim to that quality for which the latter was ever so celebrated, namely, cunning and wariness: and, though he cannot boast much resemblance to Achilles, Ajax, Patroclus, or Nestor, in courage, strength, fidelity, or wisdom, he is nevertheless a close copier of the equally renowned and more successful chief of Ithaca. He is a man *habited* like a gentleman, to be found in most societies, and who subsists by unfair play at

---

[1] Malone Society reprint (1914), lines 667, 683–5.
[2] *Poems*, ed. Grierson (Oxford, 1912), i, 78.
[3] In French *grec* was similarly used and apparently still survives. See *Littré*, s.v.; also Kastner and Marks, *A Glossary of Colloquial and Popular French* (London, 1929), s.v.
[4] Greene's *Works*, ed. Grosart, xi, 80. For an amusing example of *graeca fide*, applied to the author's praise of the red herring, see Nashe's *Lenten Stuffe* (1599), *Works*, ed. McKerrow, iii, 221 (36).

cards and *dice*, and defrauding those with whom he professes intimacy.[1]

Thackeray continued the use of the word, perhaps archaicizing. His Barnes Newcome abuses the Vicomte de Florac, declaring "he was an adventurer, a pauper, a blackleg, a regular Greek".[2]

Thus it came about that, in England, France, Italy, and elsewhere, during Shakespeare's lifetime, the Greek was a household word for a voluptuary or a crook. "Greek" never acquired such an intensively pejorative meaning as "Turk"; but the word could be used as a term of condescension, contempt, or abuse in much the same manner. These attitudes were immediately accepted as appropriate to the contemporary Greeks, who still inhabited the southern part of the Balkan peninsula and the fringe of Asia Minor. The sixteenth century, had, of course, no subtle ethnological ideas; the inhabitants of a country were, normally speaking, the aboriginals. The Ancient Britons were casually thought of as the ancestors of Queen Elizabeth's subjects; and what Julius Caesar or Dion or Tacitus wrote about the inhabitants of the island of Britannia applied, or was expected to be applicable, to their descendants in the kingdom of England. On the same principle, what St. Paul wrote about the Cretans in ancient times was supposed to be descriptive of the modern inhabitants of the island. This is precisely what happened. Compilers of lists of national characteristics accepted, with indifference, ancient testimony alongside (or in preference to) modern experience. Thus, his very name condemned the Greek before he could say anything in defence of himself—like a character in *The Pilgrim's Progress*, or in a Restoration comedy, who comes on to the stage emphatically labelled Vainlove or Sir Tunbelly Clumsy.

It was with the considerable disadvantage therefore, of a derogatory name, that the Greek nation re-entered the consciousness of Europe. Naturally, Englishmen soon discovered the characteristics implied by the label. The Greeks were (at worst) frivolous, drunken, and deceitful; or (at best) they were gay, convivial, and acute. The phrase "merry greek" occurs again and again in the early travel-books about the Levant, as if the writers had been delighted to find confirmation of a proverbial expression. Thus, Sir Anthony Sherley and his companions during their journey to the East in 1599 report that, when in Crete, they received kindly and hospitable treatment from the inhabitants, especially from "the gentlewomen, who oftentimes, did make us banquets in their gardens, with music and dancing; they may well be called merry Greeks, for in the evenings, commonly

[1] p. 413.   [2] *The Newcomes*, chap. xxxvi.

after they leave work, they will dance up and down the streets, both men and women".[1] In like terms George Sandys, who was in Greek lands in 1610, describes the people of Chios as "well meriting the name of Merry Greeks, when their leisure will tolerate. Never Sunday or holiday passes over without some public meeting or other: where intermixed with women, they dance out the day, and with full crowned cups enlengthen their jollity. . . ."[2]

These are comparatively agreeable illustrations of the way in which Greek levity impressed Englishmen. But some of the untravelled were more bitter, and eagerly revived the usual antique sneers against the modern nation. The opinionated Peter Heylyn, whose *Microcosmus. A Little Description of the Great World* was frequently reprinted during the seventeenth century, accuses the Greeks of boundless intemperance. "Hence, as I believe, sprung our by-word, *As merry as a Greek*, and the Latin word *Graecari*."[3]

The early visitors often also discovered justification for the darker interpretation of the Greek character. They found them to be "Greeks" indeed. William Biddulph, who was chaplain at Constantinople in 1599 and travelled far, reported to his correspondent that "The Greeks are very superstitious, subtle and deceitful people, insomuch that it is grown to a proverb amongst the Italians, *Cui fida in Grego sara intrego*. He that trusteth to a Greek, shall be intrigued, and still to seek."[4] The currency of this insulting Italian proverb was another blow at the reputation of the Greeks, and from now on it regularly appears in the travel-books. William Lithgow in 1610 calmly says that, in Zante, "The Islanders are Greeks, a kind of subtle people, and great dissemblers";[5] and Peter Heylyn comes out with the usual over-emphatic account of the wickedness of the Cretans:

> The people have formerly been good seafaring men; a virtue commaculated with many vices which they yet retain, as envy, malice, and lying; to which last they were so addicted, that an horrible lie was termed *Cretense mendacium* . . .

[1] From the account by George Manwaring printed in *The Retrospective Review*, vol. II (1820), p. 355; it appeared more completely (modernized) in *The Three Brothers; or, the Travels and Adventures of Sir Anthony, Sir Robert and Sir Thomas Sherley* (1825), p. 29.

[2] *A Relation of a Journey begun An. Dom. 1610* (1615), p. 14. The influence of the language of Roman comedy is apparent in the last sentence.

[3] *MIKROKOSMOS. A Little Description of the Great World* (Oxford, 1625), p. 373. This passage is not in the first edition of 1621; it remained unchanged in the later, steadily expanding, editions, reappearing in the folio *Cosmographie, in four bookes* (1652), ii, 216.

[4] *The Travels of certaine Englishmen into Africa, Asia, Troy, Bythinia* . . . (1609), p. 79.

[5] *The Totall Discourse of the Rare Adventures and Painefull Peregrinations* (1632), ii, 64 (Glasgow edition, 1906, p. 58).

and the customary quotation from St. Paul follows.[1] In spite of occasional expressions of sentiment in favour of the unfortunate Grecian Christians as inhabitants of a country once glorious in history and poetry, this view of the wickedness and perfidiousness of the Greeks was dominant in the sixteenth and seventeenth centuries and survived even longer.

It must be added that the women of Greece had a reputation that corresponded to the men's. (The complement of rogue with whore has long been usual in English literature.) Juvenal had deplored the grecizing libidinous habits of the women of his time. Every provincial girl wanted to be a "maid of Athens".[2] The traveller William Biddulph in 1599 included in his opinions of the Greeks that "many of their women [are] as light as water".[3] Peter Heylyn, in his geographical treatise, declared that in Greece, "The women are for the most part brown complexioned, exceedingly welfavoured, and excessively amorous."[4] The ladies of Chios, in particular, had great fame. One can sense the mariners' salacious yarns which lie behind Lithgow's account:

> The Women of the City Sio, are the most beautiful Dames (or rather Angelical creatures) of all the Greeks, upon the face of the earth, and greatly given to Venery. . . . If a Stranger be desirous to stay all night with any of them, their price is a Chicken [*i.e. sequin*] of Gold, nine Shillings English, out of which this companion receiveth his supper, and for his pains, a bellyful of sinful content.[5]

The beauty of the Chiot women and their lewd conduct for long remained a lively topic for travellers,[6] who thus crudely interpreted the open manners, the curiosity, and the comparative freedom enjoyed by women on the more prosperous Greek islands. But it is much in this calumniating spirit that the reputation of the women of Greece for venery appears in the literature of the sixteenth and

---

[1] *Microcosmus* (Oxford, 1621), p. 226. It may be noted how much more generous was Sir Thomas Browne: "St. *Paul*, that calls the *Cretians* liars, doth it but indirectly, and upon quotation of their own Poet. It is as bloody a thought in one way, as *Nero's* was in another. For by a word we wound a thousand, and at one blow assassine the honour of a Nation." (*Religio Medici*, Part II, sect. iv.) cf. p. 34, n. 6, above.

[2] vi, 186.

[3] *The Travels of certaine Englishmen*, p. 79.

[4] *MIKROKOSMOS* (1625), p. 373.

[5] *The Totall Discourse*, iii, 102–3 (Glasgow edition, 1906, pp. 92–3).

[6] Even the stiff George Wheler informs his readers that Chios is "renowned at present for good Wine and handsome Women, and those very kind" (*Journey*, 1682, p. 65).

seventeenth centuries. In Massinger's *The Guardian* (licensed 1633), Calipso discourses on "the garb and difference in foreign females",

> The Roman libertine, the sprightly Tuscan,
> The merry Greek, Venetian courtezan. . . .[1]

In Thomas Heywood's play, *The English Traveller* (printed 1633), the young gentleman Geraldine is asked by Prudentilla where, during his long travels through France, Italy, Spain, the Empire, Greece, and Palestine, he found the most beautiful women, and from which country he would feel inclined to choose a wife. His comments upon the Greeks contain the usual charge of profligacy:

> The Greek wantons
> Compell'd beneath the Turkish slavery,
> Vassal themselves to all men, and such best
> Please the voluptuous, that delight in change. . . .[2]

It is difficult to see any justification for these widespread aspersions on the chastity of Grecian women, for no traveller produced (so far as I can discover) any convincing testimony; hearsay, of untrustworthy origin, is all we are offered. That Grecian women to any considerable extent differed in their conduct from others in the Mediterranean lands is improbable. Antique fables about Cythera and Paphos, memories of Corinthian revels, of Phryne and Lais, of the Grecian courtesans celebrated in Roman poetry, seem to have been responsible for the calumniation. But it was unquestioned.

It is from the innocent Thomas Dallam that we probably get the truth—a delightful account of personal experience on the island of Chios in 1599. There, he tells us, "did stand the chiefest women in the town in degrees one above another, to see us at our going away; they stood in such order as we might see their faces and breasts naked, yet were they very richly apparelled, with chains about their necks, and jewels in them and in their ears, their heads very comely dressed with ribbon of divers colours; but that which made us most admire them was their beauty and clear complexion. I think that no part of the world can compare with the women in that country for beauty."[3]

On the whole, the point of view of most Western Europeans towards the Greeks was that (although it was deplorable that a Christian

---

[1] II, v. ed. Gifford (1813), iv. 168; Mermaid Series (ed. A. Symons), ii, 221.
[2] Sig. B2 (I, i); Mermaid edition, p. 162.
[3] *Early Voyages and Travels in the Levant,* ed. for the Hakluyt Society by J. T. Bent, 1893, p. 46.

people should be in servitude to the wicked and dangerous Turks)
the Greeks deserved their fate. They had degenerated so far from
their ancestors that their position was hopeless. It was God's judgment upon a decadent people. They had been, it could be assumed,
noble and virtuous in the past, but now

> their knowledge is converted, as I may say, into affected ignorance
> (for they have no schools of learning amongst them), their liberty
> into contented slavery, having lost their minds with their Empire.
> For so base they are, as thought it is that they had rather remain
> as they be, than endure a temporary trouble by prevailing succours.
> . . . Long after the loss of their other virtues they retained their
> industry. . . . But now they delight in ease, in shades, in dancing,
> and drinking; and no further for the most part endeavour their
> profit than their bellies compel them.[1]

Such opinions as these persisted for several generations. The Frenchman Jean de Thévenot, who gained fame by his oriental travels,
was in the Levant in 1655, and writes of the Greeks with great
virulence:

> As to their Customs and ways of living, they are much like the
> Turks, but more wicked. The *Greeks* are covetous, perfidious, and
> treacherous, great Pederasts, revengeful to extremity, but withal
> very superstitious, and great Hypocrites; and, indeed, they are so
> despised by the Turks, that they value not even a *Greek* that turns
> Turk. They are far greater Enemies to *Roman* Catholicks them-
> selves than the Turks are; and if it lay only in their power to hinder
> us from becoming Masters of the Turkish Countries, we need
> never expect it. Their Women are beautiful, but a little too fat,
> and very proud.[2]

John Covel, who spent seven years in the Levant (1670–6) as chaplain
to the ambassador Sir Daniel Harvey and his successor Sir John
Finch, and travelled widely, sums up his opinion: "Believe me,
Greeks are Greeks still; for falseness and treachery they still deserve
Iphigenia's character of them in Euripides, *Trust them and hang
them.*"[3]

---

[1] Sandys, *A Relation of a Journey begun An. Dom. 1610* (1615), p. 77.
[2] *Relation d'un voyage fait au Levant*, Paris, three parts 1665, 1674, 1684. Pt. 1,
chap. lv, pp. 158–9. I quote from the English translation by A. Lovell, London,
1687, p. 83.
[3] *Early Voyages and Travels in the Levant*, edited for the Hakluyt Society by
J. T. Bent (1893), p. 133.

Since these were the opinions of men who had some experience of the Greeks in the sixteenth and seventeenth centuries, we need not be surprised that the untravelled spoke in similarly censorious terms. Robert Burton thought the present low estimate of the modern Greeks was an ironical revenge for their overweening conceit in ancient times.[1] The same cruel opinion was expressed by Peter Heylyn, who writes with his usual dogmatism and blatancy. There is a kind of justice, he says, in the humiliation of the Greeks nowadays, when you remember how proud they once were. "All their neighbours and remote Nations were by them scornfully called *Barbarians*: a name now most fit for the *Grecians* themselves, being an inconstant people, destitute of all *learning*, and the means to obtain it, *Universities*; uncivil, riotous, and so lazy, that for the most part, they endeavour their profit no further than their belly compels them,[2] and so perfidious withall in all their dealings, especially towards the Western *Christians* that it is grown into a Proverb amongst the *Italians, Chi fida in Grego, sara in trigo.*"[3] None of those censorious Englishmen, so far as I have observed, remembered their Homer; Zeus robs a man of half his virtue when the day of slavery comes upon him.[4]

The moral degeneration of the Greeks was paralleled, in the minds of Western observers, by the corruption of their language. Many of the early itineraries for pilgrims to the Holy Land included lists of useful words and commonplace phrases in the contemporary Greek; and these are, in spite of their obvious inaccuracies, a very interesting revelation of the state of the language at the beginning of the modern period. Andrew Boorde, that eccentric physician, traveller, and author, gave some modern Greek equivalents of ancient Greek phrases in the *Fyrst Boke of the Introduction of Knowledge* published in 1542.[5] But there were hardly any descriptions of the contemporary Greek idiom until the seventeenth century. Probably the first popular account in English was given by Edward Brerewood, who in 1614 published his *Enquiries touching the Diversity of Languages and Religions through the chief parts of the world* (1614), a widely known book, often reprinted, and translated into French and Latin.[6]

[1] *The Anatomy of Melancholy* (1621), "Democritus to the Reader" (Everyman's Library edition, i, p. 70).
[2] Heylyn is cribbing from Sandys (see p. 44 above), as he often does.
[3] *MIKROKOSMOS* (1625), p. 373.
[4] *Odyssey* xvii, 322–3.
[5] Reprinted by the Early English Text Society (1870), ed. F. J. Furnivall, 173–5.
[6] This was reprinted in *Purchas his Pilgrims* (1625) as "Enquiries of Languages by Edw. Brerewood, lately Professor of Astronomy in Gresham College"; Glasgow edition (1905), i, 256 sqq.

He gives us a melancholy picture of the speech of the modern Greeks:

> at this day, the *Greek* tongue is very much decayed, not only as touching the largeness, and vulgarness of it, but also in the pureness and elegancy of the language . . . it is also much degenerated and impaired, as touching the pureness of speech, being overgrown with barbarousness: But yet not without some relish of the ancient elegancy.

The decay is not due, he says, merely to the invasions of barbarians, Goths, Slavonians, and Turks; "the greatest part of the corruption of that language, hath been bred at home, and proceeded from no other cause, than their own negligence, or affectation". The decay of the Greek language is the fault of the Greeks. George Sandys in 1610 agreed with this opinion; Greek had been corrupted not so much by the mixture of other tongues as through "a supine recklessness".[1] The liturgy of the Greek Church (continued Brerewood) is not understood "(or but little of it) by the vulgar people, as learned men that have been in those parts, have related to others, and to my self: which may be also more evidently proved to be true by this, because" [as every Englishman with a classical education who travels in Greece, soon learns by experience. Oh, immortal vanity of scholarship!] "the skilful in the learned *Greek*, cannot understand the vulgar". But true to the current notion that the Greeks were a kind of ancient ruin, far advanced in decay and liable to collapse, Brerewood is ready to believe that casual survivals from antiquity can be found. He had heard something of the existence of *Tsakoniká*, that dialect with curious Dorian links.

> It is recorded by some, that have taken diligent observation of that tongue, in the several parts of *Greece*, that there be yet in *Morea* (Peloponnesus), betwixt *Napoli* and *Monemabasia* (*Nauplia* and *Epidaurus* [*sic*] they were called) some 14 towns, the inhabitants where [of] are called *Zacones* (for *Lacones*), that speak yet the ancient *Greek* Tongue, but far out of Grammar rule: yet, they understand those that speak grammatically but understand not the vulgar *Greek*.[2]

In the long record of the existence of the Greeks, the sixteenth century may well be regarded as the period of their lowest condition. It is difficult to think of any other people, who, having fallen so low,

[1] *Relation*, p. 80.   [2] pp. 8, 9, 11, 12 (Purchas, i, 261–4).

rose again to achieve liberty and a respected place in civilization. They were despised by their nearest Latin neighbours as schismatics. They were degraded, humiliated, and inhumanly oppressed; and they were the victims of a hateful tax on their children. It is not for any nation, which has not endured long centuries of foreign and non-Christian oppression, to condemn the Grecian nation, in a past century or in the present. They remained faithful to their religion, to their language, and to the memory of their ancestors, although civilized Europe felt no responsibility on their behalf.

It was at this nadir of their existence that the Greeks re-entered the consciousness of Western Europe, and faced a curious variety of prejudices such as have rarely surrounded any other nation. The situation could hardly have been worse. To the English as well as to the Greeks is due some credit that it rapidly became a little better.

CHAPTER III

THE SENTIMENT OF PLACE

> Beautiful shadow
> Of Thetis' boy!
> Who sleeps in the meadow
> Whose grass grows o'er Troy. . . .
>
> Byron, *The Deformed Transformed.*

It will surprise you, perhaps, to hear, that I do not think [Byron] had much taste for the picturesque, though a very lively feeling on interesting scenes, especially where the associations were exciting: it was more associations than sights in which he delighted.

John Galt in Finden's *Illustrations of the Life and Works of Lord Byron* (1833).

WE have seen that the Romans of the Imperial period spoke with extreme disparagement of the Greeks of their time; and that this attitude was unfortunately repeated by those who came into contact with the Greeks in the sixteenth and seventeenth centuries. But although the ancient Romans were contemptuous of the nation of Greeks, they were capable of powerful sentiment about the country of Greece. They felt the emotional appeal of visiting sites with interesting historical and poetical associations; and sometimes they were capable of expressing that appeal in a curiously modern way. This sentiment for place encouraged the tourist impulse and the establishment of literary shrines for the benefit of the Romans. Sometimes the cult of curious memorials for the inspection of visitors equalled modern extravagances. At Delphi was preserved an iron chair which Pindar had used.[1] At Sparta was an egg, presumably unhatched, of Leda.[2]

The classical precedent for sentiment about places famous in history exerted a strong influence upon the attitude of Western Europeans to the Greek lands from the sixteenth to the eighteenth centuries. This is not to deny the sincerity of what the visitors from Western Europe felt; but the relevant quotations from the Roman authors helped the expression of emotion. The modern contemplative traveller was given a lead by the ancient poets with whom his

---

[1] Pausanias, X, xxiv, 5. I once knew an old lady who had, hanging from the picture-rail in her room, the seat of a chair on which Liszt had once sat when playing.

[2] Pausanias, III, xvi, 1.

education had made him familiar. He could feel, when he brooded upon the Triumphs of Time, that he was developing a theme authorized by the recognized models of culture and sensibility.

In some respects the ruins of Greece offered a more suitable theme for moralizing than Italy, where during the sixteenth century and part of the seventeenth century there existed a contemporary culture (prompted by a revival of the ancient culture) which was dominant in Europe and exciting to the traveller. But Greece offered nothing but ruined cities and an impoverished countryside, inhabited by a people in servitude to non-Christian and tyrannical rulers. The "tragic" contrast between ancient glory and modern misery was therefore more emphatic in Greece than in Rome.

One cannot take a step in Athens, wrote Cicero, without treading upon some history (*quacunque enim ingredimur, in aliqua historia vestigium ponimus*[1]). The opening of one of his dialogues charmingly describes the scene in which, in their young days in Athens, Cicero and his friends were moved by the celebrity of the places where they were talking and walking. It may be a natural instinct or it may be an illusion; but (they agree) somehow our emotions are more strongly excited by *seeing* the place where a great man of the past lived and spoke than by reading about him. Plato used to hold discussions here. Speusippus and Xenocrates used to sit on this very seat. Do we not visit the spot where Demosthenes and Aeschines delivered their famous orations? Can you pass by Colonos without thinking of Sophocles—nay, of Oedipus? Such are the powers of suggestion which places possess (*tanta vis admonitionis inest in locis*). It may be a mere fancy; but the fact remains that we really are moved (*inaniter scilicet, sed commovit tamen*); it is a usual experience that places strongly stimulate the imagination and make more vivid the ideas we have of famous men (*usu hoc venire ut acrius aliquanto et attentius de claris viris locorum admonitu cogitemus*).[2]

This sort of topographical sentiment, however, had clearly developed long before Cicero and Atticus. From the time of their wars against the Greeks, while the conquerors were preparing to capitulate to the culture of the conquered, the Romans were aware of the remarkable inheritance they were gaining by the force of their arms. After the defeat of Perseus (167 B.C.) the victorious Paulus Aemilius resolved to go through Greece to see with his own eyes those places and objects which had been ennobled by fame. The journey is described by Livy, and it reads like an account of a "classical and sentimental tour" by any eighteenth-century enthusi-ast; though the historian of Romanity tartly adds that these places,

[1] *De finibus*, V, ii (5).   [2] *Op. cit.*, V, i (2), i (3) and ii (4).

magnified by fame, appear much more impressive to the ears than
they are when seen by the eyes.[1] Paulus Aemilius went to Delphi,
Lebadia (for the Trophonian cave), Chalcis (for the tides of the
Euripus), Aulis (as the station of Agamemnon's ships), Oropus,
Athens, Piraeus, Corinth (still flourishing), Sicyon, Argos, Epidaurus,
Sparta, Megalopolis, and Olympia. The Roman proconsul was only
the first of the conquerors of Greece who viewed the cities of their
subjects with interest and admiration; in like spirit did Mahomet the
Conqueror gaze upon the Acropolis of Athens in 1460, and German
and Italian generals make archaeological tours in 1943.

An anonymous Roman poet of the age of Augustus gives a description of the cultivated tourist in Greece, which applies well
enough to the modern travellers to places made interesting by
associations from ancient history and art:

> magnificas laudes operosaque visere templa
> divitiis hominum aut arces memorare vetustas
> traducti maria et taetris per proxima fatis
> currimus, atque avidi veteris mendacia famae
> eruimus cunctasque libet percurrere gentes.[2]

The topographical sentiment is succinctly described; we gain
pleasure from a kind of participating experience of an age other than
our own (*felicesque alieno intersumus aevo*). Thebes and Thermopylae
attract the Roman, and still more does Athens; but above all Troy
where the heroes of the *Iliad* lie buried:

> miramur Troiae cineres et flebile victis
> Pergamon extinctosque suo Phrygas Hectore: parvum
> conspicimus magni tumulum ducis: hic et Achilles
> impiger et victus magni iacet Hectoris ultor.[3]

In the mood of an eighteenth-century gentleman with pretensions
to taste on his travels, the Roman (as described in this poem) visited
and admired the masterpieces of Greek painting and sculpture, the
celebrated works of Apelles, Timomachus, Timanthes and Myron.

[1] quae nobilitata fama maiora auribus accepta sunt, quam oculis noscuntur,
xlv, 27.

[2] "Having crossed the seas and faced the grim perils of travel, we hasten to visit
the far-famed wonders of the land and the temples thickly adorned by the wealth of
mankind, and to renew the historical memory of famous cities; and we eagerly
unearth ill-founded stories which have been hallowed by tradition, and take
pleasure in traversing one country after another." (*Aetna*, 569-73).

[3] "We gaze in wonder at the ashes of Troy, and at its citadel so lamentable to the
vanquished, and we think of its citizens whose hopes ended with the death of their
Hector. We inspect the little mound which covers that mighty man (Hector).
Here both the restless Achilles and the avenger of mighty Hector (Paris) lie vanquished." (590-3).

There were several eloquent models, in classical literature, for the mood of the Traveller to an Antique Land. The famous letter of consolation written by Sulpicius to Cicero on the death of his daughter Tullia contained a passage[1] which was as well known as almost anything in Latin literature and provided the material for some brilliant lines in *Childe Harold's Pilgrimage.*

> Wandering in youth, I traced the path of him,
> The Roman friend of Rome's least mortal mind,
> The friend of Tully: as my bark did skim
> The bright blue waters with a fanning wind,
> Came Megara before me, and behind
> Aegina lay, Piraeus on the right,
> And Corinth on the left; I lay reclined
> Along the prow, and saw all these unite
> In ruin, even as he had seen the desolate sight;
>
> For Time hath not rebuilt them, but uprear'd
> Barbaric dwellings on their shatter'd site,
> Which only make more mourn'd and more endear'd
> The few last rays of their far-scatter'd light,
> And the crush'd relics of their vanish'd might.
> The Roman saw these tombs in his own age,
> These sepulchres of cities, which excite
> Sad wonder, and his yet surviving page
> The moral lesson bears, drawn from such pilgrimage.

(IV, xliv-xlv)

Similarly, Ovid's great list of cities of old, now decayed, was as readily applicable to modern times as to ancient.[2] We have from

[1] Ex Asia rediens cum ab Aegina Megaram versus navigarem, coepi regiones circumcirca prospicere: post me erat Aegina, ante me Megara, dextra Piraeus, sinistra Corinthus; quae oppida quodam tempore florentissima fuerunt, nunc prostrata et diruta ante oculos iacent. Coepi egomet mecum sic cogitare: "hem! nos homunculi indignamur, si quis nostrum interiit aut occisus est, quorum vita brevior esse debet, cum uno loco tot oppidum cadavera proiecta iacent? Visne tu te, Servi, cohibere et meminisse hominem te esse natum? *Ad Fam.,* iv, 5 (Tyrrell & Purser No. 555).

[2]
>   sic tempora verti
> cernimus atque illas adsumere robora gentes,
> concidere has; sic magna fuit censuque virisque
> perque decem potuit tantum dare sanguinis annos,
> nunc humilis veteres tantummodo Troia ruinas
> et pro divitiis tumulos ostendit avorum;
> clara fuit Sparte, magnae viguere Mycenae,
> nec non et Cecropis, nec non Amphionis arces.
> vile solum Sparte est, altae cecidere Mycenae,
> Oedipodioniae quid sunt, nisi nomina, Thebae?
> quid Pandioniae restant, nisi nomen, Athenae?

Metamorphoses, xv, 420–30.

Tacitus[1] an account of that romantic tourist Germanicus, who visited the chief places of celebrity in Greece and the near East in A.D. 18. He viewed Actium with deep feeling; for to one who was the grandson of Mark Antony and the great-nephew of Augustus it was "an image of both sorrow and joy" (*magna . . . illic imago tristium laetorumque*). At Athens the inhabitants granted him special honours, adding weight to their adulation by recounting the deeds and sayings of their ancestors (*vetera suorum facta dictaque praeferentes*).[2] In Egypt he saw not only the ancient Pharaonic remains, but, of course, Canopus, the city founded by the Spartans and named after the pilot of Menelaus during the return from Troy. He journeyed among the Greek cities of Asia Minor, desiring to acquaint himself with those ancient and far-famed places (*cupidine veteres locos et fama celebratos noscendi*); here the greatest attraction was Troy, venerable for the variety of its fortunes and as the ancestor of Rome (*varietate fortunae et nostri origine veneranda*). At Troy, by the tomb of Hector, Germanicus wrote a poem which is one of the scanty fragments of his works that have been preserved. Hector can rejoice now, says the poet; for he left, as an avenger, an heir almost as great in war as he was himself. A new Troy has arisen; but the Myrmidons of Achilles have all passed away; and his Thessaly itself is ruled by the descendants of Trojan Aeneas.[3]

The feeling for Troy was something in a special category for the Romans. To the man of culture, that is, to the philosopher or the rhetorician, Athens was acknowledged to be the school of Hellas, as Pericles had said, and therefore of the world; and when the Greeks gradually gave their culture to the barbarians, it was to Athens that the young men of the Roman world came as to a kind of university. The wonders of the fine arts that the walls of Athens enclosed made it the object of pilgrimage. But the sentiment for Troy, whence they drew their origin and which they had avenged for her sorrows, was strong among the Romans. The glories of their own City were in powerful contrast to the abject decay of the Mother of their City;

---

[1] *Annales*, ii, 53, 54, 60.

[2] For the proud Roman Piso's rebuke to him for Grecizing, see p. 34 above.

[3] Martia progenies, Hector, tellure sub ima
        (fas audire tamen si mea verba tibi),
      respira, quoniam vindex tibi contigit heres,
        qui patriae famam proferat usque tuae.
      Ilios en surgit rursum inclita, gens colit illam
        te Marte inferior, Martis amica tamen.
      Myrmidonas periisse omnes dic Hector Achilli,
        Thessaliam et magnis esse sub Aeneadis.
            Anthologia Latina (Teubner edition I, pt. ii, No. 708).

1. The Acropolis in the mid-eighteenth century

2. A Street in Athens. The French Consul is sitting outside his house between a Turk and a Greek. Nicholas Revett is about to mount his horse. Behind is the Portico of the Agora (see p. 161)

3. Nicholas Revett and James Stuart (on extreme left), with James Dawkins and Robert Wood, inspecting the Monument of Philopappos near Athens (see p. 163)

4. Young ladies of the island of Chios (see p. 166)

"now low-lying Troy shows only old ruins and, instead of the riches of the men of old, funeral mounds".

> nunc humilis veteres tantummodo Troia ruinas
> et pro divitiis tumulos ostendit avorum,

wrote Ovid;[1] and in his *Heroides* are some even more touching lines which became almost proverbial; *iam seges est ubi Troia fuit.* For centuries these words were remembered by Englishmen; but fewer of our travellers nowadays read the Roman poets; and the Turks have declared the whole Troad to be a military zone inaccessible to visitors. The twentieth century is denied even the ruins of Troy; we no longer are permitted to see that the grass now grows where Troy-town stood.[2] Lucan had sent his Caesar to Troy as a tourist with an elaborate historical sense, who wanders among the relics of antiquity and who broods on the inadequacies of the rewards of Fame and on the immortality which poets give to mortal things.[3] The ruins of Troy and its glory were, in truth, a striking example of the usefulness of poetry. The great Alexander surrounded himself with writers who were to record his marvellous deeds. But when he visited the tomb of Achilles near Troy, he could not refrain from envying him his Homer: "o fortunate young man, to have such a poet to recount your merits"; but for the *Iliad* even the mound which covers his body would have lost its name.[4]

The reputation of the ruins of Troy, and in consequence its tourist traffic, continued during the first few centuries of the Christian era. In the fourth century the Ilians still did a profitable trade in attracting visitors by their pseudo-Trojan memorials. In the tenth

---

[1] *Metamorphoses*, xv, 424–5.

[2] Iam seges est ubi Troia fuit, resecandaque falce
luxuriat Phrygis sanguine pinguis humus.
semisepulta virum curvis feriuntur aratris
ossa; ruinosas occulit herba domos.
> *Heroides*, i, 53–6.

[3] Circuit exustae nomen memorabile Troiae,
magnaque Phoebaei quaerit vestigia muri.
iam silvae steriles, et putres robore trunci
Assaraci pressere domos, et templa deorum
iam lassa radice tenent; ac tota teguntur
Pergama dumetis: etiam periere ruinae. . . .
O sacer et magnus vatum labor, omnia fato
eripis, et populis donas mortalibus aevum.
> *Pharsalia*, ix, 964–9, 980–1.

[4] Atque is tamen, cum in Sigeo ad Achillis tumulum adstitisset, o fortunate, inquit, adolescens, qui tuae virtutis Homerum praeconem inveneris! Et vere: nam nisi Ilias illa exstitisset, idem tumulus, qui corpus eius contexerat, nomen etiam obruisset. Cicero, *Pro Archia*, X.

Epistle of Aeschines (these epistles are, of course, a rhetorical fabrication) we are told how the orator, after leaving Athens, arrived at Ilium, and intended to stay there until he had gone through all the verses in the *Iliad* on the very spot to which they had reference. He was prevented from getting very far in this literary exercise by the conduct of his friend Cimon, who deceived a local maiden Callirrhoe by pretending to be the river-god Scamander.[1] The other sites made famous by history and poetry for long retained their appeal to the imagination. Marathon remained "a witness of many virtues, and great ones" (*multarum magnarumque virtutium testis*).[2] Synesius in the early fifth century declared that his chief reason for visiting Athens was that he might no longer be compelled to revere those who had been there and who differed in no respect from common mortals but because they had seen the Academy, the Lycaeum and the Porch. It was he who originated the comparison (so often echoed by later writers) of Athens to the skin of a slaughtered animal; he saw the city after the passage of Alaric's army over Greece (A.D. 396).[3]

This was the classical background to the topographical ruminations of the early visitors to Greece from Western Europe during and after the Renaissance. Indeed, the feeling that the traveller in Greek lands was visiting places exciting for their associations is hardly absent even from the notes of the fifteenth-century pilgrims. In the earliest printed travel-book, the pious peregrination of Bernhard von Breydenbach, which first appeared in 1486, we are not allowed to pass the island of Cerigo without being informed that it was once called Cythera and that the goddess Venus had her name of Cytherea because she was born near there.[4] This island was, so far as Greece is concerned, probably the place on the pilgrimage route which had the greatest classical celebrity; and the manuals and travel-notes which succeed Breydenbach's generally refer to it. Indeed by the end of the fifteenth century it was firmly established that the island was also to be identified with Delphi ("the isle of Delphos").[5] In the little manual of 1498, *Information for Pilgrims unto the Holy Land*, we read: "Upon the left hand six miles within there is standing yet of the temple wherein Apollo was worshipped. . . . And the same isle where the temple was which was called of the Greeks in old time

---

[1] The story is familiar from one of La Fontaine's *Contes et Nouvelles* (V, ii, "Le Fleuve Scamandre").

[2] Pomponius Mela, ii, 3 (45).

[3] *Epistol.* liv and cxxxvi (*Epistolographi Graeci*, ed. R. Hercher (Paris, 1873), pp. 662, 722).

[4] Est insula citerea sic vocata. eoque ibi venus orta sit. (*Peregrinatio in terram sanctam*, Mainz, 1486.)

[5] See "Shakespeare's Isle of Delphos" by T. Spencer in *Modern Language Review*, XLVII (1952), pp. 199–202.

Delphos, in Latin Cerigo."[1] Similarly the chaplain who accompanied Sir Richard Guildford on his pilgrimage to Jerusalem in 1506 and wrote an account of it tells us that "the said isle Cerigo is directly against the point of Cape Malea in Morea, and in the same isle was Venus born, and in the same isle is Delphos. . . ."[2] But it was only the sites on well-defined routes that were known from personal experience. Athens for long remained comparatively unknown, because it was not itself the seat of any important trade, nor was it upon any trade-route which made travel thither secure. This is the explanation of the curious ignorance regarding the fate of Athens displayed in the sixteenth century. The learned Martin Crusius wrote to a Greek correspondent, asking if anything of the city was left. There seems to have been a notion (spread, no doubt, by sailors who had only seen Porto Leone) that nothing survived of Athens save a few fishermen's huts. This statement was true of Piraeus, but of course it was not true of Athens. Yet it was received into several important and influential books. Antoine Du Pinet, a learned geographer, stated in his folio *Plantz, pourtraitz et descriptions de plusieurs villes et forteresses* (Lyons, 1564) that nothing of Athens remained except a castle and a little village which was not free from foxes, wolves, and other savage beasts. The wild animals which infest Athens we shall meet in the writings of many ignorant commentators. Le Seigneur de Borderie, in his interesting poem, *Le Discours du Voyage de Constantinople, envoyé du dit lieu à une Damoyselle Françoise*, spares a thought for the inhabitants of what was once the most glorious city of the world; the Athenians were the first and most ancient gentlemen of Greece, but now they do not enjoy the rights of nobility.

> Athéniens qui furent les premiers,
> Et plus anciens gentilzhommes de Grece,
> User des droictz ne peuvent de noblesse. . . .

The author had, however, no personal knowledge of the city.[3]

Sometimes the inaccuracy of place-names and the repetition of seafarers' yarns makes the comments hardly intelligible, as (to quote a specimen) those of Master Laurence Aldersey who, sailing among

---

[1] Ed. E. Gordon Duff (1893), sig. ciij, recto and verso.

[2] *The Pylgrymage of Sir Richard Guylforde to the Holy Land*, A.D. 1506, ed. Sir Henry Ellis (Camden Society No. 51, 1851), p. 13.

[3] He accompanied de Saint-Blancard, who was sent in 1537 into the Levant seas at the head of the French fleet. A prose relation of this voyage was written by Jehan de Vega. Laborde, *Athènes aux XVᵉ, XVIᵉ et XVIIᵉ Siècles* (2 vols., Paris, 1854) i, 47. The poem of de Borderie was printed at Lyons (1542) and Paris (1546); and reprinted by Laborde, *op. cit.*, i, 263 sqq.

the Cyclades in 1586, reports: ". . . we passed by the Island of Paris [doubtless, Paros] and the Island of the bankes of Helicon [sic], and the Island called Ditter [perhaps a misreading of "Dilles", i.e. Rheneia and Delos], where are many boares, and the women bee witches".[1] There is a kind of disinterested bluntness in the remarks of William Harborne, the first English ambassador to the Porte, on his voyage out in the Susan in 1583; he sailed by Cythera and announced: "This Cerigo is an Island where one Menelaus did sometimes reign, from whom was stolen by Paris fair Helena, and carried to Troy, as ancient Records do declare."[2] William Biddulph, who was chaplain at Constantinople in 1599 and who went on a long journey in the Near Eastern lands in the early years of the seventeenth century is full of merely naïve comment in his letters home. "*Graecia*", he informs us, "amongst all other Countries in *Europe*, hath been accounted the most noble and most famous. . . . *Arcadia* is famous for shepherds. . . . In this part of *Graecia* is *Parnassus*, a mountain having two tops, whereon the nine Muses did dwell. . . . *Athens* is still inhabited: . . . This City was the mother and nurse of all liberal Arts and Sciences: but now there is nothing but Atheism and Barbarism there: for it is governed by *Turks*, and inhabited by ignorant *Greeks*." Biddulph recognizes Cephalonia as Ithaca, where lived Ulysses, "commended by ancient Writers, for a famous Traveller: but if he were living in these days, his travels would be counted nothing, in respect of the travels of many other now living: for he travelled but betwixt *Venice* and *Egypt*. . . ."[3]

Yet whatever the traveller might feel and admire elsewhere, it was Troy that prompted the strongest curiosity and provoked the warmest sensations. For Troy was the mother of the nations of Europe; and her fall had been enshrined in the most famous work of European poetry. To Troy every traveller went if he had the opportunity; and the untravelled made use of Troy-sentiment evocatively. The literary material about Troy, inherited from antiquity, was, as we have seen, extensive and provided a lively background for topographical sentiment. Proud Troy has fallen (*Ceciditque superbum Ilium*), Virgil had written;[4] and for Dante, Troy, having become an example of the fall of pride, is illustrated by the sculptures on the

[1] Hakluyt, vi, 41–2.   [2] *Ibid*., v, 250.
[3] pp. 5–10. The book was compiled by Theophilus Lavender from letters by William and Peter Biddulph to Bezaliell Biddulph and published in 1609 as *The Travels of certaine Englishmen*. There was another edition of 1612 with the title *The Travels of Foure English Men and a Preacher into Africa, Asia, Troy, Bythinia, Thracia, and to the Black Sea*. . . . Biddulph's travelling companions were Jeffrey Kirbie, Edward Abbot, John Elkin, Jasper Tyon.
[4] *Aeneid*, iii, 2–3.

pavement of the appropriate circle of Purgatory.[1] The references to Troyland in Renaissance literature are, of course, innumerable:

> *Troy*, that art now nought but an idle name,
> And in thine ashes buried low dost lie. . . .[2]

Every traveller in the northern Aegean seas was, therefore, eager for the experience of visiting Troy. And, as it happened, nearly all of them on their way to Constantinople had an excellent opportunity of gratifying their curiosity. The notorious current which flows almost unremittingly from the Euxine through the Bosphorus, the Propontis, and the Dardanelles, made the journey to Constantinople difficult. It was a tedious and troublesome stretch of sailing even with a favourable wind. It was almost impossible with an unfavourable wind; and the prevailing wind in summer (when most of the voyaging was done) is north to north-east. Nearly every boat had to wait at the mouth of the Dardanelles for a favourable wind, often for days, sometimes even for weeks. The most convenient station was the harbour of Tenedos. "In sight of Troy stands Tenedos, a famous island" (*Est in conspectu Tenedos, notissima fama insula*), Virgil had written;[3] and there, in full view of Tenedos, were the ruins of a great ancient city, including some buildings of stupendous size. There, obviously, was Troy; and that huge ruin, with its ponderous arches and huge lumps of masonry, what could that be but the palace of Priam? The local inhabitants and the sailors confirmed the identification; their opinion was unanimous: this was Troy. To while away the tedium of awaiting a wind to continue the journey to Constantinople, nearly every traveller went ashore and wandered over the ruins. Pierre Belon, who was there in 1546, relates that one sees the ruins from the sea, afar off, because in places the walls are still upright. There are arches made of brick with cement, wonderful to behold. How absurd, says Belon, are those who declare that the ruins have all been demolished! It took him four hours to make the circuit of the walls, on foot and on horseback.[4] It was there that Thomas Dallam, the organ-builder, in 1599 broke off a piece of

---

[1] Vedeva Troia in cenere e in caverne:
O Ilion come te basso e vile
Mostrava il segno che lì si discerne!
Purgatorio, xii, 61–3; cf. *Inferno*, xxx, 13–15:
E quando la Fortuna volse in basso
L'altezza de' Troian, che tutto ardiva. . . .

[2] *The Faerie Queene*, III, ix, stanza 33.   [3] *Aeneid*, ii, 21–2.

[4] *Les Observations de plusieurs singularitez et choses memorables trouvées en Grece, Asie, Judée* . . . (Paris, 1553), livre ii, chapitre vi (pp. 82 verso–84).

marble to take home with him as a souvenir.[1] Lithgow, who was there in 1610, had an engraving produced of himself amid the ruins of Troy, with the tombs of Priam and Hecuba in the background, and offered his readers a poem on the subject:

> Here Tombs I viewed, old monuments of Times,
> And fiery Trophies, fixed for bloody crimes:
> For which Achilles' ghost did sigh and say,
> Curst be the hands, that sakeless Trojans slay;
> But more fierce Ajax, more Ulysses' Horse,
> That wrought grief's ruin; Priam's last divorce:
> And here inclosed, within these clods of dust,
> All Asia's honour, and cross'd Paris' lust.[2]

Pietro della Valle, his mind crowded with memories of Virgil (*il nostro poeta*), is fully aware of the power of sentimental associations. He writes to his correspondent in 1614: "You could hardly believe with what tenderness I went walking over these places, being reminded at every step of all the ancient stories. As Virgil says, 'Here Achilles had his camp with his men; this was the station of the fleet; it was here that the armies used to join battle'. But when I thought how, where once upon a time were magnificent city-streets and splendid palaces, there are nowadays deserted fields and solitary waste places, my heart was filled with compassion."[3]

As a matter of fact, these travellers were standing and expending their emotions on Alexandreia Troas, a city founded by one of the successors of Alexander the Great and situated about thirty miles from the Sigean promontory. These are the ruins that are so plainly visible from the sea and that were quickly recognized as Homer's (or rather, Virgil's) Troy. The "Palace of Priam", of which three massive arches were so conspicuous and impressive to the visitors and voyagers, are really a public bath of the Roman period. Yet the travellers of the sixteenth and early seventeenth centuries were not altogether unjustified in indulging their sentiment on this place. For Troas was the prosperous city which Augustus thought of reviving as the new capital of the Empire; and the same thought was in the

---

[1] See p. 79 below.

[2] *Totall Discourse*, iii, 122–3 (Glasgow edition, 1906, pp. 109–10).

[3] V.S. non potrebbe credere con quanta tenerezza io andava camminando per quei luoghi, ricordandomi a passo a passo di tutte le istorie antiche:

> Hic Dolopum manus, hic saevus tendebat Achilles;
> Classibus hic locus; hic acies certare solebant.

Ma quando consideava, che là dove una volta erano strade magnifiche e palazzi superbi, sono adesso campi deserti e spiaggie solitarie, ne aveva gran compassione.... *Viaggi* (Brighton, 2 vols., 1843), i, 13.

mind of Constantine, who before he "gave a just preference to the situation of Byzantium, . . . had conceived the design of erecting the seat of empire on this celebrated spot".[1] Troas was a city well known, also, to St. Paul. It was there that a vision appeared to him in the night, and bade him come over from Asia to preach the Gospel in Europe.[2] But the seeds of scepticism regarding the site of Troy were beginning to be sown by the early seventeenth century. Pietro della Valle visited "the palace of Ilion, as the peasants would have us believe"; but he has the perspicacity to add "or rather something else more modern".[3] George Sandys in 1610 is convinced that Belon and the geographers are mistaken in their identification, for the ruins are "too near the naval station to afford a field for such dispersed encounters, such long pursuits, interception of scouts (then when the *Trojans* had pitched nearer the navy), and executed stratagems, as is declared to have happened between the Sea and the City";[4] and, following him, Wheler later in the seventeenth century was agreeably sceptical and recognized the ruined city as Alexandreia Troas, described by Strabo.[5] After giving an account of the building in some detail and providing both a plan and an elevation (execrably drawn), he adds: "However I believe it not the Castle of Priam, as the Country People now call it; nor of any earlier times than the Romans."

Such archaeological re-identifications, however, are irrelevant. The fact remains that a considerable number of contemporaries of Shakespeare had stood amid "the ruins of Troy", and could relate their experiences. In one of his sonnets (printed in 1604) William Alexander, Earl of Stirling, tells of travellers who visit Rome, Carthage, and Troy as the homes of three of the world's great heroes:

> Some men delight huge buildings to behold,
> Some theatres, mountains, floods, and famous springs;
> Some monuments of Monarchs, and such things
> As in the books of fame have been enroll'd:
> Those stately towns that to the stars were rais'd,
> Some would their ruins see (their beauty's gone)
> Of which the world's three parts, each boasts of one,
> For *Caesar*, *Hannibal*, and *Hector* prais'd.[6]

---

[1] Gibbon, *The Decline and Fall*, Chapter xvii; ed. J. B. Bury (1896), ii, 146.
[2] *Acts*, xvi, 8–11.   [3] *Viaggi*, i, 12.
[4] *A Relation of a Journey begun An. Dom. 1610* (1615), p. 22.
[5] *A Journey into Greece* (1682), pp. 67–72.
[6] *Aurora, Containing the first fancies of the Author's youth*, Sonnet 52 (ed. Kastner and Charlton, 2 vols., 1921–9, ii, 487).

This seems to be an exaggeration; for Carthage can hardly have been readily accessible to Scotsmen in the early seventeenth century; yet allusions to and descriptions of the ruins of Troy are numerous in Shakespeare's lifetime. Edward Barton, the second English ambassador to the Porte, had noted in his diary during his voyage in 1594 that "by the Sigean Promontory, now called Cape Janitzary, at the mouth of Hellespont upon Asia side, where Troy stood, . . . are yet ruins of old walls to be seen, with two hills rising in a pyramidal form, not unlike to be the tombs of Achilles and Ajax".[1] Moreover, even to the unlettered the name of Troy had poetical associations. The ballad tune of *Troy Town*, with its refrain

> Waste lie those walls that were so good
> And Corn now grows where *Troy* Town stood,

was a popular one in Jacobean England. The ballad *The Wandering Prince of Troy* was entered in the Stationers' Register in 1603, and may be older.[2] There is record of English *graffiti* amid the ruins as early as 1631. A young traveller at the end of the seventeenth century declares:

> One Countryman of ours has left behind him a convincing Argument of his Arrival in those Parts, for underneath the Marble Flat, which covers *Hector's* Tomb, we found these lines, upon the side of a smooth Stone; they seem'd to have been carv'd with difficulty by a Knife, and spoke their Author a Salt Water Poet.

> I do suppose that here stood *Troy*,
> My Name it is *William* a jolly Boy,
> My other Name it is *Hudson*, and so,
> God Bless the Sailors, where ever they do go.

> I was here in the Year of our Lord 1631,
> and was Bound to Old England,
> God Bless her.[3]

---

[1] Hakluyt, vi, 107.
[2] The earliest surviving text is dated about 1620. *The Roxburghe Ballads*, ed. by W. Chappell and J. W. Ebsworth, 1869–99, vi, 547. It long remained a popular ballad. It is one of those sung by the rustic minstrel Bowzybeus in Gay's *The Shepherd's Week* (Saturday, 120).
[3] Aaron Hill, *A Full Account of the Present State of the Ottoman Empire* (1709), p. 206. I am not clear from Hill's narrative where he was. If he was really standing on the tumulus which is traditionally identified as "Hector's Tomb", then he was above Bunarbashi.

"A piece of Poetry, made at *Troy* by an *English* Sailor, in the Year 1631", is the transcriber's marginal comment; and I suppose that I must record this quatrain as the first piece of English verse known to have been composed in Greek lands; a beginning.

Had some traveller to an antique land (perhaps Hugh Holland) told Shakespeare of that mood of nostalgia, that awareness of the Triumph of Time, which came upon him as he stood upon the sacred soil of Troy and viewed the scenes immortalized by Homer and Virgil and their heroes?

> When time is old, or hath forgot itself,
> When water drops have worn the stones of *Troy*,
> And blind oblivion swallow'd Cities up,
> And mighty states character-less are grated
> To dusty nothing. . . .[1]

These lines have a contemporary, as much as a classical background; the popular ballad, and Ovid, and the experiences of adventurous Englishmen in the Aegean Sea, have all gone to nourish the superb long-range irony of Cressida's words.

Certainly as early as the time of Shakespeare we have ample evidence of that romantic sentiment about Hellas which was to have such force later—the touching contrast between ancient splendour and contemporary degradation. The first serious English traveller who was capable of expressing the peculiar mood of Greece was Fynes Moryson, who spent the years 1591–7 in his wanderings about Europe (with occasional returns to England). He had an annual grant of £20 a year from his College (Peterhouse), his total expenses being about £60 a year. Never was a travelling studentship better spent. Moryson records with profound regret the situation in Greece:

> The Empire and kingdom of the Greeks from all antiquity famous (and continuing of great power till the Turks invaded Europe and took Constantinople), from that time hath been utterly abolished, and the people have been trodden underfeet. Of them some live as in exile (at Naples, in Apulia, in Calabria, at Rome, and in the City of Venice) having neither land nor coin of their own. Others live subject to the State of Venice in their own land, and enjoying Inheritances of land, but use the Coin of that State, (as in the Islands of Corfu, Cephalonia the greater and the lesser, of Zante, and of Candia). But the greatest part live in the Islands

---

[1] *Troilus and Cressida*, III, ii, 192–6.

and Continent of Greece upon their own land, yet possessing not one foot thereof by inheritance, but living as most base slaves to the Turkish tyranny. . . .[1]

George Sandys, whose folio of travels in the Levant and the Near East, *A Relation of a Journey begun An. Dom. 1610* (1615), was regarded as of special authority throughout the seventeenth century and was constantly quoted by writers who mentioned the modern Greeks, can already express the emotion of the traveller to those lands which have endured the tramplings of many conquests, the lands where the length and misery of history oppresses the imagination. In his dedication "To the Prince" in 1615, he declares that his journeys have been to countries which, "once so glorious, and famous for their happy estate, are now through vice and ingratitude, become the most deplored spectacles of extreme misery: the wild beasts of mankind having broken in upon them, and rooted out all civility; and the pride of a stern and barbarous Tyrant possessing the thrones of ancient and just dominion". Thence has come about, he continues, "that lamentable distress and servitude, under which (to the astonishment of the understanding beholders) it now faints and groaneth".

In the work of that curious writer William Lithgow, too, sentiment about contemporary Greece in relation to ancient Hellas found emphatic expression. Lithgow left Paris in March 1610 and by way of Rome, Naples, Venice, and Athens reached Constantinople; he returned home by way of Rhodes, Cyprus, and Tripoli. He travelled through Greece mostly by land; and so he was among the first Englishmen, gifted with a certain literary articulateness, who knew something more of the country than the sea-board and the ports:

> In all this country of Greece I could find nothing, to answer the famous relations, given by ancient Authors, of the excellency of that land, but the name only; the barbarousness of Turks and Time, having defaced all the Monuments of Antiquity: No shew of honour, no habitation of men in an honest fashion, nor possessors of the Country in a Principality. But rather prisoners shut up in prisons, or addicted slaves to cruel and tyrannical Masters: So deformed is the state of that once worthy Realm, and so miserable is the burthen of that afflicted people: which, and the appearance of that permanency, grieved my heart to behold the sinister working of blind Fortune, which always plungeth the most

[1] Extracts from his itinerary as printed by Charles Hughes (1903), with the title *Shakespeare's Europe*, pp. 495–6.

renowned Champions, and their memory, in the profoundest pit of all extremities and oblivion.[1]

Lithgow here cribs shamelessly from Sir Anthony Sherley,[2] but at least he manages to make his thefts into something personal. He was but little interested in antiquities. In Athens he condescends to note that there is "a Castle which formerly was the Temple of Minerva"; but the city is for him "the Mother & Well-spring of all liberal Arts and Sciences; and the great Cistern of Europe, whence flowed so many Conduit pipes of learning all where, but now altogether decayed". Yet in this spirit he has imaginative consolations for the fatigues of travelling. In Arcadia, he says,

> this I remember, amongst these rocks my belly was pinched, and wearied was my body, with the climbing of fastidious mountains, which bred no small grief to my breast. Yet notwithstanding of my distress, the remembrance of these sweet seasoned Songs of Arcadian Shepherds which pregnant Poets have so well penned, did recreate my fatigated corpse with many sugared suppositions.

Lithgow is among the first in that long line of Englishmen who, during the last three centuries and more, have made their way to Greece and recreated their fatigated corpses with such sugared suppositions.

In Shakespeare's lifetime, therefore, we may say that there was a considerable number of men to be found in England who had had some experience of Hellenic lands. However much as we may now find about Greece in the books of the period, we should, of course, have heard far more in conversation. A good deal of the information in circulation seems to be based upon hearsay. When, for example, the stay-at-home poet Michael Drayton writes,

> If *Florence* once should lose her old renown,
> As famous *Athens*, now a Fisher-Town. . . .[3]

We are in the world of seamen's confusions between the "fisher-town" of Porto Leone and Athens itself.

William Alexander, Earl of Stirling, seems to have been oddly

---

[1] ii, 71–2; Glasgow edition, 1906, p. 65.
[2] See the passage I have quoted on p. 23 above.
[3] *England's Heroical Epistles*, "Henry Howard, Earl of Surrey to the Lady Geraldine" (1598), 139–40. (Shakespeare Head edition, ed. J. W. Hebel (1932), ii, 281.)

conscious of the Levantine situation. Everyone had for centuries, of course, lamented that the holy places of the Christian religion should be in the hands of the infidel. But Stirling makes the heathen gods angry that *their* sanctuaries have been occupied by the barbarous Turk. Venus, according to one of his sonnets, deplores the loss of Cyprus in 1571, and decides to emigrate to Scotland:

> I think that *Cypris* in a high disdain,
> Barr'd by the barb'rous Turks that conquer'd seat,
> To re-erect the ruins of her state,
> Comes o'er their bounds t'establish beauty's reign. . . .[1]

Rather more conventional is the "sonnet before a poëme of *Irene*" by Stirling's friend, William Drummond of Hawthornden, beginning:

> Mourn not (fair Greece) the ruin of thy kings,
> Thy temples raz'd, thy forts with flames devour'd,
> Thy champions slain, thy virgins pure deflower'd,
> Nor all those griefs which stern Bellona brings.

These events were bad enough; but, says the poet, what is really to be deplored is that (as Gray was to write later) the Muses have abandoned Greece:

> But mourn (fair Greece) mourn that that sacred band
> Which made thee once so famous by their songs,
> Forc'd by outrageous fate, have left thy land,
> And left thee scarce a voice to plain thy wrongs.

Nowadays Greece produces no poetry; so that, to preserve her fame and to tell such stories as that of the famous Grecian lady Irene, she has to rely upon Scottish poets:

> Mourn that those climates which to thee appear
> Beyond both Phoebus' and his sister's ways,
> To save thy deeds from death must lend thee lays,
> And such as from Museus thou didst hear;
> For now Irene hath attain'd such fame,
> That Hero's Ghost doth weep to hear her name.[2]

---

[1] *Aurora, Containing the first fancies of the Author's youth* (1604), Sonnet 49 (ed. Kastner and Charlton, ii, 486).

[2] *Poetical Works*, ed. Kastner, ii, 230. It has not been ascertained who was the author of this *Irene* (to which Drummond is here writing a prefatory sonnet) and what it was. Presumably it related the story of Mahomet and the fair Irene, as told in one of Bandello's *novelle*, in Knolles, in the lost Elizabethan play of "Hiren", in Dr. Johnson's tragedy, and elsewhere. See pp. 250–5 below.

All this, however, was fruitless expostulation; Greece then had no mind to think about such things.

Other poets had their observations to make on the degradation of the once-glorious Greece in their time. In 1613 a young man, a follower of Spenser and Du Bartas and later to be eminent as a lawyer, indulged a youthful vein of poetry by publishing *The Dove: or Passages of Cosmography, by Richard Zouche, Civillian, of New Colledge in Oxford*.[1] This is a kind of poetical survey of the world, not without charm and occasionally rising to an odd kind of eloquence. His lament over contemporary Greece shows the kind of thing a young scholar would write if he remembered the present condition of the land and the people whose literature won his admiration. Even nature, says Richard Zouche (anticipating Gray in *The Progress of Poesy*), seems to mourn the calamities of Hellas:

> GREECE the dismal Sepulchre
> Of Learning, Virtue, Valour, Policy,
> Which once were flourishing and famous there,
> Since in rude Barbarism do buried lie,
> > Seems what she hath been now unapt to show,
> > Object of Fury, Image of strange woe.
>
> Olympus, unto whom the Clouds gave way,
> To upstart Tyranny submits, and bows:
> Parnassus once Crown'd with the verdant Bay,
> With saddest Cyprus shrouds his mourning brows,
> > And Tempe, robb'd of all her pleasing weeds,
> > With spiteful furrows wounded weeps and bleeds.
>
> Athens, Minerva's Chapel, *Phoebus'* Quire,
> Within whose Cloisters, those pure vestal Maids
> The Muses kept their ever-burning fire,
> Whose light, our cold dark ignorance upbraids,
> > From broken ruins and her vaults scarce found,
> > No voice but voice of horror's us'd to sound.[2]

Such expressions of concern with the fate of Greece became increasingly frequent in the seventeenth century in the writings of the learned. The laments for fallen greatness were nourished by information derived both from the ignorant compilations of geographers and from the reports of those who could write from personal experience. We have a fair estimate of the extent to which knowledge

---

[1] It was reprinted, with a memoir by Richard Walker, Oxford, 1839.
[2] Sig. C5ᵛ and 6.

about contemporary Greece was becoming available to the general reader from the references in such a work as *The Anatomy of Melancholy* (1621). Burton knows something of the beauty of Greek scenery and the most striking points of vantage. Every country (he assures us, in his discussion of the benefits to be received by the melancholic from travel and change of air) is full of "delightsome prospects, as well within land as by sea"; and among them not least remarkable are those of Greece, such as "the top of Taygetus or Acrocorinthus, that old decayed castle in Corinth, from which Peloponnesus, Greece, the Ionian and Aegean Seas were *semel et simul* at one view to be taken."[1] But, from his reading of geographers and topographers, eloquently and fervently can Burton lament the triumphs of time in the lovely and once prosperous lands of Hellas.

> May a man believe that which Aristotle in his Politics, Pausanias, Stephanus, Sophianus, Gerbelius relate of old Greece? I find heretofore seventy cities in Epirus overthrown by Paulus Aemilius, a goodly province in times past, now left desolate of good towns and almost inhabitants. Sixty-two cities in Macedonia in Strabo's time. I find thirty in Laconia, but now scarce so many villages, saith Gerbelius. If any man from Mount Taygetus should view the country round about, and see *tot delicias, tot urbes per Peloponnesum dispersas*, so many delicate and brave-built cities, with such cost and exquisite cunning, so neatly set out in Peloponnesus, he should perceive them now ruinous and overthrown, burnt, waste, desolate, and laid level with the ground. *Incredibile dictu*, etc. And as he laments, *Quis talia fando Temperet a lacrimis? Quis tam durus aut ferreus* (so he prosecutes it). Who is he that can sufficiently condole and commiserate these ruins?[2]

For Burton there is no better example of the turning of Fortune's wheel than "Greece of old the seat of civility, mother of sciences, and humanity; now forlorn, the nurse of barbarism, a den of thieves . . . Athens, Corinth, Carthage, how flourishing cities! now buried in their own ruins: *corvorum, ferarum, aprorum, et bestiarum lustra*, like so many wildernesses, a receptacle of wild beasts. . . ."[3] The fabulous wild beasts that haunt Athens may by now be a trifle irritating to my reader. But the emotion and intention is sincere enough.

[1] Pt. 2, Sec. 2, Mem. 3 (Everyman's Library edition, ii, 68).
[2] i, 89–90. Burton is here using the *Praefatio* (Basel, 1545) which Nicolaus Gerbelius wrote to accompany the map (*Descriptio Graeciae*) prepared by Sophianus.
[3] Pt. 2, Sec. 3, Mem. 3 (ii, 154).

The defect of this sort of untravelled topographical sentiment was that it relied upon sources which were not well informed. Ortelius, Gerbelius, and Sophianus were learned deposits of information collected from ancient writers; but their material was unchecked by reference even to natural geographical features which survived. However, before the end of the sixteenth century some of the humanists of Western Europe had become aware that the lands occupied by the Turk were of special interest to the classical student. Indeed, even before the Turkish conquest, Cyriac of Ancona, a Renaissance scholar with a zest for travel, had visited most of the Greek lands, collecting inscriptions and manuscripts. In 1436, 1444, and 1447, he appears to have been in Athens, then under Florentine Dukes, who were already encouraging the flow of manuscripts from Greece to Italy. Cyriac visited many of the Aegean islands and most of the important cities on the Greek mainland. At Delphi he copied inscriptions and examined the antiquities; his observations were of particular interest because, shortly afterwards and for more than two centuries, the site seems to have been lost.[1] But Cyriac was a remarkable and enthusiastic traveller, whose exploits must be regarded as exceptional. In the sixteenth century several classical scholars turned their attention to the Levant for the light that it might throw upon antiquity. The early opening of diplomatic relations by France with the Porte gave an opportunity to some *savants* of the time to acquire unusual knowledge; and when the French ambassador d'Aramont went on his second journey to Constantinople in 1546, he was the head of a kind of scientific and literary expedition, with Pierre Belon as naturalist and Pierre Gilles as antiquary. The topographical works of Gilles (*De Bosphoro Thracio* and *De Topographia Constantinopoleos*, published in 1561) were of great importance; they were justly regarded as authentic and reliable sources of information, and were included in the standard collection of antiquarian tracts made by Gronovius (1698–1702); they were constantly referred to and quoted by travellers; they were translated into English as late as 1729;[2] and they were used by Gibbon. The classical antiquary and Latin poet, Jean Jacques Boissard (1528–1602), visited the islands of the Archipelago; but his published work was principally in the field of Turkish history, rather than Greek antiquities. His *Vitae et Icones Sultanorum Turcorum* (Frankfurt, 1596) was a source commonly followed by Richard Knolles in his *Generall Historie of the Turkes* (1603).

One of the most respected Greek scholars of the sixteenth century

[1] See p. 134 below for the re-discovery by Wheler and Spon in 1675.
[2] As *The Antiquities of Constantinople*, translated by John Ball.

was Martin Kraus (latinized Crusius) of Tubingen, where he was professor of Greek from about 1556. He devoted great labour to the task of gaining information about the vanishing antiquities and present condition of the Greek lands, which he published in his massive *Turco-Graecia*.[1] His informants were largely the higher Greek clergy at Constantinople, but he had other correspondents. He made inquiries about Athens; was it replaced merely by a few fishermen's huts? He printed a letter from a Greek in Nauplia, who reported the erroneousness of this opinion: there still remained things worthy to be seen in Athens, although, to be sure, it was but the skin of an animal which had been long dead. Crusius is an interesting early example of a scholar of Greek who interested himself in the survivals in the country of Greece after the Turkish conquest.

George Does (or Dousa) made the journey to the Levant, copied classical inscriptions at Constantinople; and in his little book, published in 1599, giving the results of his travels,[2] he explains the reasons why his devotion to his studies sent him into Greek lands. Most of his countrymen go to France to study humane letters. Some go to Germany and to Italy; but, for a long time now, very few have gone to Greece. So Dousa determined to leave the beaten track and prepared to face toil and danger, in order to visit Greece, once the inventor of all humanity and the origin of all civility; but now (alas) crushed into slavery.[3]

In the early seventeenth century the topographical works of the most value to interpreters of Greece ancient and modern were those of Johannes Meursius, professor of Greek at Leyden, 1611 to 1625. In particular, his *Athenae Atticae* (Leyden, 1624) was the most comprehensive account of Athens that had yet been published, and it for long remained the most detailed. The remarkable completeness of his collection of allusions to the monuments of Athens which are found in Greek literature, makes this work of Meursius still useful to the traveller who wishes to reconstruct imaginatively the literary associations of the antiquities he sees. For at least a century after its publication *Athenae Atticae* was the usual companion of the erudite

---

[1] *Turco-Graeciae libri octo . . . quibus Graecorum status sub imperio Turcico . . . describitur* (Basel, 1584).

[2] *Georgii Dousae de Itinere suo Constantinopolitano epistola.*

[3] petunt ferè omnes humanioribus literis dediti Galliam, plurimi Germaniam & Italiam; in Graeciam tamen à longo tempore, quod sciam, penetrauere quàm paucissimi. Quod cùm animaduerterem, ipse etiam eodem studio incitatus, & quo honesto proposito plus esset adiunctum periculi & laboris, eo maius decus & pretium esse, animo reputans, relictâ communi peregrinantium semitâ, Graeciam olim omnis humanitatis inuentricem, verùm hodie (proh dolor!) Turcicâ pressam servitute inuisere malui. (p. 6.)

5. Greece invokes the spirits of the great men of old (see p. 217)

6. Pallas Athene summons the Greeks to break their chains (see p. 218)

7. Lord Byron by Thomas Phillips

student in Athens, and it enabled explorers to make many new and correct identifications. Meursius approaches his subject in the mood of the contemplative traveller, although he had never (so far as I know) visited Greece. He had what was the substitute for the modern "sense of history", namely a knowledge of the uncertainty and deplorable conclusion of human power and glory. "Why", asks Hamlet, "may not imagination trace the noble dust of Alexander, till he find it stopping a bung-hole?" The practical, unimaginative Horatio replies, "'Twere to consider too curiously to consider so." But Hamlet dissents; "No, faith, not a jot; but to follow him thither with modesty enough, and likelihood to lead it: as thus: Alexander died, Alexander was buried, Alexander returneth into dust; the dust is earth; of earth we make loam; and why of that loam, whereto he was converted, might they not stop a beer-barrel?" But it was not only the fragile human carcass that prompted such meditations. "Since brass, nor stone, nor earth, nor boundless sea, but sad mortality o'er-sways their power . . ." the poet also wrote.[1] If anyone wishes to ponder upon the instability of human affairs (Meursius declares, with the same poetic spirit, in his elegant "Epistola Dedicatoria") let him see Athens; once it was on a pinnacle of glory, now it groans in miserable servitude to the Turk; but for the immortality awarded to it by History, scarcely its name would be known.[2]

We can thus see the sentiment of place and the lament for the fallen greatness of Greece already playing its part in antiquarian inquiry. But these emotions were not something confined to secluded scholars and meditative poets. The many English merchants who were now conducting their affairs in the Levant were already, during the first few decades of the seventeenth century, becoming aware of the special interest of many parts of the lands where they sought their commercial gain.

The best and most complete account of trade in the Levant in the seventeenth century is given to us (as we have seen[3]) by the merchant Lewes Roberts, who published his fine folio, *The Marchants Mappe of Commerce*, in 1638 and a smaller work, *The Treasure of Traffike*, in 1641. Roberts had himself been a Levant merchant and had resided

---

[1] *Hamlet*, V, i, 224–35; *Sonnet* lxv.

[2] QVi incerta rerum humanarum volet contemplari . . . , is Athenas mihi videat; illas olim tam ingentes, vt ducenta ferè stadia in circuitu continerent: tam potentes, vt sibi ipsos quoq; reges tributarios haberent: tam illustres, vt splendore, gloriaq; plurimas Rerump. superarent, ipsae à nullà vincerentur: at nunc ita imminuta est magnitudo, vt consumpti animalis ossa, ac pellis, quod Synesius olim eleganter dixit, tantùm esse videantur: & potentia, adeò illis nulla restat, vt miserrimam contra seruitutem seruiant, sub Turcarum imperio sitae: gloriae, item par fortuna est; & vix nomen nunc sciretur, nisi Historia id seruasset. . . .

[3] p. 29 above.

at Constantinople for some years.[1] He affirms, with the emphasis of
italic print, that the English *"are the most eminent of all the Merchants
Christians that traffique hither"*. He was later employed in the office
of "husband" for the regulation of the trade of the Levant Company
in England.

Roberts, as revealed by these books, was a very sober merchant,
and probably a tolerably successful one. He surveys with impartial
seriousness the trade that could be conducted with the various parts
of the world. But when he comes to write of "Grecia", he cannot
refrain from reminding his reader, amid details of commodities,
moneys, weights and measures, that he is now in the classic land.
He tells us, for example, that *"Caranto*, a small Village, now supplies
the place of that ancient and famous *Corinth*, a City commodious for
the command of a brave trade, as enjoying two famous Ports into two
different Seas. . . ." (The merchant has an eye for a good trading
station.) On Acrocorinth "was seated the famous Temple of *Venus*,
near which was that notable fountain discovered by the impression
of the foot of *Pegasus*, as the Ancients did feign". (What had this to do
with trade? cries some indignant Mr. Sterling.) Moreover, "in their
continent, if the memory thereof may not here be improper", were
such remarkable places as "Misene [i.e. Mycenae] the dwelling of
Agamemnon", and "the Lake of *Lerno*, where *Hercules* slew the
Lernian seven-headed Hydra"; and Argos, Epidaurus, and Sparta.
"Here was also those pleasant *Arcadian* plains, and the places where
the *Olympian* games were solemnized; with divers other memorable
antiquities, which the injury of time hath eaten out and consumed";
[the commercial conscience now obtrudes itself] "wherefore I here
omit them, and return again to my purpose and prosecute my
method." But he is detained again when he comes to describe the
situation of commerce in central Greece:

> Here is also the mount *Helicon* and *Parnassus*, famoused amongst
> *Poets*, and the *Pythian* City accounted the midst of all the world,
> and many other remarkable places, which were here in times past,
> all having yielded to age, and therefore merit not a longer stay,
> or a more serious survey of the trade thereof.

I have only discovered one personal anecdote in Roberts's large folio;
and appropriately it relates to "the sentiment of place". Apparently
those who provided lodgings at Cerigo (the ancient Cythera) were
aware of the historical attractions of the place and were ready to
impress visitors:

[1] "The Epistle" before *The Marchants Mappe* (Sig. A2ᵛ) and p. 191.

Out of the Castle of the chief town of this *Isle*, was *Helena* the wife of *Menelaus* stolen by *Paris*, where during my abode here, the *Castelan* did shew me, and lodged me in the chamber whence, *as he would have me believe*, she was ravished; but if it were so, her lodging I am confident was better than mine, for a soft board was my best bed, & God knows with what sorry coverings and appurtenances.[1]

It is apparent from Lewes Roberts's work that the movement of Englishmen in Greek lands was increasing; they were already fully aware of the special interest of the country and beginning to be sensitive to the imaginative stimulus of sentimental associations. These Englishmen, however, were not all prudent merchants, shrewd ambassadors, or pious chaplains. It was in 1628, while Sir Thomas Roe was ambassador at the Porte, that one of the most remarkable episodes in the history of the English in the Levant took place. Sir Kenelm Digby sailed from the Downs on his famous privateering expedition on January 6th 1627/8 with his two ships, the Eagle and the George and Elizabeth; and while in the eastern Mediterranean wrote his little treatise on a mysterious passage in his favourite Spenser.[2] He dated it, on its publication in 1643, as "From aboard my ship the Eagle, the 13th June 1628", that is, two days after his notorious battle in Scanderoon harbour. Amid the Ionian and Aegean Islands and off the coasts of the Morea and Cyprus, he conducted his piracies, to the great indignation of the Venetians, as we know from the Venetian archives that have been printed,[3] and to the dismay of some of the English merchants in the Levant, who were made to suffer for his brilliant exploits.

During his voyage Digby kept a detailed log of his activities and observations, and most of it was evidently written day by day as things happened. This journal is an entertaining account of the adventure, full of bravura, courage, and vividness.[4] The factual quality of Digby's journal, very different from his other writings, sometimes gives a special liveliness to his impressions of Greece and the Greeks:

Close by Milo lies an Island that my cards call Anania [Afterwards I found they were 3 little Islands, not Anania, which lies more W.], but the Greeks I had in my ship named it *L'Isola de Diavoli*, because they say no men inhabit there, but is infested with

---

[1] *Mappe*, pp. 188, 190, 205. [2] *The Faerie Queene*, II, ix, stanza 22.
[3] See E. W. Bligh, *Sir Kenelm Digby and his Venetia* (1932), pp. 132–3.
[4] *Journal of a Voyage into the Mediterranean*, printed for the Camden Society with an introduction by John Bruce (1868).

devils; and that when they moor their cables upon the shore (for it is high land, and the water deep by the shore) they all loose of themselves, unless they make them fast, making a cross with the ends of every two cables.

He victualled at Patras and at Glarentsa; and, so far as he could, carefully observed the situation in the Morea. Almost anticipating the Venetian invasion which was to take place a generation later, he considered the Greeks as possible belligerents in a war against the Turks. As for the Morea, he declared,

> the Turk hath little force in it now, and by reason of his wars in other places could not assist it if it were invaded. One may land all about, and a castle at Corinth would preserve it from any forces to be brought by land; and the Greeks of the country would infallibly take part with a Christian invader[1] and would soon become a belliguous [sic] nation, as already the Albaneses are. . . .[2]

To Sir Kenelm may be attributed the first work of English literature actually written in Greece. On August 16th 1628 he sailed into the port of Melos[3] and had to stay there while one of his ships was being repaired. The Turkish governor, who had already heard news of the exploit at Scanderoon, made himself agreeable and "omitted nothing that might avail to divert me . . . ; and among other things, made me a liberal offer to interest me in the good graces of several of the most noted beauties of that place, who in all ages have been known to be no niggards of their favours". But Digby's mind was full of his divine Venetia; and, in order to refuse these amiable offers gracefully, he pleaded business: he had to write his dispatches. This however was quickly done ("my facility of setting down on paper my low conceptions having been ever very great"); and so, in order to fill in the time, he began to write his memoirs.[4] It is unlikely that the whole work, which tells of his early life and his love for Venetia, was completed during his few days' stay at Melos. But at any rate the mood of nostalgia, and a certain tenderness of reminiscence, perhaps

---

[1] This was contrary to what was said by other observers, for example, Thévenot, Henry Blount and Edward Browne. See pp. 44 above and 97, 119 below.

[2] *Journal*, pp. 53, 65.

[3] Sir Harris Nicolas, in his edition of the *Private Memoirs* of 1827 (introduction, p. lxxxviii), regards "Milo" as a fictitious disguise for an uncertain place, like many other names of persons and places in the *Memoirs*. But we know from the *Journal*, which was not printed until 1868 (forty years after Nicolas's edition) that Digby was, in fact, for eight days at Melos, receiving "much courtesy" from the Caya and Cadi, and there feasted the Turks "who were very barbarous and bestial in respect of others that I have seen" (pp. 53, 54).

[4] *Private Memoirs*, pp. 323, 324.

owe much to his sojourn in the enchanting Greek lands—as well, of course, as the fictional Greek setting in which he disguised his autobiography.

Almost all the writers I have quoted so far had some other interest than sentimental in journeying in the Levant. They had knowledge of Greece, and expressed opinions about it by the way. They were curious about Greece; yet it was not merely their curiosity about Greece which brought them to the Levant. But Sir Henry Blount (1602–82) in 1634–5 travelled for the sensation of it. His little book, *A Voyage into the Levant. A Breife Relation of a Iourney, lately performed by Master Henry Blount* (1636)[1] was remarkably popular; eight editions had appeared by 1671; there were German and Dutch translations; and the narrative was included in the great eighteenth-century collections of travels.[2] Blount left Venice in May 1634, and from Spalato travelled overland to Constantinople; from there he went to Rhodes and to Egypt. He was a traveller of rare quality and intelligence, and the popularity of his little book was an indication that he had something fresh to offer. He declared that he wanted to visit Turkey so that he "might satisfy this scruple, (to wit) whether to an impartial conceit the *Turkish* way appear absolutely barbarous, as we are given to understand, or rather an other kind of civility, different from ours, but no less pretending". The high quality of Blount's mind is immediately seen in his ability to conceive of the Ottoman civilization as something different from Christendom but equally valid and consistent when interpreted in its own terms. At Potarzeeke,[3] near Phillipopolis, he was persuaded by "a learned Jew" that he had come to Thermopylae, "stoutly contested for of old". Here, too, he says, "my two days abode gave me leisure to read *Caesar* his Commentary thereon, which on purpose I carried to confer upon the Place, for the better impression". Presumably Blount thought he was in the vicinity of Pharsalus. He was really hundreds of miles away. But that does not matter. The important thing is that he brought his book with him so that he could read it on the spot, for the sake of a better understanding and livelier sensations. We might have expected something good from him when he reached Troy. But there he could see nothing but an old wall, hard by the sea. "So hath that famed Town now put on *immortality*, having no *existence* but in *Poetry*; whose fictions so complying with the fancy of man, uphold themselves beyond the *Reality* of their *Subject*."[4]

[1] I quote from the second edition (1637).
[2] Churchill, Osborne, Pinkerton.
[3] The author of the life of Blount in the *Dictionary of National Biography* identified this with Tartar Bazardjik.
[4] pp. 2, 18, 20, 28.

There are other curious travellers who knew the attractions of the Levant. Charles Cavendish, a son of the second Earl of Devonshire, was an early Grand Tourist; but he went much farther afield than most of his eighteenth-century successors. In 1638, at the age of eighteen, Cavendish set out on his travels, accompanied by a tutor. He got as far as Egypt, and saw a great part of the lands ruled by the Turk. He returned to England in May 1641 and began a brilliant military career; but he was killed in his twenty-fourth year, early in the Civil War (1643). Waller's epitaph on this interesting young man supposed that his travels had had a special military influence upon him; for had he not seen the lands that Alexander the Great had conquered?

> Early abroad he did the world survey,
> As if he knew he had not long to stay;
> Saw what great Alexander in the East,
> And mighty Julius conquer'd in the West;
> Then, with a mind as great as theirs, he came
> To find at home occasion for his fame.[1]

Little is known about Charles Cavendish. But he, along with Henry Blount, Milton, and Richard Flecknoe, shows us that before the middle of the seventeenth century the lands ruled by the Turk were becoming less impenetrable. The "pilgrim of culture" was already a possibility.

[1] Epitaph v, 5–10.

CHAPTER IV

THE GIFTS OF GREECE

And here I cannot but with much reverence mention the every way Right honourable *Thomas Howard* Lord high Marshal of *England*, as great for his noble Patronage of Arts and ancient learning, as for his birth and place. To whose liberal charges and magnificence this angle of the world oweth the first sight of Greek and Roman Statues, with whose admired presence he began to honour the Gardens and Galleries of Arundel-House about twenty years ago, and hath ever since continued to transplant old Greece into *England*.

> Henry Peacham, *The Compleat Gentleman* ("The second impression", 1634).

Barbarism hath worn out all the footsteps of civility and learning: yet manuscripts are plenty, old Greek books, that are little worth. . . .

> Sir Thomas Roe in a letter from Constantinople to the Archbishop of Canterbury, December 9–19th, 1624.

Touching *Coffee*, I concur with them in opinion, who hold it to be that black broth which was us'd of old in *Lacedemon*, whereof the Poets sing.

> James Howell in a prefatory letter to Walter Rumsey's *Organon Salutis. An Instrument to cleanse the Stomach* (1657).

THERE was another motive which turned certain Englishmen's eyes towards Greece in the seventeenth century. The growth of great collections in England in that century is an interesting phase of English art-history. Such an activity as collecting ancient sculpture was, of course, limited to a small wealthy class; but it made a considerable impression on those who were interested in the fine arts. The English arrived late in the field, and for that reason the enterprising collectors were anxious to explore the possibilities of new sources of supply. By the collector of "ancient marbles", Greece was regarded definitely as only a second-best. It was taken for granted that Italy contained the great treasures, because the Romans had removed all the finer works of art from Greece in classical times. There was plenty of ancient testimony to that effect. But there might, it was thought, be something left. It was worth trying because, for the English collector, Italy had many disadvantages. The Italians were there first and had staked their claim. The competition for obtaining good statues was keen among the European princely collectors; consequently the prices of the Italian connoisseurs and dealers were high. The risk of forgery, too, was great. Greece, however, presented none of these disadvantages. It was true that the Venetians had already done something, by removing most of the visible statues from ancient sites accessible from the sea or under Venetian rule; but they seemed not to have gone beneath the surface. Much, perhaps, remained, if only the means of discovery and transport could be arranged.

The British diplomatic service and the British navy provided both. The best insight into collecting in Greece in the first half of the seventeenth century comes from the correspondence of Sir Thomas Roe (*c.* 1581–1644), who was certainly one of the most remarkable English ambassadors to be accredited to the Sublime Porte.[1] Roe was at Constantinople from 1621 to 1628; and he was commissioned firstly by Arundel and, a little later, by Buckingham to do what he could to find statues for their collections. Roe was a cultivated man, although he constantly depreciated his abilities as a connoisseur, and was by no means averse to this; "though my employment be the other end of the circle, to attend new things; yet mine own inclination is curious enough, to my means, to look back upon antiquity . . ." he wrote in a letter from Constantinople to Arundel on January 27th 1621/2. He enlisted the help of the consuls, then as always knowledgeable on local matters ("I moved our consul, Richard Milward, at Scio, whom I found prepared and ready"); and he sought the advice of Greek ecclesiastics. He was advised by the Bishop of Andros to search at "Delphos", that is, the island famous in antiquity as Delos:

> I brought with me from Messina, the bishop of Andre [Andros], one of the islands of the Arches, a man of good learning, and great experience in these parts. He assured me . . . Concerning antiquities in marbles, there are many in divers parts, but especially at Delphos, unesteemed here; and, I doubt not, easy to be procured for the charge of digging and fetching, which must be purposely undertaken.[2]

At Constantinople the Patriarch (who must be his friend the celebrated Cyril Lucaris) recommended "Delphos" to him as "a small,

---

[1] *The Negotiations of Sir Thomas Roe, in his Embassy to the Ottoman Porte, from the Year 1621 to 1628 inclusive* (1740); vol. 1 only was published. Horace Walpole was the first to use these letters for the light they throw on the history of the fine arts in England (*Anecdotes*, ed. Wornum (1888), i, 293). All the relevant extracts are reprinted by Adolf Michaelis, *Ancient Marbles in Great Britain* (Cambridge, 1882), pp. 185–205, which is a great help in finding one's way in the massive folio.

[2] *Negotiations*, p. 16 (Michaelis, p. 185).

despised, uninhabited island, in the Arches, a place anciently esteemed sacred, the burial of all the Greeks, as yet unbroken; where, he tells me, are like to be found many rare things . . . they may take without trouble or prohibition whatsoever they please, if any man of judgment to make the choice."[1]

The Roman baths at Alexandreia Troas continued to have Homeric associations; for Roe writes, "I have a stone taken out of the old palace of Priam in Troy, cut in horned shape".[2] He was particularly anxious to get the large reliefs from the Porta Aurea at Constantinople; "There are of them but six that are worth the taking down, the other being flat Gothish bodies, lame, and of later times", he writes to Buckingham on May 1st 1625.

> Promise to obtain them I cannot, because they stand upon the ancient gate, the most conspicuous of the city . . . to offer to steal them, no man dares to deface the chief seat of the grand signor: to procure them by favour is more impossible, such envy they bear unto us. There is only then one way left; by corruption of some churchman, to dislike them, as against their law; and under that pretence to take them down to be brought into some private place; from whence, after the matter is cold and unsuspected, they may be conveyed.[3]

A little later in the year he writes to tell Buckingham that his efforts have so far failed; "yet I will not leave to hope, by some art they may be made drop, and that so I may gather them".[4] But these Vandal-like proceedings came to nothing. It is a pity that Roe was not successful; for the famous reliefs disappeared not long afterwards and have never been traced.

In 1624 Arundel sent out as his agent a certain William Petty, who was given every assistance by Roe. This Petty seems to have been a remarkable character, if we may judge from Roe's correspondence. Going from Samos to Ephesus he was shipwrecked and so lost all his collection from that expedition. Having also lost his passports he was imprisoned by the Turks as a spy; but eventually he got to Chios, and then returned to the shipwreck to try to "fish for" his marbles (the phrase is Roe's). "There was never man so fitted to an employment, that encounters all accident with so un-wearied patience; eats with Greeks on their worst days; lies with fishermen on planks, at the best; is all things to all men, that he may

[1] To Buckingham, January 24th 1624–5; p. 344 (Michaelis, p. 188).
[2] p. 16 (Michaelis, p. 186). [3] pp. 386–7 (Michaelis, pp. 189–90).
[4] To Buckingham from Halchys, August 26th (O.S.) 1625; p. 434 (Michaelis, p. 192).

obtain his ends, which are your lordship's service."[1] But Roe had his difficulties. His double responsibility—both to Arundel (who had first engaged him in the search for antiquities) and to Buckingham (the reigning favourite at Charles's court) was the cause of some embarrassment to him; and he was disconcerted by his suspicions that Petty was not playing fair; "he is a close and subtle borderer, and will not brag of his prizes", wrote Roe to Buckingham[2] meaning that he feared Petty was acting independently and on behalf of Arundel alone; and he wrote a frank letter to Arundel explaining the difficulties of his own situation.[3] When he found that Petty was no longer carrying on the search in their joint interests, he employed one of his own servants to act as his agent and to travel about collecting on behalf of Buckingham. This man scoured the Aegean islands and visited Athens, Corinth, Nauplia, and Sparta, arranging for the purchase or excavation of marbles; his death at Patras, before he had arranged the shipment of what he had collected, was a source of more trouble to Roe.

Equally willing to profit by the possibilities of excavation in Greece, Charles I received "Old Greek marble-bases, columns and altars", which "were brought from the ruins of *Apollo's* Temple at *Delos*, by that noble and absolutely complete Gentleman, Sir *Kenhelm Digby* Knight".[4] This refers to the occasion when Digby was on his expedition in the Mediterranean in 1628, which we have already mentioned; he relates in his *Journal*[5] on August 28th, "I spent the day at Delos in search of antiquities". Probably he had heard of Roe's collecting activities on behalf of Arundel and Buckingham. The latter, as High Admiral, had after some coolness given Digby his commission for his expedition. At any rate, Digby, when he was amongst the Aegean islands did not let the opportunity slip. He tells us that, early in September, he wanted to keep his men from idleness and from haunting the shores of Melos or Myconos.

> I went with most of my ships to Delphos, a desert island, where staying till the rest were ready, because idleness should not fix their minds upon any untoward fancies (as is usual among seamen), and together to avail myself of the conveniency of carrying away some antiquities there, I busied them in rolling of stones down to the sea side, which they did with such eagerness as though it had

---

[1] To Arundel, March 28th (O.S.) 1626; p. 495 (Michaelis, p. 195).
[2] p. 434 (Michaelis, p. 192).   [3] pp. 444–5 (Michaelis, pp. 192–5).
[4] Henry Peacham, *The Compleat Gentleman* (1634, "The Second Impression" p. 108).
[5] *Journal of a Voyage into the Mediterranean*, printed for the Camden Society with an introduction by John Bruce (1868), pp. 55, 57.

been the earnestest business that they came out for, and they mastered prodigious massy weights; but one stone, the greatest and fairest of all containing 4 statues, they gave over after they had been, 300 men, a whole day about it. . . . But the next day I contrived a way with masts of ships and another ship to ride over against it, that brought it down with much ease and speed.

He admired the colossal statue of Apollo ("still a brave noble piece"). It was broken in two pieces about the waist; and he says that, though many have tried to take it away, all have failed.

The looting of ruins, whether by the agents of the British ambassador, by naval commanders with antiquarian tastes, or by casual vandals, belongs to the pre-archaeological stage of the interest in Greece. The Elizabethan visitors were not above bringing a keepsake home. Indeed Thomas Dallam, the organ-builder who in 1599 was sent to Constantinople with one of his instruments as a present from Queen Elizabeth to the Sultan, provides us with the first recorded example of the British souvenir-hunter in Greek lands; on the way to Constantinople he and some of the merchants went ashore at "Cape Janissary" to make a tour of the ancient sites. "We saw more at large the ruins of the walls and houses in Troy, and from thence I brought a piece of white marble pillar, the which I broke with my own hands, having a good hammer, which my mate Harvie did carry ashore for the same purpose; and I brought this piece of marble to London."[1] But, of course, serious collectors felt fully justified in rescuing ancient marbles from the lands ruled by the Turk. As Henry Peacham pointed out in *The Compleat Gentleman* (1634),

in Greece and other parts of the Grand Signior's Dominions (where sometime there were more Statues than men living, so much had Art out-stripped Nature in those days) they may be had for digging and carrying. For by reason of the barbarous religion of the Turks, which alloweth not the likeness or representation of any living thing, they have been for the most part buried in ruins or broken to pieces; so that it is a hard matter to light upon any there, that are not headless and lame, yet most of them venerable for antiquity and elegancy.[2]

A curious manuscript exists, dating from the seventeenth century,

[1] *Early Voyages and Travels in the Levant*, 1. The Diary of Master Thomas Dallam, 1599–1600 . . . edited by J. T. Bent for the Hakluyt Society (1893), pp. 49–50.
[2] "The Second Impression", p. 107.

which reveals the methods of these early explorers.[1] It gives "directions about ancient statues, in what parts of Greece they are to be found, and by what means they are to be obtained". Some of these instructions to an agent tell us the worst: ". . . if he meet with any statues or Colossus too great to be carried away whole, he must employ men to saw it asunder with iron saws and sharp sand . . .". The French, as has been usual for centuries, blamed the English for the ruthless destruction of antiquities. One Frenchman, who was in the Aegean in 1639, saw an Apollo (presumably the colossal) which, he coolly states, the English have sawn into two, from top to bottom, in order to carry away a part of it.[2] Perhaps this was a local memory of Sir Kenelm Digby's operations. Jean de Thévenot, the great oriental traveller, who was in the Levant in 1655, complained that an English gentleman was carrying off so many statues from Delos that only the colossal one was left. At Paros, too,

> there were several Statues, Marble-Chests, and other Antiquities found in this Island, which have been carried away by an *English* Gentleman, who brought off all he could find, not only there, but in the other Isles also: and chiefly in Delos, called at present *Sdrille*, heretofore so famous for the Oracle of *Apollo*.[3]

A few years later, in 1675, Sir George Wheler tells a horrific story of a nautical English visitor to Delos. The colossal statue, he says, "stood upon his Pedestal upright, until about three years ago (as Signior Georgio, our Landlord at Micone, informed me) an Englishman who was there, call'd, as he said, Signior Simon, Captain of the Saint Barbara, endeavoured to carry it away, but finding it impossible, he brake off its head, arms and feet, and carried them with him".[4] Randolph in 1687 confirms this kind of raking of Delos, which (he tells us) "is a very small Island, not inhabited, yet are there abundance of Conies. In this Island are the ruins of the Temple of Apollo. . . . The ruins are carried away by all ships who come to anchor there, so as part are in *England, France, Holland*, but most at *Venice*."[5] Within a very few generations, however, a more scholarly concern

---

[1] Tanner MSS. lxxxviii, fol. 436–42; *Catal. Codic. MSS. Bibl. Bodl.*, Oxford, 1860, Pars quarta, p. 427. It was printed in *The Gentleman's Magazine* (1793), November, pp. 986–7.

[2] Les Anglois ont sciée en deux, de haut en bas, pour en emporter une partie. This passage from *Les Voyages du sieur Du Loir* (Paris, 1654), p. 8, is frequently quoted; Laborde, i, 69, Michaelis, p. 23, etc.

[3] Pt. I, Chapter LXVII; p. 105 of the English translation (1687); French edition (1664), p. 196.

[4] *A Journey into Greece* (1682), p. 56; Spon, however, says it was a Venetian (*Voyage* (1678), i, 180).

[5] Bernard Randolph, *The Present State of the Islands in the Archipelago* (1687), p. 20.

with the vestiges of ancient Hellas became possible; and the indignation of Wheler, who was in Greece in 1675–6, is an indication that a
change of attitude had begun.

The knowledge of Greek literature during the Renaissance was
much amplified in Western Europe by the manuscripts of ancient
authors which had been brought by Greek exiles from Constantinople, Mistra, and other centres of learning. But had they brought
everything of importance? Many admirable works of Greek literature were apparently lost. Was there not a chance of their being
discoverable in Greece itself? In Constantinople, particularly, there
could not have been time, during the horrors of the siege, to remove
and safeguard the accumulation of several centuries of Byzantine
learning. The possibility of the survival of the Imperial library in the
Seraglio continued to excite speculation and to tantalize scholars for
some time. It was easy to dream of the lost works of Grecian literature that might be recovered. One Greek exile had said that a complete Diodorus Siculus was there. Others had alleged (less credibly)
the existence of a complete Livy. One hundred and twenty of the
manuscripts from the collection of the last Constantine were supposed at one time to have been preserved by the Turks. It was
well known that Mahomet II had been a man of wide culture, with
a knowledge of the languages of his Christian enemies.

The appetite had been whetted; and when Arundel's Mr. Petty
arrived in the Levant, he brought letters from George Abbot, Archbishop of Canterbury, who often interested himself in Greek matters
and who was anxious to have news of Greek manuscripts. "Barbarism hath worn out all the footsteps of civility and learning," wrote
Roe to the Archbishop from Constantinople in 1624; "yet manuscripts are plenty, old Greek books, that are little worth".[1] Roe
tried to get the patriarch to exchange the old books which England
wanted for a complete library of classic authors and learned works
that Greece really needed; Cyril promised to think it over; but little
was done. As it happened, however, Roe was to return to England
with the *Codex Alexandrinus* as a gift from the Patriarch of Constantinople to the King of England.[2]

No one, however, succeeded in penetrating to the library of the
Seraglio; and the stories of the treasures preserved there were occasionally given further credibility by the appearance of books in the
market which were alleged to have been stolen. John Greaves the
astronomer and mathematician (1602–52), who was at Constantinople
in 1638, was assured by some of the Greeks that the library which

---

[1] *Negotiations*, p. 320 (Michaelis, p. 187).   [2] See p. 90 below.

formerly belonged to the Byzantine emperors was still preserved in the Sultan's palace; and he got one book. "I have procured *Ptolemy's Almagest*, the fairest book that I have seen, stolen by a Spahy (as I am informed) out of the King's Library in the *Seraglio*."[1]

The French were eager rivals in the search for manuscripts. Even the great Colbert found time to instruct the French ambassador to buy curious books (on his behalf, and the King's), especially "authors known in antiquity, and not yet printed in Europe".[2] In 1685 the French ambassador, Girardin, bought a number of Greek manuscripts from those which were alleged to have been stolen by a renegade Italian. There were then supposed to be two hundred Greek manuscripts, in the Seraglio, all of which were removed. The Jesuit Besnier bought fifteen and the rest were sold at Pera.[3]

It was not until the early nineteenth century that an Englishman (enjoying the fruits of British prestige at the Porte after Nelson's victories) was permitted to enter the famous library; with what results we shall later see.[4]

Apart from ancient statues and manuscripts, however, the most curious contribution of contemporary Greece to English culture was coffee. The introduction of coffee into Western Europe is obscure, but the substance was known in the sixteenth century as a mysterious drug. George Sandys (whose travel-book was published in 1615) shows that the English were then unacquainted with the coffee-drink. He describes how the Turks sit in "Coffa-houses" resembling taverns, "and sip of a drink called Coffa . . . in little *China* dishes, as hot as they can suffer it: black as soot, and tasting not much unlike it". The interesting fact is that, as soon as coffee became known to Western Europe, an endeavour was made to find some classical authority for its existence; "why not that black broth which was in use amongst the *Lacedemonians*?" asked Sandys.[5] This idea was popular for some time. Henry Blount, who made his journey to the Levant in 1634, describes *Cauphe*: "It is thought to be the old black broth used so much by the *Lacedemonians*, and dryeth ill humours in the stomach, comforteth the brain, never causeth drunkenness or any other surfeit, and is a harmless entertainment of good fellowship."[6] Walter Rumsey, in his *Organon Salutis. An Instrument to*

---

[1] *A letter from Constantinople* in *Miscellaneous Works of Mr. John Greaves* (1737, 2 vols., ed. Thomas Birch), ii, 437.
[2] Dispatch dated November 1674, printed by Laborde, i, 115–16.
[3] Robert Walpole, *Memoirs relating to European and Asiatic Turkey* (1817), xvii.
[4] pp. 200–2 below.
[5] *A Relation of a Journey begun A.D. 1610* (1615), p. 66.
[6] *A Voyage into the Levant, A Breife Relation of a Iourney, lately performed by Master Henry Blount* (1636) (2nd edition, 1637, p. 105).

cleanse the Stomach (1657), says that Blount's "excellent Book of Travels hath brought the use of the Turks' Physic, of Cophie, in great request in *England*".[1] However, Pietro della Valle, writing from Constantinople on February 7th 1615, has an even more ingenious suggestion than the Spartan black broth. He suspects that *cahue* was that *nepenthe* which, as Homer relates, was drunk by Helen in Egypt. Did not *nepenthe* assuage all displeasing care? And does not this *cahue* today serve as a charm to pass the time, to encourage agreeable conversation, and to induce an oblivion of human toil? It was from Egypt that the Turks and the Greeks obtained their *cahue* (it was really of Arabian origin; but Cairo was the common emporium). This, thought Pietro, made the identification with *nepenthe* even more probable.[2]

Coffee, then, was a mysterious drug; its effect upon the animal spirits was truly remarkable. It did not, therefore, escape the scrutiny of Bacon: "This drink", he writes, "comforteth the brain and heart, and helpeth digestion."[3] It was natural for Western Europeans to describe coffee as a Turkish drink, although of course it was a beverage in widespread use among all the populations of the Levant. But the supposed classical antiquity of the drink gave the Greeks a special right to it, and it was through the Greeks that it became known and obtainable in England. It is commonly said that coffee as a beverage was first used in England by Nathaniel Kanopios (or Conopios), a Cretan, who came to England in 1637 and spent ten years at Oxford until the Puritans removed him in 1648; "he was expelled the University by the barbarians, I mean the parliamentarian visitors (wrote Anthony à Wood); while he continued in Balliol College he made the drink for his own use called coffee, and usually drank it every morning, being the first, as the ancients of that house have informed me, that was ever drunk in Oxon."[4] Evelyn likewise remembered him. "There came in my time to the College one Nathaniel Conopios out of Greece, from Cyrill the Patriarch of Constantinople, who returning many years after, was made (as I understand) Bishop of Smyrna. He

---

[1] Sig. a4.

[2] . . . se si bevesse con vino come si beve con acqua, ardirei di sospettare che potesse essere il *nepenthe* di Omero, che Elena, secondo egli racconta, ebbe già da Egitto: poichè, per la via di Egitto appunto il *cahue* qua si conduce, e così, come quello era alleviamento di ogni cura noiosa, questo ancora oggi qui serve alle genti per continuo trattenimento e passatempo, consumandosi, come ho detto, le ore in conversazione con questa bevanda, e con la mescolanza, nel simposio, di mille dilettevoli ragionamenti che inducono per avventura negli animi quella obblivione dei travagli che il poeta dice che il suo *nepenthe* cagionava. *Viaggi* (2 vols., Brighton, 1843), i, 76.

[3] *Sylva Sylvarum; or, A Natural History in Ten Centuries*, para. 738 (written c. 1624, published 1627); *Works*, ed. Spedding (1859), ii, 577.

[4] *Athenae Oxonienses*, ed. Bliss, iv, 808.

was the first I ever saw drink coffee, which custom came not into England till 30 years after."[1] Evelyn is here a little out in his dating. But at any rate the first "coffee-house" was opened in London in 1652 by a Greek who was known as Pasqua Rossie (or Rossee). He was born at Ragusa, and had come to England from Smyrna as the servant of a certain Daniel Edwards, a merchant of the Levant Company. The story is that this merchant had his coffee prepared daily for himself and for his visitors. The popularity of the new drink brought too many visitors to the house; and to obviate this inconvenience he established his Greek servant in a public coffee-house, originally in St. Michael's Alley, Cornhill.[2]

The reputation of coffee as a drug had preceded its introduction as a delicious beverage; and, as soon as coffee-houses were established, its virtues encouraged curiosity and experiment. It was still reputed to have admirable medicinal value, especially being praised for that "exsiccant quality it hath to dry up the crudities of the Stomach, as also to comfort the Brain, to fortify the sight with its steam, and prevent Dropsies, Gouts, the Scurvy, together with the Spleen, and Hypochondriacal winds (all of which it doth without any violence or distemper at all)".[3] But these important therapeutic properties were soon forgotten. The number of coffee-houses rapidly increased, and the opportunity they gave for political discussion and caballing was not unnoticed by the Government. In fact, in 1675, Charles II issued a proclamation,[4] ordering the closing of all coffee-houses as being seminaries of seditions. The unpopularity of this measure was such that within eleven days it was suspended.

Among the topics of conversation, political plans against the Turks were apparently to be heard at the coffee-houses, if we may judge from the witty parody by Montagu and Prior:

> I've heard such talk of the *Wits' Coffee-House*.
> Thither, says *Brindle*, thou shalt go and see
> *Priests* sipping *Coffee*, *Sparks* and *Poets Tea*;
> Here rugged Freeze, there Quality well drest,
> These baffling the *Grand-Seigniour*, those the *Test*.[5]

One of the most popular coffee-houses was *The Grecian*, opened by

---

[1] *Diary*, May 10th 1637; 1879 edition, i, 9.
[2] E. F. Robinson, *The Early History of Coffee-Houses in England* (1893), pp. 86–8.
[3] Walter Rumsey, *Organon Salutis. An Instrument to cleanse the Stomach* (1657), sig. b2 verso. It was reprinted as *Judge Rumsey's Instrument to cleanse the Stomack* (1664).
[4] Printed by E. F. Robinson, *op. cit.*, p. 166.
[5] *The Hind and the Panther transvers'd To the Story of The Country Mouse and the City Mouse* (1687), p. 20.

a certain Constantine Jennings (commonly known as George Constantine) early in 1665. An advertisement in *The Intelligencer* of
January 23rd 1664/5 begins: "One *Constantine* a *Grecian*, living in
Threadneedle-Street over against *St. Christopher's Church, London*,
being licensed to sell and retail Coffee, Chocolate, Sherbert and Tea.
. . ." This man is described (rather improbably) in a squib of the
time as

> Constantine the Grecian,
> Who fourteen years was th' only man
> That made Coffee for the great Bashaw
> Although the man he never saw.[1]

His coffee-house was frequented by members of the Royal Society,
and became famous for its connection with those virtuosos, as was
Wills's for its connection with men of letters. He later moved to
Devereux Court in the Strand, where we are told that as late as 1727
his name was still to be seen. *The Grecian* continued its existence into
the nineteenth century.

Thus did the black broth of the Lacedaemonians conquer British
taste.

[1] *The Character of a Coffee-House . . . by an Eye and Ear Witness* (1665)
(Robinson, pp. 221, 224).

CHAPTER V

GRAECIA SACRA

So merciful hath God dealt with this luxurious and perfidious people as not to take away their Candlestick, though he hath darkened and obscured the light thereof.

Peter Heylyn, Cosmographie (1652).

Sir Wilfull Witwoud: My Map says that your *Turk* is not so honest a Man as your Christian—I cannot find by the Map that your *Mufti* is Orthodox—Whereby it is a plain Case, that Orthodox is a hard Word, Aunt, and (*hiccup*) Greek for Claret.

Congreve, The Way of the World (1700).

THE attractions of Greece for the humanist, eager to enjoy the spectacle of lands made famous by history, literature, and the arts, were already considerable by the seventeenth century; and no one doubted that the modern inhabitants of Greece were the representatives and descendants of the ancient Hellenes whose culture was so much to be admired. But the modern Greeks had a more prominent claim upon the attention than that. To most Western Europeans it was more important that the Greeks were Christians than that they were Hellenes. The descendants of the contemporaries of St. Paul were just as interesting as the descendants of the countrymen of Socrates. Greece was, indeed, a sacred Christian land as much as a classical pagan one. It was easy to remember that the recipients of many of St. Paul's epistles were Greeks. It was at Athens that the apostle saw that strange altar dedicated to the Unknown God,[1] and that he delivered before the court of the Areopagus his famous lecture, gracefully complimenting the Athenians on being somewhat careful in religious matters and tactfully quoting from their own pagan poets. Corinth saw the foundation of St. Paul's most flourishing Greek community; and it was from that city (the Protestants could note with interest) that he wrote his expository epistle to the Romans. Nicopolis, the city that Augustus had founded to commemorate his

---

[1] For a long time the Parthenon itself was commonly regarded as the temple to the Unknown God. So says the anonymous Grecian who visited Athens about 1460 and wrote an account of the monuments of the city (printed in Laborde, i, 20). The same thing is said by Crusius (1584), Le Sieur Louis des Hayes (at Athens in 1630; Laborde, i, 64), Cantemir (1673–1723), p. 340, and others. The impudent De Guillet boldly said that the inscription *Agnôstôi Theôi* was to be seen on the façade of the Parthenon (*Athènes ancienne et moderne*, 1675, p. 191). As late as 1776 Chandler thought it necessary to deny this common error (*Greece*, p. 47).

victory at the battle of Actium, was the apostle's choice for a longer residence, as it was later to be the choice of Epictetus.

Moreover, it could not be forgotten that the Eastern Orthodox Church (the "Greek Church") represented the oldest traditions of Christianity and occupied the lands made sacred by the Founder and his apostles. In the Greek language and for Greek-speaking peoples was produced the first Christian literature, the foundations of theological investigation and the interpretation and elaboration of dogma. In the Greek lands were the sites of the first Councils of the Church (Nicaea, Constantinople, Ephesus, Chalcedon), where decisions were made which are the accepted basis of the Christian faith almost everywhere. There, too, the first five centuries of the Christian era saw great minds whose works were the basis of subsequent Christian thought, both in the Middle Ages and afterwards; and Englishmen who knew something of their own religious traditions were not ignorant of the services performed to the English Church by Theodore, a Greek of Tarsus, in the see of Canterbury.[1] For centuries, Constantinople, the foundation of the first Christian Emperor, had been the bulwark of Christendom against Islam; Constantinople had been "the eye of the world, the strongest city both by sea and by land, the bond of union between East and West, the place where the most distant extremes of the world come together, and the place to which they look as a common emporium of the faith" (as Gregory Nazianzen had once written[2]); and even after its collapse before the Ottoman, it still retained a firm hold upon the imagination of Europe. At Constantinople, as the guide to the Christian East under the Turkish yoke, the patriarchate preserved its traditions unbroken.

There is no doubt that it was an interest in the Greek Church that encouraged a large number of English people to turn their minds to Greece in the seventeenth century, and to pay particular attention to any learned Greeks who came to England. The Englishmen who, during the previous century, first came into contact with the Greek Church on their travels in the Levant are naïve in their accounts of what they saw and heard; and it can hardly be said that any intelligent interest had developed in England before the seventeenth century was well advanced. This fact is perhaps surprising, because on the Continent the leaders of the Reformation had, of course, looked hopefully to the Eastern Church. Greek, the exciting new object of study, was one of the languages of the Scriptures and of the early liturgies of the Church. Inevitably the reformers, seeking to free their religious

[1] Bede, iv, 1, etc.
[2] Oratio XLII (755). Migne, *Patrologia*, xxxvi, 469.

practices from the corruptions of time, regarded Latin Christianity of the West as a development from the Church of the Greeks. The great separation of 1054, when Leo IX excommunicated the Patriarch Michael Cerularius and the whole Eastern Church (who immediately retorted with their anathema upon the Western Church), had its origin ultimately in the Greek rejection of a system of church-government based upon the pre-eminence of the Pope of Rome. It was this system of merely ecclesiastical organization which intensified the theological differences and which led to a final separation after many mutual anathemas. The reformers in the sixteenth century, when accused of heresy and schism, looked with interest on that Church which might be supposed to preserve the primitive and apostolic traditions intact, while the Church of Rome had allegedly innovated; and should have been attracted by the centuries of protest which the Greek Church had registered against the usurpations of the Bishop of Rome. Philip Melancthon, and others, hoped to bring about a reunion of Christendom with the assistance of the Greeks. Melancthon himself dispatched, by means of a Greek deacon called Demetrius Mysus, a Greek translation of the Confession of Augsburg to Joasaph II, the Patriarch of Constantinople. Some years later Martin Kraus (Crusius), who was one of the greatest Greek scholars of the time and who in his *Turco-Graecia* (Basel, 1584) produced, as has already been related,[1] a famous work on the survivals of Greek culture after the Turkish conquest, was engaged in a correspondence with Jeremiah II, Patriarch of Constantinople (1576–81), seeking his favour for Lutheran doctrines. Jeremiah's reply in 1576, his *Censura Orientalis Ecclesiae*, emphatically condemned Lutheranism.

All this, however, seems to have made no impression upon England in the sixteenth century; and most of the early references to the Greek Church are supercilious or frankly contemptuous. The early travellers in Greece, who found the Church a living institution, failed to comprehend its ceremonies and were too hasty in their journeys to examine it seriously. John Locke, whose voyage to Jerusalem in 1553 is preserved by Hakluyt,[2] at least took notice of services in the Greek rite, but he obviously understood little of what was going on, and displays a caution excessive and disappointing. In Cyprus (which at that time had not yet been taken from the Venetians by the Turks), he says, "we went in the morning to the Greeks' church, to see the order of their ceremonies, & of their communion, of the which to declare the whole order with the number of their ceremonious

---

[1] See p. 68 above.
[2] Hakluyt (Glasgow edition, 1903), v, 76 ff., 86, 98.

crossings, it were too long. Wherefore least I should offend any man, I leave it unwritten." There is something feebly ridiculous about his comments on the Greek monastic orders: "These Greekish Friars are very continent and chaste, and surely I have seldom seen (which I have well noted) any of them fat." Edward Brerewood in his *Enquiries touching the Diversity of Languages and Religions through the chief parts of the world* (1614) endeavoured to give a balanced, though brief, account of the Greek Church[1] and a summary (fourteen points) of its differences of doctrine from those of the Roman Church. But all the information he could give was derived from second-hand sources. There is no experience, no sense of reality, behind the statements he transcribed from foreign divines. We might have expected curiosity and tolerance from Robert Burton, who was well read in such accounts as were available to him. Yet in *The Anatomy of Melancholy* (1621) he writes, "The Greek or Eastern Church is rent from this of the West . . . but as one saith, *temporis successu multas illi addiderunt superstitiones*, in process of time they have added so many superstitions, they be rather semi-Christians than otherwise." Commenting upon Strabo's ingenious comparison of Greece to the form of a man, Burton adds, "If this allusion hold, 'tis sure a mad head; Morea may be Moria [i.e. folly]; and to speak what I think, the inhabitants of modern Greece swerve as much from reason and true religion at this day, as that Morea doth from the picture of a man."[2]

The way was prepared for a better understanding by two Archbishops of Canterbury, George Abbot (1610–33) and William Laud (1633–45); and the links with the Greek Church were strengthened by the interest in England—and possibly by the presence here—of one of the most remarkable characters in the history of the patriarchate of Constantinople, Cyril Lucaris.[3] He was of Cretan origin and seems to have been born about 1572. Having travelled widely in Europe, he had become familiar with and sympathetic towards Protestantism. He was elected Patriarch of Alexandria about 1602 and Patriarch of Constantinople in 1621. He conceived the extraordinary plan of reforming the Greek Church by bringing its doctrines into harmony with Calvinism. He sent young Greek theological students to Holland, to Switzerland, and to England, to have them trained in Protestant doctrine. In 1629 he published his famous *Confession* (or summary of

[1] pp. 124–8. This tract was reprinted in *Purchas his Pilgrims* (i, 348–51 of the Glasgow edition (1905) concerns the Greek Church).

[2] Pt. 3, Sec. 4, Mem. 1, Sub. 1 (Everyman's Library edition, iii, 323); "Democritus to the Reader" (i, 39).

[3] The story of a visit by Lucaris to England seems to rest entirely upon the evidence of a statement by Ricaut, *The Present State of the Greek and Armenian Churches, Anno Christi 1678* (1679), preface, fifteenth page; and may well be doubted. If he came to England it was during the reign of Elizabeth I.

his beliefs) which includes articles openly of Calvinistic inclinations;[1] and it is evidence of the interest aroused in Western Europe that translations into Latin, French, German, and Englishappeared almost immediately. Among other innovations at Constantinople was his establishment of a Greek printing-press, which had been brought from England, complete with a fount of Greek types, by a monk called Nicodemo Metaxa in 1627. With the Patriarch's encouragement, a translation of the New Testament into modern Greek was published in 1638 by Maximos Kalliupolites; and in an appendix to the second edition of his *Confession* Lucaris recommended the general circulation of the Scriptures. An Englishman who was in the Levant in 1811–12 reports that some of the books from this press "are still to be bought in Constantinople with the English arms upon the binding".[2] The appearance of the Royal Arms of England upon the books was a device to secure some protection for the Patriarch against Turkish suspicion; for among Lucaris's warmest supporters and firm personal friends was the great ambassador, Sir Thomas Roe, who was at Constantinople from 1621 to 1628. Roe intervened to protect Cyril from his enemies on several occasions; and when the ambassador returned to England Cyril sent with him, as a present for Charles I, the *Codex Alexandrinus*, which he had brought with him either from his former see of Alexandria or from Mount Athos and which is now one of the most famous manuscripts in the British Museum. We are told of Cyril that "shortly before his death, he was present in the chapel of the British Embassy at Constantinople, at the christening of the son of the then Ambassador, Sir Peter Wych; for whom he stood godfather, named after him".[3] This godson of his was Sir Cyril Wych, who became President of the Royal Society.

His Protestant sympathies and reforming activities soon won Cyril Lucaris many enemies, especially, it was commonly said, among the Jesuits; and the French Ambassador used all his influence at the Porte against him. The Patriarch was five times deposed and reinstated; his printing press was suppressed; and finally on January 27th 1638 he was strangled by order of the Sultan Murad IV and his body was thrown into the Bosphorus. Thomas Smith, fellow of Magdalen College and chaplain of the British Embassy at Constantinople, later wrote in his well-informed *Account of the Greek Church* (1680) that the

[1] *Cyrilli Lucaris Confessio Christianae Fidei* (in Latin, 1629). An expanded version in Greek and Latin appeared at Geneva in 1633. An English translation was published in London, 1629 (*The Confession of Faith of . . . Cyrill, Patriarch of Constantinople*). For a summary of his point of view, see Philip Schaff, *The History of the Creeds* (1878, 3 vols.), i, 57.

[2] F. S. N. Douglas, *An Essay on Certain Points of Resemblance between the Ancient and Modern Greeks* (1813), p. 75.

[3] J. B. Pearson, *Chaplains to the Levant Company* (1883), p. 21.

scholar Edward Pococke lived at Constantinople at the time when the bloody deed was committed and that "he sent a long account to that excellent man, Archbishop Laud, of famous memory". The English writers were convinced that the murder of Cyril took place at the instigation of the Jesuits.[1] Thus Cyril the Patriarch came to be esteemed in England as a martyr of Protestantism within the Greek Church.[2]

One consequence of these relations between the heads of the Greek and Anglican Churches was the encouragement given to a number of scholarly Greeks who turn up in England during the seventeenth century. One of them, Christophoros Angelos from the Peloponnesus, had arrived as early as 1608. He was, wrote Anthony à Wood, "a pure Grecian and an honest and harmless man";[3] and he published between 1617 and 1619 some little tracts which have the distinction of being the first literary links between the modern Greeks and the English Universities. His first pamphlet was published at Oxford, in Greek in 1617 and in English in 1618 as *Christopher Angell, A Grecian, who tasted many stripes and torments inflicted by the Turks for the faith which he had in Christ Jesus*. He dedicates it in grateful terms to the two Universities, "most renowned and resplendent, most wise, and judicious, most learned and loving Patrons of the Greek tongue; most gracious supporters of the decayed estate of all distressed Grecians and strangers". He describes his tribulations under the Turks; he was cruelly punished as a Spanish spy in Athens; at length

> I fled from Athens, and wandering abroad, found expert Merchants, which knew well both England and many other places: and I inquired diligently of them where I might find wise men, with whom I might keep my religion, and not lose my learning: they told me, in England you may have both, for the English men love the Grecians, and their learning: and it is a monarchy, where are found many very honest, wise, and liberal men: but in Germany, France, and Italy, they have continually civil wars.

Therefore he came to England (fortified by a batch of testimonials

[1] e.g. John Covel in *Some Account of the Present Greek Church* (1722).

[2] The fullest account is given by J. M. Neale, *A History of the Holy Eastern Church*, 5 vols., 1850–73 (*The Patriarchate of Alexandria* i, 356 sqq.); but Neale's view of Cyril is highly unfavourable, being influenced by horror at his Calvinistic "heresies". This bias is interesting as a reflection of the Catholic movement in the Church of England in the nineteenth century, but it is unfortunate for the brave and likable Cyril. An interesting book is Paul Trivier's *Un Patriarche de Constantinople au dix-septième siècle* (Paris, 1877). The basic source of information from which these draw is the much earlier compilation of Thomas Smith, *Collectanea de Cyrillo Lucari* (1707), Miscellanea (Narratio de vita, studiis, gestis et martyrio C. Lucaris).

[3] *Athenae Oxonienses*, ed. Bliss, ii, 633.

from Greek clergy), arrived at Yarmouth, and presented himself to
the Bishop of Norwich.

> And he with the rest of the ministry bestowed money on me
> according to their faculties, and sent me with letters to Cambridge,
> (for he himself was a Cambridge man) and the Doctors of Cam-
> bridge received me kindly, and frankly: & I spent there almost one
> whole year, as the testimony of Cambridge can witness. Then I fell
> sick, that I could scarce breathe: and the Physicians and Doctors
> counselled me to go to Oxford, because (said they) the air of
> Oxford is far better than that of Cambridge.

After this autobiographical narrative appears "An Epistle in com-
mendations of England and the Inhabitants thereof", congratulating
England on having produced Constantine the Great and his mother
St. Helen:

> Thou art also the place of refuge, even the haven of comfort to
> poor Grecians oppressed with the tyranny of the Turks. . . . Thou
> bringest forth most wise men, yea most valiant and heroical
> captains (as heretofore Grecia did), yea and those lovers of the
> Greeks, & partakers of their former virtues.

And he will give the reason why the English are philhellenes (which
is the word he uses in his Greek version); under the Emperor
Constantine the Britons went to Constantinople and the Greeks were
sent to Britain by Constantine: "and so the Grecians and English
were mingled in blood. And for this cause the English love Grecians,
and their learning, and are beloved of them more than any other
nation."

Angell followed this tract by a more extended one in 1619, *An
Encomion of the famous Kingdom of Great Britain, and of the two
flourishing Sister Universities Cambridge and Oxford*, with Greek and
English texts vis-à-vis. His flattery now becomes somewhat fulsome,
especially in the English translation of the Greek text; but there is
feeling in his tribute to the celebrated Andrew Downes, Professor of
Greek, as one who "doth cherish, and recall as it were from the dead,
the deceased Language of the Grecians (thereby transporting as it
were Greece into Britannie, and restoring Greece to Greece)".[1]
Angelos received testimonials dated 1610, 1616, and 1617 from the
Universities of Oxford and Cambridge and from the Bishop of
Salisbury, to enable him, we must presume, to claim hospitality
as he went about England. He seems to have been at Trinity

[1] p. 10.

College, Cambridge, for more than two years, went to Oxford in 1610, and remained at Balliol teaching Greek until his death in 1638.

It was from Christophoros Angelos that the English derived their earliest first-hand information (as distinct from compilations from Crusius, Possevin, and other "authorities") of the state of the Greek Church. In 1619 at Cambridge appeared his *Encheiridion* in Greek and in Latin, a short treatise on the ecclesiastical system and practices of the Greeks. It is a careful, sincere, and rather naïve account, obviously authentic so far as it goes. Angelos was apparently known personally to Purchas, who included a version of the *Encheiridion* in his *Pilgrims*[1] "I have hither . . . translated [Purchas writes] some observations of Christopher Angelos a Greek Monk and Priest, which hath lived many years in England, and some five years since gave me a Greek Book printed by him in London, touching their present rites, both in their Churches and Monasteries." Then follows the tract, *Of the condition of life in which the Greeks now live, and of their rites of Fasts, Feasts, and other observations, gathered out of the Book of Christopheros Angelos, a Greekish Monk and Priest.* "As for dogmatical differences", Purchas wisely adds, ". . . the present Greeks are not ordinarily so learned as to give you a perfect account thereof." Yet Angelos's work was regarded as of some authority. It was reprinted at Frankfurt in 1655 (*Status et ritus ecclesiae Graecae*) and at Leipzig in 1676 (*De Statu hodiernorum Graecorum enchiridion*).

A rather more dubious character was Metrophanes Kritopoulos, who was sent by Cyril Lucaris to study in England, Switzerland, and Germany, so that he might be educated to resist Jesuitical influences in the Levant. He came from Alexandria about 1616 with a recommendation to Archbishop Abbot, who arranged for a place to be given to him at Balliol College.[2] His conduct in England appears to have merited reproach, as we learn from letters that passed between Roe and Abbot; so much so, that some have doubted whether the disreputable Greek who appears in that correspondence was really the same person as the future Patriarch of Alexandria. His subsequent conduct, however, makes the identification difficult to doubt. For Kritopoulos displayed remarkable ingratitude by later abandoning his benefactor Cyril and joining the opposing party which anathematized him. There was little justification for the triumphant remark of a Victorian writer that "Oxford educated a patriarch of Alexandria as recently as in the reign of James I".[3]

---

[1] I, chap. 14, §5; Glasgow edition (1905), i, 421–9.
[2] Anthony à Wood, *Athenae Oxonienses*, ii, 895–6.
[3] ffoulkes in *The Union Review*, vol. I (1863), p. 490.

In 1637 arrived Nathaniel Kanopios, a Cretan whom we have already met[1] as having introduced coffee into Oxford. At Laud's instigation and with his support he spent ten years in Oxford, first at Balliol College and then as chaplain or petty canon of Christ Church. After he was turned out by the Puritans, Kanopios returned to Greece and eventually (about 1650) became Bishop of Smyrna.

When Evelyn was on his travels in Italy he interested himself in the Greek churches there. In Rome on March 1st 1645, "At the Greek church we saw the Eastern ceremonies perform'd by a Bishop, &c. in that tongue"; and he noted some of the ceremonial peculiarities. In Venice he visited St. George's where he "afterwards fell into a dispute with a Candiot concerning the procession of the Holy Ghost".[2] Those English clergy who had relations with Orthodox prelates in Greece seem generally to have been regarded with friendliness, if we may judge from the experiences of the learned and adventurous Isaac Basire (1607–76). Of French origin, he settled in England and took orders in the Anglican Church, eventually becoming one of Charles I's chaplains. His devotion to the royal cause drove him from England during the Commonwealth; and, after travelling in France and Italy, he set out for the Levant in order to spread the Anglo-Catholic religious faith throughout the Near East. He pursued this extraordinary line of conduct with intrepidity and, according to his own account, in some quarters not altogether unsuccessfully. The story of his experiences is contained in a letter from Constantinople dated 1653 which is bound up with his book *The Ancient Liberty of the Britannick Church* (1661). It is described as *A Letter, Written by the Reverend Dr. Basier . . . Relating His Travels, and Endeavours to propagate the Knowledge of the Doctrine and Discipline, established in the Britannick Church, among the Greeks, Arabians, &c.*, and was addressed to Sir Richard Browne (whose daughter Evelyn married).[3] He says that, before he had been long in the Levant, he was persecuted by the "Latins" for imparting to sundry Greeks "a vulgar *Greek* translation of our *Church-Catechism*. . . . This occasioned my voluntary recess into the *Morea*, where the *Metropolitan* of *Achaia* prevailed with me to preach twice in *Greek*, at a meeting of some of his *Bishops* and *Clergy*, and it was well taken."[4] How his pronunciation of Greek was intelligible to these ecclesiastics is not recorded. When in Jerusalem, "the *Greek Patriarch* (the better to express his desire of *communion* with our old *Church* of *England*, by me declared unto him) gave me his *Bull* or *Patriarchal* Seal, in a blank (which is

---

[1] p. 83 above.　　　　　[2] *Diary* (1879), i, 208, 218, 251.
[3] This letter was reprinted in *Correspondence of Isaac Basire, D.D., with a Memoir . . . by W. N. Darnell* (1831), p. 115 sqq.
[4] *The Ancient Liberty of the Britannick Church*, sig. I7.

their way of Credence) besides many other respects".[1] But in another letter of about the same date, he gives a rather less friendly view of the Greek prelates, condemning their ignorance and deplorable superstition.[2] Basire was a religious quixote born before his time. "It hath been my constant design to dispose and incline the Greek Church to a communion with the Church of England, together with a canonical reformation of some grosser errors", he wrote. When he eventually got back to England, he was a figure of some distinction. Evelyn heard him preach at Westminster Abbey on November 10th 1661, describing him as "that great traveller, or rather French Apostle, who had been planting the Church of England in divers parts of the Levant and Asia". On October 29th 1662 Evelyn says that he had much discourse with Basire, "who shew'd me the syngraphs and original subscriptions of divers Eastern patriarchs and Asian churches to our confession".[3]

We may say that, by the middle of the seventeenth century, some knowledge of the Greek Church was available; but, on the whole, what was happening to Greek Christianity did not seem relevant to the situation of the Church in England or of any importance; nor was it in any way influential upon opinion about the prospects of the contemporary Greek nation.

In the next few decades, however, all this was changed. A real interest in the Greek Church and its relation to Western Christianity began in the seventies and had its immediate origin in an episode in France. One of the bitter controversies involving the Protestants in France was that between Antoine Arnauld (the friend of Pascal and the Porte-Royalistes) and Jean Claude (the equally famous Protestant theologian), regarding the nature of the Eucharist. Among many points at issue was the doctrine of the Greek Church: Arnauld asserted that the Greeks believed the real presence and transubstantiation; Claude denied it. The controversy immediately had wider issues, not only in France but in other countries. For on the one hand, a union with the "Greeks" was a plan which for long had received the attention of the Roman Church and was an event which would be much feared by the Protestants; and, on the other hand, the Roman Church was anxious that none of the Protestant heresies should seem to receive support from the dogmas of the Eastern Church. Information on the doctrines of the Greeks was therefore eagerly sought by both Catholics and Protestants, especially regarding the Eucharist.

Both parties, however, were gratified to find evidence to support their own cases. From the information provided by the French

---

[1] *Op. cit.*, sig. I8; *Correspondence* (1831), pp. 115–16.
[2] *Correspondence* (1831), p. 122.   [3] *Diary* (1879), ii, 138, 153.

ambassador at the Porte at this time, the Marquis de Nointel, Arnauld seemed to triumph at the Sorbonne. But the Protestants found plenty of evidence for a contrary interpretation of Greek dogma. Cyril Lucaris, of course, had expressly denied transubstantiation.[1] John Covel, who was chaplain at the Porte from 1670 to 1676, and who eventually produced a substantial folio on the Greek Church, declared: "All Greeks who Travelled or Straggled this way amongst the Europeans, were everywhere nicely Catechised and Examin'd about this Point; and I remember that about the year 1668, 1669, there was one . . . *Jeremias Germanus* here in England, at Oxford (well known to Dr. *Woodroffe*) and elsewhere, who told everybody that the Greeks believed no such thing."[2] But learned Greeks who came to Western Europe were few. The obvious thing to do was to go to Greece and find out, on the spot, what the Greeks really believed. A competently educated English theologian would surely soon be able to settle such a straightforward point of doctrine. The chaplains of the Levant Company suddenly sprang into prominence.

We may well ask why conflicting information was obtained, and why it was necessary to send to Greece to find out what the beliefs of the Eastern Church really were. Of course, anyone who was really learned in Greek theological tradition could have no doubt about the Greek position on the Eucharist. Henry More, for example, defines very simply the attitudes of the different Churches: "The *Greek* as well as the *Roman* hold *Transubstantiation*, the *Lutheran Consubstantiation*";[3] and he derides them all as guilty of *artolatria* or bread-worship. Furthermore, there existed certain joint testimonies by Greek synods issued in the seventeenth century, which could have enlightened the Western divines if they had been aware of them. These testimonies, or "Confessions", were called forth mainly by the opposition in the Greek Church both to the activities of the Jesuits in the Levant who tried to Romanize the Greek Church and to the reforming tendencies represented by Cyril Lucaris who tried to Calvinize it. But the English theologians seem to have been strangely ignorant of these Confessions or indifferent to them.

Moreover, the Protestant English divines were greatly encouraged by observing the strong antipathy of the Greeks to the Roman Church. This antipathy was based upon an inherited grievance, having its political roots as far back as the sack of Constantinople by the Latins in 1204 and the intrusion of the Venetians, Genoese, and other

---

[1] *Confessio*, Chap. 17.

[2] *Some Account of the Present Greek Church, with Reflections on their Present Doctrine and Discipline* (Cambridge, 1722), Preface, p. i.

[3] *An Explanation of the Grand Mystery of Godliness*, Book X, Chap. 2, Sec. 7 (*The Theological Works* (1708), p. 347).

tyrannical tax-gathering governments into Greek lands. In the sixteenth century the Greeks were commonly accused of having deliberately surrendered their country to the Turks out of spite towards the Latin Church. By the seventeenth century, when a reoccupation of at least part of Greece was not beyond the bounds of possibility, careful observers realized that not much reliance could be placed, by a conquering Catholic power, on the assistance of the Greeks. Henry Blount, who was on his journey in 1634, gave his opinion that "the hatred of the *Greek* Church to the *Romish* is at this day so implacable, as he who in any *Christian* war upon the Turk, should expect the least good wish from the *Christians* in those parts, would find himself utterly deceived."[1] But the hostility to the Latin Church was confused in the minds of the unfortunate Greeks with the oppression and fiscal ruthlessness of Italian governors, of which they had adequate experience. The conquest of the Morea by the Venetians in 1685 was not generally regarded by the Greeks as a liberation. The Venetians were soon alleged to be more oppressive towards the Greeks as heretics, than were the Turks towards them as contemptible infidels.

The Greek hatred towards the Roman Church was, then, encouraging to the Protestant divines. Surely some accommodation of doctrine between the Greek Church and the Anglican Church could be agreed upon. If eminent Greek ecclesiastics occasionally seemed to countenance the doctrine of transubstantiation, that could be excused as being due to ignorance or to Jesuitical influence. Other Greek ecclesiastics, equally eminent, could be found who denied transubstantiation.

It seems probable that the representatives of the Western Powers at Constantinople had to face a good deal of Greek duplicity in matters of religious doctrine, as in most other things. We need not go so far as the cynical Finlay who wrote: "So servile was the priesthood in pursuing its personal advantages, that many members of the Greek Church were found who pretended to countenance both Catholic and Protestant interpretations of the doctrines of the Church, when the influence of the French, the Dutch, or the English ambassador at Constantinople appeared most likely to advance their intrigues. Most of the disputes in the Greek Church, which during the seventeenth century induced the Catholics and the Protestants in turn to hope for the establishment of a close union with the orthodox, must be attributed to political interest, not to conformity of doctrine."[2]

[1] *A Voyage into the Levant* (1636), 2nd ed. (1637), p. 109.
[2] George Finlay, *The History of Greece under Othoman and Venetian Domination* (1856), 179–80.

It must be acknowledged, however, that the Greek ecclesiastics were in a peculiar position of power and peril which explains any crafty clinging to promises of foreign support. The Turkish conquest had actually increased the authority exercised by the Patriarch. For the world of Islam, recognizing no official division between religious and political authority, regarded the religious head of the Greek state as the political authority too; and, by means of the Patriarch, the Porte intended to rule the conquered infidels. The Patriarch became, in reality, an official of the Ottoman imperial system; and accordingly the respect of the religious Greeks for their Patriarch involved a kind of allegiance to the Sultan. The Patriarch therefore had nominally greater control over the Greeks under the Sultan than he had under the Byzantine emperors. However, the degrading venality on which the Ottoman administration depended and the capriciousness of the Turkish rulers in deposing the Patriarchs made their lot far from secure; and the history of the patriarchate under the Turks is often a shameful one; simony and the intrigues characteristic of the Phanar fill the narrative. Yet in spite of subjection to Turkish caprice, contempt, and cruelty, the Greek Church showed remarkable tenacity in all internal affairs and gradually recovered a measure of independence as a result of its obstinate conservatism. Its state may be pejoratively described as stagnation; but from another point of view it was resistance to change that safeguarded its existence in those centuries and enabled a strong national Greek Church to emerge at the time of the Revolution both with the respect of the Greek revolutionaries and with an ardent devotion to the cause of national liberty. The "stagnant" Greek Church was the champion of "liberty", as was none of the "advanced" churches of Western Christendom. The patriarchs, the metropolitans, the bishops, the monastic orders and the village-priests, were the protectors of the oppressed nation while there was none other to protect them. When the first news of the hope of liberty came, the people heard it from the clergy in the villages of Greece. In many cases it was the priest who gave the men the summons to strike for freedom; and at the monastery of Megaspelaion on April 6th (Old Style, March 25th) 1821 it was not a philhellenic enthusiast from Western Europe, but Germanos, Archbishop of Patras, who raised the standard of revolt.[1] Needless to say, one of the first orders given by Mahmud II when the Greek rebellion began was to strangle the Patriarch Gregory, together with the bishops of Adrianople and Salonica; and on Easter Day 1821 their bodies were hung outside the episcopal palace at Constantinople.

[1] Such, at any rate, is the unanimous belief of the Greeks today. What may have actually happened during the first days of the rebellion is quite another thing.

How far did the Englishmen who came into contact with the Greek Church in the seventeenth century perceive that the chief glory of the Greek ecclesiastical institutions is that in them Greek nationality itself found refuge, protection, and succour during the long humiliation of Mohammedan persecution and Turkish oppression?

Although the English writers and travellers in the seventeenth century were hardly able to see the Greek Church as a surviving representative of the Hellenic race, yet they knew that it was a living voice which had come down from the Apostolic ages. It was unquestionably a remarkable experience for these Englishmen to be present at a service in the Greek Church. In England bitter and obstinate controversy had been going on for several generations over the most rudimentary symbolical objects in the service—quarrels over a surplice or a candlestick. To even the High Churchmen from England in the seventeenth century, the services of the Greek Church must have seemed astonishingly barbaric, unintelligibly symbolical and excessively ritualistic. It is no wonder that those who penetrated beneath the sacerdotalism and felt the power of ancient traditions, were impelled to explain this Church and its liturgy to their countrymen. In the ordinary Protestant mind the appeal that the Orthodox Liturgy makes to the senses rather than to the intelligence must have provoked hostility. Although the absence of statues and crucifixes seemed encouraging to the more Protestant Anglicans, yet the worship of relics and holy pictures savoured of superstition and idolatry. The sympathetic tone in descriptions of the Greek Church which appears in the English books is therefore noteworthy. The High Church Party in England was generally friendly disposed to the Orthodox Church. Some of the English controversialists were sensitive to the accusation of illegitimacy which could be brought against the Anglican Church owing to its alleged lack of apostolic succession. It was the more distressing that strong evidence was being produced by the Romanists for an approximation of the Roman and Greek Churches in certain important points of doctrine. John Covel, the Embassy chaplain at Constantinople from 1670 to 1676 was asked by Peter Gunning (Bishop of Chichester), John Pearson (Bishop of Chester), William Sancroft (shortly to be Archbishop of Canterbury), to investigate these matters; and he obtained "A Synodical Answer to the Question, What are the Sentiments of the Oriental Church of the Grecian Orthodox; sent to the Lovers of the Greek Church in Britain in the year of our Lord 1672".[1] Thomas Smith, who had

[1] Printed in George Williams, *The Orthodox Church of the East in the Eighteenth Century* (1868), p. 67 sqq. This "answer" contains an emphatic statement of transubstantiation.

been Covel's predecessor as chaplain at Constantinople, and was later to be librarian of the Cottonian Library and a non-juring divine of some distinction, took the opportunity of the public interest to produce a Latin treatise (1676), which was translated into English in 1680 as *An Account of the Greek Church*. Moreover, Charles II is said to have interested himself in the problem and to have directed Sir Paul Ricaut, who had spent many years in the Levant, and had won some reputation by an authoritative survey of the condition of the Turkish empire, to prepare his book, *The Present State of the Greek and Armenian Churches, Anno Christi 1678*, published in 1679. Ricaut, perhaps owing to the influence of Charles II's Catholic tendencies, had no hesitation in asserting that the Greek Church held the doctrine of transubstantiation.[1] But Ricaut was well-informed. He was of Spanish origin, though his father had settled in London as a merchant. He first went to Constantinople in 1661 as a secretary to the ambassador Heneage Finch, Earl of Winchilsea, and remained there for seven years. He then lived at Smyrna as consul for eleven years. He was something of a scholar, although of a different kind from the Levant Company's chaplains, and his continuation of Knolles's history of the Turkish Empire from 1623 to 1677 (published in 1680) was a valuable work. Ricaut's *The Present State of the Greek and Armenian Churches* was important because of its fair treatment and tone of decent respect; he has feeling for the depressed situation of the Church among the Greek peoples, and for its struggle to preserve its religious existence unimpaired. The subject, he tells us, is "Tragical, the subversion of the Sanctuaries of Religion, the Royal Priesthood expelled their Churches, and those converted into Mosques; the Mysteries of the altar conceal'd in secret and dark places; for such I have seen in Cities and Villages where I have travelled, rather like Vaults or Sepulchres than Churches, having their Roofs almost levelled with the Superficies of the Earth, lest the most ordinary exsurgency of structure should be accused for triumph of Religion, and to stand in competition with the lofty Spires of the Mahometan Mosques".[2] Ricaut understood the achievement of the Greeks in retaining their religion against the almost overwhelming pressure, both economic and social, to apostatize:

It is no wonder to human reason that considers the oppression and the contempt that poor Christians are exposed to, and the ignorance in their Churches, occasioned through Poverty in the Clergy,

[1] At any rate, Lady Mary Wortley Montagu writing from Constantinople in 1718 says that his "account, I am apt to believe, was designed to compliment our court in 1679".
[2] pp. 11–12.

that many should be found who retreat from the Faith; but it is rather a Miracle, and a true verification of those words of Christ, *That the Gates of Hell shall not be able to prevail against his Church*, that there is conserved still amidst so much opposition, and in despite of all Tyranny and Arts contrived against it, an open and public Profession of the Christian Faith.[1]

Among the travellers to Greece none was more concerned with the problems offered by the Greek Church than Sir George Wheler, who was a man of strong religious sentiments and was not ashamed to express them in his book. Some readers, he writes in his preface to *A Journey into Greece* (1682), "perhaps, may not be pleased, that I have made Divine Reflections on the various events of things, and Phaenomena of nature. As to men of this irreligious temper, I make no other answer, but that I design'd to write as a Christian Traveller and Philosopher; and if my Book be unacceptable to them, because it savours of my Religion, they may leave it, as they do their Bibles, to others, who will like it better upon that account." It is not surprising that he was subsequently ordained and became a country clergyman.[2]

Wheler had therefore a taste for Church matters. In his book, however, he only gives "some short View of the State and Religion of this Church, . . . that Subject having been so amply and ingenuously handled by Mr. *Smith*, and Mr. *Ricaut*". Wheler concerns himself principally with the problem of the Eucharist, and claims that he had his "Information from Bishops, *Caloyers*, and other Religious Men of that Communion, with whom I conversed in several places of my Journey". His opinion was that the members of the Greek Church did not hold the doctrine of the Real Presence; that, indeed, they were hardly aware of the doctrine, except where their beliefs were contaminated by the influence of the Roman Church, that is, particularly at Constantinople (where a company of Jesuits and a company of Franciscans had established themselves[3]), and in Corfu,

[1] Paul Ricaut, *The History of the Present State of the Ottoman Empire* (1668), Fifth ed., 1682, p. 149.

[2] Evelyn once heard him preach at St. Margaret's, Westminster, "an honest and devout discourse, and pretty tolerably perform'd. This gentleman coming from his travels out of Greece fell in love with the daughter of Sir Thomas Higgies,* His Majesty's Resident at Venice, niece to the Earl of Bath, and married her. When they return'd into England, being honour'd with knighthood he would need turn Preacher, and took orders. He publish'd a learned and ingenious book of his travels, and is a very worthy person, a little formal and particular, but exceedingly devout." (*Diary*, October 24th 1686.)

* Really Higgons. This is the translator of Busenello (see p. 121 below).

[3] The spread of the Roman orders in the Levant about this time is noteworthy. In Athens the Jesuits had established themselves by 1645, and French Capuchins by 1658.

Zante and other places under Venetian domination or influence.
The Archbishop of Athens, with whom Wheler frequently conversed
on this subject, had been present at Constantinople when the
Patriarch signed the document given to the Marquis de Nointel,
affirming the Article of Transubstantiation; and he expressly stated
to Wheler that the word *metousiôsis* was to be understood in the
corporal and not in the spiritual sense. Wheler, however, would not
accept this plain evidence, and he found other influential churchmen
who were of quite another opinion:

> Whilst I was at the Convent of *St. Luke's* by *Livadia* in *Boeotia*,
> there happened to come thither the Bishop of *Salona*; with whom
> I had frequent discourse upon that subject [the nature of the
> Eucharist]. He seemed desirous, when I told him that I was of
> *England*, to know the Faith of our Church; of which, when I had
> given him the best Account I could, he told me that it was the same
> with theirs: For I informed him, That we believed the Holy
> Scriptures, the Apostles' Creed, the *Nicene*, and that of St.
> *Athanasius*; That our Church was governed by Bishops and Arch-
> Bishops; That our Faith was conformable to the Primitive Fathers
> and the first General Councils, until the first five or six Centuries;
> and in fine, That we were not of the *Roman* Church.

After some shallow discussion of the Eucharist the polite Bishop
declared that the English doctrine

> was the same the *Greek* Church believed; and was so obliging to me
> thereupon, that he would needs have ordained me Priest the next
> day; which, as it is really the most honourable Employment a
> Christian can be capable of, so amongst them it is most highly
> esteemed: and I had much ado to excuse myself, by acknowledging
> my Unworthiness of so great an Honour.[1]

It was not until 1920 that Constantinople sent a delegation to the
Lambeth Conference, and until 1922 that the Patriarch and his Synod
decided on the validity of Anglican orders.[2] This was contemporane-
ous with the creation, by the Holy Synod of Constantinople, of the
Metropolis of Thyatira with its see in London and its Cathedral in
Moscow Road, Bayswater, W.2.

Thus, the excitement over the religious Eastern Question seems
to have kept the wits of the chaplains and ambassadors alert when in

[1] pp. 195, 196, 198.
[2] *Documents of the Christian Church*, ed. Henry Bettenson, Oxford, 1943, p. 444.

the Levant. In the books published on the Greek Church we can see educated Englishmen for the first time looking at the contemporary Greek nation with open eyes, and inquiring into that important part of their culture, their religious beliefs. The English learnt to interest themselves in the Greek Church, and thereby became increasingly conscious of the contemporary members of it. For, with Ricaut and Wheler we begin to move away from merely doctrinal discussion and investigation, and become aware of a living religion in Greece itself. Curiously, though characteristically, it is in those very years that we come into contact with a living Greek religion in England. The metropolitan of the island of Samos, one Joasaph Georgirenes, arrived in London in 1676, having come, as he says, for the purpose of printing a book for the use of his church. He found the Greeks mostly living in a district known as Soho and records that they had a Greek priest called Daniel Voulgaris. They were anxious to build a church for themselves, and asked Georgirenes to assist them to raise the necessary funds. The Bishop of London, Henry Compton, always interested in philhellenic activities, was sympathetic, and gave them a site for a church "for the nation of the Greeks" on the west side of Charing Cross Road, then known as Hog Lane. Even Charles II is said to have contributed to the expense. The church was erected in 1677, and dedicated to the *Koimêsis* (or Assumption) of the Virgin. But its dedication to the Greek rite only lasted a few years. For in 1682, for some reason unknown, the church was seized by St. Martin-in-the-Fields, apparently without compensation,[1] and thereafter the Greeks used the chapel attached to the Russian Embassy, until about 1837 when a church dedicated to Christ the Saviour was built at Finsbury Circus.

Georgirenes published an account of the foundation of the Greek Church in London, as a broadsheet in 1682: "From the Archbishop of the Isle of Samos in Greece, an account of his building the Grecian Church in So-hoe fields, and the disposal thereof by the masters of the parish St. Martins in the fields."[2] And while he was in England the Archbishop wrote and published a book about parts of Greece that he knew and that were of religious interest, *A Description of the Present State of Samos, Nicaria, Patmos, and Mount Athos* (1677).

---

[1] In 1684 the church was taken over by the Huguenots, who owned it until 1822. This is the building which appears in Hogarth's *Noon*, where the French ladies and gentlemen are emerging from the door of their chapel. Next it was used by a body of dissenters. In 1849 it was intended to turn it into a dancing saloon, but this was prevented and it was dedicated to the Anglican rite the following year as the Church of St. Mary the Virgin. The church was knocked down in 1934 and St. Martin's School of Art built on the site.

[2] British Museum Library, 816.m. 9. (118), a broadsheet bound in *Tracts relating to London, 1598–1760*, last page.

It was translated "by one who knew the author in Constantinople" (Henry Denton), and was dedicated to James, Duke of York.

The establishment of a church in Soho for the exiles from the land of Dionysius the Areopagite, is an indication that the size of the Greek colony in London was increasing; and the name "Greek Street" nearby still testifies to the number of Greeks who resided in that part of London. After the seventeenth century, however, they moved to the City, as the centre of commerce.

Georgirenes was not satisfied merely with establishing a church for the Greek residents in London. He also wanted young Greeks to be brought from their country to England to enjoy the advantages of English education and, following the idea of Cyril Lucaris, to be equipped to spread enlightenment in Greece itself. There exists a petition from Georgirenes to Archbishop Sancroft, requesting that arrangements be made for the education of Greeks in England. The petition is not dated, but it was presumably written not long after his arrival in England in 1676.

Sheweth,
That great are the miseries and misfortunes which the Grecians at this day groan under, being prohibited the use of public Schools, and reduced to poverty by the Tyranny of the Turks; and also grown into so great Ignorance by the corruption of their Church which daily groweth more and more corrupted; That that famous nation is in great danger of being utterly lost, which is to be bewailed by all good Christians and Lovers of Learning; and to prevent which your petitioner holds it very necessary that about 12 Scholars out of Greece be constantly here to be instructed and grounded in the true Doctrine of the Church of England, whereby (with the blessing of God) they may be able Dispensers thereof, and so return into Greece aforesaid to preach the same, by which means your petitioner conceives the said people may be edified. . . .

Georgirenes hopes that his petition may be communicated by the Archbishop to the Bishop of London (the philhellenic Henry Compton) "to the intent some yearly Revenue may be allowed to carry on so pious and good a work".[1] So far as we know, however, no steps were taken immediately. A decade or so later the scheme was revived on an extensive scale. It was intended to convert Gloucester Hall (better known as Worcester College from its re-foundation in 1714) at Oxford for this purpose, and for some years that Hall was commonly known as "the Greek College". Benjamin

[1] Tanner MSS. XXXIII, fol. 57, printed in Williams, op. cit., p. lxvi.

Woodroffe became principal in 1692 and was in correspondence with Kallinikos, Patriarch of Constantinople, on the subject. Three curious documents regarding this episode have been preserved.[1] The first is "A Model of a College to be settled in the University for the Education of some Youths of the Greek Church", probably written by Woodroffe himself. The college is to consist of twenty young men who are to stay for five years; thus four men are to be sent back yearly. The Levant Company is to make arrangements for transport,[2] and the Company's chaplains at Constantinople, Aleppo, and Smyrna are to assist in the relations with the local Patriarchs who will select the young men. On arrival at Oxford they are for the first two years "to converse in Ancient Greek" and after that in Latin; "their habit is to be the gravest worn in their country". They are to study Aristotle, Plato and other ancient authors, then the Greek Fathers "as shall most conduce to the explanations of the Bible, and fit them to be able preachers and schoolmasters in their own country". Yearly reports are to be sent to the Governor of the Levant Company and to the Bishop of London. Subsequent to this "model" is a Greek letter from Woodroffe to Kallinikos, the Patriarch of Constantinople, dated March 4th 1694/5, from Oxford. We English are trying to repay to you Greeks, writes Woodroffe, the great debts we owe you, both classical and Christian: "there is nothing that we, lovers of Greece, are more ambitious of than to recompense the many things that we have received from you (or rather your forefathers), such as education, art, science, and an incredible number of other sundries, with the Evangelical word of God and the wisdom of God."[3] To educate these young Greeks, he continues, "we have established a common college at Oxford, that renewed Academy of ours, as Athens was once of yours". It is, altogether, a very handsome letter; and in the history of Philhellenism it occupies an interesting place.

The Greek prelates seem to have responded. There came over in October 1698 "divers young men from Smyrna, and others afterwards from Constantinople, and other places". But apparently the "Papal agents", who were watching the Levant very closely and were supposed to be suspicious of Protestant influence on the Greek

---

[1] They are in the Library of Lambeth Palace and were printed by ffoulkes in *The Union Review*, vol. I (London, 1863), pp. 490–500.

[2] There are references in the minutes and books of the Levant Company to these Greek youths who were sent over (Pearson, *Chaplains to the Levant Company* (1883), pp. 43–5). Wood, *Levant Company*, p. 227, says that these were sent to England at the Levant Company's expense with a view to employing them as dragomans on their return. He does not give his evidence for this, and I know of none; but he may have it from the manuscript papers of the Company.

[3] I quote from ffoulkes's translation, *op. cit.*, p. 493.

Church, arranged for the French king to establish a College for the Greeks in Paris; and, a little later, a Protestant one was established at Halle in Saxony, which seems to have been the most successful of the three. The existence of these rival establishments was a great blow to the Greek College at Oxford. Lack of funds further handicapped the project, as well as the not altogether creditable conduct of the "young Grecians" who lived in England.[1] The final blow to the Greek College was a letter from the Registrar of the Greek Church of Constantinople of March 2nd 1705. The English were politely thanked for their kind intentions, but the letter concluded, "the Church forbids any to go and study at Oxford, be they ever so willing".

Greek prelates continued to arrive in England on various occasions. In September 1701 the Archbishop of Philippopolis was in Cambridge. Archbishop Tenison knew that Covel was the man to deal with him and later wrote: "I was mighty glad that it so happened that you were in town when the Archbishop of Philippopoli came to the University; you being the person in England who could most agreeably converse with him, and in his own way." The Greek Archbishop was asked the usual questions about transubstantiation and, of course, gave the customary flattering reply. Oxford made rather a fuss of him, awarded him the honorary degree of Doctor of Divinity at a special *encaenia*, at which the Archbishop delivered a Greek oration expressing his gratitude and good will. Two rather more troublesome Greek prelates arrived in 1714, in the persons of Arsenios and Gennadios, who were also eagerly questioned. But Covel knew the true state of affairs. The Greek clergy were generally prepared to deny transubstantiation if it were in their interests to do so. In December 1714 Covel wrote to Wanley, "I long to know whether ever you tried Arsenius your Metropolite of Thebais and his associate Gennadius about their Belief of *metousiôsis* (*Transubstantiation*). I make no great doubt, but that for reward they would both declare directly against it, as Philippopoli did when lately here with me."[2] And, surely enough, Wanley managed to get a certificate from them regarding their eucharistical beliefs in the English sense.

A curious episode concerning the Greeks in England is revealed

[1] The Company wrote to Sutton, the ambassador at Constantinople, on July 6 1704 that they were not prepared to arrange for any more to come to Oxford: "those who have already been there do not give us encouragement enough to make any further trial of that kind, having no prospect of advantage, but the experience of a great deal of trouble and charge over them, for which reason we are resolved to having nothing more to do with them" (printed by Wood, *History of the Levant Company*, p. 227, from the Company's letter-books in the Public Record Office).

[2] Williams, *op. cit.*, pp. lix, lx.

by the letters of this Arsenios during his stay in England in 1714 and a few years following. Arsenios was Metropolitan of the Thebaid, and he was sent to England, together with Gennadios the Archimandrite of Alexandria, by Samuel Kapasoulis, the Patriarch of Alexandria (together with four deacons, an anagnostes, an interpreter, and a cook). They carried letters to Queen Anne; and their intention was to collect alms for their patriarchate, which was in financial difficulties. They arrived in 1714, and with the help of Henry Compton, the Bishop of London (whom we have met several decades before as supporting Georgirenes and encouraging the building of a Greek Orthodox Church in his diocese), they obtained two hundred pounds from the Queen. But they were not content with this, and remained in England collecting more money. The letters of Arsenios to Chrysanthos, the Patriarch of Jerusalem, reveal that the Greeks were tolerantly received in England.[1] "During the three years in which I lived in England", Arsenios writes, "both I and my retinue always walked about in our robes, and they held us in great favour, both the civil authorities, and the ecclesiastics." We learn that Arsenios was eager to build a Greek church in London. "Indeed, two Members of Parliament who were friends of mine told me, if I wanted them to build me a Greek Church, ... in England there is complete freedom for our religion and for anyone wishing to join our faith; only for the Latins is there any obstacle...."[2] It was more than thirty years since the failure of the first Greek church in London. But nothing came of this second attempt.

To wish to build a church for the Greek community in London is understandable. It is, at first, rather more surprising to read in Arsenios's letters that, in the reign of Queen Anne, many Englishmen apparently wished to abandon their own Church for that of the Greeks. "During the time I was in England many people asked us to receive them into the Orthodox Church. I declined to do so, however, simply because we had no church." The fact is that the presence of Arsenios and Gennadios in England gave the non-jurors an opportunity of trying to re-establish themselves.[3] About 1716 they met Archibald Campbell, Thomas Brett, Jeremy Collier,

---

[1] Extracts are given in *The Greek Orthodox Church in London*, by the Greek Archimandrite Michael Constantinides (Oxford, 1933).

[2] Constantinides, *op. cit.*, p. 10.

[3] A full account of this curious episode is given by George Williams in *The Orthodox Church of the East in the Eighteenth Century, being the Correspondence between the Eastern Patriarchs and the Nonjuring Bishops* (Cambridge (printed) 1868). This contains the original documents and the introduction is sympathetically written. See also T. Lathbury, *History of the Nonjurors* (1845). The account given by Adrian Fortescue in *The Eastern Orthodox Church* (1920), p. 258, is mildly derisive.

and other non-juring "bishops", who now projected a union between themselves (as "the Catholic remnant" in Britain) and the Orthodox. The last survivor of the canonically-consecrated bishops among the non-jurors, Thomas Ken of Bath and Wells, is well known to have said on his death-bed in 1711, "I die in the Faith of the Catholic Church, before the disunion of East and West". It was natural, therefore, that the non-juring divines should be interested in associating themselves with the great Church of the East whose claims to catholicity have always been strong, and whose apostolic succession was unquestioned. Accordingly "A Proposal for a Concordate betwixt the orthodox and catholic remnant of the British Churches, and the Catholic and Apostolical Oriental Church" was drawn up, translated into Greek, and dispatched to the Patriarch by means of Arsenios. A courteous, intelligent, and dignified reply was received from Constantinople in 1718. Considerable discussion ensued; the Czar Peter the Great became interested; correspondence with the Synod of Russia followed; and although the Greeks sent the Confession of Dositheus to the non-jurors as a kind of ultimatum to those who wished to be in communion with the Eastern Church, Brett and others continued to hope for a conference with the Orthodox synod to bring about communion. Eventually Archbishop Wake (who had been appointed to the see of Canterbury in 1716) was informed by Thomas Payne, the Levant Company's chaplain at Constantinople, about what was going on; and in 1725 he wrote to Chrysanthos[1] explaining that Collier, Campbell, Brett and the rest were schismatics posing as the representatives of the Anglican communion; and that that faithful presbyter of his, Thomas Payne, among the English merchants at Constantinople, would inform his Illustrious Reverence of the true position of those men.

By now interest in the Greek Church had declined in England. John Covel at last got his book out in 1722. But it was too late. His work was little read. The subject was dead; and until the revival of aspirations towards Catholicity in the nineteenth century, the Anglican Church no longer concerned itself with the Greek Church. There were hardly any more books published on the subject; and I am not aware of any important Greek prelates who came to England and aroused the interest of English divines. Very few eighteenth-century writers in England showed much concern with the fortunes of Greek Christianity and almost all sympathy had evaporated. Lady Mary Wortley Montagu, who was generally perceptive and sympathetic on Greek matters, declared in 1717 that "no body of men ever were more ignorant, and more corrupt" than the Greek

---

[1] The letter is in Williams, *op. cit.*, pp. lv–lviii.

priests. To her, the current religious notions of the Greeks were as contemptible as those of the Moslems:

> the Greek priests (who are the greatest scoundrels in the universe) have invented out of their own heads a thousand ridiculous stories, in order to decry the law of Mahomet. . . . There is nothing so like as the fables of the Greeks and of the Mahometans; and the last have multitudes of saints, at whose tombs miracles are by them said to be daily performed; nor are the accounts of the lives of those blessed Mussulmans much less stuffed with extravagances than the spiritual romances of the Greek Papas.[1]

Burke seems to have taken some trouble to gain information about the Greek Church and claimed to have specially authentic knowledge. The secular clergy had fallen into great disrespect among the people, he declared; and this was the cause of "a very great degeneracy from reputable Christian manners" which had taken place "throughout almost the whole of that great member of the Christian Church". He uses his information about the simony that existed among the Greeks, in order to drive home a point in his argument on the penal laws against the Irish Catholics: "The sport which they make of the miserable dignities of the Greek Church, the little factions of the harem, to which they make them subservient, the continual sale to which they expose and re-expose the same dignity, and by which they squeeze all the inferior orders of the clergy, is (for I have had particular means of being acquainted with it) nearly equal to all the other oppressions together, exercised by Mussulmen over the unhappy members of the Oriental Church."[2] The reception of Frederick North (later fifth Earl of Guildford) into the Greek Church at Corfu in January 1791 must be regarded as an example of that Englishman's eccentric philhellenism rather than as an illustration of any revival of interest.

One young English traveller, of liberal tendencies, in the later years of the eighteenth century, blurts out that the Greeks suffer from two slaveries, the Turks and their priests. If the former were taken away, the country would not be much better off; for the power would merely pass into the hands of the churchmen. "You see what a vision it is to think of seeing the ages of liberty revived here."[3] The unamiable Cornelius de Pauw, who had no personal knowledge

---

[1] *Letters and Works*, ed. W. Moy Thomas (1893), i, 371.
[2] *A Letter to a Peer of Ireland on the Penal Laws against Irish Catholics* (*Works*, ed. F. W. Raffety, 1907, v, 148, 152).
[3] *The Letters of John B. S. Morritt of Rokeby descriptive of Journeys in Europe and Asia Minor in the years 1794–1796*, ed. by C. E. Marindin (1914), p. 217.

but considerable influence, maliciously informed his readers in his *Recherches Philosophiques sur les Grecs* (1787) that the first use the Greeks would make of their liberty, if ever they acquired it, would be to start a war of religion.[1] The great philhellenic revival of the later eighteenth century was not accompanied by any reverence for the Orthodox Church on the part of Englishmen. Thornton, the misohellene, was perhaps showing especial animus when he wrote in 1807 (after fourteen years in the Levant): "I have observed the Greek religion in Russia and in Turkey. I am indeed unlearned in its peculiar doctrines, but, judging of it from its practice, I confess it to be justly characterized, as a leprous composition of ignorance, superstition, and fanaticism."[2] Equally shrewd, and more balanced, observers among those Englishmen who concerned themselves with Greek affairs, were in no doubt about the weakness and administrative corruption of the whole Greek ecclesiastical administration. Yet during the half-century from 1670 to 1720 the English concern with the Greek Church, far more than the study of classical literature, had served as a reminder of the continued existence of the Greek nation. It had prompted a series of books which were sympathetic accounts of the contemporary Greeks as human beings preserving a national culture under oppression; and although the Philhellenes of the nineteenth century had little patience with the Orthodox Church and no interest in it,[3] yet Greece as an ancient Christian land, as well as an ancient pagan land, was not forgotten by Canning when he cynically commented, at the time of the outbreak of the Revolution, that no one in England would dream of going to war on account of Aristides and St. Paul.[4]

---

[1] Berlin and Paris, 1787, 1788. Translated into English as *Philosophical Dissertations on the Greeks* (London, 2 vols., 1793), where the quoted opinion is given at i, 71.

[2] *The Present State of Turkey*, ii, 93–4.

[3] *An Apology for the Greek Church* was written by Edward Masson, the author of the volume of poems, *Philhellênika*; but it was not published until 1844, by which time religious tendencies in England were changing and a free national Church had established itself in Greece.

[4] H. V. Temperley, "The Foreign Policy of Canning 1820–1827" in *The Cambridge History of British Foreign Policy 1783–1919* (Cambridge, 1923), ii, 86.

CHAPTER VI

THE HISTORICAL SITUATION IN THE LATER SEVENTEENTH CENTURY

The *British* Monarch shall the Glory have,
That famous *Greece* remains no longer Slave;
That source of Art and cultivated Thought . . .
The banisht Muses shall no longer mourn;
But may with Liberty to *Greece* return . . .
Homers again, and *Pindars* may be found,
And his great Actions with their numbers crown'd.

Edmund Waller, *A Presage of the Ruin of the Turkish Empire* (c. 1687).

Who doubts but the *Grecian Christians*, Descendants of the ancient Possessors of that Country, may justly cast off the *Turkish* Yoke they have so long groaned under, whenever they have a Power to do it?

John Locke, *Two Treatises of Civil Government* (1690).

AN adequate picture of the state of knowledge about Greece in the seventeenth century, and the point of view of those who had no personal experience of Greek lands, can be derived from the writings of the learned Peter Heylyn, whose *Microcosmus, or a Little Description of the Great World* was first published at Oxford in 1621 and went through many editions. The insertions and deletions which were made in successive editions of the work are interesting as showing the development of knowledge about Greece and the gradual shift of opinion. In the 1625 edition Heylyn added a passage giving his views on the Turkish Empire,[1] which he considers (for sundry reasons he enumerates) to have passed the peak of its greatness. He never supposes that the nations who are ruled by the Turk should do anything to regain their liberty. He can only hope that "the Princes of *Christendom* laying aside private malice, join all in arms to strip this proud Peacock of her feathers: and (upon so blessed an advantage) to break in pieces with a rod of iron this insolent and burdensome Monarchy. A thing rather to be desired than expected. But this by way of supposition only, and as in a dream. I awake."

Of course, proposals for a holy war against the Turk had never

[1] pp. 606–9; the passage was substantially repeated in the *Cosmographie, in four bookes* (1652), part III, pp. 156–7.

III

been quite forgotten. Thus Bacon in 1617 had suggested to the king
that the intended Spanish marriage alliance might unite the two
kingdoms in such a war, "whereunto it seems the events of time
doth invite Christian kings, in respect of the great corruption and
relaxation of discipline of war in that empire; and much more in
respect of the utter ruin and enervation of the Grand Signor's navy
and forces by sea; which openeth a way (without congregating vast
armies by land) to suffocate and starve Constantinople, and thereby
to put those provinces into mutiny and insurrection".[1] Such
speculations about an offensive alliance of the Christian powers
against the Turk remained not uncommon in the seventeenth
century; and, earlier, the French monarchs, looking around for
worlds to conquer, had, besides their diplomatic enterprise at the
Porte, given thought to the possibility of expansion to the detriment
of the Ottoman empire. The crusader boastings of Francis I we have
already noticed (p. 27 above). Pierre Ronsard in *Le Bocage Royal*
(1567), after praising Greece as the mother of arts and philosophers,
suggested to Charles IX (an unstable youth who was on the throne of
France from 1560 until his death in 1574 at the age of twenty-four)
that his sovereign's very-Christian arm might well be occupied in a
Turkish war, thus removing the barbarous yoke from the neck of
Greece, the eye of the inhabitable world, which never had nor ever
will have its like; for now all her body is tortured in slavery under
the Great Turk, who has almost driven Christ out of the soul of
Greece.

> Bref cette Grèce, œil du monde habitable,
> Qui n'eut jamais, ni n'aura de semblable,
> Demande, hélas! votre bras très-chrétien
> Pour de son col deserrer le lien,
> Lien barbare, impitoyable et rude,
> Qui tout son corps gêne de servitude
> Sous ce grand Turc, qui presque de l'esprit
> Du peuple grec a chassé Jésus-Christ. . . .[2]

Similarly Malherbe, in his *Ode au Roi Henri le Grand* (1606), asks
the king to go on a crusade; and suggests, moreover, that the destinies have in store for his son both the conquest of Egypt and the
disruption of the Ottoman Empire; this includes, apparently, the
annexation of Greece. "His sword, imbrued with barbarous blood,

---

[1] *The Letters and the Life of Francis Bacon*, ed. James Spedding (1872), vi, 158.
cf. also Bacon's *Advertisement touching an Holy Warre. Written in the Yeare 1622*
(printed 1629), in *Works*, ed. Spedding (1859), vii, 9 sqq.
[2] *Œuvres complètes de P. de Ronsard*, ed. Paul Laumonier (Paris, 1914–19), iii, 241.

will one day appear to sighing Greece and bring about the downfall of the empire of the infidel Crescent."

Et que c'est lui dont l'épée,
Au sang barbare trempée,
Quelque jour apparoissant
A la Grèce qui soupire,
Fera décroître l'empire
De l'infidèle Croissant.[1]

The Greek scholar Leo Allatius of Chios (1586–1669) who settled in Rome and became librarian of the Vatican, wrote a short epic poem entitled *Hellas* in celebration of the birth of the Dauphin in 1638.[2] In this he called upon Richelieu to help oppressed Greece in her misery.

But there was one Englishman in the first half of the seventeenth century who seems seriously to have longed for the revival of the Greek nation and of the culture of her past. The first of English Philhellenes was John Milton.[3] For, with his literary inheritance from the Hellenic past Milton seems to have combined an unusual interest in the contemporary situation in Greece, and even to have envisaged possibilities for the political future of that insignificant province of the Turkish empire. A visit to Greece, as is well known, was included in his plans for his cultural Grand Tour. In December 1638 he was in Naples and was making preparations for his journey. But, as he himself later related, the sad news from England about the civil war called him home.[4] Although his intended visit was thus thwarted, Milton did not, in his admiration for Hellenism, forget that Greece remained a country on the map of Europe, a land still inhabited by Hellenes and not altogether forgetful of the past. In *Eikonoklastes* (1649) he instanced, among the crimes of Charles I, "his frequent and opprobrious dissolution of Parliaments; after he had demanded more Money of them, and they to obtain their rights had granted him, than would have bought the *Turk* out of *Morea*,

---

[1] *Poésies complètes de Malherbe*, ed. Pierre Jannet (Paris, 1874), p. 66.

[2] Printed at Rome, with a Latin translation, 1641. Leo was one of the most celebrated classical and patristic scholars of the seventeenth century. He had joined the Church of Rome and was exceedingly bitter against his schismatic countrymen. There is an edition of this curious Greek poem by Demetrios Rhodokanakis (Athens, 1872).

[3] See further T. Spencer, "Milton the First English Philhellene", in *Modern Language Review*, vol. XLVII (1952), pp. 553–4.

[4] In Siciliam quoque & Graeciam trajicere volentem me, tristis ex Anglia belli civilis nuntius revocavit. *Defensio Secunda* (*Works*, Columbia University Press, viii, 124).

and set free all the Greeks".[1] In June 1652 he wrote a letter from London to Leonard Philaras, a Greek of some distinction[2] who was in Athens at the time; and it is on the evidence of this letter[3] that the title of the first of the English Philhellenes should be bestowed upon Milton. He acknowledges his debt to the literature of ancient Athens; "When I remember how many men of supreme eloquence were produced by that city, it gives me pleasure to confess that whatever literary advance I have made I owe chiefly to my steady intimacy with their writings from my youth upwards." But he goes on from this, wishing to do something to repay the debt he has acknowledged. "Were there in me, whether by a direct gift from those old Athenians or by a kind of transfusion, such a power of pleading that I could arouse our armies and fleets for the deliverance of Greece, the land of eloquence, from her Ottoman oppressor—to this mighty act you seem almost to implore our aid—truly there is nothing which it would be more or sooner in my desire to do."[4] Hardly would the most ardent of the romantic Philhellenes of the early nineteenth century have wished to do more than to send the British Army and Navy into Greece to liberate her from Turkish tyranny. Indeed, we might be tempted to regard this merely as a flowery compliment to a Greek friend. But Milton continues more tartly; first of all, there must be rekindled in the Greeks the old valour, the old industry, the old powers of endurance (*virtutem, industriam, laborum tolerantiam*); then, he believes, they will merit their liberation, nor will other nations fail them (*neque ipsos sibi Graecos, neque ullam Gentem Graecis defuturam esse confido*).

Moreover, there is other evidence. The essential truthfulness of his statement that the plight of Greece had been long in his thoughts and in his prayers receives remarkable confirmation from an item in some "Instructions" which he prepared in 1657, when he was Cromwell's Latin Secretary, to be delivered to a new agent to the Great Duke of Muscovy: "his Highness would count it a great happiness, if he could be in any way instrumental to make peace among Christian princes, that they might turn their joint forces to

---

[1] Chap. X (*op. cit.*, v, 164).

[2] Information regarding him was collected by Masson, *Life of Milton* (1877), iv, 443–5, 637–42.

[3] *Epistolarum Familiarium Liber Unus*, 12 (*Works*, Columbia University Press, xii, 56–8).

[4] Quâ ex urbe cum tot Viri Disertissimi prodierint, eorum potissimúm scriptis ab adolescentia pervolvendis, didicisse me libens fateor quicquid ego in Literis profeci. Quod si mihi tanta vis dicendi accepta ab illis & quasi transfusa inesset, ut exercitus nostros & classes ad liberandam ab Ottomannico tyranno Graeciam, Eloquentiae patriam, excitare possem, ad quod facinus egregium nostras opes pene implorare videris, facerem profecto id, quo nihil mihi antiquius aut in votis prius esset.

set in freedom the Greeks."[1] This curious statement seems to link the Crusades with the nineteenth-century National Revolution. It was not unnatural, therefore, for Milton to think of the Grand Signior,

> the Sultan in *Bizance*,
> *Turchestan*-born,

as the infidel monarch who provided the most convenient analogy for Satan with his diabolical host:

> th'uplifted Spear
> Of their Great Sultan waving to direct
> Their course. . . .

Even the military gesture, it may be noted, becomes Islamic. In the same spirit, the deliberative assembly of the fiends is described as "their dark *Divan*".[2]

The unexpected interest which Milton showed in contemporary Greece should be remembered when we observe the intensity of feeling and of realization in that description of Athens which he gives in the fourth book of *Paradise Regain'd*:

> behold
> Where on the *Aegean* shore a City stands
> Built nobly, pure the air, and light the soil,
> *Athens*, the eye of *Greece*, Mother of Arts
> And Eloquence, native to famous wits
> Or hospitable, in her sweet recess,
> City or Suburban, studious walks and shades. . . .[3]

After the middle of the seventeenth century, the expansion of the Turkish empire was ceasing to be the terror of Western Europe. The battle of St. Gotthard in August 1664 was the first overwhelming defeat of the land armies of the Ottomans. It was the first great victory of Christendom in a pitched battle against the full force of the Turkish arms. Although the Turks outnumbered the Christians four to one and were led in person by the Grand Vizier, Köprili-Zada Ahmed, generally acknowledged to be the greatest statesman that the Ottomans ever produced, yet they left (it is said) ten thousand on the field and ignominiously retreated. It was clear to all Europe

[1] *The State Papers of John Milton* (op. cit., xiii, 504).
[2] *Paradise Lost*, xi, 395–6; i, 347–9; x, 457. It may be remembered that Dante mentions the mosques in the City of Dis (*Inferno*, viii, 70).
[3] *Paradise Regain'd*, iv, 237–43.

that military superiority had now passed from the Turkish to the Christian armies.

This was stirring news. But unquestionably it was the war which the Venetians conducted against the Turks—the long "War of Candia"—which, more than anything else, had already drawn the attention of Europe to political and military events in the Levant. In England there was a revival of interest in Venice herself,

> Europe's bulwark 'gainst the Ottomite;
> Witness Troy's rival, Candia![1]

on account of her championship of Christendom. Jean Gailhard in 1669 frankly stated that he had written and published his little book, *The Present State of the Republic of Venice, as to the Government, laws, forces, etc. of that Commonwealth: with a relation of the present war in Candia*, because "I thought that men would have the curiosity to know the condition of that Common-Wealth, which at present makes so much noise in the World, by reason of her stout and vigorous opposition to so dreadful an Enemy as the *Turk* is". His book was licensed January 9th 1668/9, that is, early in the year of the surrender to the Turks.

The Venetian forces were commanded by the great Francesco Morosini (afterwards to be the conqueror of the Morea and the bearer of the proud title of *Peloponesiaco*), seconded by the Duc de la Feuillade. French and other volunteers, we are told, flocked from every country of Christendom to Candia, as the great theatre of military glory.[2] The news of the siege of Candia was constantly reported in *The London Gazette*. In No. 400 (September 13–16th 1669—a few weeks before the fall) was advertised *An Exact Design of the City of CANDIA, with all its fortifications . . . Taken from an Original lately drawn in the said City*. This is a fine map, with an account of the history of the siege (some 6,500 words) of considerable vividness, concluding that "there is still some hope left, that this so renowned place which hath held out a longer and braver Siege than can be found mention'd in any story, may be delivered from the miseries it yet undergoes, and the ruin that seems inevitably to have attended it, and somewhat revive the ancient Glory of Christendom

---

[1] *Childe Harold's Pilgrimage*, IV, xiv.

[2] But I have not yet come across mention of names of English at the siege of Candia. The news-pamphlets that were published in England mostly came by way of France. For example, *A Relation of the Siege of Candia. From the first Expedition of the French Forces . . . to its Surrender, the 27th of September, 1669. Written in French by a Gentleman who was a Volunteer in that Service, and Faithfully Englished* (1670).

which hath been long Eclipsed by the many shameful foils it hath of late Ages receiv'd from this Common Enemy."

The conquest of Candia by the Turks in 1669, although Europe regarded it as a glorious defeat, was a calamity for the Greeks; it was the consummation of their subjection to the Turks, and seemed to rob them of any hope of a reflux of the Ottoman tide. In 1670 in Crete, 15,000 Christian children were taken from their homes, circumcised, and brought up as Moslems.[1] The ill news of further Ottoman expansion was followed by many emigrations to the West, including that of the interesting and still surviving Maniot colony which went to Corsica in 1675–6.[2]

The loss of Crete by the Venetians, the last important territorial increment of the Turkish empire, did little, however, to compensate for the defeat of St. Gotthard, and most observers, as the seventeenth century wore on, had come to the conclusion that the Turk was fast becoming a sick man, unlikely to menace Europe any longer. Busbecq in 1581 had endeavoured to arouse Christendom to face the fact that the Turk was no ordinary enemy, but one whose military strength lay in good soldiership.[3] Richard Knolles told his readers in his Preface to his *History* (1603) that, if one considered the power and strength of the Turk, nothing seemed more dreadful and dangerous. But Knolles had no personal experience of the Ottoman Empire; and those who had seen how that Empire was governed began to tell another story. Fynes Moryson, who travelled 1591–7, can give reasons for supposing that the Turkish power was on the wane. He can point to the military decline, the corruption of the administration, the degeneration in the personal ability and prowess of the Sultans. "Christians may well hope, that the power of this great enemy is declining, if not suddenly falling, which God in his mercy grant."[4] George Sandys, likewise, supposed in 1610 that the Empire had passed its zenith and was "near an extreme precipitation".[5] Bacon, as we have seen (p. 112 above), thought that the time had come when a Holy War against the Turk had a good chance of success. Sir Thomas Roe can hardly have been impressed by the stability of the Empire, when, shortly after his arrival at Constantinople in 1621, he witnessed the revolt of the janissaries, their murder of the able young Othman II (1622), the accession of the half-witted Mustafa (who

[1] A. Fortescue, *The Orthodox Eastern Church* (1920), pp. 237–8.
[2] G. Blanken, *Les Grecs de Cargèse (Corse)* (Leyden, 1951), tom. i.
[3] *De acie contra Turcam instituenda consilium*, often reprinted as his *Exclamatio, sive de re militari contra Turcam instituenda consilium.*
[4] His account as printed by Charles Hughes (1903) under the title *Shakespeare's Europe*, p. 71.
[5] *Relation of a Journey* (1615), p. 50.

had been dethroned four years before), his second dethronement in a few months, and the proclamation of his nephew Murad, aged eleven, as Sultan (1623). From Roe's correspondence we have a full picture of that intelligent and experienced diplomat's impressions of the Empire in the early years of its decay. "My last judgement is that this Empire may stand, but never rise again", was his succinct statement. The Ottoman Empire might stand, perhaps. But its early demise was just as probable. "It is impossible the empire can endure, though no stranger had a finger to help forward their destruction. . . . It has become", he wrote in 1621, "like an old body, crazed through many vices, which remain when the youth and strength is decayed." Depopulation and maladministration were continuously reducing the revenues.

> The ruined houses in many places stand, but the injustice and cruelty of the governors hath made all the people abandon them. . . . All the territory of the grand signor is dispeopled for want of justice, or rather by violent oppressions, so much as in his best parts of Greece and Natolia, a man may ride three, and four, sometimes six days, and not find a village able to feed him and his horse; whereby the revenue is so lessened, that there sufficeth not to pay the soldiery, and to maintain the court. . . . This is the true estate of this so much feared greatness.[1]

By about 1670 the feelings of uncertainty about the state of the Ottoman Empire, in spite of the loss of Crete, led to more intense speculations about the results of a war between West and East. Boileau, during the campaign of France against Holland in 1672, complains of the harsh Dutch names which he is compelled to introduce into his verses in order to celebrate the glories of the French monarch. How much better it would be if the war were taking place nearer Asia! What a pleasure to follow you to the banks of the Scamander, and to find there the poetic relics of Troy!

> Quel plaisir de te suivre aux rives de Scamandre!
> D'y trouver d'Ilion la poétique cendre!

King Louis could do more in ten days than those Greeks at Troy did in ten years; and the poet concludes that, since French arms have taken forty towns in two months, there is no reason why they should not, in a couple of years, be on the banks of the Hellespont.

---

[1] *The Negotiations of Sir Thomas Roe, in his Embassy to the Ottoman Porte, from the Year 1621 to 1628 inclusive* (1740), pp. 22, 66, 67.

Assuré des bons vers dont ton bras me répond,
Je t'attends dans deux ans aux bord de l'Hellespont.[1]

Edward Browne, the son of Sir Thomas Browne, was on his
travels between 1668 and 1673. He reached only the northern parts
of Greece; but his opinions of the results of an invasion by any of the
Western powers are especially interesting. He was sceptical of Greek
co-operation with an invader, as Henry Blount and others had been
earlier; and, remembering what happened when the Venetians
occupied the Morea in 1685, we must agree that he did not judge the
situation altogether unjustly:

> In the *European Turkish* Dominions, which I passed, I could
> not but take notice of the great number of *Christians*; for, excepting
> great Cities, or where the *Soldiery* reside, they are generally all
> *Christians*; whereof the great body is of the *Greek* Church, who
> live patiently under the *Turkish* toleration. If there should happen
> any considerable commotion among the *Turkish* powers, it is
> highly probable they would sit still, and be little active; and if any
> Forces of the *Latin* Church should attempt the Conquests of these
> parts, in all probability they would find very little assistance from
> them, and I fear they would rather adhere unto their *Turkish*
> Masters.[2]

The next few decades, following the battle of St. Gotthard, were
to see more military successes by the Christian powers. The Poles,
lead by the famous John Sobieski, won complete victories over the
Turks at Choczim in 1673 and at Lemberg in 1675. In 1679 the
Polish ambassador in England submitted to Charles II proposals for
carrying on hostilities against the Turks;[3] but nothing much seems
to have come of this plan. In 1683 the Turks made a strenuous
effort to take Vienna. When the vizier Kara Mustafa led his army
against the Hapsburgs, a number of French officers and engineers
accompanied him, lent by Louis XIV, who was glad to do something to weaken the power of the Holy Roman Empire. The price,
further Turkish expansion in Europe, seemed well worth paying.
But the Turks were repulsed by Sobieski, and in 1686 they lost Buda
itself.

The events of the year 1683, when the Turks were driven from
Vienna, certainly stirred men's minds. Edmund Waller produced a

[1] *Epitre* iv, 161–2, 171–2.
[2] *A Brief Account of Some Travels* . . . (1673); 2nd ed., 1685, p. 53.
[3] They are dated October 25th 1679 and are preserved among the Tanner MSS.
(XXXVIII, fol. 93) in the Bodleian Library.

poem *Of the late Invasion and Defeat of the Turks, in the year 1683*, in which something of the old crusaders' spirit is desiderated:

> The Turks so low, why should the Christians lose
> Such an advantage of their Barbarous foes?

Now is the time. But, as usual, the Christian states are so busy quarrelling among themselves that they are neglecting this great opportunity.

> What Angel shall descend to reconcile
> The Christian States, and end their Guilty Toil?

The answer is, of course, "Britain's king", whose greatness in the arts of war and peace peculiarly fits him for the task; and liberated Greece will honour Charles II, the queller of the Turks, more than Theseus or Hercules.

> *Charles* by old *Greece*, with a new Freedom grac'd,
> Above her Antique Heroes shall be plac'd.[1]

Charles II, however, is not known to have indulged any very serious philhellenic sentiments; although he had a Greek physician, one Constantine Rhodocanakis, who published complimentary verses in Greek on the return of Charles to England in 1660;[2] and it will be recalled[3] that the king was interested in Sir Paul Ricaut's book on the Greek Church in 1679, and that he is alleged to have contributed towards the erection of a church for the Greek community in Soho in 1677.

Waller followed this poem, a little later, by a similar one, *A Presage of the Ruin of the Turkish Empire*, addressed to the new monarch, James II. He, too, will surely reconcile the warlike princes of the Continent:

> He, Great and Good! proportion'd to the Work,
> Their ill-drawn Swords shall turn against the *Turk*.

The liberation of Greece will be the result; and, the Muses having returned, new Grecian poets will arise to sing the glories of King James:

---

[1] 33–4, 45–6, 69–70; *Poems, &c. Written upon Several Occasions* (7th ed., 1705, pp. 360–4).
[2] *Carmina graeca rythmia gratulatoria de reditu Caroli II. Magnae Britanniae . . . Regis* (Oxford, 1660).
[3] pp. 100, 103 above.

The *British* Monarch shall the Glory have
That famous *Greece* remains no longer Slave,
That source of Art and cultivated Thought!
Which they to *Rome*, and *Romans* hither brought.
The banish'd Muses shall no longer mourn,
But may with Liberty to *Greece* return;
Tho' Slaves (like Birds that sing not in a Cage)
They lost their *Genius*, and Poetic Rage,
Homers again, and *Pindars* may be found,
And his great Actions with their numbers crown'd.[1]

We must agree that Waller was too sanguine in supposing that
modern poets of a newly liberated Greece would immediately
compose Homeric epics and Pindaric odes in honour of King James II
of England.[2]

These English poems are, of course, feeble in comparison with the
six celebrated odes which Vincenzo da Filicaia wrote when his
genius was inspired by the victories of Sobieski. Filicaia pleads that
this is the moment to reunite Christian peoples under one Shepherd
by driving out the accursed Ottoman. Shall not the victorious
Christian army press forward and reach Asia?[3] For Filicaia the
usurping Turk is the defiler of Greece; with his arms he desecrates
the holy statues and treats as his insignia and booty things which

[1] 13–14, 37–46; *Poems, &c. Written upon Several Occasions* (5th ed., 1686),
pp. 263, 265.

[2] It is curious how often this Levant theme appears in Waller's poems. He had
expressed similar pious hopes for the defeat of the Turks and the recovery of "the
East" for Christendom in *To The Queen-Mother of France, upon her landing* (1638)
and in his poem addressed *To his worthy friend Sir Thomas Higgons, upon his
translation of "The Venetian Triumph"* (1658). He imitated this Italian poem, the
Prospettiva del Navale Trionfo (1656) of Gian Francesco Busenello (celebrating a
Venetian victory over the Turks near the Dardanelles on June 25th 1656, the
eleventh year of the War of Candia), in his *Instructions to a Painter, for the Drawing
of the Posture & Progress of his Majesty's Forces at Sea, Under the Command of his
Highness Royal*, written in 1665 and published the following year. See M. T.
Osborne, *Advice-to-a-Painter Poems 1633–1856. An Annotated Finding List*
(University of Texas, 1949), p. 26.

[3] Qual fia dunque, che scinto
    Appenda il brando, e ne disarmi il fianco?
    Oltre, oltre scorra il fianco
    Vittorioso Esercito, e le vaste
    Dell' Asia interne parti arda e devaste.

Canzone per la liberazione di Vienna, viii, ix. It is curious to observe how
Macaulay, when he translated this canzone in 1828, made the reference more
topical:

let the red-cross ranks
Of the triumphant Franks
Bear swift deliverance to the shrines of Greece.
        Miscellaneous Writings (2 vols., 1860), ii, 425.

were once the subject of lofty poetry.[1] Greece, the inconsolable land of Greece, says the poet, longs for the arrival of Sobieski.[2]

That these poetic aspirations for the revival of Greece were not merely fanciful writing is proved by the seriousness with which the Turkish question was beginning to be considered in diplomatic circles. The European powers were showing less timidity in their dealings with the Porte, and it became easier for the foreign ambassadors to exert diplomatic pressure at Constantinople. It was, too, a somewhat less hazardous enterprise to enter the Turkish dominions. Thus, towards the end of the seventeenth century the part played by the European powers in Turkish affairs made Greece considerably more accessible and her fate of greater interest. In 1685 an inroad upon the Turkish empire, as serious as the loss of Buda, was made when the Venetians, under Francesco Morosini, the hero of Candia, invaded the Peloponnesus and (in 1687) captured Athens. This Christian occupation of parts of Greece,

> Which, wrested from the Moslem's hand,
> While Sobieski tamed his pride
> By Buda's wall and Danube's side,
> The chiefs of Venice wrung away
> From Patra to Euboea's bay,[3]

was the most important event in the relations between Greece and Western Europe during its long subjection to the Turks. There were Scots who had joined the army of Morosini as volunteers and who served as officers in 1686 during his conquests of the Morea and Attica.[4] Moreover, the English public was kept well-informed of the progress of this interesting campaign in Greece. There was an adequate supply of news-letters, "histories", and authentic accounts, some of which were translated from the French and Italian.

The Greeks themselves, however, played no very co-operative part in the Venetian conquest of the Morea. The Maniots had

---

[1] Sallo il Sarmato infido, e sallo il crudo
Usurpator di Grecia; il dicon l'armi
Appese ai sacri marmi
E tante a lui rapite insegne e spoglie,
Alto soggetto di non bassi carmi.
                    Canzone al re di Polonia, xiv.
[2] Se'l ver mi dice un alta fantasia,
Te l'usurpata sede
Greca, te'l greco inconsolabil suolo
Chiama, te chiama solo.
                                        Ibid.
[3] Byron, *The Siege of Corinth*, ix (213–17).
[4] Finlay (1856), p. 226, on the authority of Alexander Schwenke, *Geschichte der hannoverschen Truppen in Griechenland, 1685–1689* (Hanover, 1854), p. 64.

promised to rouse the Greek population to arms, but their hopes were not fulfilled.[1] When it was clear that the Venetians were victorious, then the hatred of the Greeks towards the Turks revealed itself in horrible atrocities, which were to be repeated on an even greater scale in the revolutions of 1770 and 1821.

The Venetian conquest of Greece cannot be regarded as a "liberation"; Byron was thinking anachronistically when he wrote that Venice had once restored liberty to Greece:

> Coumourgi—can his glory cease,
> That latest conqueror of Greece,
> Till Christian hands to Greece restore
> The freedom Venice gave of yore?
> A hundred years have rolled away
> Since he refixed the Moslem's sway.[2]

The change of rulers was probably of no immediate benefit to the Greeks themselves, for the Venetians had always shown themselves to be as harsh and rapacious rulers as were the Turks, and as hateful to the indigenous population. The Venetians made no effort to establish local institutions. They ruled by military domination. And although they did much to develop trade, this was regulated for the benefit of Venice, not of the Greeks. Even the common bond of the Christian religion was of little importance, for in the eyes of the Latins the Greek Church was heretical. Yet the Venetians did something for education, during their thirty years of dominion.

> While yet the pitying eye of Peace
> Smiled o'er her long forgotten Greece:
> And ere that faithless truce was broke
> Which freed her from the unchristian yoke.[3]

Some of the more sanguine Venetians looked to a revival in Greece, which, like a new phoenix, was to be reborn to a new and glorious life under the protection of Venice.[4] It was a stirring event for the Greeks to experience this change of masters, which revealed to them the possibility of a national existence free from vassalage. "The first productive seeds of social improvement" (wrote Finlay[5] with justice)

---

[1] Finlay, p. 211.
[2] *The Siege of Corinth*, v (147–52).   [3] *Op. cit.*, ix (220–3).
[4] "La Morea, quel Paese agonizante nella Grecia; mà che spera rinascere qual nuova Fenice à vita più gloriosa sotto l'ombra de Veneti." From the dedication to *Esatta Notitia del Peloponneso volgarmente penisola della Morea* (Venice, 1687) by Girolamo Albrizzi.
[5] p. 257.

"were sown in the minds of the Greeks by their Venetian masters during the short period of their domination in the Morea. The hope, as well as the desire of bettering their condition, became then a national feeling, which gained strength with each succeeding generation, until it ripened into a desire for national independence."

The Venetian occupation of the Morea and of Attica was, therefore, the beginning of unrest among the Greeks; and it also made some of the most interesting parts of Greece more accessible to European travellers than they had ever been before. So far as the English were concerned, the war with France at that time made travelling difficult; and the number of Englishmen in Greece was then comparatively meagre compared to the list of those who had been there in the seventies. But important new geographical surveys were made under Venetian auspices, those of Albrizzi, Coronelli, and Fanelli.[1] Moreover, several remarkable men were appointed as English ambassadors to the Porte at that time; Sir William Trumbull, who was there from 1687 to 1691, is familiar in English literature; he accompanied Pepys to Tangiers; he was eulogized by Dryden; and he was the early friend and patron to whom Pope dedicated his *Pastorals*. Trumbull was succeeded by William Paget, the sixth Baron, who remained in Constantinople until 1702, when he returned to London with a present of twelve fine Turkish horses for Queen Anne from the Grand Signior. Paget's embassy marked an epoch in English influence in the Levant. The Sultan Mustafa II had in person boldly conducted a Turkish army against the Austrians; and at the battle of Zenta was completely defeated by Prince Eugène of Savoy, with the loss of thirty thousand Turks.[2] Paget, as the representative of England, a disinterested power, offered his mediation between the belligerents; and the offer was accepted. The Treaty of Carlowitz (1699) was the result of this, and forms an important landmark in the history of foreign influence in Turkey, and of English influence in the Levant.

By the end of the seventeenth century the contacts between

---

[1] Vincenzo Maria Coronelli's *Memorie istoriografiche* (Venice, 1685) was translated into English as *An Historical and Geographical Account of the Morea, Negropont, and the Maritime Places, as far as Thessalonica. Englished by R. W. Gent.* (London, 1687.) It contains many plans, maps, views, etc. Francesco Fanelli published *Atene Attica* (Venice, 1707), with plans of the town and the acropolis; also a rather comic, if melancholy, engraving of the bombardment of the Parthenon in 1686.

[2] Carlyle's lively comment upon the battle of Zenta may be recalled: "Eugène's crowning feat;—breaking of the Grand Turk's back in this world; who has staggered about, less and less of a terror and outrage, more and more of a nuisance growing unbearable, ever since that day." (*History of Friedrich II of Prussia, called Frederick the Great*, Book VII, chap. 6 (*Works*, collected edition, 1873, xxiii, 315).)

Greece and England were sufficiently strong for English people generally to be aware of the existence of that oppressed country Greece; to remember that there still lived in that country a people with whom they could legitimately feel sympathy as the descendants of the ancient Hellenes and the rightful possessors of their land. It was for this reason that Locke considered the Greeks to be a good example for his exposition of the rights of the conquerors and conquered:

the Inhabitants of any Country, who are descended, and derive a Title to their Estates from those who are subdued, and had a Government forced upon them against their free consents, retain a Right to the Possession of their Ancestors, though they consent not freely to the Government, whose hard conditions were by force imposed on the Possessors of that Country. For the first Conqueror never having had a Title to the Land of that Country, the People who are the Descendants of, or claim under those who were forced to submit to the Yoke of a Government by constraint, have always a Right to shake it off, and free themselves from the Usurpation or Tyranny the Sword hath brought in upon them.

All this, however, is rather abstract reasoning and difficult to follow. Then Locke comes down to his practical example: "Who doubts" (he continues) "but the *Grecian Christians*, Descendants of the ancient Possessors of that Country, may justly cast off the *Turkish* Yoke they have so long groaned under, whenever they have a Power to do it?"[1]

[1] *Two Treatises Of Civil Government* (1690), book II, chap. xvi (Of Conquest), para. 192.

CHAPTER VII

NEW TOPOGRAPHERS AND OLD RESIDENTS

> I am as it were sure, and do believe without all doubt, that there is
> such a City as *Constantinople*; yet for me to take my Oath thereon were a
> kind of Perjury, because I hold no infallible warrant from my own
> sense to confirm me in the certainty thereof.
>
> Sir Thomas Browne, *Religio Medici* (1642).

D URING the second half of the seventeenth century, amid religious
controversy and political speculation, the number of Englishmen who
had personal experience of Greece and the Greeks greatly increased.
Certainly even by the middle of the century the journey to the Levant
had been tolerably well described by several travellers, although
Athens itself still remained very little known. At any rate, by 1647
that tiresome person Richard Flecknoe can affect to regard the
subject as too well-worn for his lively pen; and when he made his
journey to the Levant he contented himself with a few words in
commendation of Constantinople and of the picturesque and gaily
coloured costumes of its inhabitants. For the rest, he says, "I have
nothing of rare or particular to write, but what has been heard of a
hundred times before; For that little then I have seen of *Asia*, the
Isles of the *Archipelago*, the *Dardanelles*, *Pontus Euxine*, and the
Hellespont, &c. consult *Sandys*, and other travels (if you please),
where you shall find them accurately and at large set down."[1] But
Flecknoe was not really justified in his statement. It was not until
the sixteen-seventies that Greece was adequately described. For
there is no doubt that the remarkable curiosity regarding the affairs
of the Greek Church and the military successes of the Christian
powers against the Turk had a stimulating effect upon the residents
and visitors.

The British ambassadors at the Porte during the twenty years after
the Restoration, when Charles II took over from the Levant Company
the responsibility for the appointments, were the Earl of Winchilsea
(1661–9), Sir Daniel Harvey (1669–72) and Sir John Finch (1672–81).
Winchilsea anticipated the Earl of Elgin by visiting Athens and
obtaining permission to remove ancient fragments.[2] Harvey and

[1] *A Relation of Ten Years Travels in Europe, Asia, Affrique, and America. By way
of letters to divers noble personages* (printed about 1654), p. 45, Letter XVIII (To the
Lord Thomas Somerset).

[2] Spon (ii, 187) says that the Earl of Winchilsea gained permission to remove
ancient fragments in Athens, and sent them home to England. Spon speaks of

Finch interested themselves in the controversies on the doctrines of
the Greek Church, and the latter was on good terms with his French
contemporary, the Marquis de Nointel, the outstanding personality
and patron among "the Franks" in those years. The chaplains
Thomas Smith and John Covel we have already had occasion to
mention. Many little-known and sometimes strange Englishmen
flicker for a moment in the pages of the travellers in the Levant.
There was an English surgeon called Mahomet Basha who informed
Wheler "that he was taken young, and made a slave, and brought up
in the *Mahometan* Religion". There was a Mr. Watson, a "Scotchman who hath travelled those Parts for four or five Years together".
Dr. Pickering, the physician to the English factory at Smyrna, was an
esteemed figure. At Smyrna, too, there was a certain merchant, a
Mr. Faulkener, who designed his collection of antiquities for the
University of Oxford; but this intended benefactor seems to be
unknown to fame.[1]

From an account of the English colony at Smyrna about 1675
we are provided with interesting evidence regarding the considerable
number of younger sons of the gentry who, like Tristram Shandy's
father,[2] became merchants in the Levant.

> The *English* Factory [wrote George Wheler] consist of fourscore
> or an hundred Persons, most of them younger Sons to Gentlemen;
> who give three or four hundred pounds to some great Merchant
> of the *Levant* Company; and bind their Sons Apprentices for
> seven Years; three whereof they serve in *London*, to understand
> their Masters' Concerns; and then their Masters are obliged to
> send them to negotiate in these Parts, and to find them business;
> out of which they are allowed a certain Sum *per Cent*; where by
> their Industry, in Traffic for themselves also, upon Good Gains,
> but little Loss, they live genteelly, become rich, and get great
> Estates in a short time, if they will be but indifferent good Hus-
> bands, and careful of their Owners', and their own Business.[3]

Parties of adventurous young Turkey merchants made organized
expeditions to the interesting Greek sites in Asia Minor. Thomas
Smith the chaplain joined three other Englishmen, called Lewis,

some sculptures "que monsieur le comte de Winchelseay fit enlever il y a quelques
mois, qu'il passa à Athènes, pour les envoyer par mer en Angleterre". I can find
no other evidence for this interesting visit of Winchilsea to Athens. He was
ambassador 1661–9; Spon was in Athens in 1675; and, on Spon's evidence,
Laborde (i, 178) and Michaelis (p. 48) date the visit of Winchilsea in 1675. This is
clearly wrong; Spon must be writing carelessly.

[1] George Wheler, *A Journey into Greece* (1682), pp. 199, 203, 241.
[2] Vol. I, chap. iv.   [3] *Journey*, pp. 245–6.

Rudings, and Jolly, who set out from Smyrna in April 1671 to visit the sites of the Seven Churches. He draws attention to the neglect which these important Christian shrines were suffering "by the unpardonable carelessness of the *Greeks* (unless that horrid stupidity, into which their slavery has cast them, may plead some excuse herein)". Smith was deeply moved by the experience of visiting the ruins of the Seven Churches, which had enjoyed Apostolic foundation and had once been so flourishing. "I shall not here lament the sad traverses and vicissitudes of things, and the usual changes and chances of mortal life, or upbraid the *Greeks* of luxury and stupidity, which hath brought these horrid desolations upon their Country; these are very useful but very mean and ordinary speculations."[1] What causes anxiety to Smith is the thought that the now flourishing churches of the West may suffer the same fate as the Seven Churches for their inadequacies, and that the threat that their candlestick, too, may be removed can be applied to his own countrymen. The future non-juror was already showing his sympathies.

That excellent diarist, Henry Teonge, who as a naval chaplain made two voyages in the Mediterranean,[2] arrived in Greek waters in the autumn of 1675, and astounds us by a combination of casual ignorance and amused appreciation of what he saw. "Now we are on the coasts of Sancta Maura, or Morea [*sic*], so much commended by Sir Philip Sidney for its fruitfulness and pleasant merriness of the inhabitants, and were hence called 'merry Greeks'."[3] He gives a brief geographical description of the Greek lands, inaccurate but at any rate appreciative of the survival of ancient places under modern names. He writes a poem at Zante—a kind of allegorical battle between Greek wine and Maltese wine: "A Relation of some passages happening when we were at Zante; where we tried which wine was the best."

> Two great commanders at this place fell out,
> A Malta gallant and a Grecian stout;
> True Trojans both, equal for birth and valour,
> Small difference in habit or in colour;
>   Ambitious only which should have the honour
>   To fight the Turks under the English banner.

---

[1] *Remarks Upon the Manners, Religion And Government of the Turks. Together with A Survey of the Seven Churches of Asia, As they now lye in their Ruines* (1678), pp. 206, 208, 274.

[2] His journal was printed (1825) as *The Diary of H. Teonge, Chaplain on Board his Majesty's Ships Assistance, Bristol, and Royal Oak. Anno 1675 to 1679.* I quote from the edition by G. E. Manwaring (1927) in "The Broadway Travellers".

[3] September 28th 1675, p. 79.

It is a lively and effective poem on the effects of drunkenness. The wine of Zante had for long enjoyed a reputation for potency. As early as 1517 Sir Richard Torkington wrote at Zante, "There is the greatest wines and strongest that ever I drank in my life"[1].

On October 1st Teonge confides to his journal a pretty poem to his wife beginning

> O! Ginny was a bonnie lass,
>   Which makes the world to wonder
> However it should come to pass
>   That we did part asunder. . . .

It is worth remembering that Henry Teonge was writing this charming and natural love-lyric "over against the East part of Candia" (as he describes it) in the year of *Aurengzebe* and *The Country Wife*.

Some of the British consuls in Greece were distinguished figures of the time. Bernard Randolph in his *Present State of the Morea* (1686) tells of the famous Castel Tornese, the great baronial castle of the Normans on the western shores of the Peloponnesus; beneath it was the once important port of Glarentsa[2] which is supposed to have given a title to the Dukes of Clarence. "Under the Walls is a small Town where Sir Henry Hide (who was sometimes Consul for the *English* Nation in the *Morea*) lived in great State, built a small Church, and a fair House with many Gardens and Vine-yards about it. The Church remains entire. The Situation is very pleasant."[3] It was thus possible for Englishmen to live with considerable comfort and affability in Greece. At Patras was Sir Clement Harby, Consul of the Morea and Zante, whose hospitality was grateful to passing travellers. He "entertained us" (said Wheler) "very civilly at his House". In Athens the comfort and safety of the travellers greatly increased in the latter part of the seventeenth century. This was largely due to the settlement of French religious missions there. The Jesuits arrived in 1645, but soon left for Negropont. They were succeeded in 1658 by the Capuchins, who established a convent which was familiar to every Englishman who ventured to Athens up to the time of the Revolution. In 1669 the Capuchins bought a piece of ground near, and including, the choragic monument of Lysicrates, then and for long afterwards charmingly known as "the Lantern of Demosthenes". This was where Wheler and Chandler and countless

---

[1] *Ye Oldest Diarie of Englysshe Travell*, ed. W. J. Loftie (1884), p. 18.
[2] This interesting place-name has been officially discarded and mistakenly replaced by "Kyllene".
[3] Randolph, *Morea*, 4–5. Hide is not mentioned in Wood's *History of the Levant Company*.

others stayed; and it was from here that Byron addressed many of his letters from Athens and his notes to *Childe Harold's Pilgrimage* in 1810 and 1811. His pleasure at sleeping inside the "Lantern", is more than once recounted in his letters. Moreover, the Capuchins helped the traveller in another way. About 1660 they produced a plan of the present state of the city, for the benefit of visitors who interested themselves in antiquities.[1] There had been a notable development in topographical erudition among the classical scholars of Europe. In particular must be mentioned the learned Meursius, who (although untravelled) produced a series of manuals, in which was compiled all the ancient evidence on the topography of Greece. His *Athenae Atticae* (Leyden, 1624) was in the hands of every learned traveller to Athens;[2] and Spon derived from it the evidence for some of his most intelligent identifications.

We often find mention of Jean Giraud, a Frenchman by birth, who lived for long in Athens, first as French consul and later as British consul, and was a distinguished and hospitable figure in the Levant, the host of most of the English travellers who came to Athens. He it was (said Wheler) "who with great Humanity received, and entertain'd us, during our Stay there, doing us all the Friendly Offices we could wish; and whom, in all respects, we found to be a worthy, honest, and ingenious Man, very fit for that Place, understanding the Modern Languages very well". Giraud was interested in antiquities and made available his extensive local knowledge to visitors.

To the year 1672 belongs the first detailed description of Athens from first-hand information. It is contained in a letter written by a learned Jesuit, Jacques Paul Babin. Besides antiquities, churches, and religious orders, Babin has some comments on the modern inhabitants. He quotes, of course, the Apostle's opinion on the Athenians, who however "do not retain only their curiosity as an inheritance from their ancestors; they still have a high opinion of themselves, in spite of their servitude, their misery and their poverty under the Turkish rule". But Babin is prepared to admit that "in Athens one still meets men who are courageous and remarkable for their good qualities".[3]

[1] There is a reduced reproduction of this map in Laborde, i, 78.
[2] For Meursius, see p. 68 above.
[3] Ils ne tiennent pas seulement cette curiosité par héritage de leurs ancêtres; mais encore une grande estime d'eux mêmes, nonobstant leur servitude, leur misère et leur pauvreté sous la domination Turquesque. . . . Dans *Athènes* il se rencontre encore des personnes courageuses et remarquables par leur vertu. *Relation de l'Etat Present de la Ville d'Athènes*, Laborde's reprint, i, 208, 209. The letter is dated from Smyrna, October 8th 1672, and was addressed to the Abbé Pécoil of Lyons, who accompanied the Marquis de Nointel on his tour of the

Babin's brief description, although inadequate, was at least authentic. His mistakes were the mistakes of an eye-witness. Babin had really been to Greece. But the most widely read and popular book about Athens in these years was a fraud, and a deliberate fraud. In 1675 de Guillet published his *Athènes ancienne et nouvelle*, which was immediately translated into English as *An Account of a Late Voyage to Athens, containing the Estate both Ancient and Modern of that Famous City* (London, 1676), and went through several editions. It was an ingenious fabrication from borrowed materials. De Guillet had received some information from Giraud (of whom however he writes disparagingly and scandalously) and from the Capuchins of Athens, including a copy of their plan of the city. This he amplified from learned sources, such as Meursius. But he pretended that he was basing his narrative on the observations of his brother, George de la Guilletière, who made a tour of Greece in company with an Englishman ("Mr. Drelingston"), two Germans and an Italian. It is painful for me to have to relate that this Englishman, this pioneer of cultivated travel in Greece, is a ghost, a figment of de Guillet's imposture; but for long "Mr. Drelingston" enjoyed the reputation of being "the first of our countrymen who voluntarily undertook this voyage for the mere gratification of classical taste and literary curiosity".[1] Having been successful with Athens, de Guillet turned his attention to Sparta, and in the following year produced *Lacedemone àncienne et nouvelle, Où l'on voit les Moeurs, & les Coûtumes des Grecs Modernes, des Mahometans, & des Juifs du Pays . . . Par le Sieur de la Guilletière* (Paris, 1676). This is a similar imposture. He regards it as a sequel to his *Athènes*, and in his preface promises to publish very soon the remainder of the description of Greece, particularly of Delphi and Mount Parnassus, paying careful attention all the time to the comparison between conditions in ancient and in modern times ("en gardant toûjours la comparaison des Siècles opposéz"). In spite of his disingenuousness de Guillet was an important writer on Greece. First, his book is very readable; it was, in fact, widely read, and retained its reputation for some time, even among the learned. Authentic travellers, such as Jacob Spon, in vain impugned his veracity and endeavoured to discredit his fabulous narrative. Secondly, his book was the first

Levant. It was printed (Lyon, 1674) with a preface and some notes by Spon (before his visit to Greece). A view of Athens was also added by Spon, but this is largely fantasy. There is a copy of this tiny book in the British Museum. It was reprinted by Laborde in his *Athènes*, Paris, 1854, i, 182 sqq.

[1] Edward Clarke, *Travels in Various Countries* (1810, etc.), 2nd ed., 1812, vol. III (pt. ii, sec. 2, p. 472). Clarke highly praised de Guillet's book. I do not think the surname of "Drelingston" exists. French writers of fiction are often unlucky in their inventions of English proper names.

systematic description of Athens to appear since antiquity, which was based on information (although at second-hand from Giraud and the Capuchins) about the present state of the city. Thirdly, de Guillet wrote "en gardant toûjours la comparaison des Siècles opposéz". He frequently emphasized the interest of a comparison between the Ancients and the Moderns. He was even prepared to put the folk-songs of modern Greece in the balance with the poetry of ancient Hellas; and claimed that the examples he quoted were not unworthy of the comparison.

Easily pre-eminent, however, among the visitors to Greek lands in these years, was a group of four, who travelled part of their time together; the three Englishmen, George Wheler, Francis Vernon, and Sir Giles Eastcourt; and a Frenchman, Jacob Spon, an eager epigraphist, whom Wheler took with him as his physician and amanuensis.[1] Eastcourt died in Greece during his travels;[2] but the three others have left noteworthy accounts of their experiences. In particular, George Wheler's folio, *A Journey into Greece*, which he published in 1682, remained the standard English book on modern Greece for many years, although it has never been reprinted in English. In spite of the works of Chandler and the other topographers of the later eighteenth century, a sensible traveller and author as late as 1813 could say that "perhaps, the best information we possess in our language is still to be found in the quaint relations of Sir George Wheler and Dr. Spon".[3] Wheler dedicated to King Charles II (and was duly rewarded with a knighthood) the "Observations which I made in my Travels into *Greece*; a Country once Mistress of the Civil World, and a most Famous Nursery both of Arms and Sciences; but now a Lamentable Example of the Instability of human things".

George Wheler was at Venice in June 1675. "The first thing I did there" (he tells us) "was to find out my Companion, Monsieur Spon,

---

[1] Spon has already shown his Grecian interests by publishing the letter of Jacques Paul Babin, with a preface and annotations.

[2] ". . . a small Village called *Vitrenizza*, near unto which Sir *Giles Eastcourt* was Buried, travelling in Company with Mr. *Francis Vernon*, and in his way towards Mount *Parnassus*." Bernard Randolph, *The Present State of the Morea, called Anciently Peloponnesus* (Oxford, 1686, p. 14).

[3] F. S. N. Douglas, *An Essay on Certain Points of Resemblance between the Ancient and Modern Greeks*, p. 37. William Thompson (c. 1712–c. 1766) has a poem *Coresus and Callirhoe* (Chalmers's *English Poets* (1810), XV, p. 22) based on a translation from Pausanias vii which he had found (p. 292) in "the learned and ingenious travels of Sir G. Wheler: which book, upon many accounts, deserves to be reprinted and made more common". Recently an account of the book and its author has been given by Robert Ramsey in *Essays by Diverse Hands*, XIX, N. S. (1942), pp. 1–38 ("George Wheler and his travels in Greece"). Although Wheler's travels were not reprinted in English, there were two editions of a French translation *Voyage de Dalmatie, de Grèce, du Levant*, Amsterdam, 1689, and La Haye, 1723.

Doctor of Physic, of Lyons, whom, by a particular acquaintance I had made with him at Rome, I knew to be a very discreet and ingenious person, and therefore had made choice of him, rather than any other, to be my Fellow-Traveller in this my intended Voyage." They were joined by Vernon and Eastcourt, and the four of them set out from Venice. They sailed down the coast of Dalmatia to Corfu, Cephalonia, and Zante. But here they parted company. Wheler determined to go straight on to Constantinople by sea. But Vernon and Eastcourt set out overland for Athens intending to make a tour of the Morea from there.[1] So Wheler, accompanied by Spon, sailed around the Peloponnesus. He knows of the reputation of the inhabitants of Mani; but there is nothing romantic in his description of those lovers of liberty as "famous Pirates by Sea, and Pestilent Robbers by Land". He visited several of the islands of the Archipelago, inspected Troy, and reached Constantinople, where he stayed some time.[2] He then made a long excursion into Asia Minor, visiting Smyrna and Ephesus; passed to Crete; then crossed over to the Peloponnesus to Patras, up the Gulf of Corinth to Amphissa, Delphi, Mount Parnassus, Mount Helicon, Thebes, and Athens. From Athens he made numerous excursions into Attica (including Marathon and Sunium), to Salamis and Aegina, to the northern Peloponnesus (Megara, Corinth, Sicyon), and into Boeotia. The travels of Wheler and Spon were therefore a thorough survey of the most interesting of the Greek lands. Theirs was in fact the first attempt at a systematic topographical description based upon personal exploration. Wheler and his companions were men of wide interests; and Spon, in particular, was a sound Greek scholar. Primarily, of course, Greece was to them the Classic Land. They collected marbles and inscriptions, which in 1683 Wheler presented to the University of Oxford. They made copies of numerous inscriptions which they were unable to remove, or which were considered to be of minor importance; and they made use of the collections of transcriptions accumulated by residents in the Levant, particularly that of Jean Giraud at Athens. They carried their Pausanias in their hands. They made use of ancient coins as evidence for the identification of ancient sites; and Wheler had a large number

[1] Spon, *Voyage*, i, 153.

[2] John Covel, the chaplain at Constantinople 1670–7, wrote in his diary: "I will see Nice (Nicaea), Nicomedia, Cyzicus, Mount Athos, Lemnos, Lesbos, Chios, and what else lies in my way before I leave the country, though I shall make Inscriptions and such knacks but only my pass-time. Here are every year abundance of Whifflers in those scraps of learning. Last year were here one Mr. Wheeler, a pretty ingenious youth, our countryman, and one Mr. Le Spon, a Frenchman, who certainly have made the best collection in the world..." (*Early Voyages and Travels in the Levant*, edited by J. T. Bent for the Hakluyt Society (1893), p. 278).

of "medals" engraved in his book. They saw the Parthenon before
the Venetian bombardment of 1686 had half destroyed it, and were
full of enthusiasm. To Wheler it was "absolutely, both for Matter
and Art, the most beautiful piece of Antiquity remaining in the
World. I wish I could communicate the Pleasure I took in viewing
it, by a Description that would in some proportion express the *Ideas*
I had then of it; which I cannot hope to do." He expressed the
warmest admiration for the Pheidian sculptures (now so familiar to
us as the Elgin Marbles); and he was similarly impressed by the
trunk of the colossal statue at Delos: "The beauty of it is such, that
I am apt to believe, if Michael Angelo had seen it, he would have
admired it as much as he did that Trunk in the Vatican at Rome."
Their most interesting identification was that of Delphi, which they
rightly connected with the ruins at the village of Castri, "which we
no sooner approached, but we concluded, that it was undoubtedly
the Remainder of the famous City of Delphos".[1]

The contribution of these travellers to classical studies was no
doubt admirable, although their pioneer work was perhaps not
beyond the scope of other adventurous scholars of their time. But
the special interest of their books is that they combined their classical
investigations with a full awareness of contemporary Greece. Their
enthusiasm for classical art did not blind them to the interest of the
Byzantine achievement; they visited the monastery of Hosios Loukos
("Truly, this is the finest Church I saw in all *Greece*, next to *Santa
Sophia* at Constantinople; notwithstanding it is old, and hath
suffered very much by earthquakes, and Time"); and they noted
the "ancient Mosaic Work" there. When he climbed Hymettus,
Wheler had a good opinion of the monasteries he passed; Kaisairiani
is "well enough built for that Country, where they do not strive to
excel in stately Buildings; but rather to hide themselves as much as
they can in obscurity from the world". He visited a little hermitage
on the slopes of Mount Helicon, and was there stirred to give us the
first sensitive description of the beauty of Greek scenery:

> Something below his House, descending towards the lower side
> of his Garden, is a Fountain of very good Water; and beyond that a
> River, that runneth down from the high Cliffs of the *Helicon*,
> making a natural *Cascade*, at such a convenient distance, that it
> affordeth great pleasure to the Eyes, without the least Offence to
> the Ears; until, at last, with all the murmurs of Applause, a Poet
> in his most charming Contemplations can fancy, it passeth by this
> happy Place, where Peace and Innocency seem to dwell; far out of

[1] *Journey*, pp. 47, 360, 56, 313.

reach of the Hate or Flattery of inconstant Fortune. . . . For the Quiet and Innocency of [his] Life, the natural beauty of the Place, the Rocks, Mountains, Streams, Woods, and curious Plants, join'd with the Harmonious Notes of Nightingales and other Birds, in whole Quires, celebrating and, as it were, welcoming that forward Spring, to speak the truth, so charmed my melancholic Fancy for a time, that I had almost made a Resolution never to part with so great a Happiness, for whatever the rest of the World could present me with.

This outburst is the more remarkable because George Wheler was, so far as his emotions were concerned, a rather inarticulate soul, and easily lapsed into pompousness when he felt the duty of saying something important or impressive. His comments on the Castalian spring at Delphi are not to his credit; "The Water of *Castalia* is very good and cool; fit to quench the Thirst of those hot-headed Poets, who, in their Bacchanals, spare neither God nor Man; and to whom nothing is so sacred, but they will venture to profane it."[1] Very different was the reaction of his more vivacious companion. For Dr. Jacob Spon grew poetical; the pure air on the side of Parnassus, and the imaginative stimulus of being so near to the home of Apollo and the Muses, suddenly inspired him and he made two couplets of a song in modern Greek—which he as yet only half knew.[2]

In their views of the possibilities of the Greeks' regaining their liberty, we can perceive a change from the usual indifference to such speculations displayed by most earlier travellers. Both Wheler and Spon expressed an appreciation of the vivacity of the Athenians, which would make their political improvement possible. "For this must, with great truth, be said of them", wrote Wheler; "Their bad Fortune hath not been able to take from them what they have by Nature; that is, much natural Subtilty, or Wit; of which, the Serenity and Goodness of the Air they enjoy, may be a great natural cause." He gives an indication of the contemporary emergence of political consciousness:

Although the little Hope the *Athenians* have of ever gaining their Liberty from the *Turkish* Tyranny, constrains them to live

[1] *Journey*, pp. 322, 325–6, 315.
[2] L'air épuré de ces quartiers-là, & l'imagination qu'on peut avoir, étant si proche de l'ancien sejour d'Apollon & des Muses, d'en être soudain inspiré, m'enfla d'abord la veine, & je fis deux couplets de chanson en Grec vulgaire que je ne savois encore qu'à demi. *Voyage d'Italie, de Dalmatie, de Grèce, et du Levant, Fait aux années 1662 & 1676 par Iacob Spon, Docteur Medecin Aggregé à Lyon, & George Wheler Gentilhomme Anglois* (3 vols., Lyon, 1678), ii, 55.

peaceably under their Government, without running into Rebellion against them or fomenting any Factions in the State; yet does their old Humour of Jealousy still continue: which, though they wisely moderate by Reason so far as not to be transported thereby into any Public Mutiny against the *Grand Signior*, they now own for their Emperor; yet they forbear not to shew themselves sensible of the Injuries committed by his Ministers, and to complain of them; and, with notable Industry, to prosecute the Vindication of their own Right.[1]

Spon gives a lively account of an episode illustrating this, in which the Greeks had been successful in getting rid of an odious and tyrannical ruler by applying to Constantinople. Consul Giraud told one of the Greeks who was most prominent in the affair, that he was surprised at their boldness; and the lively Greek replied in words intelligible to every student of Greek history, both ancient and modern. "Don't you see", he replied, "that we have always embroiled ourselves like this? We could never endure those who attained authority over us, and it was generally our best heads whom we banished. It is the air of our country that causes it. It is part of our heritage from our ancestors."[2] Certainly both Wheler and Spon have no hesitation about the identification of the contemporary Greeks with the ancient Hellenes. Since Athens was taken by the Turks, says Spon, it has always remained under their rule, and apparently will remain so for several centuries. For the Turks are masters of the whole of Greece, which now puts up with servitude with as much silence and timidity as it in former times displayed intrepidity and courage in maintaining its liberty.[3] Both the travellers give many pleasant accounts of details of life, amusing to the visitor in Greece today; for example, Spon relates how the resinated wine is at first very disagreeable to foreigners; but gradually they grow accustomed to the taste of the resin and eventually they do not notice it.[4] Nor do our travellers remain indifferent to the charm of the Greek folk-songs. Both Wheler and Spon concern themselves with the modern pronunciation of Greek; and Spon

[1] pp. 347, 349.
[2] Voyez-vous, dit-il, nous avons toûjours été broüillons, mais vous savez que nous n'avons jamais pû souffrir ceux qui prenoient de la autorité sur nous, & que ce ne sont d'ordinaire que nos meilleures têtes que nous avons condamnées au bannissement. L'air du pays porte cela, & c'est une partie de l'heritage de nos ancêtres. (ii, 135.)
[3] Elle est toûjours demeurée aux Ottomans, & apparemment ce sera pour plusieurs siècles, puisqu'ils sont maîtres de toute la Grèce, qui souffre cette servitude avec autant de silence & de timidité, qu'elle a autrefois témoigné d'intrepidité & de courage à maintenir sa liberté. (ii, 120.)
[4] ii, 35.

gives an excellent little dictionary of useful phrases in the demotic tongue.[1]

Francis Vernon, the companion of Wheler and Spon during the first part of their journey, was certainly the most intrepid traveller of the party. At an early age he became "possessed of an insatiable desire of seeing". During one of his youthful expeditions, he was taken by pirates, and sold into slavery; on being ransomed, he returned to Oxford to complete his master's degree. After his journey into Greece in 1675, he proceeded farther East as far as Persia; there, in 1677, he was murdered. Vernon thus had unfortunately no opportunity to prepare, at his leisure, a book of his travels like those of Wheler and Spon; and therefore the part he played in making Greece known to the English was less important. But his long letter to Henry Oldenburg (the first secretary of the Royal Society), dated January 10th 1675/6 from Smyrna, was the first descriptive account of Athens by an Englishman, and was printed the same year in the Society's *Philosophical Transactions*[2] as "Observations made during Travels from Venice through Dalmatia to Smyrna".[3] Moreover, Vernon's manuscript journal, which he began at Spalato and finished at Ispahan, reached England, and came into the possession of Robert Hooke, the famous natural philosopher, who succeeded Oldenburg as secretary of the Royal Society. In the library of that Society the remarkable document is now preserved.[4]

Towards the end of the seventeenth century Athens was apparently increasing in importance, and the number of the British there was growing. From 1678–88 an Englishman, Lancelot Hobson,

[1] Spon's *Voyage* contained several aspersions upon the book of de Guillet, who promptly published a critique of Spon's travels (*Lettres Ecrites sur un dissertation d'un Voyage de Grèce, publié par M. Spon*, Paris, 1679). Spon's own copy of this attack, with his manuscript annotations, is in the library of the University of London. Spon immediately retaliated with *Réponses à la Critique publiée par M. Guillet* (1679), in which he incorporated a translation of Francis Vernon's *Observations*. The value and trustworthy nature of Spon's travels was fully recognized; and I know of eight editions of his work, including translations into Dutch, Italian, and German. Laborde is much perturbed that his compatriots generally regard Wheler's book as better and more valuable than Spon's; and he spends many pages endeavouring to justify Spon's priority and superiority, and to prove that Wheler was a plagiarist (ii, 41 sqq). Laborde pleads strongly and sometimes unfairly (e.g. he speaks of Wheler as Spon's *jeune compagnon*; in 1675 Wheler was 25, Spon was 28). My impression is that Laborde has been successful, unjustly so. Most of those who are concerned with Athenian antiquities, and have reason to quote these travellers, now seem to prefer to quote Spon.

[2] CXXIV, 575, Abridg. ii, 284.

[3] It was reprinted in Ray's *Collection of curious Travels and Voyages* (1693), ii, and was translated in Spon's *Réponses* (1679).

[4] The epigraphical material in Vernon's MS. has been published by B. D. Merritt in *Hesperia* (1947 and 1949). I understand that the diary may shortly be printed under the editorship of Mr. S. J. Macrymichalos.

was consul, succeeding Giraud. To his time belongs a touching epitaph, the oldest British monument in Athens, now placed in the English church. It was probably brought there from the Theseum, which, as the church of St. George, was the usual place where Englishmen were buried during the Turkish rule in Athens. The inscription reads:

GEORGIOS TOU INGLEZOU
KHAIRE[1]

Here rests in hope of resurrection the body of George Stoakes
born at Limehouse in London who
after nigh seaven years appren-
ticeship in Athens unto Consull
Lancelot Hobson and learning
the Italian Greeke and Turkish
languages dyed the sixth of August
1685 in the twenty fourth year
of his age unto the inexpressible
grief of his said patron who hath
erected this monument out of true
respect unto the deceased's memory
Adjacent lyeth the bodies of Captain
Thomas Roberts commander of shipp
Recompence of Yarmouth who dyed
at Porte Leone the twelfth of May 1685:
Also Captain William Fearn commander of the Unity pink of Lon[don]
who dyed at said port the twen[ty]
sixth July 1685.

It was during Lancelot Hobson's consulship that the Venetian conquest of the Peloponnesus and of Athens took place. In fact, the first news of the Venetian invasion must have come through as poor George Stoakes of Limehouse was dying (Coron fell on August 11[2]).

The interest aroused by the Venetian expedition stimulated the pair of books which Bernard Randolph published at Oxford in 1686 and 1687 respectively: *The Present State of the Morea, Called Anciently Peloponnesus: Together with a Description of the City of Athens, Islands of Zant, Strofades, and Serigo* ... and *The Present State of the Islands in the Archipelago (or Arches), Sea of Constantinople,*

---

[1] Intended to mean "Farewell, English George".   [2] Finlay (1856), p. 212.

and Gulph of Smyrna: With the Islands of Candia and Rhodes.
Faithfully Described by Ber. Randolph. Not much is known about
Randolph;[1] but he had for some years been engaged in the Levant
trade; and he is obviously writing his rambling, disorderly account
of Greece from personal experience of many of the important
commercial centres. He is interested in modern conditions, not in
antiquities. He enjoys the spectacle of prosperity, not the Triumph
of Time; consequently he shows some real and unclassical enthusiasm
for the Greek scene. The plain of Argos "is very delightsome,
abounding with Wine, Oil, and all sorts of Grain". Likewise the
plain of Sparta "is very pleasant, full of small Villages, Olive and
Mulberry Trees".[2] Altogether, he gives an admirable account of the
conditions in Greece, during the years immediately before the
Venetian invasion; and it is a much more pleasant picture than any
visitor had given before. Here is a Greece that is beginning to thrive,
as the Ottoman empire goes on the downward path. Here is,
recognizably, the modern Greece that we know, in the pages of
this sensible, intelligent, and kind-hearted (although unerudite)
merchant.[3]

The troubles which were brought on the city of Athens by the
Venetian conquest, and the emigration of a considerable part of its
Greek inhabitants, struck a severe blow to its growing importance;
but not a lasting one. The British consulship which Lancelot Hobson
had held since 1678 lapsed in 1688, presumably when the Venetians
abandoned the city to the vengeance of the Turks; but it was revived
in 1700 in the person of Benjamin Jones and continued throughout
the eighteenth century, although the consuls were mostly Greeks.
We are told that the goods obtained by trade in Athens were oils,
aniseed, honey, wax, leather, pitch, and soap. Other cities of Greece,
too, were reviving; an English Consul at Salonica was appointed in
1715, one Richard Kemble. A vice-consul at Canea in Crete was
appointed in 1709.[4]

It was in the more favourable circumstances of increasing British
power and diplomatic influence at the Porte that Edmund Chishull
made his explorations of Greek lands while he was British chaplain
at Smyrna from 1698 to 1702. He was one of a party of eight Englishmen who in 1699 set off on "a journey round the ancient *Ionia*":

---

[1] There is a little in the *Dictionary of National Biography* under his brother
Edward Randolph.
[2] *Morea*, pp. 8, 10.
[3] Laborde (i, 176) unjustly regards Randolph as a mere copyist of Spon and
Wheler; in fact, little in Randolph's books, except his account of Athens, is not his
own.
[4] Wood, *Levant Company*, pp. 122, 123.

Whalley, Dunster, Coventry, Ashe, Turner, Clotterbrooke, Frye, and Chishull himself.[1] They visited the ruins of Ephesus and climbed Mount Tmolus, full of admiration for the scenery. Chishull was a genuinely appreciative traveller, enduring hardship and discomfort as inevitable and as worth the pleasure of enjoying the enchanting prospects of Greece. Sailing to Constantinople he feels pleased when his ship is becalmed, for that enables him to be entertained "with a fair view of the most green and fertile campaign I ever yet beheld"; and he is filled with regrets when "night now overtakes us, and deprives us of that most delicious prospect". He takes the opportunity to set down his "thoughts of *Troy*, and the whole *Trojan* shore, which for the space of three days I viewed at a convenient distance in calm and serene weather from the poop of the ship, feeding my eyes and mind with an eager and boundless curiosity". He is under no illusions, as were many previous travellers, concerning the site of Homeric Troy. He knows his Strabo, and draws the inevitable conclusion: "vain are the accounts of our modern *journalists*, who pretend to have seen the walls, the gates, or other ruins of *Troy*; that which now remains being nothing but the rubbish of new *Ilium*, or of that city once attempted there by *Constantine*".

A charming verse-epistle about his journey, *Iter Asiae Poeticum*,[2] was written by Chishull in 1701 to his old headmaster (John Horn) of Winchester School. He describes his outward voyage passing rocky Cythera and the sharp crags of Cape Malea; sailing then among the Cyclades, scattered around, and between Chios and Lesbos, until he reaches his journey's end at Smyrna. Here, in the birthplace of Homer, the English poet sits down to read his *Iliad* in a shady grove; sleep seizes him, and he is rewarded by a vision of the mighty bard.[3] Chishull thanks his old headmaster for his early initiation into classical literature, which has enabled him to enjoy to the full the sensation of being in famous places. His mind is filled with memories of Musaeus as he passes between Sestos and Abydos; he gazes upon Hero's Tower and remembers her love for Leander and the light she hung out to guide him. Above all he remembers that wonderful day which first took him to the Trojan shore, when his eyes eagerly

[1] *Travels in Turkey and back to England* (1747), pp. 17–18, 34–5, 38. This account of his journeys was published posthumously by his son Edmund, with a preface by Dr. Richard Mead.

[2] Printed in *Antiquitates Asiaticae Christianam Aeram antecedentes* (1728), extra pages (sig. Iii 1), separately paginated pp. 5–6.

[3]   nemorosâ in valle legebam
Ingentem Iliada, & resonantis ad antra Meletis
Somnia carpebam, cùm protinus alma verendi
Ante oculos stetit umbra senis, litemque diremit
Urbibus, & dixit, Sacras cave molliter herbas
Laedere, Smyrnaei quondam incunabula vatis.

wandered over the places celebrated in the *Iliad*; how fortunate he was to have had a Wykehamical education![1]

This amusing poem appeared in Chishull's learned publication *Antiquitates Asiaticae* in 1728, in which were included the inscriptions he had collected himself, and also those gathered by another Levant chaplain, Samuel Lisle, who was at Smyrna 1710–19 and later became Bishop of Norwich. Chishull's friend Dr. Richard Mead helped him in the composition of this important work. Here was given a transcript of the now famous *Monumentum Ancyranum*, which he got from Tournefort (who was in Smyrna in 1701, and mentions Chishull as "a pretty gentleman, and a good Antiquary; I communicated to him the Inscriptions I had copy'd at *Angora*").[2] There is also preserved[3] a brief account of a journey made to Aiasalúck (near Ephesus) in 1705 "from an imperfect diary, found among Chishull's papers, written in Latin by Dr. Antony Picenini, a Grison, who happening to be then at Smyrna, joined in company with consul Sherard, and other gentlemen of the English nation. . . . The other gentlemen were the Rev. John Tisser, chaplain to the English Factory; and Cutts Lockwood, and John Lethieullier, two capital merchants, of great spirit and generosity." This consul Sherard was the famous botanist William Sherard who founded a chair of botany at Oxford. He was at Smyrna from 1702 to 1716.

There were others, besides merchants and consuls and chaplains, who began to go far afield and to feel the attractions of the Levant, during the reign of Queen Anne. William Aikman, an accomplished Scots painter, after making the customary sojourn at Rome, set off for Smyrna and Constantinople about 1710 and got back to Scotland in 1712. He was, I suppose, the first British artist in Greek lands.[4] Verses by James Thomson, David Mallet, Allan Ramsay, and others, show the esteem and affection in which Aikman was held. He must have had something to tell the men-of-letters of his time.

The wars against the Turks in eastern Europe, the Venetian conquest of the Peloponnesus, and the English mediation at the

---

[1] Haeret adhuc animo conspecta Leandria Turris;
   Haeret amor, lumenque; haeret super omnia praesens
   Fausta dies, quae me Trojana ad littora primum
   Duxit, & attonitum Sigeâ in rupe locavit. . . .
   Luminibusque vagis campos permetior amens
   Iliacos. Tum, siqua fides, venerande magister,
   Hi nomen, me vate, tuum, doctosque labores
   Senserunt: & Nympha fuit mirantis in ore
   Wiccama. . . .
[2] *A Voyage into the Levant* (English translation, 2 vols., 1718, ii, 378).
[3] Chandler, *Asia Minor* (1775), p. 113.
[4] George Wheler made sketches during his tour of 1675, some of which (of very poor quality) were engraved in *A Journey into Greece*.

Porte, all played their part in promoting a revival of interest in Turkey; and whenever a special interest in the development, status, or decline of the Ottoman empire showed itself, it was generally accompanied by a concern with the most important of the subject states, Greece. Knolles's great history had been revised by Sir Paul Ricaut in 1679; another, more extensive, edition was issued 1687–1700 in three handsome folio volumes; and an abridgement by John Savage, in two octavo volumes, was published in 1701. Another history, *A Full Account of the Present State of the Ottoman Empire*, was published in 1709 by the young Aaron Hill. Hill, had, at an early age, gone to Constantinople when Lord Paget, a relative of his mother, was ambassador; and he travelled extensively in the Near East, returning to England about 1703 when he was aged eighteen. This youthful experience was the background to Hill's *Full Account* which (as he himself admits) had far more success than it deserved. Lady Mary Wortley Montagu in a letter of 1718 from Constantinople expressed herself with considerable sarcasm concerning the accuracy of its statements.[1] Yet his book must have been acceptable to many readers, for it went into a second edition within a year.

Hill's manner of writing is alternately flippant and pompous, displaying sickly errors of taste and all the kinds of false sublimity that Longinus could describe. His book is also padded out with lubricious anecdotes, which are particularly odious because they are ostensibly introduced to illustrate manners and customs in the Levant; needless to say, they are, most of them, quite incredible. Hill's folio, although I cannot bring myself to regret that it is forgotten, is certainly one of the curiosities of literature.

Like every other writer, Hill has his speculations on the consequences of the decline of Ottoman power in the Levant. As for the Turks, he says, "their declining State and Sinking Grandeur, and many reasonable Causes join to Prompt a *Christian's* hope, that he may live to Triumph in the downfall of a Throne whose Black Foundation fix'd its Greatness on the Bloody Overthrow of Injur'd Princes, and the Undistinguish'd Slaughter of Invaded Nations".[2] Many curious opinions have been held about the Greeks, ancient and modern; but Hill's notion that the Turks are the descendants of the ancient Hellenes must surely be unique: "most of the *Modern Turks*, especially those of Europe, are Descended from the *Greeks*, the old Inhabitants of that Subverted Country".[3] However, having

---

[1] *Letters and Works*, ed. Lord Wharncliffe, revised W. Moy Thomas (1893), i, 360–1.
[2] p. 37. I quote from the second edition (1710).
[3] p. 110. It is of course true that a certain portion of the Moslem population in Greece was of Greek blood, having been derived from renegades. But this is presumably not what Hill means.

described the state of the Ottoman power at some length, Hill continues: "Proceed we now to view the present State of the poor *Modern Greeks*, and see how much we find among them of the ancient Spirit of their *Glorious Ancestors*." We are then indulged with a purple passage.

> The Spacious *Earth* affords no Scene, which plainlier Represents to a Contemplative Genius the frail Foundation of all *Human Grandeur*, than the present Condition of Subverted *Greece*, that Ancient *Theatre* of *Power* and *Learning*, and *Nursery* of the most Illustrious *Propagators* of *Wisdom* and *Morality*. He who looks back on former Ages, and Traces that unhappy Nation to its Meridian Splendour, will be strangely struck with an uncommon Wonder at the Degenerate Principles of their Unmann'd Posterity. . . .

Hill has an anecdote for us, to illustrate his theme. He found a descendant of the Byzantine Emperors in employment as a stable-hand.

> I was never more Sensibly Afflicted at the Misfortunes of another, than when I saw at *Constantinople*, in the House of Mr. *Williams*, an *English* Merchant, now at *Aleppo*, one *Constantine Paleologus*, at that time a *Groom* of his Stables. This Man demonstrated by undeniable Proofs, that he was Lineally Descended from the Emperors of *Greece*; but was most sordidly Illiterate, and Inexpressibly Ignorant in anything beyond the dressing of his *Horses*; yet he had a peculiar Majesty in his Person . . . an Awful Gravity adorn'd his *Countenance*, and his silent Postures had somewhat Naturally Noble. . . .[1]

One of the effects of the slavery in which the Greeks live is that they become contented with their condition. They pay excessive taxes, "nor dare they think of shaking off the *Turkish* Yoke, by a general *Insurrection*, tho' the fairest Opportunity should Court 'em to endeavour it; choosing rather to Live Oppress'd by *Tyranny*, than by an Active *Valour*, undergo the Fatigues of a *Vigorous War*, to regain the Possession of forgotten *Liberty*".

Hill's crassness sometimes would provoke a reader possessed of the most amiable historical sense and indulgence towards misunderstandings in the past. The language of the Greeks, he declares, "is a *much corrupted Dialect*, and differs so extremely from the *ancient*

[1] pp. 172–5.

Greek, now only known to *Scholars*, that they hardly make a shift to understand one Word in ten when *Strangers* speak it". Yet Hill, who has sentiment of an inappropriate kind on most occasions, does not fail to be moved by the *genius loci*. His "sense of place" is interesting and anticipatory of the more eloquent topographical sentiment which was soon to come into English literature. He does not pass by Sestos and Abydos unmoved:

> Methinks I found a certain secret Pleasure in the *very looking* on a Place of such *Antiquity*; and while I sail'd along the *River*, the complaining Murmurs of the rolling Waters seem'd to mourn *Leander's Drowning*, and I cou'd not look upon the venerable *Turrets* of those *aged Buildings*, but they brought to my Reflection the *Idea* of those dulcid Strains, wherein *Musaeus warbles* out the Circumstances of the *melancholy Story*.

Generally speaking, of course, he spoils his effects by his exaggeration and his hopeless strivings for fine writing: "ATHENS still may call her self a *City*, but can only do it as the *Skeleton* of some *Dead Man* continues long to represent the Shape of *human Body*." But when he struggles to communicate to us how each old poetic mountain once inspiration breathed around, he at least makes us remember Gray:

> The *Mountain of Parnassus* now no more pretends to boast the *Muses' Residence*, the lofty *Songs* of ancient *Poets* are forgotten on the now-neglected Streams of *Helicon*, and the delightful *Harmonies* once celebrated there, are now converted into *Howlings* of strange Savage Beasts, and *Brayings* of *Wild Asses*.[1]

With Chishull and Aaron Hill we can take our leave of the relations between England and Greece in the seventeenth century. These two writers can be considered as the prototypes of the Englishmen who were to become the interpreters of Greece in the eighteenth century and in the early years of the nineteenth century. Chishull was an example of the scholar who brings his knowledge to bear upon his experiences in Greece and nourishes a sober excitement and erudite devotion to the places familiar to him from his reading. By his adventurousness he makes an unquestionable contribution to learning, and is capable of something like love for the strange countries of the Levant. Hill, for all his vices of style and feeling, is a romantic; he is ignorant, and what knowledge he has is frequently

[1] pp. 202, 218.

misapplied in his search for a fine sensation. If he does not shed tears over the plight of Greece, that is only because tears are not yet the fashion. He utters the commonplaces of sentiment about Greece; but they are nevertheless commonplaces that Byron was to express with so much more pathos and intensity that in his poems they seem acceptable and even exciting. Hill was an intolerable writer; but at least he said the kinds of things about Greece which better writers during the next century and a half were to refine into poetry.

CHAPTER VIII

BEYOND THE GRAND TOUR IN THE EIGHTEENTH CENTURY

It is never to be repaired, the loss that Homer has sustained for want of my translating him in Asia.

> Alexander Pope in a letter to Lady Mary Wortley Montagu (then at Constantinople), dated September 1st 1718.

We proposed to read the Iliad and Odyssey in the countries, where Achilles fought, where Ulysses travelled, and where Homer sung.

> Robert Wood, *A Comparative View of the antient and present state of the Troade. To which is prefixed an Essay on the Original Genius of Homer*, 1767.

BETWEEN 1715 and 1717 the Turks reconquered the Morea from Venice; but in the north Prince Eugène, after a fresh outbreak of hostilities, had taken Belgrade. By the Treaty of Passarowitz (1718) peace was restored; and again on this occasion, as in the case of the treaty of Carlowitz, England was the mediator, in the person of Edward Wortley Montagu, ambassador at the Porte 1716–18. It was in this favourable atmosphere, when English prestige was high, that his wife Lady Mary wrote her famous letters from Constantinople.[1] Her husband's official duties concerned (she complains to Pope) "the barbarous spectacle of Turks and Germans cutting one another's throats. But what can you expect from such a country as this, from which the Muses have fled, from which letters seem eternally banished!"[2] She herself was the first woman to give her impressions of Greek lands; and her letters, free from the pretentiousness of more learned travellers, are more sensitive and more expressive of the moods occasioned by the spectacle of the Greek people and their plight. Although Lady Mary prided herself upon her experiences of the Turks as her more remarkable achievement, yet it is clear that

[1] Although she was in the Levant 1716–18, her *Letters* were not published until 1763 (an unauthorized edition) and were not the correspondence actually written at the time. They were arranged for publication by Lady Mary in the latter part of her life (she died in 1762), from her diaries and correspondence. They are, in fact, a work of literary artifice. We cannot be sure that anything appearing in the text of her *Letters* was actually written as early as 1716–18.

[2] *Letters and Works*, ed. Lord Wharncliffe, revised W. Moy Thomas (1893), i. 337.

much of her time she spent among the Greeks, and much of her information was derived from them. She was the first consistently, and not merely incidentally, to give expression to the sentiments which were to be characteristic of Hellenic travellers during the following hundred years and after. She was, moreover, the first of the English to write verses on the modern Greeks from her own experience of them. With her the contrast between ancients and moderns in Greece comes into English poetry. The Byronic theme is firmly, and not inadequately, launched.

At Constantinople Lady Mary broods on the vanity of human pride in much the same spirit as those who contemplated the ruins of Rome. The difference is that here the Grecian glories of Constantinople have not been destroyed so much as replaced by Ottoman glories. The Greeks still live in the capital of their old empire, though now they are degraded:

> One little spot, the Tenure small contains
> Of Greek Nobility, the poor remains.
> Where other *Helens* with like powerful Charms,
> Had once engag'd the warring World in Arms;
> Those Names which Royal Ancestors can boast,
> In mean Mechanick Arts obscurely lost;
> Those Eyes a second *Homer* might inspire,
> Fix'd at the Loom destroy their useless Fire;
> Griev'd at a View which struck upon my Mind,
> The short-liv'd Vanity of Human-kind.[1]

She is sometimes mildly ironical or frankly flippant, very much in Byron's topographical manner. She is amused by her presence in famous places. Crossing the Hebrus (she writes to Pope), "the most remarkable accident that happened to me, was my being very near overturned into the Hebrus; and, if I had much regard for the glories that one's name enjoys after death, I should certainly be sorry for having missed the romantic conclusion of swimming down the same river in which the musical head repeated verses so many ages since". When she sails amongst the isles of Greece, she declares, "'tis impossible to imagine any thing more agreeable than this journey would have been between two or three thousand years since, when, after drinking a dish of tea with Sappho, I might have gone the same

---

[1] *Verses Written in the Chiask at Pera overlooking Constantinople, December the 26th 1718.* This was the kiosk of the British Embassy. The poem first appeared in *A New Miscellany of Original Poems, Translations and Imitations. By the most Eminent Hands* (1720), edited by Anthony Hammond (pp. 95–101), from which I quote. It is reprinted in the *Letters and Works*, ii, 449–51.

evening to visit the temple of Homer in Chios, and have passed this voyage in taking plans of magnificent temples, delineating the miracles of statuaries, and conversing with the most polite and most gay of human kind. Alas! art is extinct here; the wonders of nature alone remain." Then, more seriously, she tells her correspondent how much she wishes "that I might impart some of the pleasure I have found in this voyage through the most agreeable part of the world, where every scene presents me some poetical idea.

> Warm'd with poetic transport I survey
> Th'immortal islands, and the well-known sea.
> For here so oft the muse her harp has strung,
> That not a mountain rears his head unsung.

I beg your pardon for this sally, and will, if I can, continue the rest of my account in plain prose."[1]

Above all, Lady Mary has an eye for the continuity of the life of the Greek peoples from ancient into modern times; and she draws attention to the light that is thrown upon classical authors by careful observation of the manners and customs of the present day, among the Greeks and (as she wisely perceives) among the Turks who have occupied Greek lands:

> I was three days ago at one of the finest [bagnios] in the town, and had the opportunity of seeing a Turkish bride received there, and all the ceremonies used on that occasion, which made me recollect the epithalamium of Helen, by Theocritus; and it seems to me, that the same customs have continued ever since.

To those who have become familiar with country-life and its occupations in Greece, the "pastoral poetry" of the world usually seems much less "artificial" and "literary" than it does to those who write about it in their Northern studious seclusion. Lady Mary soon discovered this, and wrote to Pope:

> I no longer look upon Theocritus as a romantic writer; he has only given a plain image of the way of life amongst the peasants of his country; who, before oppression had reduced them to want, were, I suppose, all employed as the better sort of them are now. . . . The young lads generally divert themselves with making garlands for their favourite lambs, which I have often seen painted and adorned with flowers, lying at their feet while they sung or played. It is not that they ever read romances, but these are the ancient amusements here. . . .

[1] *Letters and Works*, i, 300, 375, 381.

Pope had just completed his translation of the *Iliad*, and was already engaged upon the *Odyssey*. Lady Mary writes to him:

> I read over your Homer here with an infinite pleasure, and find several little passages explained, that I did not before entirely comprehend the beauty of; many of the customs, and much of the dress then in fashion, being yet retained, and I don't wonder to find more remains here of an age so distant, than is to be found in any other country, the Turks not taking that pains to introduce their own manners as has been generally practised by other nations. . . .[1]

Pope, however, writes to her in a tone of badinage, affecting a humility he certainly did not feel. How much better, he says, his Iliad would have been if he had been able to make his translation in the localities made famous by Homer!

> I am very certain I can never be polite unless I travel with you; and it is never to be repaired, the loss that Homer has sustained for want of my translating him in Asia. You will come hither full of criticisms against a man who wanted nothing to be in the right but to have your company.

In another letter Pope writes:

> I make not the least question but you could give me great eclaircissements upon many passages in Homer since you have been enlightened by the same sun that inspired the father of poetry. You are now glowing under the climate that animated him; you may see his images rising more boldly about you, in the very scenes of his story and action; you may lay the immortal work on some broken column of a hero's sepulchre; and read the fall of Troy in the shade of a Trojan ruin. But if, to visit the tomb of so many heroes, you have not the heart to pass over the sea where once a lover perished; you may at least, at ease, in your window, contemplate the fields of Asia, in such a dim and remote prospect, as you have of Homer in my translation.[2]

This is quite a pretty letter—written to the remarkable woman towards whom Pope pretended emotions of gallantry. Lady Mary prefers to give him some sensible and useful observations on customs among the modern Grecians, which could have provided him with a valuable note to the sixth book of his *Odyssey*, but did not:

[1] i, 302–3, 361–2.   [2] *Works*, ed. Elwin and Courthope, ix, 382, 397.

Their manner of dancing is certainly the same that Diana is sung
to have danced on the banks of the Eurotas. The great lady still
leads the dance, and is followed by a troop of young girls, who
imitate her steps, and, if she sings, make up the chorus. The tunes
are extremely gay and lively, yet with something in them wonder-
fully soft. The steps are varied according to the pleasure of her that
leads the dance, but always in exact time, and infinitely more
agreeable than any of our dances, at least in my opinion. I sometimes make one in the train, but am not skilful enough to lead;
these are Grecian dances, the Turkish being very different.

On her way home from Constantinople, Lady Mary and her
husband visited the Trojan plain, Homer in hand:

Not many leagues' sail from hence, [she writes to the Abbé
Conti] I saw the point of land where poor old Hecuba was buried;
and about a league from that place is Cape Janizary, the famous
promontory of Sigaeum, where we anchored, and my curiosity
supplied me with strength to climb to the top of it, to see the place
where Achilles was buried, and where Alexander ran naked round
his tomb in his honour, which no doubt was a great comfort to his
ghost. I saw there the ruins of a very large city, and found a stone,
on which Mr. W[ortley] plainly distinguished the words of
Sigaian Polin. We ordered this on board the ship. . . .

She continues:

There is some pleasure in seeing the valley where I imagined
the famous duel of Menelaus and Paris had been fought, and
where the greatest city in the world was situate; and 'tis certainly the
noblest situation that can be found for the head of a great empire,
much to be preferred to that of Constantinople. . . . While I
viewed these celebrated fields and rivers, I admired the exact
geography of Homer, whom I had in my hand. Almost every
epithet he gives to a mountain or plain is still just for it.[1]

Wortley Montagu's successor at Constantinople was another friend
of Pope, Abraham Stanyan, a member of the Kit-Kat Club, and
brother of Temple Stanyan, whose *Grecian History* (1707) was for
long a standard work (reprinted 1739, 1766 and 1781) and was
translated by Diderot. We are also brought into the circle of Pope's
acquaintances by a minor poet, of some talent in light verse, who

[1] *Letters and Works*, i, 303, 376–8.

wrote while he was in Greece. This was Thomas Lisle[1] who became chaplain at Smyrna in 1733. He was the brother of the nine sisters for whom Pope wrote two flattering little poems, "On seeing the ladies at Crux-Easton Walk in the Woods by the Grotto" and "Inscription on a Grotto of Shells at Crux-Easton, the Work of Nine Young Ladies".[2] To these sisters in 1733 Lisle sent an amusing verse-letter describing his journey and his impressions of Greece.[3]

> The hero who to Smyrna bay
> From Easton, Hants, pursu'd his way,
> Who travers'd seas, and hills and vales,
> To fright his sisters with his tales,
> Sing, heavenly muse. . . .

From Sicily he sailed to Cerigo, where, of course, he had thoughts of Paris and Helen. But Attica was more thrilling:

> How did my heart with joy run o'er,
> When to the fam'd Cecropian shore,
> Wafted by gentle breezes, we
> Came gliding through the smooth still sea!
> While backward rov'd my busy thought
> On deeds in distant ages wrought;
> On tyrants gloriously withstood;
> On seas distain'd with Persian blood;
> On trophies rais'd o'er hills of slain
> In Marathon's unrival'd plain.
> Then, as around I cast my eye,
> And view'd the pleasing prospect nigh,
> The land for arms and arts renown'd,
> Where wit was honour'd, poets crown'd;
> Whose manners and whose rules refin'd
> Our souls and civiliz'd mankind;
> Or (yet a loftier pitch to raise
> Our wonder, and complete its praise)
> The land that Plato's master bore—
> How did my heart with joy run o'er.

---

[1] I can find no family connection between this Thomas Lisle and the Samuel Lisle who was Levant Company chaplain 1710–19 and subsequently became Bishop of Norwich; see p. 141 above.

[2] *Works*, ed. Elwin and Courthope, iv, 457–8. The latter poem appeared in Dodsley's *A Collection of Poems*, vi, 177, alongside the verses of Thomas Lisle.

[3] Dodsley's *Collection* (the "new edition" of 1782) vi, 182–8, *Letter from Smyrna to his sisters at Crux-Easton, 1733.*

After some further references to famous localities in Greece—Peneus, Delos, Ios, Naxos, and Lesbos—he laments the heavy change that has overcome these poetical places;

> Could the old bards revive again,
> How would they mourn th' inverted scene!
> Scarce with the barren waste acquainted,
> They once so beautifully painted.

He tells his sisters that they must not be too much impressed by the poetical glories of the Grecian countryside;

> And here, twixt friends, I needs must say,
> But let it go no further, pray,
> These sung-up, cry'd-up countries are
> Displeasing, rugged, black [sic] and bare;
> And all I've yet beheld or known
> Serve only to endear my own.

Lisle concludes his poem by a humorous reference to their friend Pope, who can hardly expect to compose such good poetry as one who is actually writing in the poetic Greek lands:

> Let not malicious critics join
> Pope's homespun rhymes in rank with mine,
> Form'd on that very spot of earth,
> Where Homer's self receiv'd his birth. . . .

In the 1740's and 1750's a considerable amount of up-to-date information about Greece and the Greeks was brought back by some serious and influential travellers. In 1743 Charles Perry, the author of an important book on Greece, declared that "the *Turkish* Empire . . . at least the more central Parts of it (such as *Constantinople*, the *Archipelegean* Isles, the Sea-coasts of *Asia Minor*, and of *Syria*), are now become pretty trite Subjects".[1] Richard Pococke, whose *Description of the East* was published in 1743 in three handsome folio volumes, is more important as a traveller in the Near East than in Greek lands; but he visited Cyprus, Crete (where he ascended Mount Ida), parts of Asia Minor and of the Greek mainland; he left Cephalonia, to return home, in November 1740. Although Pococke's work was aspersed by Gibbon as a "pompous folio",[2] it achieved a

---

[1] *A View of the Levant: particularly of Constantinople, Syria, Egypt and Greece* (1743), Preface.
[2] *Decline and Fall*, Chap. li (ed. J. B. Bury, 1898, v, 431), speaking of Baalbec.

great reputation, was translated into French, German and Dutch, and was reprinted in the standard collections of travel narratives.

It was about this time that a fraudulent account of Greece appears —a reliable indication that public curiosity in the country is growing. De Guillet's disingenuous treatise likewise appeared at a time of increased interest in Greece. There is no doubt about the popularity of *The Travels of the Late Charles Thompson, Esq; Containing his Observations on France, Italy, Turkey in Europe . . . and many other Parts of the World*, which first appeared in 1744, and by 1798 had gone through five editions. Whether such a person as Charles Thompson ever travelled in Greece, I can find no evidence to decide. Ostensibly, however, the author left England for his travels in 1730 and remained abroad until 1735; he left the Greek mainland for Constantinople in November 1732. But the greater part of these *Travels* is a compilation by some bookseller's hack, heavily interpolated with paraphrases and quotations from other writers; and the volume, since it lacks authenticity, is of little interest except in so far as it reflects current notions of the condition of the Greeks. After quoting St. Paul and the ancients on the vileness of the Cretans, the compiler condescends to add: "However, I am far from thinking that the present Inhabitants of the Island do in general deserve so bad a Character."[1] He appends to his history of Athens "a short Character of its ancient Inhabitants, to which that of the modern *Greeks* in many Particulars may be look'd upon as quite the Reverse".

In spite of the five editions, the *Travels* of Charles Thompson must be regarded with contempt. But a thorough and detailed account of the present state of part of the Greek nation was given by Alexander Drummond from his experiences, mostly in Cyprus, from about 1745 to 1750. In 1754 appeared *Travels through different Cities of Germany, Italy, Greece, and several parts of Asia, as far as the Banks of the Euphrates; In a Series of Letters, containing, An Account of what is most remarkable in their Present State, As well as in their Monuments of Antiquity; by Alexander Drummond, Esq., His Majesty's Consul at Aleppo*.

It is an impressive book, based unquestionably upon intimate knowledge of Cyprus, where he travelled more than six hundred miles in journeys across the island. Nevertheless, it is difficult to have much enthusiasm for Drummond as a traveller. His tone is deplorably insular; and the information his readers derived from his book can hardly have done more than make them feel the ridiculousness of manners and customs in foreign parts. In Zante he falls foul of the Greek Church, and speaks derisively especially of their

[1] i, 287, 349.

characteristic style of religious painting in "the modern Greek manner, which is distinguished by the stiffness of the figure, the harshness of the shading, a great deal of gilding, and the whole covered with a varnish like that of japan". Yet it shows some percipience in a traveller at this date so much as to mention the decayed Byzantine manner of painting, which, of course, had no place in eighteenth-century canons or fashions of taste.[1] "What a melancholy reflection it is to think that those people, who once excelled all the world in those liberal arts, are now sunk to such a degeneracy of taste and execution." Yet the ruins of antiquity could move Drummond to decent feelings:

> When we landed on Delos, mine eye was struck with the immense quantities of broken marble, and my heart was pierced with real concern, to see the devastations which have been made among such glorious edifices, and which I considered as the ruins of some friend's habitation. I therefore walked on with a kind of sullen pensiveness. . . .

At Smyrna Drummond founded a lodge of freemasons among the British merchants; it was the first, he considered, to have come into existence in the Levant, and he broke into verse for the occasion:

> For ages past, a savage race
> O'erspread these Asian plains,
> All nature wore a gloomy face,
> And pensive mov'd the swains.
>
> But now Britannia's gen'rous sons
> A glorious lodge have rais'd,
> Near the fam'd banks where Meles runs,
> And Homer's cattle graz'd;
> The bri'ry wilds to groves are chang'd,
> With orange trees around,
> And fragrant lemons fairly rang'd,
> O'ershade the blissful ground. . . .

Drummond gives a gloomy account of the Greeks of Cyprus at that time—nearly twenty years before the rebellion of 1764. In the Ottoman empire, he says, in a letter in 1745, "every man in power is a despotic tyrant by the nature of his office, and all the subjects are miserable slaves; though the Greeks, as a conquered people, are more

---

[1] Lady Mary Wortley Montagu has similar reactions to Byzantine painting. "The Greeks have a most monstrous taste in their pictures, which, for more finery, are always drawn upon a gold ground. You may imagine what a good air this has; but they have no notion either of shade or proportion." (*Letters & Works*, i, 327.)

especially exposed to their cruelty and extortion: they are now become familiarised to oppression, which hath likewise disposed them for villainy, as it were in their own defence; insomuch that they are reconciled to all manner of crimes; and mean dejection, wretchedness, or deceit, is to be read in every countenance." The poor state of agriculture in Cyprus Drummond attributes partly "to the lazy, trifling disposition of the Greeks themselves, and partly to the tyranny of the government under which they live".

Drummond is capable of writing more agreeably on more agreeable subjects. He notices the characteristic female dress in Cyprus:

> even the Frank, or European ladies, dress in the Grecian mode, which is wantonly superb; though, in my opinion, not so agreeable as our own. Yet the ornaments of the head are graceful and noble; and, when I have seen some pretty women of condition sitting upon a divan, this part of their dress hath struck my imagination with the ideas of Helen, Andromache, and other beauties of antiquity, inspiring me with a distant awe, while the rest of their attire invited me to a nearer approach.

He gives it as his opinion, moreover, that the Greek ladies "inherit the libertinism of their ancestors".[1]

It had, indeed, long been recognized that among the attractions of the Levant was the picturesqueness of the costumes of the inhabitants. The early travel-books sometimes have copper plates, but the representations are generally of extreme crudeness. In France a fine collection of engravings was published early in the eighteenth century, under the patronage of, and with explanations written by, Antoine de Ferriol, who was the French ambassador at the Porte.[2] This includes some charming specimens of Greek island costumes. In the 1730's there appears to have developed in France a frivolous craze for *turquerie*, which, of course, often included Greek costumes; and a good many Gallic trivialities are found about amorous Sultans and beautiful Greek slaves. For example, Nicolas Lancret produced a pair of paintings, *Le Turc Amoureux* and *La Belle Grecque*. The latter is in the Wallace Collection; the lady's appearance has, indeed, a few traits which resemble Greek costumes. In the engraving of this painting some characteristic verses were appended, telling the young beauty that her state of slavery does not

[1] *Travels*, pp. 96, 107, 121, 143, 150, 269.
[2] *Receuil de cent Estampes représentant différentes Nations du Levant tirées sur les Tableaux peints d'après Nature en 1707 et 1708 par les ordres de M. de Ferriol*, (1714-15). The illustrations are by J. B. van Moor (Mour). Plates 66-75 represent Greeks.

prevent her from captivating hearts; proud Sultans do her homage; and merely by the power of her enchanting eyes she triumphs over the conquerors of her nation.

> Jeune beauté, votre esclavage,
> Ne vous empêche pas de captiver les coeurs.
> Les sultans les plus fiers vous offrent leur hommage,
> Et par le seul pouvoir de vos yeux enchanteurs
> Vous triomphez de vos vainqueurs.

Similar paintings in this fashion were produced by Carle van Loo; his *Le Grand Seigneur donnant un Concert à sa Maîtresse* is in the Wallace Collection, and it originally had a companion, *Le Grand Seigneur qui fait peindre sa Maîtresse*. It seems probable that the increase of plays on Turkish themes can be attributed to this fashion. To the same time belongs Sauvé de la Noue's play, *Mahomet Second*, one of the analogues of Johnson's *Irene*, which was also written during the same decade of fashionable *turquerie*, although on quite another plane of seriousness. There was little justification for any such Gallic interpretation of relations between Turk and Greek in the eighteenth century.

The picturesqueness of the Greek costumes was something which the English, too, noticed early. The Earl of Sandwich in 1738 took with him as his draughtsman Liotard, whose task it was "to draw the dresses of every country they should go into". Sir Joshua Reynolds, in 1782, painted the Greek wife of George Baldwin, the English consul at Smyrna, in the picturesque costume of an odalisque. The travel-books begin to include more attractive representations of the costumes worn in the Levant, and some of the travellers, such as Lady Mary Wortley Montagu, the Earl of Sandwich, the Earl of Bessborough, Richard Pococke, and Richard Chandler, took pleasure in having themselves painted in their quasi-oriental clothes.

The foundation of the Levant Company had been responsible for the increase of knowledge about Greece and the Greeks in the seventeenth century, for it provided the practical machinery for the traveller. In the eighteenth century, as British naval power became dominant, the danger from pirates, the great curse of travelling in the Eastern Mediterranean, was diminished. Accordingly we find a new kind of traveller coming to Greece, the English nobleman who charters his own ship and sails through Greek seas, accompanied by his draughtsman, antiquary, classical tutor, and other members of his suite. Greece and the Levant never formed part of the Grand Tour, properly so called; but as the eastern half of the Mediterranean became more accessible, a good deal of the classical enthusiasm which had hitherto been largely devoted to Rome and Italy, was turned towards Athens and Ionia. The desire to get behind the classicism of Rome to the classicism of Greece was manifested in travel in Italy itself by the new devotion to genuine Greek remains in southern Italy and in Sicily. The great Doric temples at Paestum, which were hardly known before the middle of the eighteenth century, and the numerous genuine Hellenic remains in Sicily, were to the adventurous traveller an indication of the new architectural experiences to be found, not only in Magna Graecia, but also in Greece itself. To go farther afield, to tread classic ground unfamiliar to the Grand Tourist, became the ambition of the classically minded traveller. Lively young members of the English nobility began to make their appearance in Greece. John Montagu, the fourth Earl of Sandwich, for example, went abroad in 1737 at the age of nineteen, and in July of the following year set out on a long tour by sea from Leghorn to Sicily, several of the Greek islands, Athens, Constantinople, Smyrna and Egypt. He was accompanied by William Ponsonby, the second Earl of Bessborough, and a few other gentlemen. Among his attendants was the painter, Jean Etienne Liotard, whose task it was (wrote Sandwich in a letter) not only "to draw the dresses of every country they should go into" (as I have already mentioned); but also "to take prospects of all the remarkable places which had made a figure in history; and to preserve in their memories, by the help of painting, these noble remains of antiquity which they went in quest of". A detailed account of this tour is given in *A Voyage Performed by the late Earl of Sandwich round the Mediterranean in the Years 1738 and 1739. Written by himself*, which was published in 1799, seven years after his death.[1]

Sandwich (immortalized by the Islands and the food) has been judged by posterity largely according to his notorious vices. But his patronage of music, art, the theatre, tennis, cricket, and the voyages of Captain Cook, reflects a more admirable part of his character. He gives a reasonable and balanced estimate of the modern Greeks, who are, he says,

a people of a very lively genius, endowed with strong abilities for whatever they apply themselves to, cunning and artificial in

[1] This book purports to be the journal of the Earl kept at this time; but from its general character it seems to have been thoroughly revised and amplified, if not actually written by his tutor and chaplain, the Rev. John Cooke. Although it appeared so long after the voyage this book probably gives a fair account of the interests and activities of the party in those years. I cannot feel confident, however, that every opinion in that book dates from before the middle of the century.

their dealings, and for the most part of a temper addicted to mirth and gaiety. They are, however, very great flatterers, abject and insinuating, and generally treacherous in affairs relating to their own interests. In their diet they are sober and abstemious, and their whole way of living very frugal and sparing. The patience, with which they bear the Turkish yoke, has also been mentioned by many as one of their most shining qualities; though to me it appears in a very contrary light, since it seems rather owing to a want of spirit, than any noble motive.

The infamous but gifted peer, a prototype of Lord Byron, showed himself in the Levant, even at this early age, a patron of the arts, and brought home with him a collection of coins and minor antiquities. He was gifted with some sensibility; he observes the "grand remains" of the Parthenon, and mentions the sculptures as "excellent pieces of workmanship".[1] This classical tour was an influential experience on one who was later to be the archmaster of the Society of Dilettanti. We know less of the activities of the Earl of Bessborough during this tour; but he, too, was one of the most active collectors of art and antiquities and a prominent Dilettante.

A similar extensive tour was made by the young Earl of Charlemont, who in 1749 sailed from Leghorn in the company of Francis Pierpont Burton (later Lord Conyngham) and his classical tutor, the Rev. Edward Murphy.[2] Charlemont would seem to have gained little from his travels, if we were to judge him from the scrap of conversation related by Boswell:[3]

Johnson. How little does travelling supply to the conversation of any man who has travelled? . . .
Boswell. What say you to Lord [Charlemont]?
Johnson. I never but once heard him talk of what he had seen, and that was of a large serpent in one of the Pyramids of Egypt.

His lordship may have avoided, in conversation, the subject of his very adventurous, exciting and influential travels. Yet many years later he gave his impressions of part of Greece in a paper read to the Royal Irish Academy. His subject was the curious system of female inheritance in the island of Lesbos.[4] Here he offered an eloquent

---

[1] *Voyage*, pp. iii, 62, 203–4.
[2] Francis Hardy, *Memoirs of the Political and Private Life of James Caulfeild, Earl of Charlemont* (1810), pp. 10 sqq.; 2nd ed., 2 vols. (1812).
[3] *Life of Johnson*, ed. Birkbeck Hill, revised L. F. Powell, iii, 352.
[4] *Account of a Singular Custom at Metelin, with some conjectures on the Antiquity of its Origin*, printed in *The Transactions of the Royal Irish Academy, MDCCLXXXIX*. Dublin, 1790, "Antiquities", pp. 3–20. (This work seems to have been missed by the author of Charlemont's life in the *Dictionary of National Biography*.)

description of the scenery of this island. "Though the extreme beauty and amenity of the Grecian islands, especially those on the Asiatic side of the Aegean sea, may render it difficult to make a choice among them", yet he considers that Lesbos, that "enchanting isle, proud of the birth of Alcaeus and Sappho", is to be preferred among them all. For it "still retains those charms which gave rise and inspiration to their poetry; and though its groves no more resound with their sacred strains, the cause that inspired them still seems to exist, and love still lingers in his favourite retreat".

This lecture was prettily written, and shows that Charlemont had sensibility. Moreover, it was under Charlemont's patronage that Richard Dalton made, the first among Englishmen, detailed drawings of the monuments of ancient art in Greece. The party set out from Malta, "stopt at one or two of the Greek islands; Smyrna, the Dardanelles, Tenedos ... and the ever-interesting Troade"[1] and then stayed for a month at Constantinople. There Charlemont came of age and wrote a pleasant birthday ode to himself in imitation of *Eheu fugaces*, which could be accepted without shame into an anthology of poems written by Englishmen in Greece.[2] Then the party sailed to the islands of Lesbos, Chios, Myconos, Delos, Paros, and thence to Alexandria. In October 1749, they left Alexandria intending to go to Cyprus, but meeting with contrary winds they proceeded first to Rhodes, then along the coast of Caria, to Cnidos (where they admired the temple of Aphrodite), and to Cos. They landed at Halicarnassus, where Dalton drew, and subsequently etched, some of the great sculptures from the Mausoleum, now in the British Museum. From there they sailed directly to Piraeus, arrived at Athens, toured the Morea, and visited Corinth, Thebes and Euboea, of which Charlemont wrote an account, too long, says his biographer, for insertion in the *Memoirs*.[3]

This remarkable tour bore fruit in Richard Dalton's series of engravings of Greek antiquities and of monuments, manners and

---

[1] Francis Hardy, *Memoirs*, p. 14.

[2] I may perhaps be permitted to say, in passing, that the anthology *The Englishman in Greece* (with an introduction by Sir Rennell Rodd, Oxford University Press, 1910) is deceptive. Apart from some of Byron's philhellenic poems and a few others, it is merely a collection of miscellaneous poems on classical mythology, including such things as "Orpheus with his lute" and "Cupid and my Campaspe played ... ". The companion anthology, *The Englishman in Italy*, is authentic, and contains what its title implies. As a matter of fact, a very curious anthology of poems could be made from those written by Englishmen while in Greece, from the seventeenth to the twentieth centuries. It seems a pity that the opportunity was missed and the title preoccupied.

[3] This account of Euboea seems to have disappeared. There is no trace of it among the Charlemont Papers as listed by the Historical Manuscripts Commission (1891).

customs of Turkey and Egypt, mostly dated 1751. His collection of views of the antiquities of Athens, although not done from accurate measurements, was the first publication of its kind in England. Dalton had his architectural scenes reproduced for him by some of the eminent engravers of the day. But the sculptures he etched himself; and he did it skilfully. For the first time Englishmen were given an impression of the great sculptures of the Parthenon and the Mausoleum. The antiquities of Athens, from the mid-eighteenth century onwards were to play an increasingly important part in the history of taste. Dalton gave representations not only of the Parthenon, but also of the Theseum, the Erectheum, the Tower of the Winds, the "Temple of Hercules" (as the choragic monument of Lysicrates was called as an alternative to "the Lantern of Demosthenes"), the Arch of Hadrian, and the monument of Philopappus. He dedicated his plate of the grotto at Antiparos "to F. Pierpont Burton, in whose presence the Drawing was made". Introduced into all the engravings are charming incidents in which the "Franks" are being shown the antiquities by "natives" in various costumes. These pleasant works provided Englishmen with an adequate introduction to the Greek scene, until the vastly superior and more trustworthy volumes of Stuart and Revett began to appear in 1762.

The first half of the eighteenth century had seen a steady series of books in which contemporary Greece played a part. Descriptions and impressions of Greeks and Greece reflect the increase of knowledge which was available to the English reader. To some extent also, as we have seen, they reflect an increase of sympathy, that is, of the philhellenic sentiment. But the interest of all these works was thrown into the shade by the series of volumes produced under the patronage of the Society of Dilettanti after the middle of the eighteenth century. These English patrons of scholarship and the arts were no longer interested merely in such works of sculpture and fragments of architecture as were movable and portable within reasonable expense. They concerned themselves with the systematic investigation of the monuments. They took the lead in that subject which we now call archaeology. Their enterprise, however, did not merely produce documentation for the study of the surviving architectural monuments of the ancient Hellenic civilization. Their sumptuous folio volumes, besides accurate drawings and descriptions of ancient monuments, contained large engravings of the contemporary mode of existence. All those who appreciated the publications of the Society of Dilettanti for the sake of "Grecian Taste" were also made aware of the life of the people who dwelt around and among, and sometimes inside, the architectural glories of antiquity. The Society's faithful draughtsmen, with an eye for the picturesque, did not fail to include entertaining contemporary life in their representations.

In 1748 James Stuart and Nicolas Revett, two young architects who were in Rome, issued their "Proposals for publishing an accurate Description of the Antiquities of Athens". It was an independent venture, but their scheme soon received encouragement from some of the English Dilettanti, then in Rome, including the Earl of Charlemont, who had just returned from his journey into Greece. Stuart and Revett left for Venice to make their preparations, and there met the British Resident, Sir James Grey, who was one of the leading spirits of the Society. It was Grey, who, by his practical assistance, associated their work with the Dilettanti. Stuart and Revett were in Athens in 1751 and 1752, and, in spite of the very great difficulties of the undertaking, prepared accurate measurements and illustrations of the Parthenon and the other monuments. Their long labours in Athens gave them a particularly intimate knowledge of the inhabitants; and it is noteworthy that their account of the modern Athenians, which accompanies their learned exposition of the antiquities, contains favourable remarks. They tell their readers that the Athenians have more vivacity, more genius, and a politer address than any other people in the Turkish dominions; that they have great courage and sagacity in opposing any further burdens which the rigorous government tries to lay upon them; that they have great sprightliness and expression in their countenances; that their bodies are well-proportioned, with a due mixture of strength and agility; and that the women have a peculiar elegance of form and manners. The impression that Stuart gives was important and influential because it was based upon more detailed and more intimate knowledge than was possessed by any visitor to Athens before his time.

Stuart and Revett, however, were anticipated in publishing an account of the antiquities of Athens. Julien Davide Le Roy, a Frenchman, was in Rome in 1748 when the *Proposals* of Stuart and Revett were issued, visited Athens and other parts of Greece in 1754 (Stuart and Revett were in Greece 1751–3) and by royal patronage succeeded in getting his book, *Ruines des plus beaux Monuments de la Grèce*, published in 1758, four years before the first volume of *The Antiquities of Athens*. Le Roy makes no mention of Stuart and Revett, their proposals, or their work, although he can hardly have been unaware of them. He produced a handsome folio, and several of his engravings of Levantine life (translated into the manner of

Watteau) amid the ruins of antiquity are, for all their absurdity, full of charm. His drawings, from the architectural point of view, are in some cases seriously incorrect, and give a false impression of proportions. But there can be no doubt that Le Roy played his part in spreading information about genuine Hellenic remains. The volumes of the Society of Dilettanti were long in preparation and much delayed in publication; their superiority to any preceding work on the subject was immediately recognized; but in the meantime, while the world waited for them, the engravings of Le Roy provided a substitute.

Among the most energetic patrons of Stuart and Revett was James Dawkins (the "Jamaica" Dawkins in Boswell's *Life*), a young Dilettante who had spent several years travelling in Italy and who in 1748 was one of those assisting them in realizing their project. He also himself began his plans for a tour in Greece. He took with him John Bouverie, Robert Wood, and an Italian artist named Borra as draughtsman. Robert Wood had already been on an adventurous journey from Venice to Corfu, as far as Mitylene and Chios in the Aegean, and to Syria and Egypt in 1742-3. Dawkins with his party set out from Naples in the spring of 1750 in a ship which he had chartered from London; it was well-furnished with a library of Greek historians and poets, volumes of antiquities, and the best travel-books. They visited most of the islands of the Archipelago, part of the Greece mainland, the Asiatic and European coasts of the Hellespont, Propontis, and Bosphorus, as far as the Black Sea, and a good deal of Asia Minor. Wood declared that his principal object in their travels was "to read the Iliad and Odyssey in the countries, where Achilles fought, where Ulysses travelled, and where Homer sung".[1] Accordingly, on July 5th 1750 they anchored off the promontory of Sigeum and went ashore at the mouth of the Scamander. It was this direct experience of the Homeric environment that made Robert Wood's important *Essay on the Original Genius of Homer* (1767) quite different from all previous criticism of Homer. Written by a perceptive traveller and free from pedantry, it soon achieved a considerable reputation, and was translated into several languages. It emphatically told the reader that the geographical background of the *Iliad* was still in existence and demanded the careful study of those who wished to understand their Homer. Wood by this book began, if not the Homeric Problem, at least the Troy Problem, which (as will be related farther on) became one of the exciting literary and archaeological questions which directed the

---

[1] Robert Wood, *A Comparative View of the antient and present state of the Troade. To which is prefixed an Essay on the Original Genius of Homer*, 1767, "To the Reader".

attention of classical scholars to the Greek lands and prompted both poetry and expostulation in Byron.[1]

After their journey Dawkins and Wood returned to Athens in May 1751, where Stuart and Revett were already busy on their investigations. They made an expedition to Thermopylae; and then returned to England (Bouverie had died in Magnesia), and arranged for the printing in London of part of the "Proposals" which Stuart and Revett had issued in Rome in 1748. By their splendid publication of the ruins of Palmyra (1753) and Balbec (1757) Dawkins and Wood achieved a great reputation, for they provided authentic information regarding these relics of Graeco-Roman civilization; and the fine volumes were widely known and appreciated throughout Europe. Robert Wood there expressed with clarity and skill the imaginative appeal of the classic lands:

> It is impossible to consider with indifference those countries which gave birth to letters and arts, where soldiers, orators, philosophers, poets and artists have shewn the boldest and happiest flights of Genius, and done the greatest honour to human nature.
>
> Circumstances of climate and situation, otherwise trivial, become interesting from that connection with great men, and great actions, which history and poetry have given them: The life of Miltiades or Leonidas could never be read with so much pleasure, as on the plains of Marathon or at the streights of Thermopylae; the Iliad has new beauties on the banks of the Scamander, and the Odyssey is most pleasing in the countries where Ulysses travelled and Homer sung.
>
> The particular pleasure . . . which imagination warmed on the spot receives from those scenes of heroick actions, the traveller only can feel, nor is it to be communicated by description.[2]

It was at the expense of the Society of Dilettanti that Richard Chandler made his journeys into Greece and Ionia, and produced his two books, which were the most important description of Greece in the eighteenth century. Already at the age of twenty-five, Chandler had some reputation as a Greek scholar and antiquary by his publication, *Marmora Oxoniensia* (1763), an account and interpretation of the antiquities possessed by the University. The following year he was introduced to the Society of Dilettanti by Robert Wood, and commissioned to undertake a thorough tour of the Greek mainland and Ionia. He was accompanied by Revett, already well known as

---

[1] p. 202 sqq. below.
[2] Wood in *The Ruins of Palmyra* (1753), "The Publisher to the Reader".

Stuart's collaborator in Athens, and by William Pars, a young artist, whose task was the delineation of scenery and antiquities. The three of them were given their instructions by the Society in a document dated May 17th 1764.[1] They were to remark "every Circumstance which can contribute towards giving the best Idea of the ancient and present State of those Places". It is emphasized in their instructions that the travellers are not be to mere antiquaries:

> Though the principal View of the Society, in this Scheme, is pointed at such Discoveries and Observations as you shall be able to make with regard to the Ancient State of those Countries, yet it is by no means intended to confine you to that Province; on the contrary, It is expected, that you do Report to Us, for the information of the Society, whatever can fall within the Notice of curious and observing Travellers.

The party sailed from England in June 1764, spent about a year in Asia Minor, left Smyrna for Athens in August 1765, and arrived back in England in November 1766. The results of their labours were, firstly, the splendid folio, *Ionian Antiquities: or Ruins of Magnificent and Famous Buildings in Ionia* (1769), in which the historical part was written by Chandler, the account of the architecture by Revett, and the illustrations engraved from the water-colour drawings of Pars. This work was followed by a collection of inscriptions,[2] and then by two volumes of narrative of their travels, based upon Chandler's journals (Oxford, 1775 and 1776). By these two volumes, Chandler immediately established himself as the pre-eminent traveller in Greece. Nothing so detailed, and nothing so good, had been published since Wheler and Spon, nearly a century before. There were several editions of his work up to 1825, and translations appeared in French and German. The water-colour drawings of William Pars provided an even more complete series of views of the Greek lands than was to be found in *The Antiquities of Athens* of Stuart and Revett, in whose second and fourth volumes, in fact, some of Pars's drawings were incorporated. At the first exhibition of the Royal Academy in 1769, Pars contributed seven views from Greece, and a selection of his drawings was subsequently engraved by the eminent landscape-engraver William Byrne for the Society of Dilettanti.

There is no doubt that the journey through Ionia is the better part of Chandler's narrative. It contains the most distinguished

---

[1] Printed by Chandler before his *Travels in Asia Minor,* Oxford, 1775.

[2] *Inscriptiones antiquae, pleraeque nondum editae, in Asia Minore et Graecia, praesertim Athenis* (Oxford, 1774).

writing about Greece which had yet appeared in the English language. Like Thomas Smith a century before,[1] he finds the spectacle of the desolation of the Seven Churches profoundly moving. But Chandler has some skill in expressing his feelings. Here is his account of Ephesus:

> The Ephesians are now a few Greek peasants, living in extreme wretchedness, dependance and insensibility; the representatives of an illustrious people, and inhabiting the wreck of their greatness; some, the substructions of the glorious edifices which they raised; some beneath the vaults of the stadium, once the crouded scene of their diversions; and some, by the abrupt precipice, in the sepulchres which received their ashes. . . .
>
> Such are the present citizens of Ephesus, and such is the condition to which that renowned city has been gradually reduced. It was a ruinous place, when the Emperor Justinian filled Constantinople with its statues, and raised his church of St. Sophia on its columns. Since then it has been almost quite exhausted. Its streets are obscured, and overgrown. A herd of goats was driven to it for shelter from the sun at noon; and a noisy flight of crows from the quarries seemed to insult its silence. We heard the partridge call in the arc of the theatre and of the stadium. The glorious pomp of its heathen worship is no longer remembered; and christianity, which was there nursed by apostles, and fostered by general councils, until it increased to fullness of stature, barely lingers on in an existence hardly visible.[2]

At Laodicea the desolation was yet greater; for there

> we saw no traces, either of houses, churches, or mosques. All was silence and solitude. Several strings of camels passed eastward over the hill; but a fox, which we first discovered by his ears peeping over a brow, was the only inhabitant of Laodicea.[3]

At Chios where the British Consul was "a spare shrewd Greek", Chandler made a curious acquaintance. "An English gentleman named Bracebridge had come with the consul to visit us. He was an elderly person, who had been absent some years from his native country for the benefit of a warmer climate. After much wandering, he gave the preference to this island above any of the places which he had tried." They later visited him "at his house near the town" and were there treated with "a variety of choice specimens" of Chiot

---

[1] pp. 127–8 above. [2] *Asia Minor*, pp. 130–1.
[3] *Op cit.*, p. 228. Gibbon noticed this excellent description of Laodicea and commended it; *Decline and Fall*, Chap. ii (ed. J. B. Bury, 1896, i, 49).

wines. Chandler enjoyed Chios; and in his description of the Grecian women in their charming traditional costumes he shows more perceptiveness than any previous visitors to Greece. This is a great advance on the old scurrilous mariners' yarns about the lightness of the ladies of Chios.

> The beautiful Greek girls are the most striking ornaments of Scio. Many of these were sitting at the doors and windows, twisting cotton or silk, or employed in spinning and needlework, and accosted us with familiarity, bidding us welcome, as we passed. . . . They wear short petticoats, reaching only to their knees, with white silk or cotton hose. Their head-dress, which is peculiar to the island, is a kind of Turban, the linen so white and thin it seemed snow. Their slippers are chiefly yellow, with a knot of red fringe at the heel. Some wore them fastened with a thong. Their garments were of silk of various colours; and their whole appearance so fantastic and lively as to afford us much entertainment.[1]

Chandler's account of Athens was the most detailed that had yet appeared. Although modern Athens is (he tells us) "not inconsiderable, either in extent or the number of inhabitants", yet "Philosophy and Eloquence were exiled, and their antient seat occupied by ignorant honey-factors of mount Hymettus". Chandler devotes several interesting chapters to the manners and customs of the present inhabitants of Athens, amid his patient descriptions and elucidations of the architectural survivals; and he is well aware that the modern Grecians are, for the classical scholar, one of the most remarkable monuments of antiquity. At least they were so in the eighteenth century. Descriptions of the modern Grecians before western European civilization altered them are as valuable as descriptions of the Parthenon before the Venetian bombardment destroyed it. The Athenians were praised for their native quickness of apprehension, characteristic of all classes. But, "this aptitude not being duly cultivated, instead of producing genius, degenerates into cunning".[2]

Chandler concludes that "the traveller, who is versed in antiquity, may be agreeably and usefully employed in studying the people of Athens".

His admiration for the sculptures of the Parthenon was combined with his grief that they were steadily being destroyed. He almost provided an excuse for Elgin's appropriations a generation later:

---

[1] *Asia Minor*, pp. 50, 52, 54.   [2] *Greece*, pp. 34, 117, 121.

It is to be regretted that so much admirable sculpture as is still extant about this fabric should be all likely to perish, as it were immaturely, from ignorant contempt and brutal violence. Numerous carved stones have disappeared; and many, lying in the ruinous heaps, moved our indignation at the barbarism daily exercised in defacing them.[1]

The English poets, who have written of Greece without any experience of it, receive a tart commentary from our experienced traveller:

It may be remarked, that the poets who celebrate the Ilissus as a stream laving the fields, cool, lucid, and the like, have both conceived and conveyed a false idea of this renowned water-course. They may bestow a willow fringe on its naked banks, amber waves on the muddy Maeander, and hanging woods on the bare steep of Delphi, if they please; but the foundation in nature will be wanting; nor indeed is it easy for a descriptive writer, when he exceeds the sphere of his own observation, to avoid falling into local absurdities and untruths.[2]

The unforgettable opening of the *Phaedrus* had made the Ilissus a sacred place to the humanist; but the traveller was compelled to report that a reader must not derive his ideas of the present condition of the scenery in the neighbourhood of Athens from reading Plato, nor be disappointed when he arrives there.

The vicinity of Enneacrunus has ceased to deserve encomiums like those bestowed on it by Socrates, since it has been deprived of the waste water of the fountain, which chiefly nourished the herbage and the plane-tree. The marble-facing and the images are

---

[1] *Greece*, p. 50.

[2] *ibid.*, p. 79. Chandler is referring to a passage in Gray's *The Progress of Poetry* (II.3):

> Woods, that wave o'er Delphi's steep. . . .
> Fields, that cool Ilissus laves,
> Or where Maeander's amber waves
> In lingering Lab'rinths creep. . . .

Compare *Paradise Regain'd*, iv, 249–50:

> . . . there Ilissus rouls
> His whispering stream. . . .

I do not know who bestowed a willow-fringe on the Ilissus; Thomas Warton gave it laurel shades:

> Tho' thro' the blissful scenes Ilissus rolls
> His sage-inspiring flood, whose winding marge
> The thick-wove laurel shades. . . .
> (*The Pleasures of Melancholy*, 1747)

removed; and the place is now dry, except a pool at the foot of the rock, down which the Ilissus commonly trickles. The water, which overflows after rain, is used by a currier, and is often offensive.[1]

After his description of Athens, Chandler's narrative becomes much less interesting. Ill-health and probably some disharmony between the three men[2] made them pass through the Peloponnesus with too much haste for them to make more than rather superficial observations. Yet of great importance was his description of Bassae, which had been discovered by Joachim Bocher, a French architect, a few months before. Though he was visited in the lazaretto at Zante by Bocher and informed of the existence of the temple, Chandler felt unable to return to the Morea. His account of this remarkable and beautiful Doric temple, however, first gave the news of its survival to Europe.[3]

In spite of his obvious sincerity, accuracy, and considerable literary skill, Chandler reveals little of himself in these *Travels*.[4] We learn far more about him in a brief memoir written by Ralph Churton and prefixed to the 1825 edition, than from his journals, where he does not often allow sentiment to obtrude. In the memoir we are given some little traits of his character and incidents of his conduct, which bring him to life for us. For example, he brought home some souvenirs of Greece; among his trophies was a stuffed

---

[1] *Greece*, p. 85.
[2] The copies of the two volumes of Chandler's *Travels* which belonged to his companion Revett are in the British Museum, and contain extensive annotations. Revett corrects many of Chandler's statements with asperity.
[3] *Greece*, pp. 295–6.
[4] The only modern writer who I am aware has assessed the merits of Chandler says that the "diaries of his travels though conscientious are flat and rather uninteresting". (M. L. Clarke, *Greek Studies in England, 1700–1830*, Cambridge, 1945, p. 182.) I do not believe this judgment to be justified. Chandler's travels were admired and respected by his contemporaries. Reviewers in *The Gentleman's Magazine* and *The Critical Review* gave them detailed attention. They were reprinted in 1776, 1817 and 1825, and were translated into French and German. It is true that, twenty years later, J. B. S. Morritt writes rather harshly of Chandler; but he seems to be referring mostly to the account of the Morea, which is unquestionably the most deficient part of Chandler's tour: "He strikes me as a college fellow turned fresh out of Magdalen to a difficult and somewhat fatiguing voyage, for which he was as unfit as could be; and though very good at an inscription, was sure to go in the beaten track, and be bugbeared by every story of danger and every Turk that pleased to take the trouble." (*Letters of John B. S. Morritt of Rokeby, descriptive of journeys in Europe and Asia Minor in the years 1794–1796*, edited by C. E. Marindin (1914), p. 191 (a letter from Tripolizza, March 1795). But Morritt was a very rich young man, full of high spirits, and carrying no load of learning. Chandler was living on the equivalent of a travelling fellowship. In fact, Morritt's account of his travels compares unfavourably with Chandler's in spite of his many advantages.

owl (as related in *Travels in Greece*, p. 129, he had set at liberty another owl, with which he had been presented by a peasant); also "a drawing of a graceful Attic female, spinning, in the modern, which is believed to have been also the ancient, costume; one knee resting on a cushion, one hand a little elevated, holding the distaff, the other a little lower, drawing the thread, and twirling the spindle".[1]

Chandler subsequently became a respectable parson, and lived a life of no great distinction. But he did not forget Greece, the real Greece, where a sad historical continuity unites ancients and moderns. In his memoir Churton tells us that, when Chandler "adverted occasionally to the classic scenes, which he had visited in his travels, it was truly delightful, I had almost said enchanting, to my younger ears, to hear him tell, his bright eyes beaming with peculiar lustre, how, after a long lapse of ages of ignorance and barbarism, and under the cruel hand of Turkish tyranny and oppression, the lyre, though not now in the hands of a Tyrtaeus or Simonides, was still, however, cherished on the banks of the Ilissus".[2]

Although Greece did not form part of the Grand Tour until the later years of the century, when the wars with France closed that country and Italy to the English traveller, there was no dearth of information about the Greek lands. The important French travel-books were translated into English, as were the English ones into French. Gibbon was a judicious reader of narratives of travel in the lands which had once formed part of the Roman Empire, and he shows a detailed knowledge of the best of them. He used Spon, Wheler, Stuart, and Chandler, for example, in order to compile that polished paragraph on modern Athens which concludes the sixty-second chapter of *The Decline and Fall*:

> The Athenians are still distinguished by the subtlety and acuteness of their understandings; but these qualities, unless ennobled by freedom and lightened by study, will degenerate into a low and selfish cunning. . . . The Athenians walk with supine indifference among the glorious ruins of antiquity; and such is the debasement of their character that they are incapable of admiring the genius of their predecessors.[3]

Even among the untravelled and unlearned curiosity was aroused about Greece, as we can see from the magazines of the time. By 1757 *The Gentleman's Magazine* had a description, with a copper-plate

[1] Ralph Churton in his Introduction ("Account of the Author") to the 1825 edition of Chandler's *Travels*, Oxford, 2 vols., p. xiv.

[2] *Op. cit.*, pp. vii–viii.

[3] ed. J. B. Bury (1896), vi, 486.

illustration, of the "Tower of the Winds";[1] and even *The Lady's Magazine; or Entertaining Companion for the Fair Sex, Appropriated solely to their Use and Amusement* in 1787 and 1788 offered to its readers a "Sketch of a Voyage to Athens", including a description of the antiquities and comments upon the modern inhabitants.[2]

To visit any part of the Ottoman Empire still implied some degree of responsibility and a genuine interest in travelling, which made it unsuitable for the young sons of the gentry with their bear-leaders. Travel in Greece was more adventurous than the perambulation of France and Italy, and it was less frequent. Already to many it seemed more rewarding.

[1] Vol. XXVII, p. 176.
[2] Vols. XVIII (1787), p. 680, and XIX (1788), p. 29. The account is based on Wheler, Spon, and Chandler, some paragraphs having been borrowed verbatim.

CHAPTER IX

THE REVIVAL IN GREECE

All Greece is ready to shake off the Turkish yoke whenever a favourable opportunity offers to secure them protection.

The Gentleman's Magazine, July 1770.

The phoenix rising from its flames is the emblem invariably adopted
by the Greeks.

F. S. N. Douglas, *An Essay on Certain Points of Resemblance
between the Ancient and Modern Greeks* (1813).

Russia desires to possess, not to liberate Greece; and is contented to
see the Turks, its natural enemies, and the Greeks, its intended slaves,
enfeeble each other until one or both fall into its net. The wise and
generous policy of England would have consisted in establishing the
independence of Greece, and in maintaining it both against Russia
and the Turk.

Shelley, preface to *Hellas* (1821).

BETWEEN the end of the seventeenth century and the beginning of
the nineteenth century a great change took place in the Greek people,
which prepared the way for the national revolution and made it
possible. This gradual revival among the Greeks was the background
to a series of political events which brought the position and possibilities of Greece more and more into the consciousness of Western
Europe. When Wheler and Spon were in Greece, they observed
with interest, and with some surprise, that the Athenians still
preserved something of their old vivacity and love of independence.[1]
But a century and a half later, when Byron was living in Athens, the
liberation from the Turkish rule was a usual and frequent topic of
conversation. In 1700 the Greeks were an object of curiosity as the
degenerate descendants of the glorious creators of literature and the
arts. But by 1800 it was a matter of eager speculation and controversy
whether the Greeks inherited any of the virtues of their ancestors,
whether their language could be purified, and whether they would
owe their liberation to the kindly, but interested, arms of Russia,
France, or England, or to their own exertions.

From the treaty of Passarowitz (1718) to the Russian-sponsored
rebellion of 1770, there was peace in Greece. It cannot be doubted

---

[1] pp. 135–6 above.

that during those years there took place a remarkable development in education, which was the prelude to the national awakening and the revolutionary struggle. Pitton de Tournefort says that, when he visited Greece in 1700–2, "in the whole *Turkish* Dominions there are hardly twelve Persons thoroughly skill'd in the knowledge of the ancient *Greek* tongue".[1] This is probably an exaggeration; in any case, it depends on the meaning of "thoroughly". But it represents a genuine impression of the lack of education in Greece in the early years of the eighteenth century. Yet at Constantinople some effort was made among the Phanariot families to keep up the traditions of learning; and from the writings of that unlucky prince Demetrius Cantemir (who was born in 1673) we have an interesting account of condition of learning and education in the Phanar in his youth. "We are not to imagine," he says, "with the generality of *Christians*, that *Greece* is so far sunk in Barbarism, as not in these latter Ages to have produc'd Men little inferior to the most learned of her ancient Sages."[2] This is a large claim; and to the reader of the accounts, which I have already supplied, of the decay and degeneration of Greek civilization, perhaps it is a rather unexpected one. There is an academy in the Phanar (continues Cantemir) "built for the Instruction of Youth, by one *Manolaki* a *Greek*, who had nothing ignoble in him, but his Blood. In this Academy are taught Philosophy in all its Branches, and the other Sciences in the old uncorrupted *Greek*. In my time there flourish'd here Prelates and Doctors of great Piety and Learning." Some of these, Cantemir says, were his own teachers. He names more than a score, a few of whom we have already met in these pages, such as Kallinikos who corresponded with Woodroffe, Dositheus who compiled the Confession, Chrysanthos who received the letters of Arsenios from England, and others.[3]

Wherever there was a little liberty or a little power, the natural vivacity and self-esteem of the Greeks set them on the path of education. Whatever their state of subjection and however great their misery, the Greeks could not forget that they had once been the dominant race in the eastern Mediterranean; and the existence of their Church was a constant reminder that power and wealth had, until they were conquered by the Turks, been in their hands. Their innate self-confidence soon manifested itself in those who went abroad to seek their fortunes. This is well illustrated by an anecdote

[1] English translation of his *Relation d'un Voyage* (as *A Voyage into the Levant*, 2 vols., 1718), i, 77.
[2] *The History of the Growth and Decay of the Othman Empire*, translated by N. Tindal, London, 1734–5, p. 92.
[3] See pp. 105, 107, 108 above.

of a Greek named Dadiky, a native of Smyrna, who was resident in London when Voltaire was printing his *Henriade* there (1726) by subscription. By chance Dadiky saw the first leaf as the poem was being printed and read the line:

Qui força les Français á devenir heureux. . . .

He immediately paid a visit to Voltaire and said to him: "I am of the country of Homer: he did not begin his poems by a stroke of wit or by an enigma." The author, we are told, immediately corrected the line.[1]

Some knowledge of Hellenic literature steadily spread among the Greeks during the eighteenth century; and in the minds of the ecclesiastics and the Phanariots the prejudice in favour of "good Greek" was already strong. We can see the seeds of that unhappy "problem of the language", which has for so long troubled literary expression among the modern Greeks, when we read in Richard Pococke's narrative that in Chios "there are priests that teach the old Greek; those who understand it are reckoned to speak the best modern Greek, and often use old words; and if they would come into the custom of studying the antient Greek in all parts, it might be a great means to purify and improve the modern languages".[2] But the great centre of enlightenment was not Chios, nor Constantinople, nor Athens. It was Yannina, which became renowned for the educational opportunities it offered. Most of the Greek authors of the eighteenth century came from Yannina or were educated there; and from its schools came teachers who endeavoured to spread education and enlightenment among the Greek people. The most remarkable personality was Eugenios Voulgaris, the greatest Greek scholar of the eighteenth century. He was born at Corfu, studied in Italy, and, while remaining firm in the Orthodox faith, endeavoured to introduce something of modern Western philosophy into Greece. A more questionable contribution to Greek culture was his effort to write in a "purified" form of modern Greek, an ambition which makes him the father of *katharevousa*, the artificial literary and official language. His numerous writings include translations from Western literature, among which is a version of the *Aeneid* and the *Georgics* in Homeric verse. Thus did humbled Greece beg back a culture from the nations she had civilized.

Not only education, but also the cult of the "purified" Greek

[1] *Œuvres Complètes de Voltaire* (Paris, 1877), viii, 59. The story was familiar to English readers from Warton's edition of Pope (1822 edition, vi, 258). This Dadiky (whom I have not met elsewhere) is called "interprète du roi d'Angleterre".
[2] *A Description of the East and some other Countries* (1743–5), Vol. II, pt. ii, p. 10.

came before political emancipation. In this regard for their language, with more tenacity than in anything else have the Greeks shown their insistence on their heritage from antiquity. The effort to restore Greek linguistically to its primitive integrity (which was later to be strenuously advanced by Korais) preceded the effort to restore Greece politically to its primitive integrity.

Although the Turks endeavoured to crush any obvious rebellious inclinations among their subject peoples, they were indifferent to the more subtle signs of national revival and successful resistance, which were being shown by the Greek nation, long before the end of the eighteenth century. Unconcerned with educational matters themselves, the Turks did not discern the importance of the development of education, which was being brought to every Greek town and was being encouraged both by Greek merchants abroad, who were steadily increasing in wealth and influence, and by the great Phanariot families at Constantinople. The Ottoman government, so long as it remained strong, gave a measure of security to its subject peoples; it preserved the religious institutions of Christians and Jews, and tolerated, because of its fiscal advantages, a commerce which made it possible for some of these subjects to become wealthy. But with the decline of the government this security largely disappeared, and the subjected peoples became more than ever the victims of local officials, brigands and soldiery, unprotected by the central administration of the Porte. Apart from the hateful child-tax, the Ottoman rule was probably more intolerable to Christian subjects in the later eighteenth century than it was in the sixteenth century. This deterioration of the Ottoman government coincided with the revival of the Greeks themselves. The administration was becoming more and more intolerable, while the Greeks were becoming less and less inclined to tolerate it.

The Turks were not unaware, during the first century of their decline, of their peculiar and potentially perilous relation to the alien peoples they ruled. Köprili Mustafa took some care to propitiate the *rayas* during his brief vizierate (1689–91). He perceived, it is said, that the recent disasters of the Ottoman Empire in the wars against the Hapsburg Empire, the Russians, and the Venetians, demanded that all the Turkish resources be realized; the loyalty of the huge numbers of Christian subjects must be won. The Christian invaders of Turkey were finding everywhere sympathy and recruits among the populations of the land. The Christian Albanians had for long been enrolling themselves under the banner of Venice and were serving as mercenaries in the armies of other European states; the Servians were rising to aid the Emperor of Austria; and in Greece the victorious progress of Morosini had been aided by the readiness with which the village municipalities and the mountain tribes placed themselves under his authority, once they were convinced of his success.

During the war between the Hapsburgs and the Porte in 1716, Prince Eugène had endeavoured to rouse the Servians to co-operate with the Austrians and had promised them the aid of the Emperor's armies to shake off the yoke of Turkish oppression. The Servian youth responded and a corps of one thousand two hundred Servians successfully took part in the campaign.[1] This should have been a useful lesson to the Turks; and it is said that the Greeks benefited, in some respects, as a result. Yet whatever the Turkish fears may have been, the appeals by foreign powers to the Greeks and other Christian subjects of the Porte were not enthusiastically heeded during the early years of the eighteenth century. The Austrians' appeal to the Servians, even after Prince Eugène's victory over the Turks near Belgrade, only produced that twelve hundred, which cannot be regarded as a considerable number. There was no popular rising of the people of Hungary against the Turks during these wars which the Austrians were fighting. The Venetians received no very active help from the Greeks during the campaigns in the Morea until they were clearly victorious; indeed, there is evidence that in 1715 the Greeks welcomed the Turks as deliverers from an oppressive tyranny. The notion of liberty and national independence was premature. But soon the spread of education and the growth of a sense of nationality made hopes for the future more concrete.

It was some time before observers from Western Europe became aware of the change that was taking place; and there were evidently parts of Greece which were almost unaffected by the progress in national sentiment that was being made elsewhere. It was easy for hasty travellers to generalize from the administrative decay they observed in parts of the Greek lands. Thus Richard Pococke gives a gloomy picture of the decline of the Christians in Crete.

There were some villages where the inhabitants, who were formerly Christians, are almost entirely become Mahometans; some to avoid punishment, or to be revenged on a Turk, whom a Christian cannot strike; others are encouraged by the thriving of the renegadoes, who pay no taxes: So the Christians grow poor, the Mahometans rich, and purchase their lands; and thus the Christian religion daily loses ground in all parts of Turkey.[2]

[1] Creasey, *History of the Ottoman Turks* (1858), ii, 146–7.
[2] Vol. II, pt. i, p. 268.

Charles Perry, a sensible and intelligent writer, about the same time
as Pococke, saw little prospect of the Greeks' taking advantage of
their great numerical superiority over the Turks. The Armenian and
Greek Christians, he tells us,

> live in miserable Slavery and Subjection to the *Turks*, and suffer
> great Extortions and Oppressions from them. And considering in
> what Numbers those Christians are, in proportion to the *Turks* in
> those Parts, it is much to be wondered at, that they have not, ere
> now, endeavoured to shake off their Yoke; But their Miseries and
> Sufferings, having now endured for many Generations past, are
> become habitual; and as they have not seen or tasted better
> Fortune, and a milder Government, so they rest contented, and
> bear it with Patience.

Yet he sees some sparks of political capabilities:

> This Nation which in ancient Times made so great a Figure in
> Literature, the polite Arts and Sciences, and in military Prowess,
> is now become pretty much estranged to all those splendid Virtues
> and Accomplishments. But though Time, and Fate, perhaps, has
> divested them of these things, yet Nature still manifests herself
> in their Favour; for notwithstanding their low, abject State and
> Condition, and the great Oppressions they groan under, from their
> cruel, inexorable Tyrant, the Turk, yet they manifest a great deal
> of Cunning, Subtilty, and Dexterity, in all Parts of Life; for
> sometimes they make brave and vigorous Efforts against their
> Oppressors, we mean those of subordinate Rank, such as the
> Wayvodes, Agas, or the like.[1]

The notion that the Turkish Empire was about to crumble to pieces
had by now become widespread throughout Europe; the territories
ruled by the Ottoman would be, thought Charles Perry, "a very easy
Conquest to the united Arms and Forces of the Christian Princes".
Naturally the idea of the regeneration and revived liberty of the
Greeks came into the minds of many speculators, especially those
who were not immersed in contemporary politics. There were,
however, some shrewd interpreters of the balance of power in
Europe who were sceptical of this belief in the imminent collapse of
the Ottoman. Military observers pointed out that there was no
doubt about the continued bravery of the Turkish soldiers. It was
the administration that was faulty; courage was useless while the
military authorities in Turkey neglected or ignored the advances in

[1] *A View of the Levant* (1743), p. 23.

military science which gave tactical advantage to the Christian powers. An intelligent and enlightened vizier could very quickly change that state of affairs; and a revival of Ottoman military power seemed as probable as a collapse. Even if a military decline was inevitable, a consequent collapse of the Turkish Empire was by no means probable. Montesquieu shrewdly pointed out to his contemporaries that they would be wrong to anticipate an early disappearance of the Turk from Europe. In his *Considérations sur les Causes de la Grandeur des Romains et de leur Décadence* (published in 1734) he explained that Turkey would find champions who would maintain her against aggression; the commercial powers of Europe would prefer a weak Turkey to a strong Russia or Austria at Constantinople.[1]

Yet in spite of the growth of the opinion that "the sick man" must be bolstered up by the alliance of the great commercial powers, the usual notion in circulation was that the Turkish Empire would shortly fall to pieces, and that Europe should make plans accordingly. It was commonly supposed that the territories of the Empire would fall to one or more of the great Powers of Europe. Little attention was paid, in political and diplomatic circles, to the rights of the indigenous inhabitants of the countries which the Ottoman had conquered centuries ago. "That the submerged nationalities of the Balkan peninsula would ever again be in a position to exercise any decisive influence upon the destinies of the lands they still peopled was an idea too remote from actualities to engage even the passing attention of diplomacy", a modern historian has written.[2] This is, of course, the exaggeration of one who writes for effect; and it faithfully characterizes the attitude of those who, engaged in diplomatic activities, are therefore hardly capable of viewing other nations except as the object of their day-to-day business. As a matter of fact considerable attention was paid to the more advanced Balkan nationalities, notably the Greeks and the Servians, although only very gradually did the strength of the national feelings of subject peoples convince the rulers of Europe that self-government was the only endurable government. A particularly callous example of

[1] "L'empire des Turcs est à présent à peu près dans le même degré de foiblesse où étoit autrefois celui des Grecs; mais il subsistera long-temps: car, si quelque prince que ce fût mettoit cet empire en péril en poursuivant ses conquêtes, les trois puissances commerçantes de l'Europe connoissent trop leurs affaires pour n'en pas prendre la défense sur-le-champ." (Chap. 23; *Œuvres*, Paris, 1822, i, 364–5.) This is the famous passage to which Pitt referred in the debates on Russian intentions in 1791–2, when he vainly attempted to excite alarm on the subject of Russia's progress in south-eastern Europe. Charles Perry paraphrased this opinion of Montesquieu (without acknowledgement) in *A View of the Levant* (1743), p. 9, and helped to set it in circulation in England.

[2] J. A. R. Marriott, *The Eastern Question* (1924), pp. 5–6.

indifference to the claims and rights of the indigenous inhabitants is to be found in the plan promulgated by Cardinal Giulio Alberoni (1664-1752) for the destruction of the Ottoman Empire by the united forces of Christendom. Alberoni was a lifelong intriguer in international politics, a reactionary defying popular rights and liberties; and he was so far devoid of sentiment as even ruthlessly to endeavour to crush the tiny republic of San Marino into subjection to the Papacy, against the intentions of the Pope.[1] He cannot therefore be regarded as in any way representative of enlightened opinion in the early eighteenth century. His proposals, which were translated into English in 1736 as *Cardinal Alberoni's Scheme for reducing the Turkish Empire to the obedience of Christian Princes: and for a partition of the conquests*,[2] merit our attention as representing the views of a shrewd politician indulging in speculation on the situation in Greece. He points out the many advantages to be gained from driving the Turk out of his empire. It would be an easy task. Moreover, "the great Number of *Christians* dispersed thro' all parts of the *Turkish* Dominions, must be consider'd as another Incentive, since we may conclude, they will co-operate chearfully in all Measures consistent with their Security, for throwing off the *Turkish* Slavery" (pp. 5–6). Alberoni's scheme was to prepare an army from the states of Europe, amounting to 370,000 men, and a naval force of 100 ships of the line and 40 frigates. England was to furnish the largest contingent to this naval force: 30 ships of the line and 10 frigates. The partition of the conquests he proposed should be as follows. An Emperor of Constantinople was to be revived (in the person of the Duke of Holstein Gottorp) ruling most of the Turkish dominions in Asia and Africa and "Romania". The Hapsburg Emperor was to annex Bosnia, Servia, Sclavonia, Macedonia and Wallachia; Russia was to have Azov and Tartary; France to have Tunis; Spain to have Algiers, and Portugal to have Tripolis. The proposed partition of Greece is interesting:

> As the Maxims of *Great Britain*, being a trading Country, will not permit her People to enlarge their Dominions, it is proposed to give his *Britannick* Majesty the Island of *Candia*, and the City of *Smyrna* in Propriety (p. 39).

Holland was to have Rhodes, the King of Sardinia Cyprus, Prussia Negropont, Venice the Morea ("which was torn from her about twenty years ago"); Genoa "that Part of old *Greece* now called Livadia"; and finally the cardinal (*incredibile dictu*) proposes "that all

[1] A lively account of Alberoni is given by Simon H. Smith (1943).
[2] London, 1736; also Dublin, 1736.

the Islands in the *Archipelago*, not specified in this Partition, be reserv'd for such young Princes, and Generals, as shall be most distinguished in the Course of the War" (pp. 45–6). It must be quite clear, he continues, "that no Prince or State whatever, shall pretend to the Sovereignty of the *Archipelago*, which will, it is hoped, tend very much towards promoting Trade and preventing Disputes for the Flag" (pp. 46–7). The attack in the Mediterranean is to begin with the occupation of Coron and Modon; Mytilene and Tenedos are to be taken early, to cover the approach of the army to besiege Constantinople. The campaign, Alberoni calculated, would soon be over; and so, for a comparatively small expenditure of money and manpower, the states of Europe would be able to acquire extensive and valuable dominions. Any question of the legality of the proceedings need not be considered; for the enemy was merely the Turk; and it had for long been a principle of international law among the Christian nations that a war against the Turk was always just.

From all the information available about the state of the Ottoman Empire and the administration at Constantinople in the years following the great revolt of the janissaries in 1730, it seems that Alberoni's scheme was feasible. But it depended upon the concerted action of the united forces of the states of Europe; a mere dream. And long before Alberoni prepared his plan, one of the Great Powers had already decided upon her own claims to supersede the Ottoman Empire. In fact, the future of the Greek lands was, from the later seventeenth century onwards, generally supposed to be determined by Russian aggression. In these years Russia boldly came forward as the champion of the Greeks. She had begun to take the place of Venice as the main opponent of the Ottoman Empire; and looked forward to inheriting the Byzantine throne at Constantinople, controlling the Bosphorus and thence the Eastern Mediterranean, and getting rid of all Turkish sovereignty in Europe. Already in 1668 Sir Paul Ricaut wrote: "the *Greeks* have also an inclination to the *Moscovite* beyond any other Christian Prince, as being of their Rites and Religion, terming him their Emperor and Protector; from whom, according to the ancient Prophecies and modern Predictions, they expect delivery and freedom to their Church".[1] A few years later Aaron Hill drew attention to "the *Universal Disposition* of the *Greeks*, to look upon *that Nation*, as their *long-decreed Deliverers*". He offered to his readers his conjectures about Peter the Great's aggressive designs, based upon the "*Conspicuous Probability*" of the *approaching Downfall* of the *Turkish Empire*", which "at *present* seems so weaken'd,

[1] *The History of the Present State of the Ottoman Empire* (1668), 5th ed. (1682), p. 177.

by the *Natural Corruption*, and *Infirmities* of *Age*, that Terrible
Convulsions shake its Frame, as if 'twere hastening onwards,
towards a *sudden Period*".[1]

For so long as Venice and Catholic Europe were the main opponents of Turkey, the Greeks were indifferent to the results of their
conflicts. At the Battle of Lepanto, for example, more Greeks are
supposed to have fought on the side of the Turks than in the Venetian
squadron.[2] But with Russia it was different. Towards Russia the
Greeks felt a far greater sympathy, because with Russia they had the
bond of a common Byzantine religion, and the relics of Byzantine
culture. It was easy for the Russians to use the Greeks as a convenient tool for their meditated plan of expansion in the Mediterranean. The Russian propaganda had begun as early as the time of
Peter the Great, who had issued proclamations and presented
portraits of himself as "Emperor of the Russo-Greeks" to Christians
in the Turkish dominions.[3]

It is probable that the writings of the unhappy Prince Demetrius
Cantemir of Moldavia (1673–1723) had a great influence upon the
views held in Europe in the eighteenth century regarding the future
of the Turkish Empire. Cantemir (wrote Voltaire) was "a Greek by
birth, who had the talents of the ancient Greeks together with a
knowledge of letters and of arms". Convinced of the decay and
imminent ruin of the Turkish empire, Cantemir had deserted from
his Turkish overlordship in Moldavia (to which he had been
appointed in 1710), and joined the Czar Peter the Great. "He
reckoned on all the Greeks joining his faction, and the Greek patriarchs encouraged him in his defection" from the Porte, wrote
Voltaire with his customary pose of turcophilism.[4] After the failure
of his schemes and the defeat of the Czar at the Pruth in 1711,
Cantemir remained in Russia and settled down to write his history of
the Turkish Empire. The manuscript was brought to England after
his death, and was translated into English in 1734–5 by N. Tindal
as *The History of the Growth and Decay of the Othman Empire*.[5]

Cantemir worked in part from Turkish sources; and therefore his

[1] *A Full Account of the Present State of the Ottoman Empire* (1710), pp. 338, 339.

[2] Finlay (1856), p. 98, says there were twenty-five thousand in the Ottoman
fleet and five thousand in the Venetian, making a total far exceeding in number that
of the combatants of any of the nations engaged. This fact, of course, gives Finlay
a kind of angry pleasure.

[3] Wm. Miller, *The Turkish Restoration in Greece* (1921), p. 18.

[4] *Histoire de Charles XII* (*Œuvres Complètes de Voltaire* (Paris, 1878), xvi, 273, 274).

[5] His son Antiochus was "Minister Plenipotentiary from the Czarina to King
George, and brought with him into *England* the *Latin* manuscript of his father's
Othman History, from whence the *English* Translation was made" (life of Cantemir
appended to *History*, p. 459). The MS. was given to King George. ("The Translator to the Reader", p. iii).

history seemed to be especially authoritative. Gibbon, for example, frequently quotes Cantemir as representing the Turkish accounts of events. The supposed authenticity of the narrative and the picturesque personality of the author gave his *History* a wide circulation, and a well-merited one, among those who were interested in Levantine affairs. The second part of Cantemir's work ("The History of the Decay of the Othman Empire, from the Reign of Mahomet IV to the Reign of Ahmed III. Being the History of the Author's own Times") is, of course, indirectly a defence of his own political conduct. Cantemir had calculated on the collapse of the Turks in the face of the determined aggression of Peter the Great; and he had calculated wrongly. His *History* gives the background to his decision, and endeavours to justify it, in spite of his failure. Cantemir's testimony regarding the state of Turkey seemed convincing; and neither the defeat of Peter the Great at the Pruth in 1711, nor the reconquest of the Morea from the Venetians in 1715, nor the fact that in 1717 the extent of the Turkish dominions was greater than it had ever been before, nor the Treaty of Belgrade in 1739 (by which both Austria and Russia were frustrated), convinced Europe that the Ottoman Empire was not tottering to its downfall. Generally speaking, the English politicians, like the "enlightened" French writers, approved of the expansion of Russia. But the fact that other opinions were already held in some quarters is evident from Goldsmith, who in his *Citizen of the World*, which was published in 1758, many years before the great military expeditions of Catherine in the war of 1765 to 1774, wrote: "I cannot avoid beholding the Russian empire as the natural enemy of the more western parts of Europe; as an enemy already possessed of great strength, and, from the nature of the government, every day threatening to become more powerful."[1]

From the pen of a British ambassador at the Porte shortly before the first national uprising of 1770, we have a lively account of the Greeks, which displays the typical qualities of its origin. Sir James Porter (1710–86) was at Constantinople for many years (1746–62)—longer, in fact, than any other ambassador until Stratford Canning. He knew the Greeks of the Phanar thoroughly. It is not clear that he had much experience of any other Greeks; that is the chief defect of his book. But his cynical pen points out, not so much the similarity of the modern Greeks to the ancient, but rather the similarity of the ancients to the moderns:

> The modern Greeks are a near image and resemblance of the ancient. Too crafty and subtle, too intriguing, vain, and vindictive,

[1] Letter lxxxvii (Globe edition, ed. Masson, p. 227).

either to support and maintain the interest, reputation, and glory
of a republic; or to share with, and submit to Government under a
monarch of their own; their busy spirit seems exactly formed and
adjusted to live no where tranquil but under a foreign subjection;
where the heavy hand of power can depress the soaring ambition
of their genius, and curb the violence of their passions; where
severity can awe them to obedience, and if not to social virtue, at
least to social quiet.[1]

This ingenious opinion—that the most appropriate political condition for the Greeks was one of subjection to a despotic foreign
nation—was often to be expressed during the next half-century.

> Whoever could live among the Greeks, and observe their refined
> intrigues, their eternal and continued contests for these ecclesi-
> astical and civil dignities, would see a true portrait in miniature
> of the worst Peloponnesian republics, and a most striking resem-
> blance of their abominable practices under their own emperors
> from Constantine to the last of the Palaeologus's.[2]

There is some skilful malice here.

From about the middle of the eighteenth century the new spirit
among the Greeks themselves began to be noticed by many visitors
and intelligent observers; and towards the end of the 1760's a feeling
that a new phase in the history of the Greeks was beginning can be
discerned. In 1764, the extortions of the Turkish administration
caused a rebellion amongst the Greeks in Cyprus.[3] It was savagely
suppressed; but it was the first sign of a spirit of active hostility to
Turkish rule. In 1738, when Russia was conducting her aggressive
war against the Porte, the Russian general Munnich arranged for
agents to be sent into the European provinces of the Turkish Empire
to stir up the Christian *rayas* against the Turk. These agents had
little success. But thirty years later matters had changed. Chandler,
when he visited Greece in 1767, heard the people frequently discuss
their approaching liberation from Ottoman rule by the arms of
Russia. The appearance of a cruciform light over Aya Sophia had
created the impression that the liberation of Constantinople was at
hand.[4]

---

[1] *Observations on the Religion, Law, Government, and Manners of the Turks*
(2 vols., 1768), ii, 110. There was a second edition, augmented, in 1771, doubtless
prompted by political events. It was reprinted in 1854 in *Turkey: its History and
Progress, from the Journals and Correspondence of Sir James Porter* (2 vols.), by
which time it was obsolete and useless.

[2] *Op. cit.*, ii, 112.   [3] Finlay (1856), p. 96.

[4] Wm. Miller, *The Turkish Restoration in Greece* (1921), p. 18.

In 1769, the year before the outbreak of the first serious uprising among the Greeks, a writer in *The Annual Register* informs his readers that "the affairs of the Turkish empire are at present in a very critical situation". The lack of military exercise among the Turkish soldiery, since the Turks ceased their career of conquest, was something that the Greeks were well aware of. Peace was ruining the Ottoman Empire; and the Greeks were ready for revolution.

To this long peace may also be attributed that disposition to revolt which seems at present so prevalent among the Greeks. The terror with which they first regarded their fierce and haughty conquerors, was kept up by seeing them continually in arms, and by being witnesses that the same courage which first made them irresistible, still made them terrible to their most warlike neighbours. These ideas being worn off, by a long knowledge and acquaintance in the softness and weakness of peace; they now dare to reflect upon the wretchedness of their own condition, and to repine at the oppressions which they suffer.

This malcontent temper of the Grecian Christians, and the strong attachment which from religious and political principles they bear to the Russians, are circumstances much more alarming to the Ottoman empire, than any consequences that could result from the ill conduct of the last campaign, or the military prowess of their enemies. The Greeks are not only numerous, but most of the provincials are fierce and warlike; so that the Turks are indebted to the bigotry and oppressive disposition, which so uniformly disgraced the councils, both of the house of Austria and the republic of Venice, for most of their European provinces. The people, from this cause, generally preferred a submission to the Mahometan government (which was favourable enough to them in religious matters, and perhaps not more oppressive in civil) than to the intolerant principles of their Christian neighbours. Now that Russia is arrived at great power and dignity, these people look up to her, not only as the preserver of their religion, but as their natural protector, and the restorer of the Greek empire.[1]

Russian agents were active throughout Greece in stimulating the rising which began in the Morea in 1770, and the Russians sent a fleet from the Baltic into the Aegean, landed small numbers of troops in several places and indulged in a few naval demonstrations.

[1] *The Annual Register*, 1769, pp. 4–5.

The part played by British naval officers serving in the Russian navy during these years was of great importance. The fleet which appeared in the Mediterranean was under virtual, though not nominal, command of Admiral Elphinstone, supported by numerous British officers—it was said that every vessel had one on board. The service of these officers with the Russians in the Mediterranean must have been with the cognizance of the English Government, which at that time approved of the political advances and aggrandizement of Russia. Elphinstone commanded the Russian squadron which arrived off the Peloponnesus in 1770; and shortly afterwards, another admiral, Samuel Greig, brought a contingent, and served with Elphinstone under Orloff and Spiritoff at the naval battle near Chios, where two of the three fire ships which succeeded in burning the Turkish fleet in the bay of Tchesmé were commanded by officers named Dugdale and Mackenzie.[1] But the incompetence of the Russian admirals who were nominally in command of the expedition thwarted the seamanship of their British subordinates; and the Greeks of the Morea, who had risen against the Turks, were quickly overpowered. The small Russian force hastily withdrew, leaving the Greeks to the savage vengeance of their conquerors.

These events in Greece in 1770 were of much interest in England. For the first time for many centuries the Greek nation was appearing as belligerents; the names of places once glorious for military exploits, and familiar to every educated person, were being mentioned in the news. The periodical-writers quickly seized the opportunity for expatiating on this interesting situation. In July 1770, *The Gentleman's Magazine* commented: "As a bloody war is now raging between the Russians and the Turks in the Morea, a brief description of that celebrated Country with a Map of its coasts and the adjacent Islands, must at this time, be subjects of Curiosity, and therefore are here inserted." Readers were then given a short account of the principal places in the Morea which were in the news, with their ancient and recent history. The writer is tolerably well informed; but already uneasiness is shown at Russian intentions. Half a century ago, he says, no one would have believed that these savages could have risen to such heights; "and who knows, but that the same people, in a like period of time, may contend with the other maritime powers for the empire of the sea!"

As it was expected that the Russians would at any time begin an attack upon Constantinople, readers were, in December, offered a

---

[1] When war was renewed in 1787, this Greig was put in command of the fleet that Catherine intended to send to the Archipelago. Lives of John Elphinstone and Samuel Greig are in the *Dictionary of National Biography*.

description of that city, with a plan of the surrounding country; and in a Supplement for the same year was given "A Review of the present State of the War between the Russians and the Turks, with an accurate Map of the Turkish Dominions in Europe". The horrible campaign in the Morea is related at some length:

> On the first appearance of the Russian succours, the Greeks, who had long groaned under the tyrannical yoke of the haughty Ottomans, assumed for a moment the appearance of the manly bravery of their renowned ancestors, and fell upon their oppressors with all the violence of vindictive rage.

But the writer severely reprimands the conduct of the Greeks in massacring all Turks without distinction of age or sex: "their boasted victories were the frantic exploits of enraged madness, and not the deliberate enterprizes of men, determined to die or shake off their bondage".

The writer agrees that Russian success is very probable, in spite of Turkish achievements in reconquering the Morea. Russia is speedily expanding at the expense of the Ottoman empire; and "all Greece is ready to shake off the Turkish yoke whenever a favourable opportunity offers to secure them protection".[1]

The writer in *The Annual Register* for the year 1770, while admitting that "it had become the policy of the great European commercial powers, long before Russia was the mistress of a single ship, to suffer no new maritime state to spring up amongst them", yet declared that Great Britain can behold "without uneasiness, the aggrandizement of a power, in whose alliance she is to look for a balance to the family compact". But the Russian attitude to the Greeks is another matter:

> It does not indeed appear to have been good policy in Russia, to have made so fatal and useless a trial of the disposition of these unhappy people. It was natural enough that they should wish for a deliverance from their oppressors, and that, vain of their antient national glory, they should think themselves possessed of the virtue of their ancestors.

Badly misinformed, he praises the moderation of the Porte in reacting to Greek excesses: "notwithstanding the rebellion of the Greeks, and the unheard of violences and barbarities they committed, we hear of no vengeance that he has taken, either upon the persons or goods of their inoffending brethren" (p. 6). It would be absurd to imagine,

---

[1] pp. 289, 290, 617, 619, 620.

he declares, that the Greeks, "a people immersed in a corruption of two thousand years, broken by long slavery, and sunk thro' every state of degradation; whose depravity, and total insensibility of condition, were become proverbial, and whose imaginary bravery only depended upon their having never seen the face of an enemy, should all at once do more than inherit the valour of their ancestors" (p. 4). This has a kind of superficial shrewdness about it, in the manner of leader-writers. But it already contains the seeds of that attitude to the Greeks which was for long to mar not only English public opinion, but also much intelligent observation and speculation. The idealization of Antiquity has permeated our consciousness. To be sentimental about the Greeks is deplorable, doubtless. To be cynical about the Greeks shows the same kind of weakness and partiality; for the cynics are the sentimentalists who feel that their emotions have been betrayed. To expect the modern Greeks to display the virtues of Pericles and Leonidas is foolish. To consider it ridiculous that the modern Greeks do not display those virtues is bad taste.

There exists a curious body of correspondence between Voltaire and the Empress of Russia during these years, a correspondence discreditable to both parties, but interesting as revealing in a hypocritical form those sentiments which half a century later were to inspire the literature of philhellenism and which were not to be entirely without an influence upon practical affairs. Already in a letter of November 15th 1768 Voltaire contemplates the possibility that Constantinople will soon become the capital of the Russian Empire; and in May 1770 Catherine writes to him that Greece is on the point of being free; however, it is nowadays far from being what it once was; yet it is pleasant to hear named the places which were so much beaten into our ears when we were young.[1] Voltaire soon broke into a pindaric ode on these glorious events; Pallas Athene exclaims that she wishes to resurrect Athens. "Would that there were a Homer to sing your combats, and a hundred orators like Demosthenes to give you courage. Revive, o ye Fine Arts, from underneath the deplorable ruins which have hidden you . . ."

> Je veux ressusciter Athènes.
> Qu'Homère chante vos combats,
> Que la voix de cent Démosthènes
> Ranime vos coeurs et vos bras.

[1] Voilà la Grèce au point de redevenir libre, mais, elle est bien loin encore d'être ce qu'elle a été: cependant on entend avec plaisir nommer ces lieux dont on nous a tant rebattu les oreilles dans notre jeunesse.

Sortez, renaissez, Arts aimables,
De ces ruines déplorables
Que vous cachaient sous leurs débris;
Reprenez votre éclat antique. . . .

But in September, after the news of the cruel fiasco in the Morea, Catherine changed her attitude and wrote that the Greeks, the Spartans, had much degenerated; they preferred booty to liberty. Consequent upon the failure of the Russian activity, Voltaire "with prompt servility altered the tone of his correspondence concerning Greece. He began to defame the Greeks, in whose favour he had previously affected great enthusiasm. Perceiving that Catherine was no longer eager to support their cause, he now spoke of them as unworthy of freedom, which, he says, they might have gained had they possessed courage to support the enterprises of the Russians. . . . Voltaire expected the Greeks would fight like heroes to become serfs of a Russian favourite."[1] Next year, when peace was being discussed, Voltaire writes: "What will become of my poor Greece? What will become of this fair land of Demosthenes and of Sophocles? I shall always be grievously afflicted to see the theatre of Athens turned into kitchen-gardens and the Lyceum into stables. I had every hope that you would rebuild Troy, and that Your Imperial Majesty would sail in your barge on the river Scamander."[2]

Voltaire, in one of his Lucianic dialogues, certainly had some fun at the expense of the unfortunate and humiliated Greeks; this is so characteristic, cruel, ill-informed, and amusing, that it merits a short quotation. In Hades Pericles is engaged in conversation with a Greek and a Russian:

Pericles. I have some questions to ask you. Minos informs me that you are a Greek.

Greek. Minos has told you truth, I was the most humble slave of the Sublime Porte.

Pericles. What do you say of slavery? A Greek a slave!

Greek. Can a Greek be anything else?

Russian. He is right; Greek and slave are the same thing.

Pericles. Just heaven! How I deplore my poor countrymen!

---

[1] Finlay (1856), p. 321.

[2] Que deviendra ma pauvre Grèce? que deviendra ce beau pays de Démosthène et de Sophocle? . . . je serai toujours douloureusement affligé de voir le théâtre d'Athènes changé en potagers, et le Lycée en écuries . . . Je comptais bien que vous feriez rebâtir Troie, et que Votre Majesté impériale se promènerait en bateau sur les bords du Scamandre. *Œuvres Complètes de Voltaire* (Paris, 1882), vol. xlvi (Correspondance xiv), 170; vol. viii, 492–3; vol. xlvii (Correspondance xv), 90, 219, 487.

Greek.   They are not so deplorable as you imagine; for my part I was
well enough content with my situation; I cultivated a little
plat of land which the Pacha of Romella had the goodness to
give me; and for which I paid a tribute to his highness.

Pericles is naturally astounded and incensed at this intelligence.

Pericles.   Oh Destiny!—But tell me, is not my memory still held in
veneration among the Athenians in that city into which I
introduced magnificence and good taste?
Greek.   I cannot inform you concerning that.   I dwelt in a place
called Setines, it is a poor miserable village which is falling
into ruins, but which I have been informed was once a
magnificent city.
Pericles.   So you know as little of this superb and famous town, than
of the names of Themistocles and Pericles!   You must have
lived in some subterraneous place or unknown quarter of
Greece.
Russian.   Not at all; he lived at Athens itself.
Pericles.   How!   Did he live in Athens and knows it not?   He does not
even know the name of this famous town.
Russian.   Thousands of men live actually in Athens, and know it no
more than him.   This city once so opulent and stately, is
now no more than a poor and dirty town called Setines.
Pericles.   May I believe what you tell me?
Russian.   Such are the effects of the ravages of time, and the inunda-
tions of barbarians still more destructive than time itself.[1]

It was long before the Greeks forgot their desertion by the Russians
in the Peloponnesus in 1770, although some of them entered a Greek
regiment which was formed by the Russians and used in their
campaign against the Persians.   Many Greeks were now serving as
mercenaries in European armies; this was the reason why Rhegas, their
patriotic poet, admonished his countrymen that it was better to die
for their own country than to wear a foreign tassel on their swords.

Some of the foreign advisers of the Porte suggested that the time
was ripe for a reform of the political relations between the Moslem
and the *giaour*.   Among these was the Baron François de Tott
(1733–93), who lived at Constantinople 1755–63 and was later
(1769–76) in the service of the Porte, engaged in establishing a
military academy in Constantinople and supervising the fortifications

[1] *Philosophical, Literary, and Historical Pieces*, translated from the last edition of
M. De Voltaire, by W. S. Kenrick, Second Edition, 1780, pp. 293–5.   Perhaps I
may comment on one piece of misrepresentation: "Setines" was a Frankish corruption of the name of Athens, not a modern Greek.

of the Dardanelles against the Russians. One foreign correspondent of a London magazine in February 1755 reported that "the zeal of the famous chevalier Tott for the glory of the Porte" had led him to submit several projects by which the Ottoman Empire might be made to flourish again. One of these projects was "to give education to the Greeks, which M. Tott thought would be a means to make them better subjects, and that privileges would make them attached to the government by gratitude".[1] Of course, the Porte was indifferent to such schemes.

In spite of its failure, the rising of 1770 was not altogether fruitless. It was an anticipation of what was to come in the nineteenth century. It drew the attention of the world to Greece. It reminded them that the restoration of the Greeks as an independent nation in Europe was a possibility. Incidentally the whole history of the episode makes it very difficult for us to agree with the point of view of those who regard the Greek national movement of the early nineteenth century as merely a result of the backwash of the French Revolution. The rising of 1770 took place two decades before the Greeks had heard of the French Revolution.

The Peace of Kutchuk-Kainardji in 1774, moreover, produced some very positive results for the Greeks. By this treaty the Russians were allowed free navigation for merchant ships in Turkish waters, and Russian consuls were appointed in the main ports. The consuls were in most cases Greeks; and the right to carry the Russian flag was granted to Greek vessels almost indiscriminately. The consequences were obvious. Greek commerce increased enormously, and before long a merchant navy had come into existence, which made the Greeks a match for the Turks at sea when the Revolution began. The Greek mariners in these years became more skilled, more adventurous, and (needless to say) more unscrupulous. Many of them corresponded to the character of Haidée's father, in whom

> something of the spirit of old Greece
> Flashed o'er his soul a few heroic rays,
> Such as lit onward to the Golden Fleece
> His predecessors in the Colchian days;

[1] In the "Foreign News" in *The Lady's Magazine*, 1775 (vol. VI, p. 106). Baron de Tott published his *Mémoires . . . sur les Turcs et les Tartares* (4 vols., Amsterdam, 1784). There were two different translations into English (2 vols., London) published in 1785 and 1786. His memoirs are highly readable; but Gibbon chastised him several times for his frivolity (". . . He seems to write for the amusement, rather than the instruction of his reader. . . . That adventurous traveller does not possess the art of gaining our confidence. . . . Always solicitous to amuse and amaze his reader." *Decline and Fall*, ed. J. B. Bury, vi, 3; vii, 170, 181).

'Tis true he had no ardent love for peace—
Alas! his country showed no path to praise:
Hate to the world and war with every nation
He waged, in vengeance of her degradation.[1]

Undeterred by the failure of 1770 and its miserable consequences
for the Greeks, Catherine for long clung to her ambition to inherit
the Byzantine Empire from the Ottomans. Her second grandson,
born in 1778, was named Constantine, and everything was done to
prepare him for his future as king of a restored Greek kingdom.
"Greek women were given him for nurses, and he sucked in with his
milk the Greek language, in which he was afterwards perfected by
learned Greek teachers: in short his whole education was such as to
fit him for the throne of Constantinople." Thus writes William Eton
in his *Survey of the Turkish Empire* (1798), and he had excellent
opportunities for being informed on these matters. He also tells us
that Potemkin had a scheme for aiding England in her war against
the American colonists in exchange for British assistance against
Turkey. The British help was to consist of the cession of the island
of Minorca (then a British possession) as a station for the Russian
fleet in the Mediterranean and as a rendezvous for the insurgent
Greeks.[2] In the plan which Catherine offered to her ally the Emperor
Joseph II in 1782, she impudently proposed that, on the successful
conclusion of a war against the Turks, the Morea, Crete and Cyprus
should go to Venice, while her grandson Constantine should sit on
the throne of a revived Greek empire at Constantinople, holding
dominion over northern Greece, Macedonia, Thrace, Bulgaria and
Albania.[3] The Prince de Ligne was present at this meeting, and he
has left an account of the mood of the partitioners. He himself, as a
lover of antiquity, wanted to see the Greeks re-established. Catherine
spoke only of new Solons and Lycurguses. But Joseph, who was
much more matter-of-fact, only said, "What the devil are we going
to do with Constantinople?"[4] The complete neglect of any respect
for the nationality of the peoples to be governed or any wishes they
might express about a choice of tyrant is noteworthy; it was as Byron

---

[1] *Don Juan*, III, lv.   [2] p. 409.
[3] J. A. R. Marriott, *The Eastern Question* (1924), pp. 155–6.
[4] Leurs Majestés Impériales se tâtoient quelquefois sur les pauvres diables de
Turcs. On jetoit quelques propos en se regardant. Comme amateur de la belle
antiquité et d'un peu de nouveautés, je parlois de rétablir les Grecs; Catherine, de
faire renaître les Lycurgue et les Solon; moi, je parlois d'Alcibiade; mais Joseph II,
qui étoit plus pour l'avenir que pour le passé, et pour le positif que pour la
chimère, disoit: "Que diable faire de Constantinople?" Letter from Baktcheserai
(in the Crimea), June 1st 1787. *Lettres du Prince de Ligne à la Mise de Coigny
pendant l'année 1787*, publiées avec un préface par M. de Lescure (Paris, 1886), p. 24.

wrote, forty years later, scathingly of the Czar Alexander, who had

> no objections to true Liberty,
> Except that it would make the nations free.
> How well the imperial dandy prates of peace!
> How fain, if Greeks would be his slaves, free Greece![1]

The northern Balkan nations were, perhaps, still inarticulate. But the Greeks were a different problem; and Catherine's views of man and society, speciously "enlightened" but really autocratic, were to be finally disproved by the influence of the outbreak of the French Revolution. It was too late in the day to regard Greece merely as attractive and interesting plunder for an expanding imperialistic power. Educational zeal was prompted by wealthy Greek merchants. Schools were being established in every Greek town. The commercial colonies abroad—notably Vienna, Venice, Trieste, Paris, and London, were growing in wealth and influence. Books were issued from the presses at Venice, Trieste and Vienna; and translations were made of influential works in the languages of western Europe.[2] Young Greeks went abroad to study in the Western universities; and when they returned to Greece, they were the champions of a new civilization for their countrymen. After the fall of Venice (1797), Vienna became the most important centre of enlightenment; and there in 1793 the first Greek newspaper had already been established.[3] James Dallaway, who was chaplain to the ambassador at the Porte and produced his book *Constantinople, Ancient and Modern* in 1797, gives a convincing picture of the Greeks of the Phanar towards the end of the eighteenth century; their pride and covetousness; their peril and their ambition. He recognizes that they have some claims to represent the more advanced and polished element in the Greek nation at that time. He acknowledges their faults and their follies; but he knows that they have pretensions to literature and to education. Moreover, their political curiosity is (as every Frank knows) intense.

> Degraded as the modern Greeks are in the political scale of Europe, no people are more apparently anxious with respect to pending transactions. Credulous in the extreme, or ingenious in inventing circumstances, the current news engrosses every conversation, and the gazette, published in Greek at Vienna, their grand oracle, is read or repeated with the greatest avidity (p. 105).

[1] *The Age of Bronze* (1823), x (442–5).
[2] It is a curious fact that Oliver Goldsmith's *Grecian History* (2 vols., 1774) was translated into modern Greek and published at Vienna in 1806.
[3] John Mavrogordato, *Modern Greece* (1931), p. 2.

Most of the travellers, however much they may seem to be absorbed in their investigation of classical antiquity, report conversations with the inhabitants of Greece who lament their misery and foretell their liberation. Edward Clarkē in 1801 was spending a night at Nemea with some peasants. "As soon as the men had taken a short nap, they sate up, and began talking. The conversation turned upon the oppressions of their Turkish masters." The owner of the hut in which they were staying the night related the unendurable taxes he was compelled to pay to the Turks. "He toiled incessantly with his children to gain enough to satisfy their demands, but found himself unable, after all his endeavours. Having said this, the poor man shed tears; asking us if the time would ever arrive when Greece might be delivered from the Mahometan tyranny: and adding, 'If we had but a leader, we should flock together by thousands, and soon put an end to Turkish dominion.'"[1]

This was the kind of discussion among the Greeks that Byron, too, knew well. Among Selim's men are some who are not merely self-seeking but who "to higher thoughts aspire".

> The last of Lambro's patriots there
> Anticipated freedom share;
> And oft around the cavern fire
> On visionary schemes debate,
> To snatch the Rayahs from their fate.[2]

The new spirit among the Greeks was manifested by the appearance of their first modern national poet. Before he was put to death in 1798 Rhegas had acquired some reputation in Europe, and had projected the *Hetaireia*. He had not many connections with the English; but he met Frederick Hervey, the famous Earl of Bristol, at Venice. Rhegas, like many Greeks, was profoundly moved by the French Revolution; and, from being a teacher in his native Thessaly, he wandered about Greece encouraging revolutionary sentiments in his compatriots. He went to Vienna in order to solicit help from the important Greek colony there for organizing an insurrection. But the Austrian government handed him over to the Turks, by whom he was put to death in 1798. His special interest for us is that, as a Greek, he gave expression to the earnest patriotic sentiments which derive from the contrast between the ancient glories and contemporary degradation of Greece, and which we naturally regard as

---

[1] *Travels in Various Countries* (1810, etc.), vol. III (pt. ii, sec. 2) (2nd ed., 1812), pp. 715–16.
[2] *The Bride of Abydos*, II, xx (862–6). Byron gives a note about Lambro Canzani, emphasizing his patriotism rather than his piracies.

characteristic of philhellenism. His splendid War Song contains the commonplace exhortations to the moderns to follow the examples of the ancients; but it was encouraging to philhellenic foreigners to hear those sentiments so powerfully communicated by a modern Greek: "Would that the spirits of our ancestors could arise to help us to free ourselves from the Turkish yoke; Sparta and Athens, Leonidas and ye who fought with him at Thermopylae against the Persians, it is your spirit we need; but we must ourselves fight until we conquer and are free." The poem was vigorously translated by Byron,[1] and it became well known to other English poets and scholars in Greece. The reviving Greek nation had produced its own national poet who was a martyr to his patriotism while Byron was a schoolboy in Aberdeen.

[1] *Poetical Works*, ed. E. H. Coleridge, iii, 20.

CHAPTER X

HELLENISM AND PHILHELLENISM

It is one thing to read the *Iliad* at Sigaeum and on the tumuli, or by the springs with Mount Ida above, and the plain and rivers and Archipelago around you; and another to trim your taper over it in a snug library—*this* I know.

> *Childe Harold's Pilgrimage*, canto iii, note 19.

Ah, Athens! scarce escaped from Turk and Goth,
Hell sends a paltry Scotchman worse than both.

> *The Curse of Minerva* (1811), a cancelled couplet.

I cannot forbear mentioning a singular speech of a learned Greek of Ioannina, who said to me, "You English are carrying off the works of *the Greeks*, our forefathers—preserve them well—we Greeks will come and re-demand them!"

> John Cam Hobhouse, *A Journey through Albania and other Provinces of Turkey in Europe and Asia* (1813).

ALTHOUGH our view nowadays of Greek civilization may be very different from that current at the beginning of the nineteenth century, there can be no doubt that the eighteenth century enjoyed a fuller appreciation of ancient Greece and her achievement than had existed since Roman times; and the result was an enthusiasm that was both intense and contagious. Greece was the new focus of attention for classical studies. The "second Renaissance" which took place in the later eighteenth century and which both stimulated and was nourished by the researches of ardent antiquaries, above all, Winckelmann, made the very word "Grecian" full of emotional overtones. The Abbé Barthélemy's *Anacharsis*, and its imitators, were educating Europe to an appreciation of the life and "sensibility" of the ancient Greek. The background to the more generous attitude to the modern Greeks was the idealization of the ancient Greeks. The new Hellenism was, in England and in France, but not in Germany, a powerful companion of Philhellenism, principally because it took the enthusiasts to Greece and created a demand for information about the country.

What had been recovered during the Renaissance in the fifteenth and sixteenth centuries was more of a Roman culture than a Greek culture. It was generally assumed that the Romans had learnt their arts from the Greeks; and that therefore the accessible Roman remains of sculpture, architecture and literature were adequate models of Greek excellence. Classical enthusiasm hardly distinguished between Greek and Roman. It took several centuries to discover that Greek art and literature, and Roman art and literature, were fundamentally different from each other. The discovery came first, of course, in literature; as regards the fine arts, it was necessary to reveal the survivals in Greece itself. The growing enthusiasm for the Greek arts meant an expanding interest in Greece.

In architecture the first stage in the revelation of "the true Greek genius" was the discovery of Doric. When at Verona, Addison had noticed "the ruin of a triumphal arch erected to Flaminius, where one sees old Doric pillars without any pedestal or basis, as Vitruvius has described them";[1] but the modern world knew practically nothing of the Doric order (except from the descriptions of Vitruvius and from travellers' inadequate accounts of the Parthenon) until the discovery of Paestum about the middle of the eighteenth century[2] and the increase in the number of visitors to the Grecian temples of Sicily. Although the toast of the Society of Dilettanti was, from its earliest days, "Grecian Taste and Roman Spirit", the first part of this aspiration was imperfectly or negligibly realized for some years. Only after they had organized their expeditions to Greece and Ionia and arranged for their magnificent publications, did the Dilettanti reveal to themselves and to the world what Grecian Taste was. The notion of "The Antique" was undergoing a fundamental change. "Classicism" gradually came to mean a devotion to purely Greek ideals, in so far as those ideals could be discovered. The taste for Roman antiques, although still widespread, became much more discriminating. It was a common opinion that Rome had been inferior to Greece in all spheres of the arts; and Roman objects were of interest only so far as they could be relied upon as a just reflection of Greek art. The Portland Vase could be regarded as sufficiently Hellenic to provide patterns for decorative porcelain and the background to an ode on a Grecian Urn. The reputation of the Apollo Belvedere, the Venus dei Medici, and the Discobolus could be saved because they were supposed to be examples of Greek workmanship.

The new Hellenism, which developed in the latter part of the eighteenth century, thus directed towards Greece a good deal of the enthusiasm which had hitherto been concentrated upon Rome. The movement which Stuart and Revett had accelerated by their

[1] *Remarks on several parts of Italy . . . in the years 1701, 1702, 1703.* (*Works,* ed. Hurd, Bohn's Library (1854), i, 378.)

[2] See S. Lang, "The Early Publications of the Temples at Paestum" (*Journal of the Warburg and Courtauld Institutes,* XIII (1950), 48–64).

important pioneer publications had provoked, in many quarters, an enthusiasm for "pure Grecian" architecture. Some eminent architects, it is true, warmly opposed the growing fashion. The Grecian style did not grow up unopposed or uncondemned. Sir William Chambers, trained in the old Vitruvian and Palladian styles, emphatically rejected this new classicism, and proclaimed the superiority of the Roman remains in Italy and France over any surviving examples of Grecian architecture in Greece; and, without, of course, having seen any of the Athenian buildings, he ventured to assert that St. Martin-in-the-Fields was superior to the Parthenon. It should be remembered, however, that the source of information about the Doric order was, for many years, Le Roy's *Ruines des plus beaux Monuments de la Grèce* (1758), the incorrectness of which is obvious to modern eyes (see p. 162 above). The first volume of the Society of Dilettanti's work on Athens by Stuart and Revett (1762) contained no important specimen of Doric. It was not until the second volume (twenty years after Le Roy's *Ruines*) that the world had an accurate account of Doric monuments. The rejection and contemptuous treatment of "Grecian" by many artists who were trained in the Palladian style becomes more intelligible when we remember that they had no material more authentic or accurate than Le Roy's to base their opinions upon. But the third volume of Stuart's work (1794) contained, for the first time, full delineations of Doric architecture; and this may be regarded as marking the turning-point in the reputation of "Grecian". After that date a visit to Greek lands and the careful study of the surviving monuments came to be regarded as an important part of the training of a young architect. With the decline of the taste for the Palladian style, the authority of the *dicta* of the Italian architects of the Renaissance weighed less heavily. Greater emphasis was placed on the actual study of extant remains. The Buildings of the Ancients, Robert Adam had written, "are in Architecture, what the works of Nature are with respect to the other Arts; they serve as models which we should imitate, and as standards by which we ought to judge: for this reason, they who aim at eminence, either in the knowledge or in the practice of Architecture, find it necessary to view with their own eyes the works of the Ancients which remain, that they may catch from them those ideas of grandeur and beauty, which nothing, perhaps, but such observation can suggest".[1] Fired with ideas like these, a visit to Greece for the purpose of studying the extant remains became the ambition of all the more adventurous young architects; and those who were unable to make the journey studied the records which had been made by

[1] *Spalatro* (1764) (ad init.).

others. The result is the large number of buildings in London and elsewhere based on Hellenic models, and incorporating memories and motifs brought back from Greece. Of course, the arguments against the adoption of an authentic Grecian style were strong. The method of construction which was appropriate to the climate of Greece is hardly suitable, or rarely suitable, in England. The porticos are unattractive and wasteful in a country where the inhabitants look for sunshine not shade. The pitch of the roof is not high enough to get rid of the snowfall in northern latitudes. The windows characteristic of pure Grecian buildings are ludicrously inadequate on the frequent sunless days. Yet none of these practical objections was sufficiently strong to overcome the romantic appeal of the Grecian manner; and buildings deriving their form from the Parthenon, the Erectheum, etc., filled the towns of Europe. It was a startling new architectural style. We have forgotten how strongly it once stirred the imagination.

Willey Revelly (d. 1799), one of Chambers's pupils, accompanied Sir Richard Worsley, the great collector of antiquities, during his tour of Greece in 1785–7, as architect and draughtsman; and on his return immediately began producing buildings in the Grecian style. It was he who edited the third volume of Stuart's *Antiquities of Athens* (1794), and in the preface he replied to Chambers's strictures on Greek architecture. Sir Robert Smirke was in Greece in 1802, before he was twenty-one; published his *Specimens of Continental Architecture* in 1806, and later designed the British Museum and the Royal College of Physicians in Trafalgar Square in the new Greek style. William Wilkins, in his early twenties, was also in Athens; he published his *Atheniensia, or Remarks on the Topography and Buildings of Athens* in 1812, and later designed the façade of the National Gallery and University College, London, where he reproduced the Choragic Monument of Lysicrates on the top of the dome. These are some famous characteristic London buildings. But there were many other architects in the first two decades of the nineteenth century, whose travels to Greece gave them a style which filled town and country with romantically Grecian buildings.

It was the architect Thomas Harrison (1744–1829) who urged Lord Elgin, on his appointment as British Ambassador at Constantinople in 1799, to obtain casts and drawings of works of art at Athens and other places in Greece. For during the first few years of the nineteenth century conditions in the Turkish dominions gradually became especially advantageous to the English. The favourable issue of the struggle against Napoleon impressed the Porte, which became anxious to placate the government of the nation whose sea-power was dominant in the Mediterranean. Nelson was already a popular hero amongst the Greeks. He was presented with a golden-headed sword by the people of the Zante, together with a truncheon studded with all the diamonds that the island could furnish. It was on account of the enhanced prestige of Britain after the Battle of Copenhagen (1801) that Elgin was eventually able to obtain a firman from the Porte which allowed his agents to "fix scaffolding round the ancient Temple of the Idols [i.e. the Parthenon], and to mould the ornamental sculpture and visible figures thereon in plaster and gypsum". This was not all. They were also given permission "to take away from the Acropolis any pieces of stone with old inscriptions or figures thereon". Elgin wrote in his report: "In proportion with the change of affairs in our relations towards Turkey, the facilities of access to the Acropolis were increased to me and to all English travellers, and about the middle of the summer of 1801 all difficulties were removed." The story of the removal of the sculptures from the Parthenon, their shipment to England, their shipwreck off Cerigo and recovery after three years, and the eventual purchase for the British Museum for £35,000, is well known.[1] It was one of the events which were bringing Greece into the English imagination in the early years of the nineteenth century. Plaster casts of most of the frieze were probably to be seen in London before Elgin's cases were unpacked. For W. R. Hamilton (who was Elgin's secretary during his embassy, and later minister at Naples, secretary of the Society of Dilettanti, and a trustee of the British Museum) had had casts made of the marbles before they were dispatched to England and these casts were visible in London before the marbles.[2]

Elgin's activities in Greece were notorious before Byron went to Athens and wrote his scathing attacks on the second destroyer of the Parthenon. Already in *English Bards, and Scotch Reviewers* (1809) he had expressed his derision of the Grecian cult:

> Let ABERDEEN and ELGIN still pursue
> The shades of fame through regions of Virtù;
> Waste useless thousands on their Phidian freaks,
> Misshapen monuments and maim'd antiques . . . (1027–30).

[1] See Courtenay Pollock, "Lord Elgin and the Marbles" in *Essays by Divers Hands being Transactions of the Royal Society of Literature*, New Series, vol. XI (1932), pp. 41–67; Michaelis, p. 132 ff.; A. Hamilton Smith in *The Journal of Hellenic Studies*, XXXVI (1916).
[2] Hamilton purchased Stanley Grove in Chelsea about 1815 and added a large East Room to accommodate them. They are still there, now that the house has become part of the College of St. Mark and St. John.

Thus Byron joined in the fashionable contempt for the Elgin marbles. which, led by Payne Knight, was then usual in England. But after he had lived in Athens and could see with his own eyes the devastation that Elgin's agents had caused, his language acquired a personal bitterness:

> Come then, ye classic Thieves of each degree,
> Dark Hamilton and sullen Aberdeen,
> Come pilfer all the Pilgrim loves to see,
> All that yet consecrates the fading scene.[1]

But we need not trouble to come to Elgin's defence; it is clear that, during the first twenty years of the nineteenth century, the eagerness to obtain genuine examples of Grecian sculpture was so great that, if one despoiler had not succeeded, another would have taken his place. The sentiments of the Greeks on the matter were noted, but not taken very seriously. Hobhouse, who was in Athens in 1810 with Byron, gave his readers a thoughtful discussion of the rights and wrongs of removing the sculptures, but concluded:

> I have said nothing of the possibility of the ruins of Athens being, in event of a revolution in the favour of the Greeks, restored and put into a condition capable of resisting the ravages of decay; for an event of that nature cannot, it strikes me, have ever entered the head of any one who has seen Athens, and the Modern Athenians. Yet I cannot forbear mentioning a singular speech of a learned Greek of Ioannina, who said to me, "You English are carrying off the works of *the Greeks*, our forefathers—preserve them well—we Greeks will come and re-demand them!"[2]

"No circumstance", wrote James Dallaway, "has tended so much to improve the national style of design and painting as the introduction of so many genuine antiques or correct copies of them."[3] But until towards the end of the eighteenth century, Italy, and Rome in particular, had remained the principal source of antiquities for the English collectors. The ancient marbles derived from Italy were almost all late copies of Greek originals or mere imitations by sculptors of the Roman period. From the beginning of the nineteenth century, however, Greek sculpture of the finest periods

[1] *Childe Harold's Pilgrimage*, from a cancelled stanza after II, xiii. (*Poetical Works*, ed. E. H. Coleridge, ii, 108.)
[2] *A Journey through Albania and other Provinces of Turkey in Europe and Asia* (2 vols., 1813), i, 347–8.
[3] *Anecdotes* (1800), p. 269.

(according to nineteenth-century taste) began to arrive in the country; and the British Museum acquired a series of marbles which have made it one of the greatest depositories of Greek art in the world. More and more did Greece romantically fill the imagination. "My spirit is too weak", wrote the Greekless poet contemplating the wonders of Greek sculpture:

> Such dim-conceived glories of the brain
>   Bring round the heart an indescribable feud;
> So do these wonders a most dizzy pain,
>   That mingles Grecian grandeur with the rude
> Wasting of old Time—with a billowy main
>   A sun, a shadow of a magnitude.[1]

Moreover, new Greek arts were being discovered and appreciated. The vases which for long had been known as "Etruscan" and collected by English connoisseurs in Italy, such as Sir William Hamilton, were now recognized as Greek. An English gentleman called Stephen Graham was noted as a highly successful excavator, having secured nearly a thousand vases near Athens.[2] Another collector was a merchant of the Levant Company, Thomas Burgon (1787–1858), the nephew of that Greek lady, Mrs. Baldwin, whom Reynolds painted in 1782,[3] and father of the author of Petra ("a rose-red city half as old as time"). Burgon made an important collection of vases, and conducted excavations on Melos. Two travellers named Berners and Tilson returned from Greece about 1795 with a large collection of vases. The old error, that the pottery which we know as a characteristic product of Greek art of its finest periods was of "Etruscan" origin, was soon exploded; and the way was prepared for the interpretation of Greek literature and culture with the help of ancient vase-painting, a field of scholarship that has borne fruit ever since.

The idea that the library of the Grand Seraglio contained some valuable Greek manuscripts had long been held;[4] it was thought, too, that the libraries of some of the mosques which had been converted from Christian Churches, especially that of Aya Sophia, might contain lost treasures of Greek literature. It had also been reported, at various times, that the monasteries of the Levant contained manuscripts, which might represent unknown and important ancient

[1] Keats, Sonnet v, "On seeing the Elgin Marbles for the first time", Poems, ed. de Sélincourt, p. 275.
[2] Clarke, Travels in Various Countries (1810, etc.), 2nd ed., 1816, IV, preface and p. 25.
[3] See p. 156 above.   [4] See pp. 81–2 above.

writings. When Elgin was sent out as British ambassador in 1799, it was decided, therefore, that a suitably erudite person should accompany him who might explore these unknown literary treasures. "The plan originated with Mr. Pitt and the Bishop of Lincoln, who thought that an embassy sent at a time when Great Britain was on the most friendly terms with the Porte, would afford great facilities for ascertaining how far these hopes of literary discovery were well founded. They trusted that the ambassador's influence would obtain permission for the transmission at least, if not for the acquisition of any unpublished work that might be found."[1] The choice fell upon the professor of Arabic at Cambridge, Joseph Dacre Carlyle, who joined Elgin's entourage as his official chaplain,[2] and it was he who by an extraordinary concession, the result of Elgin's pressure and the prestige of the English at the Porte, was admitted to the sealed library of the Seraglio. A full account of his remarkable achievement was sent home by Carlyle to the Bishop of Durham and the Bishop of Lincoln; and his letters make amusing reading. He was interviewed by Youssouf Aga, probably the most influential person at the Porte at that time; and Carlyle had to persuade the Turk that this activity of hunting for old books was of great importance to the Franks, even to the politicians. "I observed" (Carlyle wrote home) "that different nations possessed different customs; that my discovery of one of these ancient authors would be looked upon in England as very important; and I took the liberty of adding, that no person felt more interested in subjects of this kind than Mr. Pitt. Youssouf Aga replied, that nothing could give them greater pleasure than to gratify the British nation, and particularly Mr. Pitt; and that if they could give any intelligence where such books were deposited, I should not only have the liberty of inspecting them, but of carrying them along with me to England."

Thus fortified, and trembling with anticipation, Carlyle was ushered into the room which no infidel (it was supposed) had entered since the Turk had been at Constantinople; and there he found, amid large numbers of Persian and Arabic books, not one manuscript in Greek or Latin. The dream was at an end. Had he come upon the poems of Sappho or a codex of the comedies of Menander, Carlyle would have been famous; and Elgin would have been better known for his success in bringing Greek literature to England than in bringing Greek sculpture. But not a single classical

[1] Robert Walpole, *Memoirs* (1817), p. 84.
[2] Carlyle is in the *Dictionary of National Biography*; but this episode is misunderstood and slighted because the author (Stanley Lane-Poole, who should have known better) has missed the letters of Carlyle printed in Robert Walpole's *Memoirs* (1817).

fragment of a Greek or Latin author was found in any of these vast collections.[1]

Topographical investigation became especially important during the last decade of the eighteenth century and the beginning of the nineteenth century owing to the rise of the great Homeric Problem or Trojan Puzzle. The trouble began with Robert Wood, whose tour of Greece and Asia Minor in 1750–51 resulted in his book *A Comparative View of the Antient and present State of the Troade. To which is prefixed an Essay on the Original Genius of Homer* (1767). In this work (which went through five editions and was translated into French, German, Italian, and Spanish) Wood discussed, among other things, whether the art of writing was known to Homer; and he came to the conclusion that it was not. His book was well-received in Germany and enthusiastically reviewed by Heyne, the foremost German humanist; and Wood's view of writing became the chief evidence on which F. A. Wolf, in his *Prolegomena* (Halle, 1795), based his theory of multiple authorship of the Homeric poems. Meanwhile in 1775, Wood's book was edited by his untravelled friend, Jacob Bryant, a somewhat disputatious scholar, known in literary history as the author of a strongly written defence of the authenticity of the Rowley poems. But other travellers were visiting the Troad and coming to conclusions about the topography, in relation to Homer's poems, very different from the opinions of Wood. The French traveller Choiseul-Gouffier made an important survey of the region, and concluded that Homer's Troy was not at New Ilium but at Bunarbashi. These ideas were communicated, without acknowledgement, to the Royal Society of Edinburgh by another Frenchman, J. B. Le Chevalier; and the account was translated, with annotations by Andrew Dalzel, the respected Professor of Greek at Edinburgh, as a *Description of the Plain of Troy, translated from the original not yet published* (Edinburgh, 1791), in which Wood's account was condemned. Bryant responded not merely with his *Observations* (Eton, 1795) on Le Chevalier's treatise, but followed this by a work which began an acrimonious controversy lasting for many years, *A Dissertation concerning the War of Troy, and the Expedition of the Grecians as described by Homer. Showing that No Such Expedition Was Ever Undertaken, and that No Such City of Phrygia Existed* (1796). The title explains itself. Naturally Bryant was immediately attacked, both by those who (like himself) had never seen the Troad with their own eyes and by those who brought their first-hand impressions to the problem. The impetuous Gilbert Wakefield hastily produced a pamphlet (*A Letter to Jacob Bryant, Esq.*, 1797) and William Vincent

[1] Walpole, *Memoirs*, pp. 86, 173.

reviewed Bryant's book unfavourably in *The British Critic* (January 1 and March 1, 1799; the reviews were also printed separately as a pamphlet). Meanwhile, James Dallaway in his important and veracious book *Constantinople, Ancient and Modern, with Excursions to the Shores and Islands of the Archipelago and to the Troad*, had written agreeing with Le Chevalier on the topography of Troy; and J. B. S. Morritt of Rokeby, fresh from his adventurous tour in the Levant (1794–6), leaped to Homer's defence in his *Vindication of Homer and of the Ancient Poets and Historians who have recorded the Siege and Fall of Troy* (York, 1798). Bryant replied to all attacks, often with great bitterness of tone, and republished his book in 1799 with corrections and additions. Replies, Vindications, Observations, and further Observations followed one another. New topographers set out to examine the evidence once again. William Francklin, in company with Henry Philip Hope, the brother of the author of *Anastasius*, re-surveyed the site and published his *Remarks and Observations on the Plain of Troy, made during an Excursion in June 1799* (1800), corroborating Morritt's views. In 1804 Sir William Gell produced his folio *Topography of Troy*; Edward Clarke, Dodwell, Leake, and many others during the next few years gave the world the benefit of their observations on the problem.

"These tedious and pedantic productions" are the words used by one of the few modern scholars who have had occasion to mention the series of books and pamphlets which Wood and Bryant provoked.[1] This judgment is unfair. Of course, any entirely obsolete controversy will seem tedious to later generations. But the Troy Problem was an exciting development in Homeric studies in those years; and, so far from being pedantic, the whole movement to relate the Homeric poems to a real environment was the very opposite of pedantry. Pedants did not make the difficult, troublesome, and sometimes dangerous journeys to the Trojan plain. It mattered intensely to many people of the time—and not merely to scholars—whether or not the Homeric environment could be made to fit the actual topography. Suggestions to the contrary provoked a characteristic outburst from Byron, who was not one to waste energy on pedantic controversies and who detested "antiquarian twaddle". To those who declared that it did not really matter whether the tale of Troy was authentic or not, Byron had nothing but scorn.

We *do* care about 'the authenticity of the tale of Troy'. I have stood upon that plain *daily*, for more than a month in 1810; and if any thing diminished my pleasure, it was that the blackguard

[1] M. L. Clarke, *Greek Studies in England, 1700–1830* (Cambridge, 1945), p. 184.

Bryant impugned its veracity. . . . I venerated the grand original as the truth of *history* . . . and of *place*; otherwise it would have given me no delight.[1]

It is this reborn Troy-sentiment—now Homeric, no longer Virgilian—which provides one of the most telling poetical localizations in Byron's poetry:

> The winds are high on Helle's wave,
>   As on that night of stormy water
> When Love, who sent, forgot to save
> The young—the beautiful—the brave—
>   The lonely hope of Sestos' daughter. . . .
>
> The winds are high, and Helle's tide
>   Rolls darkly heaving to the main;
> And Night's descending shadows hide
>   That field with blood bedew'd in vain,
> The desert of old Priam's pride;
>   The tombs, sole relics of his reign,
> All—save immortal dreams that could beguile
> The blind old man of Scio's rocky isle.
>
> Oh! yet—for there my steps have been;
>   These feet have pressed the sacred shore,
> These limbs that buoyant wave hath borne—
> Minstrel! with thee to muse, to mourn,
>   To trace again those fields of yore,
> Believing every hillock green
>   Contains no fabled hero's ashes,
> And that around the undoubted scene
>   Thine own "broad Hellespont" still dashes,
> Be long my lot! and cold were he
> Who there could gaze denying thee.[2]

Nor was his experience of the Troad forgotten when Byron was writing *Don Juan*:

> High barrows, without marble, or a name,
>   A vast, untill'd, and mountain-skirted plain,
> And Ida in the distance, still the same,
>   And old Scamander (if 'tis he), remain;

---

[1] Diary, January 11, 1821; *Letters and Journals*, ed. Prothero, v, 165–6.
[2] *The Bride of Abydos*, canto the second, i–iii, 483–7, 502–20.

The situation seems still form'd for fame—
A hundred thousand men might fight again
With ease; but where I sought for Ilion's walls,
The quiet sheep feeds, and the tortoise crawls. . . .

(IV, lxxvii)

Although Troy provided the most interesting problem of topography, the whole of Greek studies, both history and poetry, was being enlightened by the detailed inquiries into the country of Greece and the remains of antiquity which were conducted during the dozen years before the arrival of Byron in Greece. By the end of the eighteenth century it was still possible for those who concerned themselves with classical geography to present their ideas to the world without having seen the places they were writing about. Thus, Jacob Bryant evolved his ideas about the topography of Troy without any personal experience; and one of his opponents, Thomas Falconer, later to be celebrated as a student of Strabo, produced *Remarks on some Passages in Mr. Bryant's Publications respecting the War of Troy* (1799), being equally inexperienced. Occasionally a brilliant guess might be made by an untravelled scholar, as, for example, when Arthur Browne revealed the situation of the Vale of Tempe in his *Miscellaneous Sketches, or Hints for Essays* (2 vols., 1798). But on the whole the time had passed when the learned could write about the geography and topography of Greece as if it were a place built to music, therefore never built at all, and therefore built for ever; and it was now fully appreciated that the country itself must be investigated for the light it might be expected to throw on the history and literature of the ancients.

The most ardent and assiduous of those who came to Greece in these years left his bones in Athens. Among all the Englishmen in Greece none seems to have caught the imagination of the learned world like the unfortunate and all-accomplished Tweddell. His was a name (it is accented on the first syllable) which once, whatever it may sound like now, was associated with every pathos and every grace. John Tweddell, fellow of Trinity College, Cambridge, having been crossed in love,[1] set out on his European travels in September 1795, at the age of twenty-six. He traversed the north of Europe and parts of the Near East, and arrived in Greece. "Athens especially, is my great object", he wrote in a letter from Tenos in December 1798. "I promise you that those who come after me shall have nothing to glean. Not only every temple, but every stone,

[1] Some love-letters are printed by "George Paston" in *Little Memoirs of the Eighteenth Century* (1901).

and every inscription, shall be copied with the most scrupulous fidelity."[1] He had engaged the French artist Preaux, whom he had met in Constantinople, to accompany him through Greece as his draughtsman and artist. They reached Athens early in 1799. Tweddell was there for four months, diligently pursuing his researches. He died on July 25th 1799, in the arms of the faithful Fauvel, in the house of Spiridion Logothete, of a "double tertian fever". Tweddell seems to have been genuinely regretted in Athens. The Turkish commandant of the city wished his funeral to be accompanied by his own guard. He was buried in the Theseum, at his own request—precisely in the middle, because Fauvel hoped to find some traces of Theseus while Tweddell's grave was being dug. The Archbishop of Athens, the Archons, and a great crowd of people, formed the funeral procession; and as it was lowered into the grave, three salvos of musketry saluted his corpse—an unprecedented honour.[2] The arrangements for a monument were a topic of discussion and rivalry among the Englishmen in Athens for several years. When Edward Clarke was there in 1801, he found that the burial had been carelessly made. Fearing foraging animals, he had the coffin re-interred more efficiently; and a lump of Pentelic marble from the Parthenon, left by Elgin's agents, was used for a tombstone. A creditable epitaph in Greek was written by Robert Walpole in 1805 as an inscription, concluding that it was some solace to his friends that Athenian dust was strewn upon this cultivated Briton's head.[3] Although the poem was certainly inscribed on the marble soon afterwards (Edward Clarke, who has preserved it, says so), the tombstone itself appears to have now disappeared. When Byron was in Athens in 1810, he and one of his friends, John Fiott of St. John's, exerted themselves to get something done about Tweddell's grave. Eventually a Latin inscription also was placed in the Theseum. Fragments of this Latin monument are still preserved in the English Church at Athens, whither they have been removed from the Theseum.[4] Many memorial verses were composed in his honour by scholars of both Universities. Among the

[1] *Remains of the late John Tweddell Fellow of Trinity College Cambridge* (1815), p. 268.
[2] Letter from Preaux to Spencer Smythe, *Remains*, p. 395.
[3] Printed in Edward Clarke, *Travels*, iii, 534.
[4] The following can be read:

O H S S   (=Ossa Hic Sita Sunt)
Johannis Tweddell An(gli)
Provincia Northumbria
Canta(bri)giae Literis in
(Thomas de Elgi)n Comes
(Amico Optimo Op)timeq(ue) Merito
(M. C. F.) C.

I adopt the reconstruction of the late William Miller.

prettiest was that of his friend Abraham Moore in 1799. If Tweddell must die, where but in his beloved Athens would he wish to rest? "Happy art thou, if perchance it is permitted to thee to retain any feelings in the grave; for the bones of how many great men rest here! and does not thine own Athens cover thee too?"[1] Yet in spite of the interest and affection Tweddell had aroused, all the papers which he had collected, all his journals and drawings, unaccountably disappeared, after being sent by the British consul in Athens to the ambassador at the Porte. The loss was regarded as a severe one to the cause of learning, and for the next twenty years it provoked an acrimonious controversy. Tweddell's friends demanded some explanation from Elgin, who, however, denied all knowledge and resented the accusations made by Clarke, Thornton, Spencer Smith, and others. The complete loss of all Tweddell's extensive literary labours seemed a cruel blow after his unhappy death; and this, too, encouraged the University Muses to deplore "the exemplary and lamented Tweddell".[2]

Others, however, were more fortunate. William Martin Leake, the most accurate and indefatigable of the old topographers of Greece, was in 1799 sent on a military mission to Constantinople to instruct the Turkish troops in the use of modern artillery; for the Porte was anticipating aggression from the French. It was a time when, as we have seen above, in every province of the Turkish Empire, the English had an advantageous position; and Leake as a topographer (like Elgin as a collector) seized the favourable opportunity and travelled extensively throughout Greece and Asia Minor. In 1802 he was in Athens; and in September that year he sailed with Hamilton from the Piraeus in the boat which was conveying the Parthenon marbles from Athens and which was wrecked off Cythera. In 1809–10 he was British Resident in Yannina, much respected by Ali Pasha. Here Byron met him.[3] He returned to England in 1815 and henceforth devoted himself to the preparation of a series of topographical writings on Greece, which are still of the greatest value to the modern scholarly traveller, for Leake records much that has now been destroyed.

Another serious and voluminous traveller was Edward Daniel Clarke, who, as the travelling tutor to a succession of young noblemen, made extensive journeys in the Levant. He was in Greece in

---

[1] Felix! si tibi forsan inter umbras
Persentiscere fas sit, ossa tecum
Illo marmore quanta conquiescant,
Tuae te quoque quod tegant Athenae! *Remains*, p. 23.
[2] Edward Clarke, *Travels*, iii, 532.
[3] *Childe Harold's Pilgrimage*, ii, note B.

1801–2, collecting coins, ancient manuscripts (of which he secured some great prizes), statues (his colossal "Ceres" now in the Fitz-william Museum was his greatest achievement), pottery, and other antiquities. It is said that, when Clarke published his *Travels* in 1810 and the following years, he made nearly £7,000 from the sale. Greece and the Near East were certainly the subjects of popular interest. Byron rarely spoke with much enthusiasm of his fellow-travellers in the Levant; but a letter to Clarke dated December 15th 1813, is highly complimentary.[1]

The year 1801 was indeed a remarkable one for the English in Greece. In that year William Wilkins began his four years' tour in the Levant, preparing material for his *Antiquities of Magna Graecia* (Cambridge, 1807) and his *Atheniensia, or Remarks on the Topography and Buildings of Athens* (1812). Edward Dodwell arrived in Greece in 1801 and made a second journey in 1805–6. He was a prisoner-of-war in the hands of the French government, and, through the good offices of Le Chevalier, the topographer of Troy, he had been granted leave of absence to travel. Dodwell was a cultivated traveller and an ardent collector of the usual type in those years. It took him some years to get his travel-book ready for the press; it eventually appeared in 1819 as *A Classical and Topographical Tour through Greece*, in two quarto volumes. Sir William Gell accompanied Dodwell from Trieste to Greece in April 1801,[2] and began a great series of topographical surveys, which, but for the fact that he has been somewhat outshone by Leake, would be regarded as a remarkable contribution to classical studies.

> Of Dardan tours let Dilettanti tell,
> I leave topography to classic Gell,

wrote Byron in *English Bards, and Scotch Reviewers* (1809), although his manuscript originally referred to him as "coxcomb".[3] Gell was among the first seriously to study the topography of Ithaca for the sake of its Homeric associations and elucidations. He went to the island, in company with Dodwell, in 1806 and published his *Geography and Antiquities of Ithaca* in 1807, the first attempt to localize the Homeric descriptions. Gell, of course, carried to impossible lengths

---

[1] *Letters and Journals*, ed. Prothero, ii, 308–11; a better text is in *Byron, A Self Portrait; Letters and Diaries*, edited by Peter Quennell (1950), i, 204–5.

[2] Dodwell, *Tour*, i, 2.

[3] 1033–4. In the fifth edition of the poem, Byron, now better acquainted with Greece, again altered the epithet, this time to "rapid Gell", with the note: "Rapid indeed! He topographized and typographized King Priam's dominions in three days!" (*Poetical Works*, ed. E. H. Coleridge, i, 379.)

his identifications of the smallest allusions by the poet to the topography of Odysseus's kingdom. His *Ithaca* and his *Itinerary of Greece* (1810) had the honour of a detailed and skilful review by Byron in *The Monthly Review* for August 1811.[1] From Patras in October 1810 Byron had written to Hobhouse, "I have some idea of purchasing the Island of Ithaca; I suppose you will add me to the Levant lunatics."[2]

Robert Walpole returned from extensive travels, apparently about 1808, and began his collection of papers on the antiquities and modern conditions of Greece and the Greeks which appeared in two parts in 1817 and 1820 (*Memoirs relating to European and Asiatic Turkey; edited from manuscript journals* and *Travels in Various Countries in the East; being a continuation of Memoirs relating to European and Asiatic Turkey*). Most of this impressive collection of essays and journals belongs to the pre-Byronic years. Here were printed papers by many of those Englishmen who had devoted themselves to the study of modern Greece in the early years of the century; the Earl of Aberdeen, John Sibthorp, John Hawkins, W. M. Leake, John Squire, C. R. Cockerell, William Wilkins, Henry Raikes, J. B. S. Morritt, W. G. Browne, William Haygarth, and others. Here, too, appeared a street-plan of contemporary Athens which had been prepared by the industrious and amiable Louis-François-Sébastien Fauvel (1753–1838), the cicerone of every learned traveller to Athens in those years. Fauvel had been taken into his service by Choiseul-Gouffier, the French ambassador, and eventually became consul.[3] He was an eager and skilful excavator (by the standards of the age), and a paper on his work around Athens was printed in Robert Walpole's *Memoirs* in 1817. Among his many talents was some skill in landscape painting, in which he is no inconsiderable figure.[4] Fauvel was Byron's guide to the antiquities of Athens and its neighbourhood, as he was for many others.

Byron, of course, had his joke against all this devoted inquiry into ancient Greek ruins; and he is reputed to have said, when standing before the Parthenon, "Very like the Mansion House".[5] In some cancelled lines, which originally formed part of his allusion to the celebrated temple of Corinth in *The Siege of Corinth*, he wrote of

---

[1] Reprinted in *Letters and Journals*, ed. Prothero, i, Appendix III (pp. 350 sqq.).

[2] *Op. cit.*, i, 305.

[3] See an account of him by Phillipe Ernest Legrand, "Biographie de Louis-François-Sébastien Fauvel, Antiquaire et Consul", in *Revue Archaeologique*, Ser. 3, XXX and XXXI (1897).

[4] Two of his water-colours were exhibited at Burlington House in the Exhibition of French Landscape Painting 1950 (nos. 432, 442, representing the east front of the Parthenon and the temple of Bassae).

[5] *Recollections of the Table-Talk of Samuel Rogers* (1856), p. 238.

Monuments that the coming age
Leaves to the spoil of the season's rage—
Till Ruin makes the relics scarce,
Then Learning acts her solemn farce,
And, roaming through the marble waste,
Prates of beauty, art, and taste.[1]

But, as a matter of fact, Byron saw all the usual things, and made all the usual expeditions as well as several unusual ones. Moreover, he employed a "famous Bavarian artist taking some views of Athens, etc., etc." for him, as he wrote home to his mother.[2] He was sufficiently proud of his painter (Jacob Linckh) to mention the fact in a note to *Childe Harold's Pilgrimage*: "I was fortunate to engage a very superior German artist, and hope to renew my acquaintance with [Cape Colonna], and many other Levantine scenes, by the arrival of his performances."[3] Nearly all the travellers in Greece took with them their own draughtsman, or employed one of those who had settled in the Levant, whose task it was to record the beauties of Nature and the relics of Antiquity. Fauvel played his part in this pictorial record of Greece, although he was not a professional artist; and many of his representations were engraved in the travel-books of the time. But there were several professionals who made their living by accompanying English gentlemen on their travels in Greece. Most of these were of Italian origin, but there were some Frenchmen and others. Dawkins and Wood had an Italian named Borra. Sir Robert Ainslie, who was ambassador at the Porte 1776 to 1792, employed Luigi Mayer to make drawings, which were subsequently engraved in a splendid series of books which Ainslie sponsored. Gaetano Mercati accompanied Liston on his embassy to the Porte 1793 to 1796; and from his drawings the engravings in Dallaway's book were made.[4] John Sibthorp the botanist, who in 1794 began his second extensive tour of Greece collecting materials for his famous *Flora Graeca* (1806, etc.) had with him one Francis Borone. J. B. S. Morritt in 1794–6 had a Viennese artist (unnamed).[5] Tweddell employed Preaux, who, on Tweddell's death in 1799, was taken over by Thomas Hope of Deepdene.[6] Many of Preaux's drawings were engraved in Clarke's *Travels*. Agostino Aglio was met by Wilkins in Rome in 1801, travelled with him in Greece, and subsequently

---

[1] *Poetical Works*, ed. E. H. Coleridge, iii, 470; the lines follow section xviii.
[2] A letter dated January 14th 1811; *Letters and Journals*, ed. Prothero, i, 309–10.
[3] Note 6 to Canto ii (*Poetical Works*, ed. E. H. Coleridge, ii, 170).
[4] *Constantinople*, Advertisement, p. xii.
[5] Some feeble drawings are reproduced in Morritt's *Letters* (1914).
[6] *Remains*, pp. 402, 440.

came to England to help Wilkins in the production of his *Magna Graecia* (1807), in which the illustrations were executed in aquatint by Aglio. A Neapolitan draughtsman, Lusieri, was employed by Elgin and Hamilton in Athens after they had failed to enlist the services of Turner for the task; Turner proved to be too expensive. Dodwell was accompanied by Pomardi, who made 600 drawings while in Greece; Dodwell himself made 400.[1]

In 1634, Henry Peacham had praised the Earl of Arundel for transplanting old Greece into England (p. 75 above), but the transplantation really took place in the latter years of the eighteenth century and the early years of the nineteenth century. This eager exploring, excavating, transcribing, depicting, and collecting was fully developed before Byron went to Greece; and it forms the background, and the explanation, of many of his most characteristic utterances and attitudes while he was there. The revival of the Greek nation was taking place at a time when ancient Greece had become, more than it had ever been before, vividly resurrected in the imagination of Europe. There were thus many Englishmen in Greece to observe the stirrings of Greek national consciousness, and to form their opinions about the nature of a Greek revival, the possibility of a revolution, and the consequences of political independence. Some of the Englishmen were champions of the modern Greeks; some were sceptical of the Greek capacity for self-government. But both enthusiastic champions and cynical sceptics were expressing their opinions against a background of romantic attitudes to the ancient Greeks, as well as of the social and commercial advances which were being made by the modern Greeks. The opinions of these champions and sceptics we must now investigate.

[1] *Tour*, preface, p. ix.

CHAPTER XI

PROPHETS, SCEPTICS, AND CHAMPIONS OF GREECE

The melancholy reflection of its departed glory succeeded the joy
I at first felt. I looked steadfastly upon it, my remembrance made my
sorrow insupportable, and I burst into tears. No man ever knew the
Greeks who did not admire them above all other people: how then
could I behold their country without lamenting the loss of such
inhabitants?

Thomas Watkins, M.A., in 1788.

Travellers, and especially our own countrymen, fresh from the study
of classical literature, and glowing with those principles of freedom
which form its peculiar merit, excite by their pity the exertions of the
modern Greeks.

F. S. N. Douglas, *An Essay on Certain Points of Resemblance
between the Ancient and Modern Greeks* (1813).

It can hardly be expected that any of us should live to see that interesting time when Greece shall be enabled to resume an independent
place in the great family of Europe.

The Quarterly Review, July 1814.

So far in this book we have come across no trace of a doubt that the
inhabitants of Greece in modern times were other than the descendants of the glorious Hellenes of old. It could be deplored that
the Greeks were unworthy of comparison with the mighty figures
who walked the earth in those days. But mankind is prone to
degeneration, as certain philosophers had explained; and the decay
of Greece, though regrettable, was explicable. It was not altogether
due to their Turkish slavery. The seeds of their decline had been
sown long before that. The Muses had left Greece for Rome (the
poets declared) when Liberty was lost; and even if something of
literary splendour was retained during the centuries that followed
the Roman domination of Greece, at any rate under the Byzantine
empire (whose contemptible existence had been enshrined for all to
read in the greatest historical work of the eighteenth century) any
vestiges of classic splendour had departed. As Sir James Porter,
ambassador at the Porte, wrote in 1768:

Whatever arts and sciences, whatever virtues might have been found in ancient times among the Greek republicans, seem to have been obscured, or totally lost, under their emperors. The present Greeks have not a trace of them remaining.[1]

But (it was pointed out) although the modern Greeks are almost strangers to the virtues, the arts, and the learning of the ancients, yet other less dignified qualities were retained; especially their natural vivacity of temperament. Sir James Porter continues, "Without the least knowledge of Homer, Anacreon, or Theocritus, they abound in poetry, such as it is, love-songs, ballads, and pastorals; they are eternally singing or dancing." Thus the amusements of the ancient Greeks survive, if not their moral and intellectual qualities; and in the amusements of the modern Greeks the attentive observer might discern much of interest, as Lady Wortley Montagu had already shown. The world gradually became convinced that it was here that one should look for the survivals of the Ancients in the Moderns. The Greeks have carefully preserved, added the British ambassador,

the Cretan Lyre, and Pan's pipe, the *septem imparibus calamis*, "seven unequal reeds", and also the pipe of the Arcadian Shepherds. They still use the ancient long dance led by one person, either with women alone, or intermixed with men and women, called by pre-eminence the *Romeika*, or Greek dance. They have also the manly martial Pyrrhic dance, and those more obscene infamous love-dances, accompanied with the *Ionici Motus*, offensive to all modesty and decency.[2]

This sort of evidence for the survival of ancient amusements could support an interesting argument. Since the modern Greeks had preserved so much from antiquity, why had they not preserved everything? The ready answer was: they have tenaciously preserved what they could. Were it not for the intolerable servitude under which they groan, perhaps other ancient qualities would be displayed. Their true nature was permanent; their apparent degradation was accidental. The sympathetic traveller observed countenances worthy of Homer in the streets of the villages. His heart responded to Greek maidens with figures worthy (allowing for the difference of clothing) of the Venus of the Medici. In the last quarter of the eighteenth century, the *continuity* of the Greek nation became the ordinary

[1] *Observations on the Religion, Law, Government, and Manners of the Turks* (2 vols., 1768), ii, 123.
[2] *Op. cit.*, ii, 132, 133.

object of exploration and interest, and provided the background for the eager discussion of the political future of the Greeks.

There is no doubt that, from about 1770 onwards, the influence of a series of French travel-books of a remarkably sentimental kind was very great in establishing opinion about the Greeks. We have good reason to suppose that the writing of Guys, Savary, Sonnini and Choiseul-Gouffier were as widely read as that kind of book ever is, and directly and indirectly disseminated romantic views of the modern Greek nation and therefore romantic suggestions for their revival. It was Pierre Augustin Guys (1722–1801) who began the elaborate comparison of the Ancients and the Moderns, which was to exercise the ingenuity of many writers for the next two generations. His remarkable work, *Voyage Litteraire de la Grèce, ou Lettres sur les Grecs Anciens et Modernes, Avec un Parallèle de leur Moeurs, Par M. Guys, Négociant, De l'Académie de Marseille*, appeared in 1771,[1] that is, when the first Greek uprising was already causing interest throughout Europe. In his "Avertissement" Guys claims that these letters were really written on the site of places seen by the author. This is, for the most part, credible; for they seem genuinely expressive of moods which had their origin in the contemplation of splendours and miseries, imaginary and real. On some occasions Guys makes little advance upon the conventional lamentation for fallen Greece, which we have found during the last few centuries;[2] but he becomes interesting when he occupies himself, not in composing laments for ruined greatness and departed dignity, but in recounting anecdotes, drawn from his own experience, of the love of country which was to be found among the Greeks of his time. "La Grèce moderne, couverte du long voile des esclaves, est une Mère captive, affligée, que ses enfants embrassent avec tendresse, & promettent de ne point abandonner."[3]

Guys, as his title-page promised, set out to make an elaborate parallel between the ancient and modern Greeks. His argument (which was not, of course, new, but had never before been so thoroughly expounded) was that the moderns had preserved many interesting customs from antiquity, unchanged or at least not essentially modified; the moderns help us to understand the ancients, and the ancients help us to understand the moderns. Although Guys

---

[1] 2 tom., Paris; 3rd edition, 1783.

[2] Les Grecs ne conservent plus que le triste souvenir de ce qu'ils ont été, & des traits auxquels on ne peut les méconnoître. Dans les isles de l'Archipel, c'est un vil peuple livré à la misère, à l'ignorance & à la servitude; dans les villes, ce sont des esclaves riches & orgueilleux. A Athènes, un Papas ignorant harangue encore ce peuple, qui a eu des Eschines & des Démosthenes pour Orateurs: *tristes relliquiae Danaum.* (i, 18.)

[3] ii, 184.

thus had a good idea, his defect is that he exaggerates. He credulously seizes upon every resemblance that he can himself discover or that has been related or suggested to him. His thorough-going belief in tradition naturally brought upon him some sceptical criticism. The poet William Haygarth, who was in Greece with Byron, speaks of his "rage for assimilating every thing ancient to modern appearances and customs in Greece".[1] Finlay tartly wrote in his copy of the book (now in the library of the British School of Archaeology, Athens): "Some Antiquary says Guys would have employed his time better looking after the figs and raisins of Smyrna than writing this book." The truth is that the Frankish merchants in Greek lands were rarely so gullible as Guys. They were mostly pro-Turk, rather than pro-Greek, having had quite enough experience of the commercial dexterity of the Greeks to rob them of all philhellenic sympathy. Sentiment about Greece was expressed by the superficial travellers rather than the merchants who had resided amongst the representatives of the ancient Hellenes, and found it very difficult to make money out of them. Guys, like his fellow-merchants, has few illusions about the modern Greek character; he is prepared, however, to explain it in terms of the ancients. He finds the Greeks such as their historians have painted them, and especially Thucydides—artificial, vain, subtle, inconstant, avaricious, lovers of novelty, and little scrupulous in their words.[2] The antiquaries (says Guys) search for the relics of antiquity in famous sites; but the real survivals from ancient times are the men, not the buildings. The men are ruins which are in a much better state of preservation than the cities. His conclusion seems to be that the modern Greeks are entitled to receive the same sort of inquisitive research as ancient monuments. They are in fact a kind of ancient monument; and Guys sets out to describe them in much the same spirit. He is writing, therefore, with something of the method of those who, in more recent times, have sought for remnants of ancient religion in the folk-lore of the Balkans.

Guys's book attracted considerable notice. He sent a copy of the second edition, with a flattering little poem, to Voltaire and received a reply in 1776 from Ferney. Voltaire regrets his lack of travel, not only in Italy but also in Greece. He knows nothing more than the name of Greece, that cultivated place; the Inquisition prevents his making even a tour of Italy; how sad that he will have to die without having seen the places where lived Virgils and Platos!

[1] *Greece, a Poem, in three Parts* (1814), p. 215.
[2] One is reminded of the fact that Venizelos spent his years of exile in translating Thucydides into modern Greek for the benefit of the political education of his countrymen.

Il ne connoissait que le nom
De votre Grèce si polie.
La bigote Inquisition
S'opposait à sa passion
De faire un tour en Italie.
Il disait aux Treize-Cantons:
"Hélas! il faut donc que je meure
Sans avoir connu la demeure
Des Virgiles, & des Platons."

However, concludes Voltaire, by the advantage of reading Guys's book, he can imagine himself in the land of these demi-gods; in fact, he now knows the places much better than if he had made the journey himself; for he sees them through the eyes of Monsieur Guys.

Il les reconnaît beaucoup mieux
Que s'il avait fait le voyage,
Car il les a vus par vos yeux.[1]

In a subsequent edition Guys included two letters (one on Greek dances and one on funerals) by Madame Chénier, the Greek mother of André Chénier. She compliments the author on his work and on his devotion to Greece; the parallel which he has made between the ancient nation which attained to such celebrity and the modern Greeks enslaved and subjugated by a barbarous people is of the greatest justness. Greece, she says, having lost its liberty, cannot have the same ornaments of culture which make the ancient country so admirable; but Nature, who is not a cruel stepmother, has preserved for them their genius; and it can no longer be denied, now that Guys has written his book, that the Greeks, disfigured though they are, are yet still recognizable.[2]

The work of Guys was typical of what was being thought about the Greeks throughout Europe, and it was the most extended treatment of the Harmony of the Ancients and the Moderns. Anecdotes were in circulation which were supposed to reveal the continuity of classical and contemporary national sentiment. The philosopher James Harris (1709–80) gave his readers a typical story of this kind:

... even among the *present Greeks*, in the day of *Servitude*, the remembrance of their *antient* Glory is *not yet* totally extinct.

---

[1] *Œuvres Complètes de Voltaire* (Paris, 1877), x, 450–1. Guys printed the poems in his third edition, iv, 238.

[2] La Nature, qui n'est point marâtre, lui a conservé son genie, & l'on ne peut disconvenir, d'après vous, que les Grecs, tout défigurés qu'ils sont, ne soient encore reconnoissables. (3rd edition, i, 187.)

When the late Mr. *Anson* (*Lord Anson's* Brother) was upon his Travels in *the East*, he hired a Vessel, to visit the Isle of *Tenedos*. His Pilot, an *old Greek*, as they were sailing along, said with some satisfaction,—*There 'twas our Fleet lay*. Mr. *Anson* demanded, *What Fleet?*—What Fleet, replied the old man (a little piqued at the Question)—WHY OUR GRECIAN FLEET AT THE SIEGE OF TROY.[1]

This sort of experience could give an exquisite pleasure to the classical traveller; and it still does so nowadays. But there is no need to be impressed; the shrewd Greek pilot had picked up the remark from one foreign traveller, and repeated the information for the benefit of the next—a tiresome practice which, in truth, makes any reliance upon Greek *traditions* impossible,[2] and any conclusions from the stories collected by Guys and others unwarranted. Whether the stories were true or false is hardly worth deciding. What is interesting is that the world was now prepared to believe that sort of thing about the modern Greeks.

Choiseul-Gouffier was a much more distinguished person than Guys, and his *Voyage Pittoresque de la Grèce*, the first volume of which was printed in folio at Paris in 1782,[3] was one of the most splendid books that have been published about Greece. It does not rival the publications of the Society of Dilettanti as regards scholarship, accuracy, or good sense. But it was probably more attractive to the ordinary rich collector of books, who would not be aware how hollow were some of its pretensions. Choiseul-Gouffier was in Greece in 1776, that is, shortly after the first national uprising; and his consideration of the hopes, and the duties, of the Greeks is written very much under the influence of that stirring event. On the title-page of his book, Choiseul-Gouffier offers a lively emblematic vignette. Greece, a gracious lady in semi-oriental robes, has her arms chained. Around her are funerary monuments to the great men of Antiquity, who were devoted to the Liberty of Greece—Lycurgus, Miltiades, Themistocles, and the rest. On a stele is

[1] *Philological Inquiries* (1781), pp. 320–1. Harris adds, "This story was told *the Author* by *Mr. Anson himself*".

[2] Travelling through Arcadia, on the track to the remote temple of Bassae, I was asked by a lonely shepherd, "Are you going to Apollo?" It was gratifying, it was delightful, to recognize in the mouth of this indigenous inhabitant, the ancient idiom, used in addressing one on his way to the temple of the god. Calmer consideration, however, made one wonder from what passing foreigner the shepherd had picked it up. This illustrates the defect of the earlier study of the survival of ancient "traditions" in a country so fascinating to erudite travellers and inhabited by a nation so quick-witted as the Greeks.

[3] A second volume of the work appeared in 1809 and a third (really the second part of vol. ii) in 1822. It was re-edited, with augmentations, 4 vols., Paris, 1842. These later volumes are not to our purpose.

inscribed the epitaph by Simonides on those who fell at Thermopylae. Greece seems to be evoking the *manes* of these great men; and
on a neighbouring rock are inscribed words summoning an avenger,
EXORIARE ALIQUIS (the Latin—Dido's prophecy of Hannibal—perhaps
strikes a somewhat barbarous note in the composition). There are
other ominous emblems in Choiseul-Gouffier's splendid volume.
At the head of the first chapter Pallas Athene, waving the *bonnet
rouge* (it appears to be) on the point of her spear, seems to be arousing
the Greeks, who rush forward breaking their chains. Behind her
march the serried ranks of the Russian army with fixed bayonets.
In the foreground, along with military trophies, lies a plan of the
town of Coron.

In spite of the enthusiasm which the author feels for the classic
land, there succeeds a more dolorous sentiment, caused by the
excessive contempt and humiliation into which the descendants of
men so celebrated have fallen. In the midst of the degradation before
his eyes, he seeks to disentangle some hereditary traits of the character
of the Greeks, as one seeks the imprint of an ancient medal beneath
the rust which covers it and is devouring it. He analyses the gradual
loss of liberty by the Greeks from the time they were conquered by
the Romans; and opines that there is good hope for the future in the
fact that they have never really at heart submitted to the Turks.
They have kept themselves separate, in religion, manners and
customs; and after nearly four centuries they hate their conquerors
as much as they did at first. This long-preserved antagonism has
prevented the Greeks from having degenerated so much as one might
have feared. The cause of the failure in 1770 was lack of unity; if
only we could get the Greeks of the Morea to unite, they would soon
achieve their liberty, "cet object éternel de tous leurs voeux". He
concludes by a touching appeal to the feelings. "If any of my
readers has travelled among the Greeks; if, in living among them
under that beautiful sky and upon that favoured soil, he has felt the
charm attached to the development of their spirit, their character
and their lovable qualities; if he has received from them that ancient
and touching hospitality which was every day offered to me; finally if
he has for a long time borne the weight of that afflicting contrast
between their ancient glory and their present humiliation, he will
cry out, perhaps, with them and with me, Let the avenger arise. . . ."[1]

[1] . . . si quelqu'un de mes Lecteurs a voyagé chez les Grecs, si en vivant parmi
eux sous ce beau Ciel & sur cette terre favorisée, il a senti le charme attaché au
developpement de leur esprit, de leur caractère & de leurs qualités aimables; s'il a
reçu d'eux cette antique & touchante hospitalité qui m'a été offerte tous les jours;
enfin s'il a long-tems porté le poids de ce contraste affligeant de leur ancienne
gloire & de leur humiliation actuelle, il s'écriera peut-être avec eux, avec moi,
Exoriare aliquis. . . . (pp. xv–xvj.)

Choiseul-Gouffier became French ambassador at Constantinople in 1785; and was soon, therefore, at some pains to disown the philhellenic sentiment expressed in his *Voyage Pittoresque* of 1782, especially as the British ambassador (Sir Robert Ainslie) promptly presented a copy of the book to the Grand Vizier to reveal what a danger the Frenchman was.

The new travellers, inspired by "sensibility" and depressed by the picture of administrative decay in the Greek lands and by the great contrast between the present unproductiveness and the fertility of the land as described by ancient authors, had little good to say of the Turks. Oppression and corruption seemed to have reduced Greece to unparalleled poverty; this was not the fault of the Greeks, who were unable to do anything against the system of government. The people, wrote Claude Etienne Savary in 1788,[1] are in despair and "are everywhere ripe for rebellion, and shake the throne with violent concussions. The empire, tottering to its foundations, is on the brink of ruin. Such are the effects of despotism." Sailing from Rhodes, he cannot but lament its destiny; and, as a man of sensibility of the new type, he can utter his lament with more verbosity than his half-articulate predecessors.

> Will those happy days never return, when every polished nation did homage to this island? . . . When science has once ceased to enlighten a country, must it remain for ever obscured by barbarous darkness? No: I would rather wish to believe that the glorious days of Greece will again return, and that a people inimical to despotism, again establishing a wise system of government, will restore its sciences and arts. Such were my reflections as we sailed.

From his observations of life on the island of Casos (which preserved its local independence without much interference from the Turks, none of whom lived on the island), he draws the conclusion that the evil character which is attributed to the modern Greeks is not their own fault; it is solely due to their condition of servitude under the Turks.

> Travellers, who have made observations on the character of the Greeks under the Ottoman yoke, justly reproach them with

---

[1] *Lettres sur la Grèce* (Paris, 1788). He was travelling in 1779, but he was preparing his letters between that date and his death in 1788. This fact doubtless explains a certain amount of mild revolutionary sentiment. An English translation appeared the same year; *Letters on Greece . . . containing travels through Rhodes, Crete, and other islands of the Archipelago: with comparative remarks on their ancient and present state and observations on the government, character, and manners of the Turks and modern Greeks.* From this I quote (p. 103).

hypocrisy, perfidy, and meanness. These vices are not inherent in their nature, but are the consequence of the servitude in which they live. The inhabitants of Casos are also Greeks; but, enlightened, and warmed, by a ray of liberty, they possess industry, sensibility, and integrity.

The consequences of this opinion are obvious. Let all the Greeks be warmed by the rays of liberty, and they will all possess industry, sensibility, and integrity. The Greeks, Savary adds, may have good hopes of a favourable opinion from western Europe, where more and more of the enlightened people were becoming convinced of "the first and most sacred of political truths; that, in general, man is virtuous in proportion as he preserves his liberty and natural rights, and that as he is deprived of these, he becomes vicious and degenerate". This theme runs through the whole of Savary's book. The "deplorable debasement" of the Cretans from their ancient vigour and glory "can only be attributed to the extinction of their liberty"; and since the Turks are entirely devoid of the notion of "liberty", all their actions are given the worst interpretations. "Fraud and force are the two means they employ to accomplish their designs; but" (he adds grimly) "the time is certainly not far distant, when they will be compelled to restore their unjust conquests." The tyranny of the Turkish government must alone be considered as the cause of the complete decay of agriculture in Crete (p. 386); and Savary contemplates for a moment, in his imagination, what the happiness of that island would be, if only it were ruled by a polished nation. Were commerce and agriculture to revive,

> men would multiply without end, in the finest climate in the world; villages and impoverished towns would again become populous cities; again would the arts return to their native country; again would they flourish; and, in a word, the superb island of Crete revive out of her ashes. To produce this extraordinary, this happy change, nothing is necessary, but the encouragement and protection of a wise government.

Savary concludes his book with some strong words against the Turk:

> Let me not be accused of painting the Turks in colours blacker than they deserve. I have travelled through their empire, I have seen the injuries of every kind which they have done to the sciences, the arts, and the human race. . . . At the sight of these melancholy spectacles my heart groans, and is filled with indignation; my

blood boils in my veins, and I would wish to excite all Europe to combine against these Turks, who, descending from the mountains of Armenia, have crushed the nations in their passage, and waded through rivers of blood to the throne of Constantinople. Nor have the beautiful countries they inhabit been able to soften the ferocity of their character.[1]

It is easy to understand how the feelings of hostility towards the Turks and their ways, which were nourished in the sentimental traveller in Greece, were easily combined with a faith in the Greek powers of regeneration. The miso-turk becomes the philhellene.

It is probable that the sentimental and interested philhellenism of some of the French writers did a grave disservice to the cause of Greece, and earned the derision of many Englishmen, especially after the French Revolution. But meanwhile the English had a very fine specimen of the type in Thomas Watkins, who made an eight-months tour of the Levant in 1788. Watkins is otherwise unknown to fame and his account of his travels is completely forgotten;[2] but never before (I believe) had so many tears been shed over the fate of Greece. His excitement is touching, if not exactly infectious.

> When I got up on the morning of our arrival, I beheld the object I most desired to see, I beheld, oh let me write it in Italicks, *The main Land of Greece the Peloponnesus.*[3]

He seizes every opportunity for the exercise of his sensibilities. No historical association of the place he visits fails to stir profound emotions in him.

> It is impossible, my dear sir, for any body who has not experienced the same pleasure as I have in reading the fragments of Sappho, to conceive what I felt on beholding Leucas, the northern promontory of this island, from which that tenth muse . . . *etc.*[4]

We need not continue the quotation, because Byron, a quarter of a century later, did this sort of thing so much better;[5] and, in the

[1] pp. 106, 141, 189, 194–5, 387–8, 406–7.
[2] *Travels through Switzerland, Italy, Sicily, the Greek Islands, to Constantinople, through Part of Greece, Ragusa, and the Dalmation Isles. In a Series of Letters to Pennoyre Watkins, Esq., from Thomas Watkins, M.A., in the Years 1787, 1788, and 1789.* (2 vols., 1792.) A second edition was published in 1794. His letters from Greece are in the second volume.
[3] ii, 666.
[4] In a letter from Zante, July 28, 1788.
[5] *Childe Harold's Pilgrimage*, ii, stanzas 39, 41.

manner of Byron, Watkins constantly links his historical emotions with the lamentable prospect of the country before his eyes.

> As I gazed upon the coast of Elis, not many miles from that sacred place in which the Olympic games, the nurse of Grecian virtue and enterprise, were celebrated, the melancholy reflection of its departed glory succeeded the joy I at first felt. I looked steadfastly upon it, my remembrance made my sorrow insupportable, and I burst into tears. No man ever knew the Greeks who did not admire them above all other people: how then could I behold their country without lamenting the loss of such inhabitants?

He observed the countrywomen of the future Haidée with a favourable eye. On Melos

> the women are in general well-made and beautiful. Their hair is dark, their eyes large, with more languor than expression in them. They are uncommonly full in the bosom, reminding me of Homer's descriptive epithet *bathukolpos* and their loose and airy manner of clothing themselves heightens that voluptuous appearance for which they have ever been distinguished.[1]

The sight of Troy had, for about two thousand years (with a Dark-Age interval), aroused profound feelings. But Watkins was stupefied with emotion when he "at length ascended an easy eminence, from which (oh grand and affecting object!) I looked over the plain, the very plain, which was the scene of Homer's battles. Those who read the Iliad with *enthusiasm*, and those *only*, can conceive *my sensations*. I was for some time motionless. . . ." He climbed Mount Ida and there "read many passages of Homer, descriptive of the sacred spot, and the surrounding scenery—which is divine". He is enchanted by the scenery around Troy; "Yet when I look upon them, I sigh at the melancholy change that has taken place from the former to the present inhabitants of this renowned land." On arriving at Piraeus he kissed the ground, and on catching the first glimpse of Athens, "I stopped and gazed, but was too full to speak, yet thankful to the Supreme Being that he had permitted me to visit the place, which of all others I most desired, but least expected, to behold"; and then went to find the house of the British consul, Mr. Macri, with whom he lodged, and who had three sisters "the most pleasing and amiable Greek women I know". Macri was, of course, the father of Byron's Maid

[1] Watkins, *Travels*, ii, 166–7, 177.

of Athens; it is interesting that the three beautiful aunts of Macri's three beautiful daughters made a great impression upon a susceptible English traveller in Athens a generation before Byron.[1]

Watkins climbed Lycabettus and then "looked over Athens with a mixed sensation of affection and sorrow: of affection . . . [he relates the usual reasons]; and of sorrow, because it is now sunk into barbarism and misery. Is it not surprising that this same Athens, which sacrificed every thing for liberty and the preservation of Greece, which treated with virtuous contempt both the enmity and friendship of a despot, who led millions of troops against it, should now be the property of the Kislaar Agà, a castrated black slave of the Seraglio? Its temples are mouldering to the breath of time, and in another century perhaps, the remains of its beauty will be lost for ever." He left Athens on December 26th 1788 on his way to Patras; and, after climbing the hills to the west, "sat down to take one parting look of the city. I was happy in the reflection *that the general appearance of the country was the same as ever*, but alas! how changed is Athens. I doted over the prospect above an hour—the fleetest hour I ever knew, and . . . I *tore* myself from the happy spot on which I lay, never, never to be forgotten."

It is tempting to linger with Watkins in his emotions over Athens; but let us pass to Sparta, where sterner feelings prevail. His boat coasts along the seaboard of Laconia, and he recalls that this was the region of Sparta: "my mind was all reflection, dwelling upon its former race of men, their laws, their discipline, their abstinence, their patience, their modesty, and their valour". Moreover, he declares, "there is a strong similarity of character" between the ancient and the modern inhabitants of Sparta. Here dwell the "Magnotti", who "are as free and independent as the ancient Spartans . . . still wearing on their heads iron helmets, in which they occasionally boil their black broth". Six of these men came in a boat to sell fish, and he thought that he had never beheld men to such advantage; their aspect and lofty demeanour seemed to tell him that glorious Sparta was their land of birth. These Magnotti, however, "are the only Greeks who resemble their predecessors".[2]

Although Watkins never visited the Maniots, his attitude to that remarkable tribe of Greeks probably represents the culmination of the romantic legend of their virtues and vices. Their reputation had been high for more than two centuries. Already in the time of Pietro della Valle, as is evidenced by a letter of 1614, they were known as

---

[1] ii, 188, 198, 203, 280–1, 316. His letter from Athens is dated December 4th 1788.

[2] ii, 170–2, 313–14, 318.

"a fierce and brave people who, under the dominion of the Turk, keep themselves almost in liberty; and often, for the sake of their liberty, they make war upon the Turks themselves, for they still retain part of their ancient valour".[1] Opinion about them, however, varied; to some they were "famous Pirates by Sea, and Pestilent Robbers by Land";[2] but, on the whole, the favourable interpretation was strong in the eighteenth century. Prince Cantemir declared that the *"Mainottae"* were "the Descendants of the ancient *Lacedaemonians*, who are at this day the bravest People among all the *Greeks*. Though they are not reckoned to have above twelve thousand soldiers, they never were subdued, nor made tributary by the *Turks*: neither could the *Venetians* ever give them law at pleasure."[3] The Earl of Sandwich, who was in Greece in 1738-9, writes with greater sobriety. Yet we can already see the influence of the romantic attitude to these noble exceptions to the degeneration of the Greeks:

> All this part of the country is at present inhabited by the descendants of the ancient Lacedemonians, who still preserve their love of liberty to so great a degree, as never to have debased themselves under the yoke of the Turkish empire; but flying to the mountains, which are almost inaccessible, live in open defiance of that power, which has found means to enslave all the rest of Greece. ... Their poverty makes them guilty of a vice, which probably, were they in a more flourishing condition, they would abhor. They are extremely given to thieving, though they seldom murder but upon an absolute necessity; abstracting this, they are a very tractable people, and endowed with many good qualities, of which the more refined part of the world are destitute.[4]

Choiseul-Gouffier in his *Voyage Pittoresque* of 1782 is even more emphatic, for he there describes the Maniots as "robustes, sobres, invincibles, libres comme au tems de Lycurgue" (p. ix). But the malicious and paradoxical Cornelius de Pauw, in his *Recherches Philosophiques sur les Grecs* (Berlin and Paris, 1787-8), gave a horrifying account of their conduct, accusing them, among other things, of cannibalism ("It is probable, that the Mainots of Laconia have

---

[1] gente feroce e brava che sotto il dominio del Turco, si conserva quasi in libertà; e spesso per la libertà fa guerra agli stessi Turchi, ritenendo ancora parte del valore antico. Let. 1, par. 4; first printed at Rome in 1650 (*Viaggi*, 2 vols., Brighton, 1843, i, 6).

[2] George Wheler in 1675, *A Journey into Greece* (1682), p. 47.

[3] *The History of the Growth and Decay of the Othman Empire* (1734-5), p. 325.

[4] *A Voyage Performed by the late Earl of Sandwich round the Mediterranean in the Years 1738 and 1739. Written by himself* (1799), p. 31.

likewise in their fits of fanatical fury devoured several Mahometans of the Morea . . ."[1]).

J. B. S. Morritt, who journeyed in Greece in 1794–6, thought that he was the first really to penetrate into Mani. Everyone had recounted to him the perils of such a journey, but he was quite undeterred. He first obtained in Kalamata letters of recommendation to powerful Maniots, and then set off for the peninsula. His confidence was justified. He soon wrote home:

If I see any danger of not getting out of it, it is not from banditti, but from the hospitality and goodness of its inhabitants, and we really have thoughts of domiciliating, and staying in Maina. We are in the territory of Sparta, and have found the descendants of the ancient Spartans the terror of all their neighbours, and free in the midst of slavery.

Nearer acquaintance only confirmed him in his belief that here at last were the true representatives of the glorious Hellenes of old:

Though the Turks made a prey of Greece and the Grecian Islands in general, yet it is not commonly known that one little district has always resisted all their efforts. What is still more interesting is that this district is the ancient Laconia, and that the men who have defended their freedom are the descendants of the heroes of Greece, for there is no place where families are less mixed or have gone on for generations more than here.[2]

In these letters Morritt gives a glowing account of the manners of the Maniots and his hospitable reception. The women were beautiful and had all the dignity of the ancient Spartans. He found, in the first house he stayed in, a copy of *Belisarius* and of Rollin's *Ancient History* in Romaic. His host "talked to us a vast deal about ancient Greece, of which he knew the whole history as well or better than us . . . and his eyes sparkled with pleasure when he talked of the ancient Spartans". There are few antiquities remaining in Mani, he reports. But the Ancients "survive here in a nobler manner, since certainly these people retain the spirits and character of Grecians

---

[1] English translation as *Philosophical Dissertations on the Greeks* (2 vols., London, 1793), ii, 303. His view of the modern Greeks is succinctly expressed: "So far from being excited by patriotism, or the love of glory, they are now a burden to the earth, and a disgrace to their ancestors, whose very tombs they neither know nor remember" (i, 70). De Pauw had no personal experience; and he earned the derision of Byron (*Poetical Works*, ed. E. H. Coleridge, ii, 196).

[2] Letter from Kitris (i.e. Kitriais) in Maina, April 18th 1795, in *Letters of J. B. S. Morritt of Rokeby*, ed. C. E. Marindin (1914), pp. 194–5, 198.

more than we had ever seen, and their customs and language are
transmitted with greater purity". He writes flippantly to his sister:

> You were in great danger of losing us, for we were very often
> asked to marry and settle, and think we should have made excellent
> captains of a Mainote band. I have bespoke a very handsome
> Mainote lady's dress. . . . You will look very well in a muslin
> chemise and a blue silk pair of trousers. We will attend Ranelagh
> as Mainotes. . . .[1]

When we study Morritt's route, we can see that he did not, in fact,
penetrate very far south; and he did not reach the Kakivouni; his
route was merely Kitriais, Kardamyli, Itylo, Marathonisi. But it was
an original exploration of an interesting district.

An account of Morritt's visit to the Maniots in 1795 was printed
at the beginning of Robert Walpole's *Memoirs* (1817). Although he
is here writing more solemnly than in his letters to his family,
through this account, too, there blows a breath of enthusiasm and
honest appreciation, in great contrast to the usual sordid accounts
of the relations of Greeks and Turks, and to the facile regrets of more
casual travellers. (We must add, in parenthesis, that Morritt at this
time held Whiggish opinions.) "Their freedom, though turbulent
and ill regulated, produced the effects of freedom; they were active,
industrious, and intelligent. . . . Their independence and their
victories had given them confidence, and they possessed the lofty
mind and attachment to their country which has everywhere distinguished the inhabitants of mountainous and free districts, whether
in Britain, Switzerland, or Greece" (p. 43). But in spite of the
excellence of Morritt's narrative of his adventurous journey, it was
not made available to his immediate contemporaries. It is a matter
for regret that his brief account was not published until more than
twenty years after his visit, and his letters to his family not until
modern times. Therefore, by the end of the eighteenth century,
there was still no authentic information available about the Maniots.
Napoleon introduced still more confusion into the sources of information; for his attitude to the Greeks seems to have been as romantic
and as cynical as that of Catherine of Russia had been. His imagination had been stirred by the travel-books on the Near East; and his
remark about Constantinople ("it is the Empire of the World")
shows in what directions his ambitions were prompting him. In
1797, the collapse of Venice as a political power was followed by the
French occupation of the Ionian Isles. "Be careful", he wrote to the

---

[1] *Op. cit.*, pp. 203, 206, 208.

general whom he sent to arrange the French rule of the Islands, "in issuing your proclamations to make plenty of reference to the Greeks of Athens and Sparta."[1] To arouse the Greeks to rebellion was part of Napoleon's scheme, as it had been part of Catherine's, for an aggressive war against the Turk; and French agents were dispatched to Greece to further this project of his romantic imagination.

Such was the origin of the book about the Maniots which the two Stephanopoli (uncle and nephew) gave to the world. Their exertions were not disinterested and independent, like the adventurous travels of Morritt. The Stephanopoli were tools, and very suitable ones, for Napoleon's plan of giving as much trouble to the Turk as possible. For they were themselves Corsicans of Maniot origin, being descended from the Greeks who left Vitylos in 1675–6 and settled in Corsica.[2] At Milan they were invited to a dinner-party with Napoleon, where Augereau proposed the toast, *Au rétablissement de la République Grecque!*; and later in the evening Napoleon made known his wishes to Dimo; it was a proposition of greater significance than their intended botanizing on the isles of the Levant, although the botanizing was to be continued as camouflage. Said Napoleon:

> ... il est une tâche bien plus importante, bien plus utile que vous pouvez remplir, celle de répandre les semences de la véritable liberté, de rendre les enfans de la Grèce digne de leurs ancêtres et de la grande nation qui vient de briser leur chaînes. ... [3]

We can hear the tones of Volney, Savary and Choiseul-Gouffier behind this uncandid conversation (it need not have been a genuine report, of course). So the Stephanopoli set out for Greece. They carried with them a letter from Napoleon to the Maniots, who were addressed as "worthy descendants of the Spartans, who alone among the ancient Greeks knew the secret of preserving political liberty". They distributed portraits of Napoleon to those Greeks whom they thought particularly meritorious; and informed them that the French general was in politics an Athenian, in valour a Spartan, and as a military strategist a Theban.[4]

The impressions and adventures of the two Corsican Greeks on this mission were allegedly the source of the published account,

[1] J. A. R. Marriott, *The Eastern Question* (1924), pp. 20, 167.
[2] For this colony see G. Blanken, *Les Grecs de Cargèse (Corse)* (Leyden, 1951), tom. i. See also p. 117 above.
[3] *Voyage de Dimo et Nicolo Stephanopoli en Grèce* (1800), i, 71, 72.
[4] "Athénien pour la politique, Spartiate pour la valeur, et Thébain pour la manœuvre militaire" (i, 189).

Voyage de Dimo et Nicolo Stephanopoli en Grèce, pendant les années V et VI, (1797 et 1798 v. st.) D'après deux missions, dont l'une du Gouvernement français, et l'autre du général en chef Buonaparte. . . . A Paris . . . an VIII (1800).[1] This raised great expectations of authenticity. A writer in *The Monthly Review* in 1801 declared that "the publication of travels in Greece, by Greeks, might naturally lead us to hope for an acquisition to letters, and a treat for curiosity". It had long been a legend that the Maniots were genuine representatives of the ancient Spartans, retaining much of their language and original manners; but there was no account of a visit to them in print; now here were the Stephanopoli who, themselves of Maniot origin, seemed to provide a genuine and first-hand narrative of this strange and interesting place and its inhabitants. Moreover their description fully confirmed the stories that were in circulation. In Mani lived a people who had preserved their patriarchal way of life and, consequently, the virtues of the time of Homer. Their inheritance, you see, was not merely Lycurgan. It was Homeric.

It is, on the whole, an unpleasing book; its political tendentiousness obtrudes itself constantly, in a manner reminiscent of some travel-books produced in the twentieth century by obsequious citizens of totalitarian states. The authors were, apparently, gullible to an amazing degree, unparalleled, I think, in any other book about Greece I have mentioned. They relate, for example, how they were shown the basin in which, during an enforced stay upon Cythera, "the ungrateful wife of Menelaus washed, with her own hands, the linen and the tunics of her lover".[2] After all, the Maniots preserved the traditions of Sparta unimpaired.

The *Voyage* of the Stephanopoli has generally been regarded as a source-book by those who have been interested in the Greek nation and in the Eastern Question at this period. Is the book genuine? My opinion, after a comparison with other and unquestionable material, is that the book is largely a fake. On its title-page it is admitted to have been "redigé par un des professeurs du Prytanée", who has been identified as Antoine Sérieys.[3] I consider it to be largely a compilation by some skilled government propaganda-writer in Paris. I do not doubt that the Stephanopoli went to Mani, and that their report to Napoleon's officials, and even their written notes, were used as the basis of the book. But some hack padded out this material with unauthentic conversations and descriptions, political disquisitions which are quite out of character, and an

[1] There was also an edition "à Londres", 1800, i.e. printed in Paris.

[2] "l'ingrate épouse de Ménélas blanchit, de ses propres mains, le linge et les tuniques de son amant" (i, 105).

[3] He produced a *Voyage en Orient* (Paris, 1801), a sickly work.

absurd love-story about the younger Stephanopoli and a Maniot maiden who bade him liberate her country ere he laid claim to her Spartan heart.

The crude ambitions of France, ignoring all the sentiment that French writers had expended upon Greece during the last few decades, is well represented by the negotiations between Napoleon and Alexander of Russia in 1807. On their raft on the River Niemen, they discussed two plans for the dismemberment of the Ottoman empire. The first plan, which left to the Turks the greater part of their Asiatic and some of their European territories, gave Greece, Albania and Crete to France. The second plan was much more uncompromising and was intended to push the Turk beyond the Taurus; it gave to France the Greek mainland, Albania, Crete, the Aegean islands, and Cyprus.

Nevertheless, the English conflict with France was responsible for sending more Englishmen to Greece than ever before. When France and Italy were closed to the young English gentleman, it was natural for him to turn farther afield; the Levant had now become as famous for its classical antiquities as Rome herself, and it was, moreover, the area of stirring events. As a reviewer of Leake's *Researches in Greece* in *The Quarterly Review* in 1814, surveying the English habits of travelling during the last two decades, wrote:

> The exclusion of Englishmen from those parts of the continent which were formerly the chief objects of inquiry to the curious, has of late years induced many of our travellers to direct their attention to a country highly interesting from the wrecks which it contains of ancient grandeur, and from the contrast between its former state of glory and its present degradation. No man is now accounted a traveller, who has not bathed in the Eurotas and tasted the olives of Attica; while, on the other hand, it is an introduction to the best company, and a passport to literary distinction, to be a member of the "Athenian Club", and to have scratched one's name upon a fragment of the Parthenon.[1]

The Englishmen in Constantinople in those years of war with France (1792 onwards) were so numerous that the chargé d'affaires (Spencer

---

[1] *The Quarterly Review* (July 1814), XI, p. 458. Compare F. S. N. Douglas, *An Essay on Certain Points of Resemblance between the Ancient and Modern Greeks*, (1813), pp. 6–7: "The political circumstances of the last twenty years . . . have so entirely excluded us from the greatest part of the continent, that the love of travelling inherent in an Englishman was to be directed in a new channel, and, in consequence, the shores of the Mediterranean, and particularly the regions under our consideration, have been visited by more British subjects during that period than had ever approached them before."

Smith, the husband of Byron's "fair Florence") formed an association called "the Ottoman Club", which was intended to renew acquaintance among them in England. Its members were most of those who played their part in making Greece and its inhabitants better known in England; Sibthorp, Hawkins, Liston, Dallaway, Wilbraham, Morritt, Stockdale, Tweddell, Clarke, and many others.[1] Chateaubriand in 1806 gives his testimony to the presence of the Englishmen in Greece; there were always some of them to be met on the roads of the Peloponnesus. At Mistra there was even a Greek house which called itself "The English Inn", and there the visitor ate roast beef and drank port. Travellers throughout Europe owe a great debt to the English, continued Chateaubriand, for establishing good inns wherever they go; there is now comfort for the traveller at Constantinople and at Athens, and even—in spite of Lycurgus—at Sparta itself.[2]

I have not, however, noticed this "English Inn" mentioned by any other traveller. "Athens is at present infested with English people", wrote Byron in 1810;[3] and his companion Hobhouse confirms his account: "Attica at present swarms with travellers, and several of our fair countrywomen have ascended the rocks of the Acropolis."[4] Already Greece was beginning to collect English eccentrics, still the delight and horror of their race. Byron, it will be remembered, thought of buying the island of Ithaca; "I suppose you will add me to the Levant lunatics", he wrote to Hobhouse. He was offered the plain of Marathon for about nine hundred pounds.[5]

The young Englishmen who were travelling about Greece during those years form an agreeable contrast to the Grand Tourists of the eighteenth century, who were conducted around France and Italy by their bear-leaders. Travel in Greece was still comparatively hard; and it was rewarding. A few years later, when living in Albany, Byron looked back with something like nostalgia upon these vigorous, happy days in Greece (*et in Arcadia ego*):

---

[1] Tweddell, *Remains*, p. 337.

[2] Il y a toujours quelques Anglois sur les chemins du Péloponèse. . . . Il y a même à Misitra une maison grecque qu'on appelle l'*Auberge angloise*: on y mange du roast-beef, et l'on y boit du vin de Porto. Le voyageur a sous ce rapport de grandes obligations aux Anglois: ce sont eux qui ont établi de bonnes auberges dans toute l'Europe . . . à Constantinople, à Athènes, et jusqu'aux portes de Sparte, en dépit de Lycurgue. *Itinéraire de Paris à Jérusalem* . . . (in 1806; published 1811) (*Œuvres Complètes* (Paris, 1836), ii, 238; *Itinéraire*, ed. Emile Malakis (2 vols., Baltimore, 1946), i, 221).

[3] *Letters and Journals*, ed. Prothero, i, 305.

[4] *A Journey through Albania and other Provinces of Turkey in Europe and Asia* (2 vols., 1813), i, 302.

Poetical Works, ed. E. H. Coleridge, ii, 187.

In the year since Jesus died for men,
Eighteen hundred years and ten,
We were a gallant company,
Riding o'er land, and sailing o'er sea.
Oh! but we went merrily!
We forded the river, and clomb the high hill,
Never our steeds for a day stood still;
Whether we lay in the cave or the shed,
Our sleep fell soft on the hardest bed;
Whether we couch'd in our rough capote,
On the rougher plank of our gliding boat,
Or stretch'd on the beach, or our saddles spread
As a pillow beneath the resting head,
Fresh we woke upon the morrow. . . .[1]

Alastor himself in Shelley's poem (whatever his symbolic or allegorical meaning may be) is in some respects a typical traveller of the early nineteenth century, going far beyond the stale Grand Tour in search of deeper experience:

His wandering step
Obedient to high thoughts, has visited
The awful ruins of the days of old:
Athens, and Tyre, and Balbec. . . . (106–9)

From the letters of J. B. S. Morritt, whom we have already quoted on his visit to the Maniots, we can derive a full and agreeable picture of the new kind of traveller who turned to the Levant because the usual tour of Europe was closed to him by the French Wars.[2] Morritt set out early in 1794, immediately after leaving Cambridge, at the age of twenty-one. He had all the advantages that make a good traveller; among them, plenty of money and good spirits. He was young, strenuous, unperturbed by danger real or imaginary; and the account he has left us is not the pretentious efforts of a book-maker to impress the reading public, but the personal letters he wrote to his mother, sister, and other members of his family. We shall not compare him with Byron fifteen years later. But at any rate he has Byronic attributes. He has a similar flippancy in the treatment of the most difficult and even dangerous situations; and like Byron he grew up during the course of his travels. He shows himself to be genuinely appreciative of the scenery of the places he visits, especially that of Mount Athos; he is, of course, educated in Mr. Gilpin's picturesque.

---

[1] *The Siege of Corinth*, opening lines.
[2] *Letters of John B. S. Morritt of Rokeby, descriptive of journeys in Europe and Asia Minor in the years 1794–1796*, edited by C. E. Marindin (1914).

He scribbles a gaily doggerel poem to his sister Anne in a cave on Mount Mycale. He has a pleasant reception in the Islands; he gives balls for the fair Greek ladies; and there is dancing and singing from morning to night. He writes to his sister from Athens (January 18–22, 1795) that he will be very pleased to answer the learned questions of the Archbishop of York (William Markham) "anent Grecian anti-quities, and to give Miss Markham any hints in my power on the varieties of Grecian dress, of which I shall bring a pattern from the Islands. I must observe, however, that the English ladies were very accurate in the shape of it, though the *belles Grecques* are much less exposed" than was the English fashion in imitation. All this is amusing epistolary badinage. But, more seriously, Morritt in the early stages of his travels is little impressed by the prospects of liberty for the Greeks. Travelling between Mount Athos and Salonica he finds that the Greeks have there a good deal of local autonomy, as a kind compensation for their working in the mines. Their power they exercise in a most rascally way; "I assure you the Turks are so much more honourable a race that I believe, if ever this country was in the hands of the Greeks and Russians, it would be hardly livable". You see what a mere vision it is, he declares, to think of seeing the ages of liberty revived in Greece. "Upon my word, but for the Turks I do not believe the country would be fit to be visited. The Greeks would not be able to hinder the corsairs and robbery, would cheat with more impunity, and have no masters more honest than themselves to appeal to."

Morritt seems to have matured in character towards the end of his two years' travel (he was now nearly twenty-three, not twenty-one), and the member of a party which "agreed at Vienna to be as great fools as they possibly could, which those who know our talents will own to be a good deal", ended by expressing great impatience at signs of frivolity among the Greeks. At Pyrgos his host the Aga

was surrounded by Greeks and Zantiots, who laughed, sang, danced, and wrestled as he bid them. Good God! if a free ancient Greek could for one moment be brought to such a scene, unless his fate were very hard in the other world I am sure he would beg to go back again. An old Lacedemonian, on his return from Athens, made a remark, which may very truly be said on leaving Turkey, "that he came from a country where nothing was thought dis-honourable", and this is the character I shall give of the Levant.

Morritt often made the customary contemptuous remarks about the Greeks; but his opinion gradually improved when he began to have experience of those who lived in greater independence of the Turks. They have, he writes "improved in our opinion very much, as independence to a certain degree has made men of them".[1]

But would the Greeks really be improved by independence? Could one feel confident? It was becoming clear to all that the days of the Turks in Europe were numbered; and what would then happen to the Greeks? In 1797 Mrs. Piozzi scribbled in her journal:

> The Mutiny at Sheerness was a horrid Thing: every Nation seems struck in the *vital* part: France loses her Loyalty, Italy its Ecclesiastical Splendour, Holland her Bank of Amsterdam—& we our boasted Navy. Greece will be free soon, the Turks are at length scooping ye Red Apple and covering their Heads with the Peel—What could yt Prediction have meant if it was not the Bonnet Rouge? Their Empire is going—The End is at hand.[2]

The feeling that a crisis in the history of the Greek nation had now approached was widespread before the end of the eighteenth century. What hopes had Europe of seeing a regenerate Greece following the expulsion of the Turk? It was of importance, in view of the anticipated conflict, to form a just estimate of the respective national characters of the Turk and the Greek. But this, observers declared, was not altogether an easy thing to do. Neither "the haughty uncommunicative Turk" nor "the boasting uncandid Greek" was capable, according to the standards of Western Europe, of liberal intercourse with those who sought the truth about them. James Dallaway, who was chaplain at Constantinople in the last decade of the eighteenth century and produced his book, *Constantinople, Ancient and Modern, with Excursions to the Shores and Islands of the Archipelago and to the Troad* in 1797, kept a reasonably balanced view of the problem.

> Of the Greeks, it is usual to make a comparison with their ancestors. As the possessors or the vassals of an empire, under those rulers who encouraged literature, arts, and elegance, or those who have debased the mind by maxims of abject slavery, it is easy to conclude how differently they have been affected. Though in the present age, in some respects, they experience greater toleration than the conquered subjects of any other nation, they have in no

[1] *Op. cit.*, pp. 83, 120–2, 152, 156, 181, 198, 217, 245.
[2] *Thraliana*, ed. K. C. Balderston (Oxford, 1942), ii, 972, note 4 (September 1st 1797).

degree recovered their former energy. The richer Greeks, for that
constitutes the sole distinction, are versatile and intriguing, and,
with very [misprinted "every"] limited exception, only less
ignorant than their masters. The lower ranks have an instinctive
cheerfulness, and are the merriest creatures imaginable, but are
prevaricating, and awake to every advantage.[1]

Like most of his compatriots, Dallaway assumes that he possesses a
detailed knowledge of the physical appearance of the ancient Greeks
—based very largely, it is hardly necessary to add, upon notions
derived from Greco-Roman sculpture (and its imitations), coins,
and such literary references as were found in the Anacreontic
poems.

> The contour of Grecian statues, and the profiles on their medals,
> are still to be seen in the faces of their degenerate successors; and
> there is sometimes even yet a marked resemblance between those
> of heroes, which have been transmitted to us, and the peasant, or
> the mariner. In the islands, especially of Chio, all that symmetry
> of features, and brilliancy of complexion, which inspired the
> poets and heroes of old, still flourishes in a delightful degree.

With this background of delighted recognition of the old in the new,
the philosophical observer readily comes to the conclusion that the
defects of the modern Greeks, including those darker faults of a moral
kind, are to be attributed to the relentless tyranny to which they are
inured, rather than to the genius of the Greek nation, were it free and
uncontrolled. "For by those, at least, who visit them under the
influence of a classical partiality, it will be thought that no people on
earth are more liberally endowed by nature", Dallaway asserts.
It is but Fortune, all is Fortune. Accidents of history alone have
brought the Greeks to their present deplorable condition. Thus,
before the end of the eighteenth century it could be excitedly claimed,
in a tone not of contempt, but of excited anticipation, that the Greeks
were Greeks still: ". . . debased as the modern Greeks are, no one
who has been conversant with them can suppose that, had the
political character and fortune of their nation been propitious,
nature should oppose any prevention to their maintaining their
original excellence."[2]
    An uncompromising champion of the Greeks and their claim to
liberation by Europe—and by Britain in particular—came forward
in the person of William Eton, whose book *A Survey of the Turkish*

[1] pp. 5–6, 21.   [2] pp. 6, 356, 414–15.

Empire was published in 1798.[1] We have the testimony of De Quincey, writing in 1833 that "the once celebrated work of Mr. William Eton" was "a book which attracted a great deal of notice about thirty years ago".[2] Not much is known about Eton,[3] but we learn a certain amount from his book, which was based upon long and intimate experience of the Levant. He spent twenty years abroad, and in 1792 he was in the French service as an interpreter, in which capacity he visited Ali Pasha.[4] It was commonly said that Eton was pro-Russian; and that, owing to "the splendid chimeras of Catherine" which had aroused controversy about the real nature of the modern Greeks, Eton had "described their character with all the feelings of a devoted courtier of that empress; and it is vain to expect a correct estimate of the Greeks from an author, whose every sentence shews his original intention to have been the eulogium of the Russians, and the satire of their enemies".[5] Certainly Eton had spent time at the court of St. Petersburg and had been intimate with Potemkin and other Russian political leaders. His evidence of Russian ambitions against Turkey is valuable because of his very prejudice in favour of Russia.[6]

Be that as it may, Eton provided a seriously argued statement of the necessity of philhellenism. "The expulsion of the Turks from Europe, and the re-establishment of the Greek empire" would be (he declares in the preface to his work) "more the advantage of Britain than even of Russia itself." It would be "an act of justice"; but it would be more than that. For it is quite certain that the Greeks will soon emancipate themselves from the yoke of Turkey; if this happens through the assistance of the French, "we shall *certainly* have an *enemy* in Greece". In his book "there will be found much matter wholly new to the Public, but not to the Directory; for no one was better informed of the state of Greece than citizen (heretofore chevalier de) Truguet, lately minister of the marine department. He was for a long time employed in the Archipelago, under the direction of Mr. de Choiseul-Gouffier."[7]

Eton fully acknowledges the defects of the Grecian character; but, of course, these defects (in so far as the evil reputation of the

---

[1] There was a second edition in 1799 and a French translation by C. Lefebure appeared in the same year.

[2] *Works*, ed. Masson (1897), vii, 289, 293. De Quincey was reviewing Thomas Gordon's *History of the Greek Revolution* (2 vols., 1832) in *Blackwood's Magazine*, April 1833.

[3] He is not in the *Dictionary of National Biography*.

[4] *Survey*, p. 372.

[5] F. S. N. Douglas, *An Essay on Certain Points of Resemblance between the Ancient and Modern Greeks* (1813), pp. 35–6.

[6] See p. 190 above.   [7] *Survey*, pp. viii–x.

Greeks is not due to the calumnies of their mortal enemies, the French) arise from the long humiliation and depression they have endured under the Turks.

> This degradation and servility of their situation has operated for centuries, and has consequently produced an accumulated effect on the mind; but were this weight taken off, the elasticity and vigour of the soul would have wide room for expansion. . . . It is rather astonishing that they have retained so much energy of character, and are not more abased, for like noble coursers they champ the bit, and spurn indignantly the yoke; when once freed from these, they will enter the course of glory.

The Greeks are obviously superior to the Turks in knowledge and in intelligence; "they possess a great degree of genius and invention, and of so lively an imagination, that they cannot tell the same story twice without varying the embellishments of circumstance and diction". They talk "with wonderful volubility and boldness, and no people are such natural orators". (However, another interpretation could be put upon these two Grecian virtues.) They bear the Turkish yoke with impatience, and they "possess a spirit of enterprise, which, however ridiculed by some authors, often prompts them to noble achievements. The ancient empire is fresh in their memory; it is the subject of their popular songs, and they speak of it in common conversation as a recent event." Eton gives the now customary hostile picture of the Phanar, where lives "a race of Greeks who call themselves nobles, and affect to despise those of the islands". He describes their vicious and intriguing nature and their oppressiveness when in office under the Porte. Then, amusingly, the tables are turned on the Phanariots, who claimed to be the most advanced of the Greek nation and to be the true representatives of the oldest Greek traditions; "They are the only part of their nation who have totally relinquished the ancient Grecian spirit." He tries to characterize the various Greeks:

> Those of Macedonia, &c. are robust, courageous, and somewhat ferocious; those of Athens and Attica are still remarkably witty and sharp; all the islanders are lively and gay, fond of singing and dancing to an excess, affable, hospitable, and good natured; in short, they are the best. . . . Albania, Epirus, and in general the mountaineers, are a very warlike, brave people, but very savage. . . .

Like Dallaway, Eton assures us that the moderns even resemble the ancient Greeks in physiognomy:

In general, the people of the islands have grand and noble features. From different faces you may put together, in walking through a market-place, the heads of Apollo and the finest ancient statues.

Greece, cries Eton, "can no longer submit to the Turkish yoke; she pants for emancipation, and already aspires to be ranked among the independent states of Europe".[1] The ardent views of Eton found expression with even greater emphasis in the *Voyage en Grèce et en Turquie*, of Sonnini de Manoncourt (1751–1812). His book appeared in 1801 (Paris, 2 tom.) doubtless prompted by political events, but his journeys in the Levant had taken place in 1777–80.

Equally convincing, authentic, and first-hand information was, however, becoming available which supported quite a different point of view regarding the modern Greeks. The Baron Felix de Beaujour was for some time French consul at Salonica and published his *Tableau du Commerce de la Grèce* in 1800, immediately translated into English as *A View of the Commerce of Greece* (London, 1800). Beaujour was responsible for some lively sneers. Greece, he tells us, has returned to its heroic age; its inhabitants are only shepherds and brigands; unfortunately for us, however, there is no Hercules and no Theseus.[2] Those merchants, and their consuls, who were actively engaged in trade in the Levant were quite unable to share any romantic notions about the modern Greeks. Beaujour bluntly wrote that they were the moral pests of commerce; his soul was sickened at being obliged to become familiar with their profound immorality. In their commercial dealings, they are bold in their enterprises, persuasive in their discourses, and seductive by their promises. Nevertheless, in spite of this blackening evidence, Beaujour testifies to the new spirit which had arisen among the Greeks and to their now fully awakened patriotism: the modern Greek, he says, regards Greece as his own country, and thinks of the Turk as a troublesome but temporary guest.[3]

Beaujour was writing, so far as I can judge, quite independently of Eton, although his miso-hellenic sentiments form an effective contrast to Eton's enthusiasm. In 1807, Thomas Thornton published a weighty work in two volumes, *The Present State of Turkey*, which

---

[1] *Op. cit.*, pp. 334, 339–46.

[2] La Grèce est revenue à ses temps heroïques. On n'y rencontre plus que des bergers et des brigands; et par malheur pour nous, il ne naît plus d'*Hercule* ni de *Thésée*. (*Tableau* i, 135.)

[3] *Op. cit.*, ii, 209, 213, 223; ". . . regarde la Grèce comme sa *patrie propre*, et le Turc comme un *hôte incommode et passager*".

was written, as he declared on his title-page, "from observations made during a residence of fifteen years in Constantinople and the Turkish provinces". It is a valuable contemporary study of the situation in the Levant, severely attacking the philhellenism of Eton; for Thornton writes in favour of the Turks, and protests against the abuse which they have suffered in England during those years owing to their alliance with, and dependence upon, France. He argues with calm emphasis against the notion that the modern Greeks are likely to display the virtues of their alleged ancestors. After ten centuries of Byzantine torpor (the authority is, of course, Gibbon) the Greeks have since lain "through the long space of three hundred and fifty years, lost even to the love of liberty or the faculty of employing it; can such men suddenly recover from the stupor of so tremendous a fall, and emulate the virtues of their remote and illustrious ancestors?" If indeed (adds the sceptical Thornton) "they be the descendants of the ancient Greeks. . . . Who are the modern Greeks? and whence did Constantine collect the mixed population of his capital; the herd of dogmatists, and hypocrites, whom ambition had converted to the new religion of the court? Certainly not from the families which have immortalized Attica and Laconia" (ii, 68–9). Thornton writes very much in the spirit which animated the disappointed George Finlay, when forty years later and after the Revolution, he composed his great *History*; and he repeats with approval a remark by a Greek that "his nation in nothing resembled the ancient empire of the Greeks, except in the pride and fanaticism which caused its ruin".

The darkest interpretations of the Greek character were as common as ever, especially among those with no classical prejudices. A respected naval officer, one Captain John Stewart, who had seen a good deal of service in the Eastern Mediterranean, succinctly gave his views in a letter dated November 15th 1807:

> My opinion of the Greeks is, that they are a faithless, sordid, cruel set. I never, if possible, would trust to, or deal with any one of them. Their meanness may indeed be attributed to their fear of the Turks; but I cannot give the latter the credit of causing those other bad qualities, which I hold them to possess.

He coasted along Mani and observed the romantic inhabitants; "they were the most savage-looking animals I ever saw, very dark coloured and ill clad".[1] While the cultivated philhellenes and the shrewd Turcophils disputed, the simple-minded Englishmen in foreign parts thus drew their conclusions from what they were pleased

[1] *The Naval Chronicle*, vol. XXVIII (July 1812), pp. 30, 31.

to call "their own personal observations". Such visitors were (and
they still remain) an influential and unreliable source of current
opinion. From the Prussian J. L. S. Bartholdy, who was in Greece
in 1803 and 1804, we have an amusing anecdote of an Englishman of
this kind who, moreoever, brought pious sentiments to reinforce his
moral condemnation. Bartholdy relates that at Gastouni he heard a
conversation between an Englishman and two Greeks (a monk and
their host, who was the doctor in the place). The two Greeks
complained bitterly of the Turkish yoke which weighed upon their
countrymen. "God", said the Englishman, "has deprived the Greeks
of their freedom because they did not deserve to have it" (*c'est parce
que les Grecs en sont indignes, dit l'Anglais, que Dieu leur a ôté le
bienfait de la liberté*).[1] The Greeks replied that, in that case, the
English deserved their freedom still less, since in their country
there were more than thirty religious sects, of which, evidently, at
least twenty-nine were accursed of God. We need not believe the
second part of this anecdote, which belongs to a well-known type of
continental joke against the English; but the first part has the ring
of truth. I cannot identify this Englishman who displayed insight
into Divine Judgment upon the Greek nation.

From this Prussian Bartholdy we have, indeed, independent and
comparatively disinterested evidence about the attitude of the chief
European nations towards Greece, now perceptibly stirring for her
revolution. The French translator (Auguste du Coudray) in 1807
assures his readers that this is a moment when Greece, along with the
other countries subject to the Turk, occupies more than ever the
attention of Europe; with the classical interest, which is for all time
attached to this country of mighty memories, is nowadays joined the
political interest, which nowadays fixes all eyes upon Greece and her
destiny. Bartholdy declares that the English are the most numerous
of all travellers in Greece and that their numbers are steadily increasing; their education encourages them to go there and prepares them
for the experience better than any other nation. Moreover, by the
Turks they are given preference to all other nations; they enjoy, he
says, at this time (1803–4) a high degree of confidence at the Porte,
and have even been given permission to visit the white slave market,
a thing refused to all the rest of the world. Bartholdy is rather
hostile to the English; he complains of their arrogant conduct
towards the Greek local notables, and, of course condemns the
"incredible barbarity" of Elgin.[2] He gives us some interesting

[1] J. L. S. Bartholdy, *Voyage en Grèce, fait dans les années 1803 et 1804*, traduit
de l'Allemand, Paris, 1807, 2 pts., i, 13.
[2] *Op. cit.*, i, 42, 44.

evidence that the ideas of Korais were beginning to be a powerful influence upon opinion, even in the early years of the nineteenth century. Korais had read a paper in 1803 to the "Société des Observateurs de l'Homme" in Paris, on the subject of the present state of civilization among the Greek nation. The greater part of the second volume of Bartholdy's *Voyage* is, by way of commentary on Korais's discourse, a detailed study of the degenerate condition of the contemporary Greeks. His opinions of those with whom he came into contact are not favourable. His disapproval of the pride and intriguing nature of the Phanariots is usual enough; more interesting is his account of the inconvenience of lodging with the richer Greeks—the insupportable monotony of their conversation, their outrageous pride, the foolish vanity with which they boast of their glorious ancestors (of whom they know neither the names nor the history), the ridiculous affectation they sometimes indulge in imitating European ways of living.[1] Nevertheless, Bartholdy gives a not unsympathetic account of contemporary Greek culture. He describes Greek dances, and accompanies his description with three pieces of music. He knows something of sculpture and painting. His account of Greek poetry even includes a summary of *Erophile*. But he combats the notion that the modern Greeks have any intellectual genius left; he is not of the opinion of those who think that to the lack of a political existence must be attributed the feeble condition of the arts and sciences in Greece, and who conjecture that a reestablishment of the Eastern Empire will be the epoch of their regeneration. He writes sarcastically of those enthusiasts who "see in the least intellectual movement among the modern Greeks a spirit which is about to lead them to the Temple of Genius, and who suppose that, because this people was once great and glorious, as soon as they awake from their long lethargy they will restore themselves with equal rapidity and brilliance". But neither is he among those who regard the Greeks as an exhausted nation, having no hope of regeneration or renaissance. He has great expectations of a new existence for the Greeks, although it is hard to conjecture how and when it will come about. The expulsion of the Turks from Europe will only be the first condition of a Greek revival.[2]

During the fifteen years which preceded the publication of *Childe Harold's Pilgrimage* this controversy was conducted with great eagerness and some acrimony. A certain Englishman named Griffiths, wishing to obtain accurate and unbiased information about manners and prospects in the Levant, travelled as a Greek. It was a great mistake, coolly remarked Thornton, to assume a

[1] *Op. cit.*, ii, 55.   [2] *Op. cit.*, ii, 156–7.

character so little respectable.[1] Dr. William Wittman was included in a British military mission, numbering seventy, which assembled at Constantinople in 1799 under General Frederic Koehler and was intended to encourage and advise the Turks in their campaign against the French in Syria and Egypt. In his *Travels* (London, 1803) Wittman inserted "a very florid panegyric on the modern Greeks", which he attributed to (of all improbable people) Thornton. When Thornton published his book in 1807 he emphatically rejected this conversation as wholly inaccurate.[2] Sir William Gell, the energetic topographer in Greece from 1801 onwards, was in his early years a champion of the rights of the Greeks; but later he retracted. "I was once very enthusiastic in the cause of Greece", he wrote in his *Narrative of a Journey in the Morea* (the journey was made in 1804–6 and his account published in 1823 in order to damp enthusiasm for the revolution); ". . . it is only by knowing well the nation that my opinion is changed." Gell caused some offence by declaring that he knew no lot "which must be so desirable to any Mainote of common sense, if such existed, as that of being suddenly placed under the dominion of Russia".[3]

Byron pertinently and shrewdly summarized the controversy in one of his long notes to *Childe Harold's Pilgrimage*. Fauvel, the consul and antiquary in Athens had frequently declared in Byron's hearing that the Greeks did not deserve to be emancipated, because of their "national and individual depravity". But all the Franks who disparage the Greeks base their opinions, writes Byron, "on much the same grounds that a Turk in England would condemn the nation by wholesale, because he was wronged by his lacquey, and over-charged by his washerwoman". Byron had, of course, read the books on the subject of the modern Greeks and had formed his opinions of the writers: "Eton and Sonnini have led us astray by their pane-gyrics and projects; but, on the other hand, De Pauw and Thornton have debased the Greeks beyond their demerits." He expresses a lively impatience with the self-righteous censoriousness of those who tax the Greeks with perfidy and ingratitude.

Where is the human being that ever conferred a benefit on Greek or Greeks? They are to be grateful to the Turks for their fetters, and to the Franks for their broken promises and lying counsels. They are to be grateful to the artist who engraves their ruins, and to the antiquary who carries them away; to the traveller

[1] *The Present State of Turkey*, i, 85.
[2] *Op. cit.*, ii, 8.   [3] pp. 295, 306.

whose janissary flogs them, and to the scribbler whose journal abuses them. This is the amount of their obligations to foreigners.

Avoiding both animosity and credulity, Byron is prepared to indulge "a reasonable hope of the redemption of a race of men, who, whatever may be the errors of their religion and policy, have been amply punished by three centuries and a half of captivity". He adds, with more characteristic irony, that he is loth to hazard a conclusive opinion on the Greeks, "knowing as I do, that there be now in MS. no less than five tours of the first magnitude, and of the most threatening aspect, all in typographical array, by persons of wit and honour, and regular common-place books".[1]

The most accurate and balanced book about Greece during these years was unquestionably that of Frederick S. N. Douglas (1791–1819), who published *An Essay on Certain Points of Resemblance between the Ancient and Modern Greeks* in 1813; his book enjoyed a second edition in the same year. He followed the usual path of travellers from England during the Napoleonic domination of Europe: Portugal, Spain, Malta, Sicily, the Ionian Isles, Prevesa, Yannina, etc., the route which was very soon to be immortalized by Byron in *Childe Harold's Pilgrimage*. He travelled for two years (1810–12), arriving in Greece in April 1811. Part of the time he was in the company of Frederick North, the eccentric philhellene; in Crete he also travelled with Cockerell and Foster, the architects.

There is no special reason why Douglas's book should not have been forgotten. Yet one cannot help regretting that the best book that was written on modern Greece before the time of the Revolution should so completely have sunk into oblivion.[2] Douglas writes well, and he writes sanely; and his interesting work was much quoted and probably influential among those who concerned themselves with Greece during his generation. It therefore deserves some quotation. Douglas has a clear idea of his purpose in writing the book.

> It cannot surely be deemed useless to exhibit the little that still exists of the most splendid of people, to point out to other nations the causes of their fall, and to canvass the possibility and means of their restoration. The degeneracy of the descendant may be traced to the corruption of his ancestor, and Greece, whence all our brightest instances of excellence are drawn, may still be an example, even in her decay.

[1] *Poetical Works*, ed. E. H. Coleridge, ii, 190, 191, 196.
[2] It is ignored, for example, by the *Cambridge Bibliography of English Literature*; and Douglas only gets into the *Dictionary of National Biography* as a brief addendum to the life of his father Sylvester Douglas (1743–1823).

He is neither cynical nor sentimental. He has sensibility, and he does not fail to express it, as an inevitable background to the consideration of Greece and the Greeks.

> The remembrance of the first Greek sentence I heard upon landing in that beautiful island [Zante] will never be effaced. I doubt whether the *thalassa!* of Xenophon's soldiers was productive of more lively sensations than those I experienced at the first sight of the Morea.

The old lament for the fall of greatness of Grecian cities, which had been expressed for centuries, was transformed by Douglas's pen into something more precise and more humane; for the emotion becomes directed towards the inhabitants, not towards the lumps of stone:

> . . . though I do not pretend to a particular degree of sensibility and enthusiasm, it was impossible to see, without a pang, Corinth, *Olbia Korinthos*, Corinth, the seat of all that was splendid, beautiful, and happy, degraded to a wretched straggling village of two thousand Greeks, whose pale countenances and emaciated figures proved the deadly influence of the atmosphere which surrounded them.

Douglas gives us an attractive picture of one of those whom Byron called "the Levant lunatics":

> It is difficult to fancy a life more attractive than that which has been selected by a countryman of ours among the islands of the Archipelago. A fortune considerable anywhere, but very great in relation to the mode of life which he pursues, has enabled him to give effect to the liberality of his mind by conferring so many benefits upon the people among whom he lives, that they fear him as a king and love him as a father. Having acquired property and houses in the islands to which he is particularly attached, he visits each of them in the season of its peculiar excellence; Santorin affords him grapes, Mycone is the nurse of his sailors, Syra gives him wine; and there are now twelve years that he has never rested without the magic circle of the Cyclades.[1]

This illustrates the spirit in which Douglas writes his book on the theme of the Ancients and the Moderns. Whoever, he says, has

[1] pp. 3, 9, 18, 21.

viewed Greece "in the tints of a Mediterranean spring, will agree with me in attributing much of the Grecian genius to the influence of scenery and climate". He acknowledges his debt to Guys, justly describing that book as "amusing though in many cases fanciful". But, in reality, Douglas writes in a mood entirely different from Guys, for he knows that "the Greek blood in the greater part of the peninsula is now so corrupted by intercourse with foreigners, that we may be rather surprised in finding so many of its ancient characteristics than disappointed at not discovering them all". Douglas has, on the whole, a fairly favourable view of contemporary Greek culture, declaring that "the purity of diction, the extent of learning, and the knowledge of the world, that distinguish its society, make Joannina the Athens of modern Greece". He condemns the *Erotocritos*, rather oddly, as "a vapid pastoral"; but he fully appreciates the importance of Korais, whose "merits are enthusiastically extolled by his countrymen", so that (he continues) "we may fairly expect the restoration of Greece, as much from the writings of Koray, as from the arms of the Mainots or the commerce of Hydra". He declares that he is, naturally, unwilling "to repress in the least degree the exertions of a rising nation, and to chill, by dull and abstract reasoning, the longing for independence, and the hope of a speedy restoration, which hourly increases in the minds of the Greeks". For "the phoenix rising from its flames is the emblem invariably adopted by the Greeks".[1] But he thinks that the Greeks were not yet ready for liberty; they must proceed farther along the path of education and enlightenment before they will be ready for a free existence. This was also the opinion of Korais, from whose writings, indeed, Douglas may well have derived it. The next half-century were to prove that Korais was a shrewd observer of his countrymen.

Douglas was also concerned about the present state of the Greek language, which was increasingly recognized, during those years, as an important relic of antiquity. A few conventional remarks on the degeneration of the Greek tongue from the glories of the past no longer suffice. It is difficult to ascertain how far the earlier travellers troubled to learn Romaic. Their remarks on the subject are vague; and in the absence of positive statements we may perhaps justly conclude that they, for the most part, remained in ignorance of more than a few phrases and common words, content to rely upon Italian, the *lingua franca* of the Levant. This is true even of the more scholarly travellers, although perhaps not all and not the best. The early pilgrim-books had lists of words and useful phrases; but the first widely available account of the state of the language was contained in

[1] pp. 40, 52, 74, 76, 78, 146, 176, 182.

Spon's *Voyage* (1678), where we are given a vocabulary or "Petite Dictionnaire". There were, however, earlier and more complete grammars, notably that of Simon Portius, whose *Grammatica linguae Graecae vulgaris* had appeared in 1638. But by the time of James Dallaway (1797) quite a respectable account of the language, including some of its phonetic peculiarities, can be given; and when Byron arrived in Athens, he settled down seriously to master 'Romaic', and wrote an elaborate appendix to the second canto of *Childe Harold's Pilgrimage* on the modern language, with lists of Greek authors, Rhegas's war song, and extracts from various translations and original works.[1]

The pronunciation of ancient Greek had for long been a subject of controversy. The Greeks from whom the Renaissance humanists learnt the language naturally taught them the pronunciation they were familiar with; that is, they pronounced ancient Greek precisely as if it were modern Greek. Grocyn, who seems to have learnt most of his Greek from Chalcocondylas, and his contemporaries introduced this pronunciation into England and it remained usual until Sir John Cheke and Sir Thomas Smith succeeded in ousting it in favour of what was supposed to be a more authentic phonetic system, corresponding more closely to the orthography. Such was the pronunciation which has prevailed (falling into line with the phonological changes that have taken place in the English language during the last few centuries) in English schools and universities, until more recently an effort to bring the customary pronunciation of ancient Greek into line with linguistic scholarship has led to a change in most teaching institutions.

But who has ever persuaded a Greek that the ancients spoke in a way different from himself? The modern educational system in Greece is based upon inculcating the belief that the only correct way to pronounce the ancient language is to treat the words as if they were modern Greek words. Greek children are taught this as an unquestioned and unquestionable fact. It is a cause of embarrassment to a foreign scholar in Greece; and if he is foolish he may endeavour to talk rationally and persuasively on the problem of the pronunciation of the Greek tongue in fifth-century Athens. He will soon find that discussion of the evidence is regarded as either the ridiculous ignorance of the foreigner, or the insulting disparagement

---

[1] It is unfortunate that in the standard edition of Byron's works this excursus has been omitted as being "remarkable rather for the evidence which it affords of Byron's industry and zeal for acquiring knowledge, than for the value or interest of the subject-matter". (*Poetical Works*, ed. E. H. Coleridge, ii, 208.) Some information is collected by Panos Morphopoulos in "Byron's Translation and Use of Modern Greek Writings" (*Modern Language Notes*, LIV (1939), 317–26).

of the miso-hellene. He will learn, if he is wise, to preserve silence on this subject which touches national pride.[1] The Greek opinion is a very old one and it was widespread in the eighteenth century. There were treatises written by Greeks to prove the authenticity of the modern pronunciation; and among the educated Greeks of Constantinople it was already a matter of national pride. Dallaway informs us in 1797 that "the more learned of the inhabitants of the Fanal strongly contend that, however their language has been debased by the alloy of others, the pronunciation of the remotest times is continued to them, pure and without variation".[2] Commenting on the revival of the Greek language and its apparent purification, Douglas in 1813 prophesied with greater truth than he was ever to know (for he died in 1819, aged twenty-eight) that "in half a century more the language of her ancient poets and historians may again be heard within the walls of Athens; though I fear we shall still have to regret that it is not so easy to revive the genius, the courage, and the love of freedom, as to restore the language through which those virtues were encouraged or inspired".[3]

[1] There are of course linguists in Greece who are free from this delusion and treat phonological history in a scientific manner. The history of the Greek language from the earliest times to the present day by Manoles Triandafillides is a work of which any country might be proud. But Professor Triandafillides was, I believe, trained abroad.

[2] *Constantinople*, p. 400.

[3] *An Essay on Certain Points of Resemblance*, p. 106.

CHAPTER XII

BYRON'S POETICAL INHERITANCE OF PHILHELLENISM

> Perhaps the flood of time now rolls towards Us
> A Signal Hour marked out by pitying Heav'n
> To raise our prostrate Country from its ruins
> And add new lustre to the Grecian name.
>
> Samuel Johnson, *Irene* (an unused fragment).

> The traveller will be struck with the beauty of the prospect over
> "Isles that crown the Ægean deep": but, for an Englishman, [Cape]
> Colonna has yet an additional interest, as the actual spot of Falconer's
> shipwreck. Pallas and Plato are forgotten in the recollection of
> Falconer and Campbell.
>
> *Childe Harold's Pilgrimage*, canto II, note 6.

THE consequence of all this specialized interpretation of Greece, the
numerous travel-books, the speculation about the fate of the Turkish
empire and the future of its subject people, was, generally speaking,
a growing interest in the representatives of the ancient Hellenes.
The casual references to contemporary Greece in eighteenth-century
literature by writers who had no personal experience of the country
and of the people reflect this gradual change. The contrast, and the
comparison, between Ancients and Moderns becomes more precise
as more knowledge becomes available. It was not long before the
comparison, as well as the contrast, became an influential factor in
determining opinion; and, on the whole, increasing knowledge produced increasing sympathy.

Such an increase of sympathy had not reached James Thomson
in his *Liberty, A Poem*, of which the second part was entitled *Greece*,
published separately in 1735. The poet listens to the goddess Liberty,
who gives him a long account of the glories of ancient Greece concluding:

> These were the Wonders that illumin'd GREECE,
> From End to End—Here interrupting warm,
> Where are they now? (I cry'd,) say, GODDESS, where?
> And what the Land they Darling thus of old?

In reply, the goddess begins an emphatic and vituperative discourse regarding contemporary Greece, a country which (it is hardly necessary to say) was quite unknown to Thomson personally; yet that ardent reader of travel-books might have been expected not to darken the picture excessively.

> Sunk! she resum'd, deep in the Kindred Gloom
> Of *Superstition*, and of *Slavery* sunk!
> No Glory now can touch their Hearts, benumb'd
> By loose dejected Sloth, and servile Fear;
> No Science pierce the Darkness of their Minds;
> No nobler Art the quick ambitious Soul
> Of Imitation in their Breast awake.
> Even, to supply the needful Arts of Life,
> Mechanic Toil denies the hopeless Hand.

The poet's archaeological information is hardly adequate:

> Scarce any Trace remaining, Vestige grey,
> Or nodding Column on the desart Shore,
> To point where *Corinth*, or where *Athens* stood.

Both trade and travel are deterred in frightful Greece:

> A faithless Land of Violence, and Death!
> Where Commerce parlies, dubious, on the Shore;
> And his wild Impulse curious Search restrains,
> Afraid to trust th'inhospitable Clime.

Nonsense, cries my reader (interrupting warm). Even Nature, which, on the testimony of Lady Mary Wortley Montagu and Byron, was as wonderful as ever in Greece, even Nature the poet says has deteriorated:

> Neglected Nature fails; in sordid Want
> Sunk, and debas'd, their Beauty beams no more.
> The Sun himself seems angry to regard,
> Of Light unworthy the degenerate Race;
> And fires them oft with pestilential Rays:
> While Earth, blue Poison steaming on the Skies,
> Indignant, shakes them from her troubled Sides.[1]

[1] ll. 391–417.

Such was the turgid hyperbole about Greece that could be offered the reader of poetry in 1735. The next twenty years were to see a remarkable change; and scarcely was Thomson's *Liberty* published when Samuel Johnson began work upon a poem which was perhaps the most curious and unexpected expression of interest in the Greek situation before the middle of the eighteenth century.

Although Johnson himself never travelled much farther south than Paris, his interest in travel-books, travellers, and travelling remained constant throughout his long life, as we can see from his writings and from the records of his conversation preserved by Boswell and others. For Johnson "the grand object of travelling is to see the shores of the Mediterranean. On those shores were the four great Empires of the world; the Assyrian, the Persian, the Grecian, and the Roman. All our religion, almost all our law, almost all our arts, almost all that sets us above savages, has come to us from the shores of the Mediterranean."[1] To go to Italy was the limit of any definite plans he made for travel; but he could at least imagine himself in Greece, inspired by what he called "local emotion"; and it was the plain of Marathon which came into his mind when he wrote that sublime paragraph in *A Journey to the Western Islands of Scotland in 1773*, a passage much admired by his contemporaries.[2]

> To abstract the mind from all local emotion would be impossible, if it were endeavoured, and would be foolish, if it were possible. Whatever withdraws us from the power of our senses, whatever makes the past, the distant, or the future, predominate over the present, advances us in the dignity of thinking beings. Far from me, and from my friends, be such frigid philosophy, as may conduct us indifferent and unmoved over any ground which has been dignified by wisdom, bravery, or virtue. That man is little to be envied, whose patriotism would not gain force upon the plain of *Marathon*, or whose piety would not grow warmer among the ruins of Iona.[3]

On the subject of travelling Johnson is emphatic that there are two objects of rational inquiry, "the Christian world and the Mahometan world. All the rest may be considered as barbarous."[4] Johnson himself was, of course, always interested in the East, especially those lands where (as he once wrote in a Latin poem) the Turk exercised his unjust dominion.[5] He had no hesitation in regarding the

[1] Boswell's *Life*, ed. Birkbeck Hill, iii, 36.   [2] *Op. cit.*, v, 334.
[3] *A Journey to the Western Islands of Scotland in 1773* (1775), "Iona".
[4] Boswell, iv, 199.
[5] Imperium qua Turca exercet iniquum. *Geographia Metrica*, 5. (*The Poems of Samuel Johnson*, ed. D. Nichol Smith and E. L. McAdam, Oxford, 1941, p. 230.)

contemporary Greeks as the descendants of the ancients; and he used his knowledge of the two to illustrate the great changes that can take place in national characteristics over a period of time. He expressed opinions which are almost like those of a modern determinist, when in 1772 (during the Turkish reaction against the first Greek revolution) he said: "there is no permanent national character; it varies according to the circumstances. Alexander the Great swept India; now the Turks sweep Greece."[1] Johnson knew at least one learned Greek, who came to England; this was Nicolaides, nephew of a patriarch of Constantinople.[2] Moreover, when his pension was granted to him in 1762, he said, "Had this happened twenty years ago I should have gone to Constantinople, to learn Arabick, as Pococke did."[3] He warmly praised the Turkish history of Richard Knolles as possessing "all the excellencies that narration can admit",[4] an opinion which Dr. Johnson and the present writer can only justify (against the ridicule of Gibbon) by their prejudice in favour of the unpopular subject-matter.

It was Johnson's reading in Turkish history that provided him with the material for his tragedy *Irene*, which he had begun to write about 1736 and which was produced at Drury Lane in 1749. This curious and justly neglected poem, with which the young Johnson hoped to conquer the literary world of London on his arrival, was based on an incident which he had found in Knolles. The action takes place during the reign of Mahomet II, very soon after the fall of Constantinople. The Grand Vizier at that time was Khalil (Johnson's "Cali"), of the famous family of Djenderelli; shortly after the fall the Sultan had him executed, having reason to suspect him of treasonable dealings with the last Byzantine Emperor.[5]

The story of Mahomet II's love for the fair Grecian Irene and of her tragic death had been put to theatrical use many times before Johnson found it in Knolles.[6] From Bandello the anecdote had passed to the accumulations of stories by Boaiastuau (1559), Belleforest (1564) and Painter (1566), and thence, like many stories of that kind, to the Elizabethan drama; Peele's lost work, "the famous play of the Turkish Mahomet and Hiren the fair Greek" was popular, if we may judge from Pistol's allusion ("Have we not Hiren here?").

---

[1] Boswell, ii, 194. [2] *Op. cit.*, ii, 379.
[3] *Op. cit.*, iv, 28. He means, of course, Edward Pococke (1604–91) who was a Levant Company chaplain 1630–6, not the Richard Pococke (1704–65) whose travels I have mentioned on pp. 152, 173, 175 above.
[4] *The Rambler*, No. 122 (1751). [5] Finlay (1856), pp. 20–1.
[6] The history of the Irene-story has been well studied; see D. Nichol Smith's introduction to Irene in *The Poems of Samuel Johnson* (Oxford, 1941); also "Johnson's 'Irene'" in Bertrand H. Bronson, *Johnson Agonistes & Other Essays* (Cambridge, 1946).

It also found its way into more serious historical compilations, such as the *Turco-Graecia* of Martin Crusius, and so into *The Generall Historie of the Turkes* by Knolles (1603).

The subsequent dramatic treatment of this story provides interesting evidence for us in writing the history of opinion of the Greeks. The events related take place at one of the supreme moments in the history of the Greek nation, the fall of Constantinople; Greeks and Turks are brought together in belligerent opposition for the last time in this phase of their history; and the downfall of the Greeks brought them to that condition of subjection and political insignificance which they were to endure from the fifteenth to the nineteenth centuries. How far do those who re-tell the story of Irene associate the stirring events which surrounded her to the continuity of Greek history and to the historical realities of the reviving Greek nation?

We know nothing of the Elizabethan *Hiren the fair Greek*, nor of the *Irene* by William Drummond of Hawthornden.[1] Gilbert Swinhoe, whose *Tragedy of the unhappy fair Irene* was published in 1658, offers us very little. The play contains a few hints that these Greeks of the last days of the Byzantine empire are essentially the same as the heroes of ancient Hellas. Mahomet tells his "sweet Greek", Irene, the news of fresh rebellions:

> Harsh News, my Love:
> Your unbridled colts of *Greece*, not brooking yoak,
> Act to disquiet my tranquillity and peace,
> And lame the greatness of my dear Enjoyments of thee.
> But it shall not be so; thou'st go with me unto the *Grecian* Empire,
> And there be crown'd the Empress of thy Native Soil.

These honourable intentions (very un-Turkish) are thwarted because (as we are told by one of Mahomet's followers)

> the *Paeloponesian* Lords in general Rendezvous, with a great force, March to indanger his New Conquests.[2]

Such conduct from the despots of the Morea is amusing enough; it is noteworthy, too, that although the name of Irene's betrothed is one Paeologus [*sic*], his servant is called Demosthenes.

There is very little advance in Charles Goring's *Irene; or The Fair Greek: a tragedy* (1708), in which the Greek characters are mainly Byzantine; and hardly more frequently than in Swinhoe's play do

---

[1] Or by a friend of his; see p. 64 above.   [2] pp. 22, 23.

they betray any affinity with the Ancients. Irene, who is described by the Vizier as "the *Grecian* Wonder of the Age", upbraids Mahomet as being

> My Countries Plague! My Faith's inveterate Foe!
> Horrid with Stains of all my slaughter'd Race!

Asked by the Sultan why she is wearing black, Irene replies:

> This annual Debt I to my Country owe,
> My murder'd Parents, and extinguish'd Race.
> This fatal Day the Grecian Empire fell.

Irene's former betrothed, Aratus (described in the *dramatis personae* as "Captive Prince of Corinth" and apparently the heir to the Byzantine empire), inveighs against Pyrrhus, the apostate brother of Irene, as "Eternal Shame of Great *Justinian's* Race". Mahomet bids Irene dress herself in her best, for he designs signal honours for her:

> *Justinian's* Race shall Mount the Ott'man Throne,
> And *Greece* Triumphant Boast an Emp'ress of its own.

Nevertheless, when Irene converses with her lover Aratus (who talks wildly of revenging himself upon Mahomet) she raises the tone somewhat by a hint of Antique Magnanimity:

> A base Revenge *Aratus* will not take,
> Nor act beneath the noble Character
> A *Grecian* Worthy bears.[1]

But the personages of the play are almost entirely envisaged in conventionally theatrical forms; they are merely inhabitants of the world of refined tragedy. The situation becomes slightly more *actuel* in the *Mahomet Second* of Jean Sauvé de la Noue, first acted in Paris in 1739. In this play Irene expresses her hopes that, since she enjoys the Sultan's favour, she can do something to succour "malheureuse Byzance". Her confidante Zamis replies that to free the Greeks from their oppressive yoke would be a magnanimous intention:

> J'approuve avec transport ce dessein magnanime.
> Détournez loin des Grecs le joug qui les opprime.
> Qui le peut mieux que vous? (II, i.)

[1] pp. 6, 12, 14, 26, 30, 40.

There is no reason to suppose that Johnson had any knowledge of the earlier Irene-plays which the piety of modern Johnsonian scholars has resurrected. He shifts the emphasis of the story away from Irene. His action concerns the conspiracy of two Greeks, Leontius and Demetrius, together with the Vizier Cali and a supporter named Abdalla, to murder the Sultan, who is at that time infatuated with his Greek captive, Irene. With Irene is her friend, Aspasia, the betrothed of Demetrius but also, unfortunately for the conspirators, the object of Abdalla's passion. The conspiracy fails, owing to the vigilance of one of the Sultan's followers; Cali is executed; Demetrius and his Aspasia escape; and Irene, who is really guiltless of any treasonable conduct, loses her life owing to the misunderstanding and hasty wrath of the Sultan.

This dramatic plot, which is neither subtle nor well arranged, is given a curious contemporary quality by being converted into the theme of a struggle for Liberty against Tyranny, and, in particular, Grecian liberty against Turkish tyranny:

> . . . the glorious Cause,
> The Cause of Liberty, the Cause of Nations. (I, ii, 8.)

By a strange anachronism the plot is conducted on behalf of the liberty of Greece, where (says Demetrius)

> Now ghastly Desolation
> In Triumph sits upon our shatter'd Spires,
> Now Superstition, Ignorance and Error,
> Usurp our Temples, and profane our Altars. (I, i, 66–9.)

The two Greeks almost became Plutarchan worthies with

> The gloomy Resolution, horrid Greatness,
> And stern Composure of despairing Heroes. (II, vi, 82–3.)

Demetrius and Leontius have a ship, manned by trusty Greeks and concealed nearby; and this will enable the conspirators to escape. Cali says:

> What Passions reign among thy Crew, Leontius?
> Does cheerless Diffidence oppress their Hearts?
> Or sprightly Hope exalt their kindling Spirits?
> Do they with Pain repress the struggling Shout,
> And listen eager to the rising Wind?

Leontius replies:

> All there is Hope, and Gaiety, and Courage,
> No cloudy Doubts, or languishing Delays;
> Ere I could range them on the crowded Deck,
> At once a hundred Voices thunder'd round me,
> And every Voice was Liberty and Greece. (II, iv, 21–30.)

Aspasia encourages her lover to have the purest motives in his assassination of the tyrant:

> Approving Justice smiles upon your Cause,
> And Nature's rights entreat th'asserting Sword.
> Yet when your Hand is lifted to destroy,
> Think—but excuse a Woman's needless Caution,
> Purge well thy mind from ev'ry private Passion,
> Drive Int'rest, Love, and Vengeance from thy Thoughts,
> Fill all thy ardent Breast with *Greece* and Virtue,
> Then strike secure, and Heav'n assist the Blow.
> (IV, i, 2–9.)

Moreover, Demetrius occasionally apologizes for the way in which his love for Aspasia at times interferes with "the cause of Greece":

> Reproach not, Greece, a Lover's fond Delays,
> Nor think thy Cause neglected while I gaze,
> New Force, new Courage, from each Glance I gain.
> (III, xi, 19–21.)

He confesses a little shamefully that, in addition to patriotism, a desire to free Aspasia from her slavery encourages him in his dangerous task:

> His groaning Country claims Leontius' Aid;
> And yet another voice, forgive me *Greece*,
> The pow'rful Voice of Love inflames Demetrius,
> Each ling'ring Hour alarms me for Aspasia. (II, iv, 17–20.)

Further (as had been hinted in the earlier plays) when the Sultan is persuading Irene to apostatize, he flatters her with the suggestion that her influence can ameliorate the lot of the subservient Greek nation:

O seize the Power to bless—Irene's Nod
Shall break the Fetters of the groaning Christian;
Greece, in her lovely Patroness secure,
Shall mourn no more her plunder'd Palaces. (II, vii, 75–8.)

It is in corresponding terms that Irene excuses herself to her friend Aspasia for indulging the Sultan's amorous advances; it is all done for the sake of Greece:

O! did Irene shine the Queen of *Turkey*,
No more should *Greece* lament those Prayers rejected.
Again should golden Splendour grace her Cities,
Again her prostrate Palaces should rise,
Again her Temples sound with holy Musick:
No more should Danger fright, or Want distress
The smiling Widows, and protected Orphans.
(III, viii, 51–7.)

After the conspiracy has failed, Demetrius enters.

Is *Greece* deliver'd? is the Tyrant fall'n?

Aspasia asks; and he replies:

Greece is no more, the prosp'rous Tyrant lives,
Reserv'd for other Lands, the Scourge of Heav'n.
(V, iii, 3–5.)

and she laments,

O *Greece*! renown'd for Science and for Wealth,
Behold thy boasted Honours snatch'd away. (V, iii, 42–3.)

What Johnson has done is to exemplify the conventional "classical" theme of resistance to tyranny in the conflict between the Greeks and the Turks. The scene of the play is set shortly after the middle of the fifteenth century; and there had been little change in the political relations between Greeks and Turks from that time until Johnson's own day. But by anachronism he attributes to Greeks of the fifteenth century feelings of devotion to the Liberty of their country which were, in fact, coming into existence among the Greeks contemporary with Johnson; and which were to be given revolutionary expression before Johnson's death.

It is curious to observe that there is hardly anything of this Greece-and-Liberty theme in the "first draft" (or rather, set of rough notes for the composition of the play) which is bound up with a copy of *Irene* in the British Museum.[1] Most of the details of the plot (the development of the action and the emotions of the persons) are to be found in these notes; and there are drafts and prose versions of many of the speeches; but there are only the barest hints of the many references to Greek liberty and liberation which are in the final version.[2] It seems that at some definite stage in the composition of the play Johnson saw the situation from a new point of view, and changed his dramatic intentions. The chronological relations of the composition of the early notes and the play as we have it are very difficult to decide. How did it come about that Johnson made the change? Was it an accession of new knowledge that made him begin writing more like a philhellenic poet of the nineteenth century than a Drury-Lane tragedian? My guess (though I have not the evidence) is that it was a reading of Prince Demetrius Cantemir's *History of the Growth and Decay of the Othman Empire* (1734) that made him see the conflict of Greeks and Turks in a new light. It seems improbable that an admirer of Richard Knolles and an author of a play on a Turkish theme would have ignored a recent and reputable book that had been written about the Turks by a well-known and picturesque figure of almost contemporary history.

Johnson's extended treatment of the Greece-and-Liberty theme was certainly unusual (I believe it to be unique) in the eighteenth century. Nothing so "prophetic" was to appear in English poetry before the end of the century. Yet it is not to be regarded as merely

---

[1] See Boswell, i, 108–110, for an account of this. The notes have been printed, but unfortunately not in their original order (whatever that may have been), in *The Poems of Samuel Johnson*, ed. D. Nichol Smith and E. L. McAdam (Oxford, 1941), pp. 336–77.

[2] The following are the only hints at the "Greek-and-Liberty" theme, in the forty pages of the notes:

"Mentioning the Miseries and Slavery of the [Greeks]" (p. 351).

"Irene's Smile
Shall break the fetters of the Groaning Christian" (p. 354).

"Vices will have their effect then particularises the faults that brought on the Greek fall" (p. 360).

"Think on Revenge and Glory, Greece and Love" (p. 361), which was used at I, ii, 146 ("Remember Freedom, Glory, *Greece* and Love") with the significant replacement of "Revenge" by "Freedom".

"Ye venerable Ghosts of noble Patriots" (p. 374).

"Greece and Revenge" (p. 375).

"She (Aspasia) relates Abdalla('s) offers of Love, he (Demetrius) informs her (When she expresses her fears of him) that the Greeks are all devoted to him, that if they cannot serve Greece or live secure there they will go into Italy and spread Learning over the West" (p. 376); this was used for IV, i, 34–123.

Another quotation is given at the head of this chapter (p. 247).

eccentric; for many of the eighteenth-century poets remembered Greece, and remembered her plight with tenderness. That lazy poetaster Sneyd Davies wrote a verse-epistle *To his Friend and Neighbour Dr. Thomas Taylor* in 1744 and at least shows that he has been reading the travel-book of George Wheler. For he follows his panegyric of the glories of ancient Greece by an account of the present misery of the country:

> The sad reverse might start a gentle tear.
> Go, search for Athens; her deserted ports
> Enter, a noiseless solitary shore,
> Where commerce crouded the Piraean strand.
> Trace her dark streets, her wall-embarrass'd shrines;
> And pensive wonder, where her glories beam'd.
> Where are her orators, her sages, now?—
> Shatter'd her mould'ring arcs, her tow'rs in dust,—
> But far less ruin'd, than her soul decay'd.
> The stone, inscrib'd to Socrates, debas'd
> To prop a reeling cot.—Minerva's dome
> Possess'd by those, who never kiss'd her shield.
> —Upon the mount where old Musaeus sung,
> Sits the gruff turban'd captain, and exacts
> Harsh tribute!—In the grove, where Plato taught
> His polish'd strain sublime, a stupid Turk
> Is preaching ignorance and Mahomet.[1]

Collins in the *Ode to Pity* appropriately alludes to his favourite Euripides as the poet of pathos; then remembering Otway, he exclaims

> But wherefore need I wander wide
> To old *Ilissus'* distant Side,
>   Deserted Stream, and mute?

The other river of Athens comes to his mind when he conjures Simplicity

> By old *Cephisus* deep,
> Who spread his wavy Sweep
> In warbled Wand'rings round thy green Retreat,
>   On whose enamel'd Side
>   When holy *Freedom* died
> No equal Haunt allur'd thy future Feet.[2]

[1] Printed in Dodsley's *Collection of Poems*, vol. vi (the "new edition" of 1782, p. 160).
[2] *Ode to Simplicity*, 19–24 (*Odes*, 1747).

In his *Newmarket, A Satire* (1751)[1] Thomas Warton expressed
the usual, and now rather trite, enthusiasm for ancient Grecian
culture:

> *Greece!* how I kindle at thy magic Name,
> Feel all thy warmth, and catch the kindred Flame.
> Thy Scenes sublime, and aweful Visions rise,
> In ancient Pride before my musing Eyes.

With Miltonic echoes in his diction, he imagines the scene where
lived the sages he admires; for example:

> lo, where rapt in Beauty's heavenly Dream
> Hoar *Plato* walks his oliv'd *Academe.*

Warton has the customary procession of classical worthies. But
he sets against this glowing picture the present desolation of
Greece:

> Yet, ah! no more the Land of Arts and Arms
> Delights with Wisdom, or with Virtue warms.
> Lo! the stern *Turk*, with more than *Vandal* Rage,
> Has blasted all the Wreaths of ancient Age:
> No more her Groves by Fancy's Feet are trod,
> Each Attic Grace has left the lov'd abode.
> Fall'n is fair *Greece!* by Luxury's pleasing Bane
> Seduc'd, she drags a barbarous foreign Chain.

This is, at least, sympathetic. Perhaps the moral he draws from the
contemplation of fallen Greece is hardly justifiable: his own country
must maintain a high standard of public and private morals lest she
go the way of Greece:

> *Britannia* watch! O trim thy withering Bays,
> Remember thou hast rivall'd *Graecia's* Praise,
> Great Nurse of Works divine! Yet oh! beware
> Lest thou the fate of *Greece*, my Country, share.

More imaginatively and with a poetic skill that made his lines
memorable in eighteenth-century poetry, Gray drew attention to
contemporary Greece in *The Progress of Poesy*, written 1754 and
published in 1757:

[1] Printed in *The Oxford Sausage* (London, 1764), pp. 188–97.

Woods, that wave o'er Delphi's steep,
Isles, that crown th'Egæan deep,
Fields, that cool Ilissus laves,
Or where Mæander's amber waves
In lingering Lab'rinths creep,
How do your tuneful Echo's languish,
Mute, but to the voice of Anguish?
Where each old poetic Mountain
Inspiration breath'd around:
Ev'ry shade and hallow'd Fountain
Murmur'd deep a solemn sound . . . (II, 3.)

The author of *The Fleece* was unlikely to forget that pastoral poetry
had its origin in Greece and that Arcadia was (as our Elizabethan
traveller once said) "famous for shepherds".[1] But John Dyer
informs his readers that things are not what they were in those
favoured climes, among that once-happy people.

Proud tyranny devours their flocks and herds:
Nor bleat of sheep may now, nor sound of pipe,
Soothe the sad plains of once sweet Arcady,
The shepherds' kingdom: dreary solitude
Spreads o'er Hymettus, and the shaggy vale
Of Athens, which, in solemn silence, sheds
Her venerable ruins to the dust.[2]

All these, however, are incidental poetic allusions to the Greece
of modern times; and although at least half a dozen English men and
women had already achieved the writing of verses while actually in
Greece (Henry Teonge, Edward Chishull, Lady Mary Wortley
Montagu, Thomas Lisle, Alexander Drummond, Lord Charlemont
and others), the poet who must be credited with the first elaborate
treatment of modern Greece in English poetry was William Falconer.
His only important work, *The Shipwreck, a Poem in Three Cantos by
a Sailor*, first published in 1762, did much to familiarize the reading
public with those sentiments which Byron was to express with far
greater power half a century later. Falconer was born in 1732 and
spent most of his life at sea; he was one of those self-educated poets
in whom the eighteenth century took special interest. He became the
second mate of a vessel engaged in the Levant trade; and on one
voyage, towards the end of 1750, the ship, intending to proceed from
Alexandria to Venice, was caught in a storm south of the Morea.

[1] See p. 56 above.   [2] *The Fleece: a Poem. In Four Books* (1757), i, 520–6.

Driven far from its course, it was wrecked off Cape Colonna (anciently
and nowadays named Sounion), that treacherous promontory which
has brought many a good ship to ruin. Only Falconer and two others
of the crew escaped with their lives; and they were befriended by some
Greek peasants on the coast. This experience, and the emotions it
aroused, were the materials of his poem. Falconer had, of course,
many limitations as a poet; but his descriptions of what he knew well,
the plight of the sailors in the storm, the agonizing expectancy as the
battered ship approaches the rocks of Cape Colonna, the misery of
the three survivors and their gratitude to the kindly Greek peasants,
these things no artificiality conceals. The poem achieved great
popularity; about a dozen editions were published before 1800, and
it became one of the accepted classics of English poetry, included in
the collections of Anderson, Chalmers, and others. It was much
admired by Campbell, who introduced a famous allusion to it in the
second part of *The Pleasures of Hope* (1799):

> Yes, at the dead of night, by Lonna's steep,
> The seaman's cry was heard along the deep. (149–150.)

Byron knew the poem well; and in one of his notes to *Childe Harold's
Pilgrimage* he wrote:

> In all Attica, if we except Athens itself and Marathon, there is
> no scene more interesting than Cape Colonna. To the antiquary
> and artist, sixteen columns are an inexhaustible source of observa-
> tion and design; to the philosopher, the supposed scene of some of
> Plato's conversations will not be unwelcome; and the traveller will
> be struck with the beauty of the prospect over "Isles that crown
> the Aegean deep": but, for an Englishman, Colonna has yet an
> additional interest, as the actual spot of Falconer's shipwreck.
> Pallas and Plato are forgotten in the recollection of Falconer and
> Campbell.[1]

Falconer was an innovator, and he used his material, the picturesque Greek scene, with full effect. The poem opens in Crete, where
off Candia his ship lies; and the poet and a companion go ashore.
The bright attractiveness of the island is (provided that we accept
the limitations of eighteenth-century diction) strikingly expressed:

> Olive and cedar form'd a grateful shade,
> Where light with gay romantic error stray'd:
> The myrtles here with fond caresses twine;

[1] Canto ii, note 6 (*Poetical Works*, ed. E. H. Coleridge, ii, 169).

> There, rich with nectar melts the pregnant vine:
> And lo! the stream renown'd in classic song,
> Sad Lethe,[1] glides the silent vale along.[2]

His picture of the Greek scene is often glittering and evocative, as in such a couplet as:

> The golden lime and orange there were seen
> On fragrant branches of perpetual green.

But this delight in the lovely aspect of Greece only arouses his pity and indignation at the humiliation of her people, the devastation of her countryside, and the melancholy loss of her ancient glories. The harsh moralistic attitude of James Thomson has given place to a series of sentiments which (if we ignore the British self-congratulation) are little different from those expressed by Byron.

> Eternal Powers! what ruins from afar
> Mark the fell track of desolating War!
> Here Art and Commerce, with auspicious reign,
> Once breath'd sweet influence on the happy plain! . . .
> For wealth, for valor, courted and rever'd,
> What Albion is, fair Candia then appeared.—
> Ah! who the flight of ages can revoke?
> The free-born spirit of her sons is broke:
> They bow to Ottoman's imperious yoke!
> No longer Fame the drooping heart inspires,
> For rude Oppression quench'd its genial fires,
> But still her fields, with golden harvests crown'd,
> Supply the barren shores of Greece around.
> What pale distress afflicts those wretched Isles!
> There Hope ne'er dawns, and Pleasure never smiles.
> The vassal wretch obsequious drags his chain,
> And hears his famish'd babes lament in vain.
> These eyes have seen the dull reluctant soil
> A sev'nth year scorn the weary lab'rer's toil.
> No blooming Venus, on the desart shore,
> Now views, with triumph, captive Gods adore . . .
> Here sullen Beauty sheds a twilight ray
> While Sorrow bids her vernal bloom decay.[3]

---

[1] Lethaeus flows south past Gortyna; this is not the famous Lethe, of course, which is in Portugal.

[2] i, 450–5. I use the edition of 1803. There are many verbal differences in the various editions of the poem.

[3] i, 162–6, 171–7, 192–3, 738–9.

The famous siege of Candia (1669) was comparatively recent history
when Falconer wrote; and it is with interest that the sailor observes
the ruined fortress,

> . . . the shore with mournful prospects, crown'd;
> The rampart torn with many a fatal wound;
> The ruin'd bulwark tottering o'er the strand;
> Bewail the stroke of War's tremendous hand.

Falconer (in the character of Arion, which is the name he assumes,
with some relevance, in the poem) describes himself as having
deliberately sought the eastern Mediterranean on account of his
interest in the remains of ancient civilization:

> Hither he wander'd, anxious to explore
> Antiquities of nations now no more.

But a sailor has little chance of seeing anything more than the shores
of the countries he visits.

> In vain!—for rude Adversity's command,
> Still on the margin of each famous land,
> With unrelenting ire his steps oppos'd.[1]

His ship, the Britannia, affectionately and admiringly described by
the poet, sails from Suda Bay past Rethymno and Cape Maleka,
until Cape Spada is sighted. There are amusing incidents of a
voyage in the eastern Mediterranean (as familiar then as they are
now, when our steamer takes us from island to island in the Aegean):
the water-spout, the "shoal of sportive dolphins", the "troop of
porpoises". But off Cape Spada a storm arises, which drives the ship
out of her course, due north towards "Athens' rocky strand". The
men are helpless; for it becomes impossible to steer the ship, which is
driven before the wind. The captain tells his men that at any rate
there is one danger they need not fear on the coasts of Greece, a
danger which was common enough on the British coast—the men who
wait on land during a storm and murder the shipwrecked sailors for
the sake of plunder. But this, he says, is

> a crime to Greece unknown!
> Such bloodhounds all her circling shores disown;
> Her sons, by barb'rous tyranny opprest,
> Can share affliction with the wretch distrest:
> Their hearts, by cruel fate inur'd to grief,
> Oft to the friendless stranger yield relief.

[1] i, 314–15, 318–20, 438–41.

Clearly Falconer experienced kindly treatment from the Greeks when he was shipwrecked.

The wind shows no sign of abating. By good fortune the ship escapes the rocks of "Falconera's rugged height" (now renamed Gerokounia), where, it is surprising to learn, there was a lighthouse:

> High o'er its summit, thro' the gloom of night,
> The glimm'ring watch-tow'r casts a mournful light.

With great difficulty they steer clear of "the steep St. George" (the little island Hagios Giorgios); greater danger awaits them:

> But now Athenian mountains they descry,
> And o'er the surge Colonna frowns on high;
> Beside the cape's projecting verge is plac'd
> A range of columns, long by time defac'd;
> First planted by devotion to sustain,
> In elder times, Tritonia's sacred fane.

The ship is shattered to pieces on the rocks; and most of the crew are drowned or crushed to death by the breakers against the cliffs. Three wretched survivors reached the shore exhausted. Meanwhile

> A troop of Grecians who inhabit nigh,
> And oft these perils of the deep descry,
> Rous'd by the blustering tempest of the night,
> Anxious had climb'd Colonna's neighb'ring height.

The Greek peasants watch the wreck helpless; and hasten down the cliff to rescue the survivors:

> The generous natives, mov'd with social pain,
> The feeble strangers in their arms sustain;
> With pitying sighs their hapless lot deplore,
> And lead them trembling from the fatal shore.[1]

Falconer's *Shipwreck* has a few powerful moments even for the modern reader when he penetrates the conventional diction and tolerates the frequent feebleness of phrase; and we know that eighteenth-century readers found the work profoundly moving. The popularity of the poem, and the frequent references to it in connection with Greece, make it seem probable that Falconer played his part in awakening the minds of English people to the condition of Greece

[1] ii, 864–9; iii, 121–2, 526–31, 763–6, 915–18.

and to the oppression under which Greeks lived. For the first time in English poetry, contemporary Greece was celebrated at some length by a poet who was familiar with the country and its habitants. In the misery of the approaching disaster the poet's mind turns to the famous places of the land towards whose coasts the ship is being helplessly driven. Several hundred lines in the third canto are devoted to sentimental descriptions of the famous places of Greece; and, it must be confessed, these quasi-Byronic emotions interrupt the narrative of the shipwreck very inappropriately. The poet's admirer, Byron, knew this and wrote:

> In what does the infinite superiority of Falconer's *Shipwreck* over all other shipwrecks consist? in his admirable application of the terms of his art; in a poet-sailor's description of the sailor's fate. These *very terms*, by his application, make the strength and reality of his poem. Why? because he was a poet, and in the hands of a poet *art* will not be found less ornamental than nature. It is precisely in general nature, and in stepping out of his element, that Falconer fails; where he digresses to speak of ancient Greece, and "such branches of learning".[1]

But, however absurd the digressions may be, the difference from previous attempts at this sort of thing in English poetry is that Falconer was actually familiar with the sites (at least, some of them) which he was writing about. We, who know our Byron on these themes, find Falconer tame as a poet of topographical sentiment. But Falconer's originality and his position as Byron's predecessor deserve to be recognized.

First, there is Athens, the home of Socrates and Plato, Solon and Aristides; what of those glories of the past?

> Of all her tow'ring structures, now alone
> Some scatter'd columns stand, with weeds o'ergrown.
> The wandering stranger, near the port, descries
> A milk-white lion of stupendous size;
> Unknown the sculptor; marble is the frame;
> And hence th'adjacent haven drew its name.

Strict veracity compels us to say, however, that although the Piraeus was still called Porto Leone in Falconer's time, the marble lion had long disappeared. It had been taken to Venice by Morosini in 1687;

---

[1] "Letter . . . on the Rev. W. L. Bowles's Strictures on the Life and Writings of Pope", 1821 (*Letters and Journals*, ed. Prothero, v, 551).

and there, with its runic inscription, it remains, outside the Arsenal. Next, Corinth, once so famous for its "gorgeous fabrics";

> But now, in fatal desolation laid,
> Oblivion o'er it draws a dismal shade.

He does not forget that interesting town of medieval, not of classical, origin, where

> further westward, on Morea's land,
> Fair Misitral thy modern turrets stand.

Like most travellers, he associates Mistra with ancient Sparta.

> But ah! how low her free-born spirit now!
> Her abject sons to haughty tyrants bow;
> A false degenerate superstitious race,
> Infest thy region, and thy name disgrace!

Arcadia was once serenely gay:

> Now, sad reverse! oppression's iron hand
> Enslaves her natives, and despoils the land.
> In lawless rapine bred, a sanguine train
> With midnight-ravage scorn th'uncultur'd plain.

Argos and the Argolid plain, once the scene of tragic events, is now "forgotten and unknown":

> Fast by Arcadia stretch these desert plains;
> And o'er the land a gloomy tyrant reigns.

Similarly Ithaca, Delos, Lemnos, Delphi, Parnassus, and so on, are objects of the poet's sentimental reflections; and he struggles to give ornate expression to the old tag *iam seges est ubi Troia fuit*:

> And now, by Time's deep ploughshare harrow'd o'er,
> The seat of sacred Troy is found no more;
> No trace of all her glories now remains!
> But corn and vines enrich her cultur'd plains.[1]

For Byron, as we have seen, the merit of Falconer's poem was such that Cape Colonna acquired a fame from the British poet equal to that bestowed on Greece by her ancient deities and worthies;

[1] iii, 184–9, 196–9, 220–3, 234–7, 261–2, 303–6.

"Pallas and Plato are forgotten, in the recollection of Falconer and Campbell". This hyperbole is altogether consistent with Byron's temperament. It is the associations of a place that primarily give it interest and beauty; not merely natural beauty, but also poetical associations, were the object of the sentimental traveller's search. Byron himself elaborately insisted on the importance of this, in 1821, when his Grecian experiences had had plenty of time to mature in his mind.

> Ask the traveller what strikes him as most poetical—the Parthenon, or the rock on which it stands? The COLUMNS of Cape Colonna, or the Cape itself? The rocks at the foot of it, or the recollection that Falconer's *ship* was bulged upon them? There are a thousand rocks and capes far more picturesque than those of the Acropolis and Cape Sunium in themselves. . . . But it is the "*art*", the columns, the temples, the wrecked vessel, which gives them their antique and modern poetry, and not the spots themselves.[1]

Between the time of Falconer and the publication of *Childe Harold's Pilgrimage*, modern Greece came to play an increasing part in the imagination of Europe, although it was not until after 1790, I believe, that English poets were again writing from personal experience of the country. In the year of the foundation of the Royal Academy of Arts, the poet laureate, William Whitehead, wrote a Birthday Ode (1769) congratulating the King on his patronage of the fine arts. But will there be (the poet asks) no need in future, now that instruction in the arts is available in England, for artists to travel to Italy and Greece?

> —And shall each sacred seat
> The vales of Arno, and the Tuscan stream,
> No more be visited with pilgrim feet?
> No more on sweet Hymettus' summits dream
>   The sons of Albion? or below,
>   Where Illyssus' waters flow,
>   Trace with awe the dear remains
> Of mould'ring urns, and mutilated fanes?

(It would assuredly be deplorable if the sons of Albion ceased to dream on sweet Hymettus' summits.) On the contrary, the studious youth of England will go more than ever to places famous for the monuments of the fine arts,

---

[1] "Letter . . . on the Rev. W. L. Bowles's Strictures on the Life and Writings of Pope", 1821 (*Letters and Journals*, ed. Prothero, v, 546–47).

And rich with spoils from every coast
Return, till Albion learn to boast
An Athens of her own.[1]

The Quaker poet John Scott of Amwell (1730–83) draws a contrast between ancient and modern Greece, but there is little more than poetical clichés in his poem; the glory of the past is followed by the misery of the present:

> But, oh! what darkness intervenes!
> But, oh! beneath, what different scenes!
> What Matron she, to grief resign'd,
> Beside that ruin'd arch reclin'd?
> Her sons, who once so well could wield
> The warrior-spear, the warrior-shield,
> A turban'd Ruffian's scourge constrains
> To toil on desolated plains!——[2]

A similar sympathy, modified by the inevitable reproof that the woes of Greece were due to the decline of military prowess among the Greek youth, was expressed by William Julius Mickle (the translator of the *Lusiad*). Mickle sailed to Portugal in 1779 and there wrote *Almada Hill: An Epistle from Lisbon*, printed at Oxford in 1781, which contains the lines:

> Alas! how waste Ionia's landscapes mourn;
> And thine, O beauteous Greece, amid the towers
> Where dreadful still the Turkish banner lowers;
> Beneath whose gloom, unconscious of the stain
> That dims his soul, the peasant hugs his chain.
> And whence these woes debasing human kind?
> Eunuchs in heart, in polish'd sloth reclin'd,
> Thy sons, degenerate Greece, ignobly bled,
> And fair Byzantium bow'd th'imperial head. (p. 17.)

One of the youthful poems of George Canning, who was later to play such an important role in the resurrection of Greece, seems to link the old and the new: the hopeless lament for fallen greatness, the stinging description of contemporary servility, the hope for the future, all appear here enveloped in the characteristic Byronic

---

[1] *Ode XVIII. For His Majesty's Birth-Day, June 4, 1769.* (Chalmer's English Poets, xvii, 260.) The first meeting of the Academy had taken place towards the end of 1768.
[2] *Ode XVII. After reading Akenside's Poems* (Poetical Works, 1782, p. 242).

sentiment. Canning's poem, *The Slavery of Greece*, is no prophecy of the Revolution. It reads rather like an exercise on a theme, a prize poem on a prescribed topic of contemporary interest. Yet it is hard not to believe that the subject meant something to Canning and that this early rhetorical introduction to the plight of Greece left an impression upon his mind.

> Unrivall'd Greece! thou ever honour'd name,
> Thou nurse of heroes dear to deathless fame!
> Though now to worth, to honour all unknown,
> Thy lustre faded, and thy glories flown;
> Yet still shall Memory, with reverted eye,
> Trace thy past worth, and view thee with a sigh.[1]

This is no advance upon what everyone had been saying about Greece for several centuries. Omitting the customary panegyric on the glory that was Greece, we come to its present condition:

> This was thy state! But oh! how chang'd thy fame,
> And all thy glories fading into shame.
> What? that thy bold, thy freedom-breathing land,
> Should crouch beneath a tyrant's stern command;
> That servitude should bind in galling chain,
> Whom Asia's millions once oppos'd in vain;
> Who could have thought? Who sees without a groan,
> Thy cities mould'ring and thy walls o'erthrown?
> That where once tower'd the stately solemn fane,
> Now moss-grown ruins strew the ravag'd plain;
> And unobserv'd but by the traveller's eye
> Proud vaulted domes in fretted fragments lie;
> And thy fall'n column on the dusty ground,
> Pale ivy throws its sluggish arms around.

This displays an adequate eloquence; and the poetic contrast between the Marathonian virtues of the past and the Levantine servility of the present has something of the spirit of "The Isles of Greece", including the taunting lines:

> The glittering tyranny of Othman's sons,
> The pomp of horror which surrounds their thrones
> Has aw'd their servile spirits into fear;
> Spurn'd by the foot, they tremble and revere.

[1] *Poetical Works, with a biographical memoir of the author* (1823, p. 13).

But Canning, like the sentimental travellers, cannot refrain from paying his tribute; for Greeks a sigh, for Greece a tear!

> Disastrous fate! still tears will fill the eye,
> Still recollection prompt the mournful sigh,
> When to the[1] mind recurs thy former fame,
> And all the horrors of thy present shame.

More remarkable than Canning's poem was a curious work of the Cornishman Richard Polwhele (1760–1838), whose *Grecian Prospects: a Poem, in Two Cantos* was published at Helston in 1799. This relates the ruminations of a bard, Celtic in sensibilities, who wanders over Greece. It is deliberately archaic in language, and it is written in the Spenserian stanza; consequently, it has a strange appearance of familiarity to the reader. Surely we have read this sort of thing before? It is, of course, surprisingly like weaker parts of *Childe Harold's Pilgrimage*, or like stanzas in the first draft of that poem which Byron later had the good sense to cancel. We have to remind ourselves that Polwhele's poem was published thirteen years before its illustrious successor and in a year when Byron was a schoolboy of eleven who had not yet been sent to Harrow.

> From Cambria's wizard hills, a hallow'd bard
>   Travelling o'er Greece, had nurs'd the heroic Muse;
> Each classic isle surveyed with fond regard,
>   And caught, at every step, sublimer views. . . .[2]

This elder brother of Childe Harold sits on a Grecian isle one evening:

> High on a tower, that overtopp'd the trees,
>   His wild harp whispering a congenial sigh,
> He ravish'd inspiration from the breeze,
>   As stretch'd afar, beneath a golden sky,
>   The varied mountains charm'd his wandering eye. . . .

Nature is wonderful here still; and the relics of ancient art inspire the soul. But where are the men? The modern Grecians have

---

[1] Misprinted *thy*, which gives quite a different sense, attributing these sentiments to the Greeks themselves; the word was corrected in the next edition of Canning's poems, Bohn's "Cabinet Edition of the British Poets", 1851, IV, sig. GG2 (p. 2), and there can be little doubt about Canning's meaning.

[2] I quote from the edition of Polwhele's poems in 1806 (London, 3 vols.); there *Grecian Prospects* appears in iii, 68–89.

similar features to those of the ancients. Of what good is the face without the soul?

> . . . the Semblance of the Grecian mien,
> The Grecian face arrests the poet's eye.
> . . . a Homer's head we oft descry
> In many an aged peasant, silver-grey:
>   Yet where, alas! that spirit mantling high,
> That genius flashing an immortal ray,
> That independent soul which spurns despotic sway?

The isles of Greece are beautiful yet, and fertile with orange-groves and citron-bowers, pomegranates and figs.

>   Lo, the poor inhabitant looks coldly round,
> And slights his long hereditary claim
> To nature's liberal gifts, nor heeds his former fame.

> Midst the wide prospect, can the Muse discern
>   One mental feature of the Grecian mould?
> If Macedon still rage, in conflict stern,
>   She rages, in her robbers, uncontroul'd:
>   And free-born Athens, to the despot sold,
> Grovels amidst the intriguing and the base:
>   And in piratic plunder only bold,
> The dark Morea boasts no Spartan trace;
> And half the verd'rous isles embower the assassin race.

His poetic reverie is rudely interrupted by a horrible scream. Some murder is being perpetrated? What a country it is! And the poem ends on a note which seems to discourage philhellenic sentiment.

>   By terror chill'd, the fond enthusiast stood;
> And, as cold shadows o'er the portrait flew,
> Saw, but in glimpses pale, his own ideal View.

Polwhele was untravelled; the pilgrimage of his Cambrian bard was a flight of fancy. But the next English poet of modern Greece had remarkable experience of the country. We have already met Joseph Dacre Carlyle (1759–1804), the scholar who accompanied Elgin as chaplain on his embassy to the Porte in 1799–1801 and who was entrusted with the search for unknown works of Greek literature in the library of the Seraglio. Carlyle was also something of a poet, in the early romantic style; and his *Poems, suggested chiefly by scenes in Asia-Minor, Syria, and Greece* were posthumously published in 1805, together with interesting extracts from his journal. Carlyle gave expression, in by no means contemptible verses, to most of the emotions about Greece and Grecian culture which were of special interest to Englishmen who visited the land. Like Byron, for example, he was one of those who felt incapable of doubts about the authenticity of Homer's narrative when they were actually in the Troad. His poem *On Visiting the Source of the Scamander after having ascended Ida*, illustrated by an appropriate engraving, is interesting as having put into verse some of the feelings of a visitor to Homeric lands who faced up to the current scepticism. Even the Scamander, which still preserves its name in a modified form, and Mount Ida (says the poet) have been doubted:

> Yet hallow'd stream! there are who've shed
> Thine honours o'er a subject rill,
> The chaplet torn from Ida's head
> To bind it on a nameless hill; . . .

But to read Homer is enough to dispel these doubts:

> Oh! mighty master of the lyre,
> By rapture's magic fingers strung,
> Who, who can drink thy strains of fire
> And listen to the critic's tongue?

And appealing to (apparently) the Poetic Genius, he concludes:

> Tell, as thou will'st, the streams to glide,
> The plains to spread, the hills to rise,
> Bid Argive fleets, in myriads ride,
> And Ilium's bulwarks pierce the skies—

> Let me, great Bard, but catch the lay
> Wafted thro' time, on transport's wings,
> And every raptur'd sense shall say,
> *Truth* can but speak as *Homer* sings.[1]

Carlyle visited Athos and was appreciative both of scenery and hospitality. At Batopade (if we can trust the extracts given from his journal of 1801) he was somewhat perturbed by a rowdy group of Albanian pilgrims, obviously Christians from Epirus:

[1] pp. 40, 43–4.

they sung, danced, and drank, and in the intervals of their
amusement fired their guns continually over the windows. What
a strange picture did these fellows exhibit? Most of them were
robbers, and the greatest part of their songs recounted the thievish
exploits which they had accomplished;—their appearance was
more ferocious than any thing I had ever before seen. . . . They
are no doubt very savage, but might they not be still more so, were
the little civilization withdrawn which they derive from the
existence of the monasteries?

Carlyle then versified his ideas, not without feeling. He at least
perceives the debt which Greek nationality owes to the ecclesiastical
institutions.

> Oh! when the hour shall come, as soon it must
>   When Othman's tottering empire prostrate lies,
> When the pale Crescent hides its head in dust,
>   And Moslem splendour sinks no more to rise,
>
> May no reforming fiend of Gallic brood,
>   O'er these sad seats his blasting wings expand. . . .

(Napoleon had, of course, recently effected a thorough reformation
of monastic institutions in Italy.)

> Then shall these seats once more the blessings shed,
>   Again through Greece diffuse her ancient lore—
> Cherish her offspring—raise her drooping head—
>   And Truth revive, and Faith's pure light restore![1]

His poem *On viewing Athens from the Pnyx, by the light of a waning
moon* has an interesting and romantic title, even if it has not much
more. The suggestive scenery is made appropriate to his emotions:
the permanence of Athens even amid its ruins, the transience of the
poet and his friends. His meditations on Athens in its early glory
lead him to think of himself in his eager undergraduate days at
Cambridge (Carlyle was now forty-two):

> Some fond remembrance—some connected thought
>   Hovers around each antiquated stone—
> Each scene retraced with conscious pleasures fraught,
>   And Athens' youth recall'd recalls my own.

[1] pp. 48–9, 53–4.

Apparently he was prevented from journeying into central Greece by dangers from bandits, and he consoled himself by writing a poem, *On being disappointed in a prospect of Parnassus, from the heights betmeen Eleusis and Megara*. Most of this is merely a hymn of gratitude to the poet's muse. But at times he remembers the scene in which he is writing, the enchanting prospect over the Saronic Gulf:

> That island's Salamis—where fame
>   In noontide splendour shone,
> And blaz'd on Greece the deathless name
>   That dawn'd at Marathon—
>
> Touch'd by the Muse, th' heroic train
>   Still in the battle breathes—
> The years roll back, and Greece again
>   Is deck'd in all her wreaths.

The most remarkable of all his poems, however, is merely entitled *Written on the Banks of the Bosphorus*. It is an historical medley of thoughts on the age-long conflict between East and West, Asia and Europe, some hints being taken from Lycophron's *Cassandra*.

> In predatory war
>   The hostile bands engage—
> And Greece alike, and Asia long must share
>   Alternate ravages, alternate rage,
> Till swell'd by mutual wrongs and mutual hate,
>   The poison'd cup boil'd o'er in Ida's vale,
> And Ilium's sorrows, Hector's hapless fate,
>   And the sad Conqueror's ills shut up th' afflictive tale.[1]

His visions of Darius and of Xerxes at the Hellespont are exercises in the historical imagination, of a kind which Byron was later to make peculiarly his own.

In relation to Byron's poetical inheritance on the subject of modern Greece, the poems of Carlyle are interesting as having been derived from personal experience of the country. But, in spite of the similarities with what Byron was to write later, I have no reason to believe that the poems of either Polwhele or Carlyle were known to him. In the case of W. R. Wright, however, whose *Horae Ionicae* was written, or at least begun, in 1800–4 and published in 1809, Byron not only knew the work of his predecessor but regarded himself as a

---

[1] pp. 59, 69, 80.

rival. In one of the long notes to the second canto of *Childe Harold's Pilgrimage*, he mentions *Horae Ionicae* as a "beautiful poem" and its author as "a good poet and an able man".[1] Wright was consul-general of the Ionian Isles in the early years of the nineteenth century. He was still there in 1804, when his papers and books were rifled by the French in Zante and all the materials he had collected for a book on the Greek islands were destroyed or removed. His poem, however, seems to have been kept safe; at any rate, Wright declares that a considerable part of his verses in *Horae Ionicae* were "written amidst the scenes which they profess to describe"; the remainder was composed at leisure in England from his recollections. He claims that his poem "faithfully records the train of reflections suggested to his own mind by such historical events or poetical descriptions as more peculiarly relate to the islands of the Ionian Sea".

There was a time (says the poet) when "the sun of freedom" cheered these lovely places:

> Now, sunk in shades of intellectual night,
> Extinct for ever is that golden light:
> Forlorn and wither'd lies the Muse's bow'r;
> For stern oppression blasts each op'ning flow'r.

Genius has gone. But Greece is still a land which inspires a poet:

> Yet in unfading bloom the scene appears,
> All glowing with the pride of distant years;
> And still, by nature and the Muses dress'd,
> Might waken rapture in a poet's breast.

Wright adapts his faded, apostrophic eighteenth-century style tolerably skilfully to the new material:

> Ye isles beyond the Adriatic wave!
> Whose classic shores Ionian waters lave;
> Ye plains of Greece! the Muse's ancient pride,
> Whose rising beauties crown the western tide. . . .

Historical and literary associations and allusions are his principal poetic topics. Corfu ("blest Phaeacia!") is where Nausicaa was greeted by Odysseus; but the old prosperity and glory of Corfu is gone;

[1] *Poetical Works*, ed. E. H. Coleridge, ii, 202.

> nor can my searching eye
> One relic of thy former pomp descry:
> Save, that yon rising bank of olive shows
> Where once the stately theatre arose;
> Thine ancient harbour chok'd with rising sand,
> No footstep marks the solitary strand;
> While finny shoals through desert waters stray,
> And sea-gulls hover o'er their destin'd prey.[1]

This is an interesting description of Palaeopoli. The part played by Corcyra in the Peloponnesian war, and the valiant repulse of the Turk when Corfu was besieged in 1645–50, equally provide material for his ruminations. The poet then begins an imaginary voyage among the islands. He sails to Paxos, where once, in the reign of Tiberius Caesar, was heard the voice crying that Pan was dead, as Plutarch had related[2] and as Milton had remembered:

> The lonely mountains o'er,
> And the resounding shore,
> A voice of weeping heard, and loud lament.

Here the poet looks over towards Suli, where

> The last of ancient Greeks, unknown to fame,
> Her sons preserv'd th' unconquerable flame
> That erst on freedom's sacred altar glow'd.

Then he passes to Leucas (from whose cliff Sappho . . . etc.), to Ithaca (where Ulysses . . . etc.), Cephalonia, Zacynthos, and Cythera, which is an island now noted for other things than the seat of Love:

> Forsaken isle! around thy barren shore
> Wild tempests howl and wintry surges roar.
> Th' Aegean pilot, hence, with cautious heed
> Doubles the cape, and plies with trembling speed
> His westward course; or scuds beneath the land.

The derivation of Wright's style is, of course, unmistakable. But he has been stimulated by his environment, and there is sincerity and affection in his poem. He regrets, like many another who

---

[1] pp. v–vi, 2, 3, 10.
[2] *De Defectu Oraculorum*, xvii. Byron's fragment, *Aristomenes*, may be compared (*Poetical Works*, ed. E. H. Coleridge, iv, 566).

arrives in Greece, that he has sadly neglected his classical studies; he
was one

> whose thriftless hand for many a day
> Had cast the half-form'd classic wreath away.[1]

Byron had already written in commendation of Wright's *Horae
Ionicae* in *English Bards, and Scotch Reviewers* (1809), as "a very
beautiful poem, just published"; this was before Byron went to
Greece; and we can see in the jejune couplets of his satire something
of his ambition to rival Wright in the same field:

> Blest is the man who dares approach the bower
> Where dwelt the muses at their natal hour;
> Whose steps have pressed, whose eye has marked afar,
> The clime that nursed the sons of song and war,
> The scenes which Glory still must hover o'er,
> Her place of birth, her own Achaian shore.
> But doubly blest is he whose heart expands
> With hallowed feelings for those classic lands;
> Who rends the veil of ages long gone by,
> And views their remnants with a poet's eye!
> WRIGHT! T'was thy happy lot at once to view
> Those shores of glory, and to sing them too;
> And sure no common Muse inspired thy pen
> To hail the land of Gods and Godlike men.[2]

These lines are prophetic. Byron was soon to drive all competitors
from the field; so that the world, forgetting his dozen puny predecessors, supposes that he discovered modern Greece for English
poetry.

Strange to relate, this Byronic distinction might have fallen to
Coleridge. For it is one of the curiosities of Coleridge's biography
that he nearly accompanied the great topographer Leake from Malta
to the Levant. In his dispatch dated January 2nd 1805 to the
Secretary of State, the Governor of Malta, referring to a commission
which had been issued by him to Captain Leake, R.A.,[3] to proceed
to the Black Sea to buy oxen, says that he takes with him "a Mr.
Coleridge". Southey wrote to a friend in February of that year that
Coleridge "is going with Capt. ——— into Greece, and up the Black
Sea to purchase corn of the Government. Odd, but pleasant enough,
—if he would but learn to be contented in that state of life into which

---

[1] *Horae Ionicae*, pp. 3, 24, 49–50.　　[2] ll. 867–80.　　[3] See p. 207 above.

it has pleased God to call him."[1] But the sudden death of the Public Secretary at Malta gave Coleridge a temporary post of more importance, and prevented his excursion into Greece in the company of the greatest topographer of the age. Any regrets we may feel that Coleridge did not enjoy this experience must be modified by our doubts whether he would have profited by it. For, did he not declare his apathy to topographical sentiment? "I believe I should walk over the plain of Marathon without taking more interest in it than in any other plain of similar features."[2] Of course, Coleridge was on this occasion provoked by his recollection of Dr. Johnson's remark in 1773 that a man is little to be envied whose patriotism would not gain force as he stood on the plain of Marathon.[3] But his professed insensibility to the romantic appeal of Greece does not encourage us to speculate about Coleridge as a poet of philhellenism.

The growing interest in Greece, and the developing awareness of its hopes and sorrows, were reflected in the prize poems at the Universities. At Cambridge in 1800 Francis Wrangham, later to be a scholar of distinction, won a prize for his poem on *The Holy Land*; thither his muse makes her aerial flight touching down briefly in Greece:

> Across th'Ionian next, by Delphi's steep,
> The forked mount, and fam'd Castalia's spring
> To Athens, scene of all her infant joys,
> Anxious she speeds. But there nor pictur'd porch
> Glowing with various life, nor virgin's fane,
> Meets her sad eye. By Rome's fell lightning scar'd
> With partial blast, at Othman's withering touch
> Th'Athenian amaranth died; the servile brow
> No chaplet binds.

His general lament for Greece, however, is made more poignant by the Cambridge poet's grief for Tweddell.

> Yet other sorrow's wound,
> With keener pang, the Muse's gentle breast.
> There in his early bloom, 'mid classic dust
> Once warm with grace and genius like his own,
> Her favorite sleeps; whom far from Granta's bowers
> To Attic fields the thirst of learning drew,
> Studious to cull the wise, the fair, and good.

---

[1] *Life and Correspondence of the late Robert Southey* (6 vols., 1850), ii, 315.
[2] *Table Talk*, August 4th 1833.   [3] See p. 249 above.

He could have taught the echoes of old Greece
(Silent since Freedom fled) their ancient strains
Of liberty and virtue, to his soul
Strains most congenial! But high heaven forbade.
Rest youth belov'd. . . .[1]

Oxford preferred rhymed couplets to blank verse; and it is notable that the subjects of the prize-poems at Oxford, as well as the poems themselves, become noticeably more Hellenic in the early years of the nineteenth century. In 1806 the subject was "A Recommendation of the study of the Remains of Ancient Grecian and Roman Architecture, Sculpture, and Painting"; and the successful competitor, John Wilson (later to be celebrated under his pseudonym "Christopher North"), bade slumbering Genius

> turn the eye, where, spurning time's controul,
> Art stamps on stone the triumphs of the soul:
> With trembling awe survey each hallow'd fane
> Ennobling Greece mid Desolation's reign.[2]

In 1811 the subject proposed was the *Parthenon*; and the winner, Richard Burdon (otherwise, I believe, unknown to fame), produced some meditative and descriptive lines on the building whose

> beauty still appears
> Amid the wreck of thy forgotten years.
> Though rude barbarian mosques profane thy site,
> And cells unveil'd now mingle with the light.

The sculptures are movingly described as if they were still in their positions, although by this time they had been removed by Elgin and were being displayed in Park Lane. No mention is made of these depredations; but

> Such Fancy paints thee, Parthenon, and pours
> Meridian splendor on thy waning hours.

In 1815 Samuel Rickards of Oriel College (he later became a divine of some distinction) won his prize with some verses on the *Temple of Theseus*.

---

[1] Text from *The Remains of the late John Tweddell* (1815), pp. 389–90.
[2] *Oxford Prize Poems: being a collection of such English Poems as have at various times obtained prizes in the University of Oxford*, fifth edition, Oxford, 1816, pp. 105–6.

Amid the wrecks of age, o'er wasted lands,
Fix'd as his fame, the Hero's Temple stands:
Though many a pile, wide mould'ring on the plain,
Mark the dread scene of Desolation's reign;
Though desert fields, and rifted towers declare
The shocks of nature, or the waste of war;
Yet rear'd in monarch state that fane appears
Proud o'er the lapse of twice ten hundred years,
And seems to live an emblem to the brave,
How Time reveres the Patriot Hero's grave.

Rickards, too, takes the opportunity of making a pathetic allusion to the death of Tweddell, buried in the Theseum:

Such the fair pile, where, shrin'd in holy cell,
The slumb'ring ashes of the mighty dwell,
Where Tweddell, youthful shade, to classic rest
Sinks, like a wearied child, on Science' breast,
And in the sacred scenes he lov'd to roam,
Finds the last honors of a kindred home,
While Muses, mourning whom they could not save,
Still guard his fame; for Athens is his grave.[1]

It becomes even more clear that Byron was writing his impressions of Greece in a well-established literary genre when we read a curious poem entitled *A Letter from Athens, addressed to a Friend in England*, which appeared anonymously in 1812. This consists of more than eight hundred lines, in rhymed couplets of the manner of Goldsmith, and it was printed as a substantial quarto with notes and disquisitions very much in the manner of *Childe Harold's Pilgrimage*. The author was Charles Kelsall, who was responsible for a few other minor works of scholarship and travel; and in his "Advertisement" to the poem he says that "the following lines were partly composed abroad to break the taedium of solitary travel". Like the other poets who were meditating poems on the attractions and desperations of Greece —including Byron himself—he brought back with him from his travels a half-completed manuscript to be augmented and polished at leisure in England.

Charles Kelsall supposes that his poem will be useful to travellers in Greece, who are so numerous nowadays.

An excursion to Athens has become of late so much the object of those who have a relish for antiquities, or classical recollections,

[1] *Op. cit.*, pp. 173, 176, 198–200.

that though the Author is sensible of the insufficiency of his poetical powers, he cannot help flattering himself with the hope of his composition proving an acceptable companion to those who purpose visiting that interesting city.

The poet conducts his reader on a tour of the famous places in Athens, expressing the appropriate emotions each time he places his foot on some history.

> For wheresoe'er my devious footsteps tread,
> Some sage has reason'd, or some patriot bled,
> Some bard has here been crown'd with deathless bays,
> Some statesman there has won his country's praise.

As he contemplates the present condition of Athens his mind vacillates between sympathy and censoriousness.

> Degen'rate Athens! in my breast, by turns,
> Compassion stirs, and indignation burns,
> When I thy sons behold by Turks enslav'd,
> The sons of those who erst all Persia brav'd,
> Rul'd by the very dregs of human kind,
> In mien disfigur'd, and debas'd in mind.

He bitterly upbraids the servile subjects of the Turks, and expostulates:

> Hide from my sight that slave in fetters bound,
> Close to the dwelling where great Phocion own'd.

Marathon ought still to be an inspiration to the men of Greece and to encourage them to the performance of great deeds:

> Cannot the sight of Marathon's famed plain
> Stir thy great efforts, Attica, again?
> Nor patriotic zeal, nor thirst of praise,
> Kindle that flame which blaz'd in ancient days?

The poet now rises to the climax of his philhellenic sentiment. It is the duty of Britain to give back liberty to Greece:

> Rise, Britain, rise! (for to thy sons is giv'n
> That high prerogative of fav'ring Heav'n,
> To rescue nations from the tyrant's lust,
> To scourge the guilty, and avenge the just,)
> Pour forth thy dauntless legions, and release

The fetter'd Hellespont—ah! rescue Greece!—
Through thee, let Actè's sons assert their cause,
And own no other but their Solon's laws.
Let youths from Athens borrow as of yore
The patriot's ardour, and the sage's lore. . . .[1]

Charles Kelsall cannot be described as a shrewd observer of the modern Greek situation; but he was certainly an emphatic philhellene of the literary kind.

But of all the philhellenic poets of the first two decades of the nineteenth century, the one who was most cruelly crushed out of poetical existence by the reputation of Byron was William Haygarth. His substantial and dignified work, *Greece, a Poem, in Three Parts; with Notes, Classical Illustrations, and Sketches of the Scenery*, was (as the author declares in his preface) "designed in the country which it attempts to delineate and a part of it was written at Athens in the middle of 1811". It was published, a splendid quarto, in 1814—too late; for the sun of Byron was already above the horizon.

Very little seems to be known about Haygarth.[2] But I can bring him to life for a moment by identifying him with an anonymous victim of Fanny Burney's amusing pen. In a letter of June 1817, she writes to her husband (General d'Arblay):

> . . . we jointly spent an evening with Miss Maltby to meet the two Mrs. Bowdlers and a young man who is celebrated for a poem called "Greece", which he has published; and for "Letters to his Friends *from* Greece", which are *un*published, but highly esteemed. He added, however, nothing to the entertainment of the evening, for he avoids making a parade of his travels and knowledge, by a contrary extreme; that of a reserve that leads him only to speak when spoken to, and only to answer concisely to the propositions presented to him; so that all conversation drops with his first answer, or is to be renewed at the expense of a fresh interrogatory.[3]

The poem *Greece* was his only work to be published; but four of his drawings (comprising a panoramic view of Athens from the Museion

---

[1] pp. 5, 7, 29, 33, 37.

[2] Neither the *Dictionary of National Biography* nor the *Cambridge Bibliography of English Literature* condescends to him. Borst, in his *Lord Byron's First Pilgrimage*, knows his dates, his school and his college (p. 135 footnote); and Larrabee in *English Bards and Grecian Marbles* is aware of his existence.

[3] *Diary and Letters of Madame d'Arblay*, ed. Austin Dobson, 6 vols. (1905), vi, 309. Presumably she could not remember his name.

hill) were engraved, with descriptive notes, in Robert Walpole's *Memoirs relating to European and Asiatic Turkey* (1817).[1] He appears to have been on good terms with Byron when they were in Greece together in 1811, and so he is occasionally mentioned in Byron's letters.

Haygarth says, "I have ventured to predict in poetry what I certainly should not be so hardy as to foretell in prose—the moral regeneration of Greece."[2] Yet in spite of this disclaimer, Haygarth clearly reveals himself as one of the enthusiasts. The Spirits of the Great Hellenes of the past will inspire the modern Greeks if only these descendants can become worthy of their glorious ancestry:

> When Hellas dares be free, when the deep sigh,
> Heaving her breast, proclaims that she can feel
> A wish to emulate your glorious deeds;
> When her dark eye returns the glance of scorn
> On her oppressor—when her mind, long chill'd
> And palsied by the icy grasp of vice,
> Revives again in virtue's spring, and bears
> The bloom of fancy and of reason; then
> Your spirits shall awake and save her sons.[3]

In Athens,
> near thy fanes
> And marble monuments the peasant's hut
> Rears its low roof in bitter mockery
> Of faded splendour.

But although it is difficult, says the poet, to be happy in Greece (for who can enjoy the beauty of nature and the splendid relics of antiquity while he is conscious of the misery in which the present inhabitants exist?), yet no one can live there without being convinced that the spirit of the place survives.

> Genius of Greece! thou livest, though thy domes
> Are fallen; here, in this thy lov'd abode,
> Thine Athens, as I breathe the clear pure air
> Which thou hast breath'd, climb the dark mountains' side
> Which thou hast trod, or in the temple's porch
> Pause on the sculptur'd beauties which thine eye
> Has often view'd delighted, I confess
> Thy nearer influence.

[1] p. 550 sqq. (2nd edition, 1818).   [2] *Greece, a Poem*, p. 276.   [3] I, 803-11.

But what is to be made of the contemporary Athenians? The soul of a true-born Briton is nauseated by their ignominy, their obsequiousness, their vanity:

> And lo! he comes, the modern son of Greece,
> The shame of Athens; mark him how he bears
> A look o'eraw'd and moulded to the stamp
> Of servitude. The ready smile, the shrug
> Submissive, the low cringing bow, which waits
> Th' imperious order, and the supple knee,
> Proclaim his state degen'rate: pliant still
> And crouching for his gain, whether in vest
> Of flowing purple, and with orange zone,
> And saffron sandal, and a coif of fur,
> He apes the Archon's state.[1]

The poet would have little pleasure, too, in recalling the glories of the Spartans of old, were it not that

>   still their spirit walks the earth,
> Their martial shouts are heard from Maina's rocks,
> Where, still unconquer'd, thousands rally round
> The spear of Grecian Freedom. Hardy race,
> How wild the dauntless glances of your eye
> Midst slav'ry's tears; how sweet your war-notes swell
> Upon the ear, long us'd to slav'ry's moan!
> Sparta's true progeny!

The plight of Corinth reduces this poet to tears:

> Hard is his heart, O Corinth! who beholds
> Thee bow'd to dust, nor sheds one pitying tear.

But, as well as shedding tears, Haygarth forsees that Corinth is likely to be a rallying-point for the liberators of Greece. The great siege of 1715 was not forgotten (Byron was soon to remind everybody of it, when *The Siege of Corinth, a Poem* was published in 1816). Moreover, Haygarth informs us, a party of British engineers had recently made a careful survey of the Isthmus to determine the practicability of its defence. Corinth, the poetical prophet exclaims, will soon again have a part to play.

[1] II, 16–19, 50–7, 222–32.

And yet thou art not cast for ever down;
Thro' the dark night of time the Muse beholds
Thy glory's second morn; thy lofty rock
Gilded by liberty's returning day,
Shall be the point to which awak'ning Greece
Shall turn her anxious eye; upon thy shores
Battle shall wave her banners, and with shouts
Of martial preparation call thy sons
To burst their chains, and meet the foe in arms.

Whatever the faults of Greece may have been, her centuries of
suffering have purged her from the guilt of the past:

Thou hast aton'd,
By a long age of agony and grief,
For all thy former vices, and the tears
Pour'd down thy bosom, in the bitter hour
Of thy captivity have wash'd the stains
Of guilt which sullied thy historic page.

Yes, Greece shall be free. Who can doubt it? for the manly forms
of the best of her sons still

Attest the progeny of those who bled
At Marathon.

Who can listen to Rhegas's great ode "calling on Sparta's children
to be free" without believing in the future of Greece? And new
poets (abandoning, of course, the "barb'rous jar of gingling dis-
sonance" characteristic of modern Greek songs) will arise to sing
the happiness of regenerated Hellas. But what part shall Britain,
the home of liberty, play in the regeneration of Greece? The poet
hopes that diplomatic alliances between England and the barbarous
Turk will count for nothing against the overwhelming claims of
Greece for sympathy and assistance. British generals and volunteers,
surely, will be the right persons to direct the revolutionary struggle
by the Greeks against their cruel and vile oppressors. May Britain
respond to the appeal and be worthy of it!

And O my country! let thy voice be heard
Amidst the din of battle, like the cry
Of the wild eagle in the tempest's roar;
When Hellas rises to assert her rights,

Be not far from her: let thy chieftains sage
Direct the onset, and thy hardy sons
Be foremost in the fight which Britons love,
The fight for liberty. When tortur'd Greece
Raises her supplicating eyes to thee,
Turn not away, nor let thy virtuous name,
Pledg'd to a faithless horde of infidels
Be made the safeguard of her tyrants.

With prophetic fervour, the poet exclaims:

Yes, wretched Greece! beneath my country's shield
Thou still mayst vanquish and be free again.[1]

With his *Greece* Haygarth printed a shorter poem entitled *Cassandra*,
which is a pindaric ode in the prophetic style which had already been
used by Carlyle in his lines *Written on the Banks of the Bosphorus*.[2]
The genre derives from Gray's *Bard*, incorporating material from
Aeschylus's *Agamemnon* and Lycophron's *Cassandra*. Haygarth can,
of course, continue the prophetess's visions into later history than
could Lycophron, and therefore allows her to omit the tedious events
between the death of Agamemnon and the fall of Constantinople.
Vengeance will one day be exacted for the destruction of Troy,

Land of my fathers, cradle of the brave,
Pearl of the Eastern billow, beauty's gem,
Refulgent set in Asia's diadem. . . .

Cassandra foretells that Agamemnon will be murdered and that
Mahomet II will crush Greece. She apostrophizes the Ottomans,

Hail! Destroyers of this land
Ilion's stern avengers hail![3]

It must have been nearly two centuries since any writer thought of
the Turks as the avengers of the Trojans.[4] But this is consistent
with Haygarth's sense of the unity of Greek history. The battle of
Marathon, he says, was the most important event in the history of
the world; "Had Greece been overwhelmed by the host of barbarians
which then assailed her, she would have been erased from the list

[1] III, 524-31, 626-7, 646-54, 706-11, 723-4, 662-73, 703-4.
[2] See p. 273 above.   [3] *Greece, a Poem*, pp. 229-30, 304.
[4] See p. 8 above.

of nations. . . . The day of Grecian slavery would in short have been accelerated above two thousand years; and before she had acted her great part on the theatre of the world, she would have sunk to her present abject condition—the province of an Eastern empire."[1] William Haygarth disappears into oblivion and died young.   But he lived until 1825, and we may be permitted to hope that he followed with interest the news of the Greek Revolution, the first exploits of the British and American philhellenes, and the career of his friend Byron.

Amid these poetical philhellenes, the authoress of the first novel set in Athens may intrude, especially as her work was well known to Byron. Miss Sydney Owenson (later Lady Morgan) followed her success *The Wild Irish Girl* with a four-volume romance *Woman: or, Ida of Athens* in 1809. Through all this gushing story there is expressed a profound, or at least unquestioned, faith in the rights of the Greek people and in their future liberation. Although she had no personal knowledge of Greece or the Greeks, she took the trouble to learn all she could from travel-books; and she lays on the local colour with a thick brush. In her notes she quotes, as authorities for her descriptions and opinions, the travellers Spon, Lady Mary Wortley Montagu, Guys, the Baron de Tott, Sonnini, Olivier, Choiseul-Gouffier, the art-historian Winckelmann and the ancient historian John Gillies.[2] Above all, she has faith in woman, natural woman; and in her preface she justifies her choice of a maid of Athens in modern times as her heroine:

> According to the testimony of all modern travellers, the complexional character of the Greek women is now, as anciently, highly favourable to that poetic idea of female fascination so bewitching to the fancy, and to that moral view of female influence so gracious to the mind. But that nice power of development which would justify the intentions of nature in their favour, is denied them by the oppression of the government under which they live, and the ignorance of those with whom they associate. And many a fair Leontium, and many a charming Aspasia, may still exist in Athens, unconscious of the latent powers of their own ardent minds. . . .

[1] *Greece, a Poem*, p. 241.
[2] Guillaume Antoine Olivier, *Voyage dans l'Empire Othoman, l'Egypte, et la Perse* (3 tom., Paris 1801, 1804, 1807). An English translation began to appear in 1801. Olivier travelled mostly in 1793, and his account of parts of Greece is in volume i and the last few pages of volume iii. John Gillies produced *The History of Ancient Greece* (2 vols., 1786), a large work which had some reputation being awarded several reprints, and translations into French and German; it was reasonably well-informed, but I find hardly any allusion to contemporary Greece.

This is not intended to be improper. Her Ida of Athens is a young lady of the highest moral character, as well as of the most exquisite refinement and sensibility.

Yet it cannot be doubted that Sydney Owenson exercised sound judgment in selecting modern Greece as an appropriate environment for her romance. The reasons she offers in her preface read like a justification of the Levantine fictions with which Byron, a few years later, was to capture the reading public:

> the nation which mourns over its sufferings, without the power to re-dress its wrongs, which faintly struggles in an interval of hope against the oppression which would impose a permanent despair, must even-tually give rise to a romance of incident, to a boldness of character, and a vicissitude of event, which bestows on the wildest fiction of the novelist the sanction of probability and the authority of fact.

Byron in a note to the second canto of *Childe Harold's Pilgrimage* made gentle fun of Miss Owenson and her heroine Ida, and pointed out the inaccuracies in the narrative.[1] But in this novel (which was in print before Byron reached Greece) one of the prominent char-acters, who is enamoured of Ida with not altogether honourable intentions, is a certain English traveller in Athens, blasé, sophisti-cated, susceptible, aristocratic. By a curious coincidence his name is Lord B——.

Byron, when he set out on his travels in 1809, like many other young men about that time and during the previous twenty years, followed the sea-route to Constantinople instead of the path to Rome which had been so common in the eighteenth century. Anyone who has read through the lively letters which Byron wrote during those two years of travel will be in no doubt that the lands of the Levant provided a most exciting episode in Byron's life, the experience which made him a poet. When he looked back, Byron thought that, from his early years, his interests had gravitated to the Near East; certainly he was, I believe, excellently prepared to travel in the Levant. For, the books which I have most frequently quoted were the boyhood and manhood reading of Byron. He himself wrote, "Knolles, Cantemir, De Tott, Lady M. W. Montagu, Hawkins's translation from Mignot's History of the Turks,[2] the Arabian Nights—all travels or histories, or books upon the East, I could

---

[1] *Poetical Works*, ed. E. H. Coleridge, ii, 187–8.
[2] Vincent Mignot's *Histoire de l'Empire Ottoman* (Paris, 1771) was translated as *The History of the Turkish or Ottoman Empire from its foundation in 1300 to the peace of Belgrade in 1740* by A. Hawkins (4 vols., Exeter, 1787). It seems to me to be an uninspired compilation, justly forgotten.

meet with, I had read, as well as Ricaut, before I was *ten years old*".[1]
He read and formed opinions on the merits of most of the champions,
prophets and sceptics of the previous few decades: Cornelius de
Pauw, Savary, Eton, Thornton, Miss Owenson, Edward Clarke,
de Tott, W. R. Wright, Gell, Leake, Robert Walpole, and the rest
of the names that have filled my pages. Byron could not compare in
classical erudition with several of his contemporaries in Greece;
but few of them were so well equipped by a knowledge of recent
history of the Levant. Byron knew the charm of being in places
celebrated by ancient history and poetry, without being fussily
engaged in identifying everything and wasting his energies and
impressions upon anxious interpretations of ancient texts and elucidations of geography and topography. In many of his letters Byron
wrote flippantly about his own activities in Greece; but it is clear
that he took considerable trouble to increase his knowledge, learning
the modern language and canvassing the contemporary state of
culture of the Greeks. He described Greece as "a country replete
with the *brightest* and *darkest*, but always most *lively* colours of my
memory";[2] and this intensity of his reactions to the physical appearance of Greece is constantly exemplified in his poetry:

> Fair clime! where every season smiles
> Benignant o'er those blessèd isles,
> Which, seen from far Colonna's height,
> Make glad the heart that hails the sight,
> And lend to loneliness delight.[3]

Byron could write as sarcastically as any miso-hellene about the
contemporary inhabitants of Greece; and he was as familiar as other
travellers with the difficulties, inconveniences and even dangers,
which beset the Frank. And yet . . .

> And yet how lovely in thine age of woe,
> Land of lost Gods and godlike men art thou!
> Thy vales of evergreen, thy hills of snow,
> Proclaim thee Nature's varied favourite now:
> Thy fanes, thy temples to thy surface bow,
> Commingling slowly with heroic earth,
> Broke by the share of every rustic plough.

The imagination of every visitor to Greece was stimulated by the
memory of antique glory:

[1] Written in the margin of his copy of Isaac D'Israeli's *Essay on the Literary
Character* (*Byron's Works* (1837), p. 62).

[2] Diary, December 5, 1813 (*Letters and Journals*, ed. Prothero, ii, 361–2).

[3] *The Giaour* (7–11).

Where'er we tread 'tis haunted, holy ground;
No earth of thine is lost in vulgar mould,
But one vast realm of Wonder spreads around,
And all the Muse's tales seem truly told,
Till the sense aches with gazing to behold
The scenes our earliest dreams have dwelt upon.[1]

Because of his intense receptiveness to what he saw in Greece, Byron provided a new reality for much of the old-fashioned poetic diction of a classicizing kind, by giving it a local habitation and a name in the Greek environment with which he was familiar. *Childe Harold's Pilgrimage* opens with an invocation to the Muse, in the traditional manner—an appeal to her to aid her poet from Parnassus and to inspire him from her fountain of Castalia. But Byron immediately makes this old-fashioned jargon more effective by giving it, in the very first stanza, a context in the experience of the sentimental traveller in Greece:

> Yet there I've wander'd by thy vaunted rill;
> Yes! sigh'd o'er Delphi's long deserted shrine,
> Where, save that feeble fountain, all is still.

The trite items of schoolboy learning, and the battered ornaments of schoolboy verse-making were revivified, when they had become hopelessly trivial even to the schoolmasters. The memory of Coleridge's James Bowyer at Christ's Hospital is irresistible: "Lute, harp, and lyre, muse, muses, and inspirations, Pegasus, Parnassus, and Hippocrene, were all an abomination to him. In fancy I can almost hear him now, exclaiming, '*Harp? Harp? Lyre? Pen and ink, boy, you mean! Muse, boy, muse? Your Nurse's daughter you mean! Pierian spring? Oh, aye! the cloister-pump, I suppose!*'"[2] But Byron writes avowedly and deliberately in a manner which makes emotive use of these trite recollections. All the rant about Parnassus may be old stuff. But, listen, reader, I have been there; in fact, I am writing this stanza, I assure you, in full view of the mountain in December 1809:

> Oh, thou Parnassus! whom I now survey,
> Not in the phrensy of a dreamer's eye,
> Not in the fabled landscape of a lay,
> But soaring snow-clad through thy native sky,
> In the wild pomp of mountain-majesty!
> What marvel if I thus essay to sing?

---

[1] *Childe Harold's Pilgrimage*, II, lxxxv, lxxxviii.
[2] *Biographia Literaria*, Chap. i (ed. J. Shawcross, Oxford, 1907, i, 5).

The full emotional effect is extracted from the contemplation of
Parnassus, so much lauded by the poets, so rarely seen by them, and
still so beautiful:

> When I recount thy worshippers of yore
> I tremble, and can only bend the knee;
> Nor raise my voice, nor vainly dare to soar,
> But gaze beneath thy cloudy canopy
> In silent joy to think at last I look on Thee![1]

In later years, Walter Scott, writing rather regretfully, contrasted
his own claims to poetical success with those of his formidable rival,
when he published *Rokeby* in the same year (1812) as that which saw
the first two cantos of *Childe Harold's Pilgrimage*: "Lord Byron was
also a traveller, a man whose ideas were fired by having seen, in
distant scenes of difficulty and danger, the places whose very names
are recorded in our bosoms as the shrines of ancient poetry."[2] This,
as Scott knew, was Byron's great advantage at that time. No Northern
mythology or topography or history could make such a strong appeal
to the imagination of an educated reader. Byron wrote his poems
about "the scenes our earliest dreams have dwelt upon". But he was
following in the footsteps of scores of other Englishmen in Greece,
including at least a dozen minor poets. His links with the many
writers of the preceding centuries who gave their opinions, and
recounted their emotions, about Greece, were obviously considerable,
as he himself acknowledged. But Byron could express these opinions
and emotions with an intensity hitherto unknown.

> Cold is the heart, fair Greece! that looks on Thee
> Nor feels as Lovers o'er the dust they loved. . . .

It is superbly done; the old attitudes are suddenly revivified; the
eighteenth-century images are translated into a style with a bravura
that captured Europe.

> 'Tis Greece, but living Greece no more!
> So coldly sweet, so deadly fair,
> We start, for Soul is wanting there. . . .[3]

We know from the discrepancies between the opinions Byron
expressed in his letters, in his poems, and in the notes on his poems,

[1] *Childe Harold's Pilgrimage*, I, lx, lxi.
[2] Introduction to the 1830 edition of *Rokeby*.
[3] *Childe Harold's Pilgrimage*, II, xv; *The Giaour*, 91–3.

that he had some difficulty in making up his mind about the merits of
the modern Greeks and their prospects of freedom. But whatever
the fluctuations in his opinions may have been, his attitude was never
that of the scholar who casually notes the disappearance of a nation
from the world and exalts the past by spurning the present. For
Byron, the past glories should be the stimulus to achievement among
the Greeks now.

> Fair Greece! sad relic of departed worth!
> Immortal, though no more; though fallen, great!
> Who now shall lead thy scatter'd children forth,
> And long accustom'd bondage uncreate?

To answer this his mind inevitably turns to the old comparisons.
The heroes of Thermopylae did not act thus.

> Oh! who that gallant spirit shall resume,
> Leap from Eurotas' banks, and call thee from the tomb?

Those heroes of antiquity who knew the spirit of freedom, what
would they think now, if they could see the plight of Greece? What
would Thrasybulus, with his little band at Phyle?

> Not thirty tyrants now enforce the chain,
> But every carle can lord it o'er thy land;
> Nor rise thy sons, but idly rail in vain,
> Trembling beneath the scourge of Turkish hand,
> From birth to death enslaved; in word, in deed, unmanned.

> In all save form along, how chang'd! and who
> That marks the fire still sparkling in each eye,
> Who but would deem their bosoms burned anew,
> With thy unquenchéd beam, lost Liberty!
> And many dream withal the hour is nigh
> That gives them back their fathers' heritage:
> For foreign arms and aid they fondly sigh,
> Nor solely dare encounter hostile rage,
> Or tear their name defiled from Slavery's mournful page.

> Hereditary bondsmen! know ye not
> *Who* would be free *themselves* must strike the blow?
> By their right arms the conquest must be wrought?
> Will Gaul or Muscovite redress ye? no!

True—they may lay your proud despoilers low,
But not for you will Freedom's Altars flame.
Shades of the Helots! triumph o'er your foe!
Greece! change thy lords, thy state is still the same;
Thy glorious day is o'er, but not thine years of shame.[1]

It was *Childe Harold's Pilgrimage* which, read throughout Europe, made Byron the poetic champion of modern Greece; and the passages of similar import in the "Tales" that followed *Childe Harold* only emphasized his philhellenism, and quite cancelled out any jeers and sneers about Greece and the Greeks that the author permitted himself in private. Who could not respond to these stirring strains?

Clime of the unforgotten brave!
Whose land from plain to mountain-cave
Was Freedom's home or Glory's grave!
Shrine of the mighty! can it be,
That this is all remains of thee?
Approach, thou craven crouching slave:
    Say, is not this Thermopylae?
These waters blue that round you lave,—
    Oh servile offspring of the free—
Pronounce what sea, what shore is this?
The gulf, the rock of Salamis!
These scenes, their story not unknown,
Arise, and make again your own. . . .[2]

Greece was the mother of Freedom; but does not Freedom still hope for something from the Greece of our days?

Oh! still her step at moments falters
O'er withered fields, and ruined altars,
And fain would wake, in souls too broken,
By pointing to each glorious token:
But vain her voice, till better days
Dawn in those yet remembered rays,
Which shone upon the Persian flying,
And saw the Spartan smile in dying.[3]

All the old anecdotes about the continuity of national consciousness among the Greeks have fed Byron's poetry—the Greek pilot who

---

[1] *Childe Harold's Pilgrimage*, II, lxxiii, lxxiv–lxxvi.
[2] *The Giaour*, 103–15.   [3] *The Siege of Corinth*, xiv (382–9).

pointed to the harbour where his countrymen berthed their ships at the siege of Troy; the Maniots of Spartan lineage who related how "we conquered Messenia"; the Athenian who explained that the air of Attica had always given vivacity to his countrymen. Byron himself gives a moving account of the influence of his surroundings upon a modern Greek, who, like Alp in *The Siege of Corinth*, is sensitive to the history of the nation; the spirits of the great figures of the past live on:

> The very gale their names seemed sighing;
> The waters murmured of their name;
> The woods are peopled with their fame;
> The silent pillar, lone and grey,
> Claimed kindred with their sacred clay;
> Their spirits wrapped the dusky mountain,
> Their memory sparkled o'er the fountain;
> The meanest rill, the mightiest river
> Rolled mingling with their fame for ever.
> Despite of every yoke she bears,
> That land is Glory's still and theirs!
> 'Tis still a watch-word to the earth:
> When man would do a deed of worth
> He points to Greece, and turns to tread,
> So sanctioned, on the tyrant's head:
> He looks to her, and rushes on
> Where life is lost, or Freedom won.[1]

The sudden growth of Byron's reputation as a poet among his contemporaries had, no doubt, a variety of causes. But as the poet of modern Greece one important source of his success was the fact that the feelings he described, and aroused, were authentic. We need have no doubt about that, when we have observed English writers during the preceding two or three centuries attempting to attain a lucid description of the emotions which a classically educated person nourished in Greece. The land which had gained a stronger and stronger romantic appeal during the eighteenth century was present in Byron's poetry amid all its sorrows and humiliations, never forgetting the splendours and glories of its past, and therefore making memory, indignation, and sympathy more poignant. The natural scene in Greece is, in itself, enough to stimulate any writer, as it had done many times before Byron and as it will doubtless continue to do. But Greece was always more than scenery; for it was peopled in the

[1] *Op. cit.*, xv (407–23).

imagination with forms which are derived from poetry and mythology and history, familiar to everyone. Byron's poetry of Greece was based upon the moving comparison between what Greece then was, and what Greece had been and always will remain in the imagination. Shelley knew this comparison; but Byron had seen it and felt it.

> Greece and her foundations are
> Built below the tide of war
> Based on the crystalline sea
> Of thought and its eternity.
> Her citizens, imperial spirits,
>   Rule the present from the past,
> On all this world of men inherits
>   Their seal is set.[1]

That was what Shelley wrote. But in Byron's poetry the Greece of the imagination and the Greece of observation were one; and this unity of vision was the culmination of three centuries' increasing awareness. Byron appeared just in time, a few years before the Revolution. There was not likely to be another English poet of Greece; at least, not of that kind. For the Revolution inevitably gave Greece the ambition to be a modern nation, educated, proud, perplexed, bankrupt. The antiquities remained; they were tidied up, and a charge was made for admission. But Greece and the Greek people ceased themselves to be antique ruins where the sentimental traveller could contemplate the instability of human things, and enjoy the exquisitely painful contrast as he considered, first, the ancient inhabitants (in his fancy), philosophers and heroes; and then, the contemporary Grecians, either crushed into subservience by their harsh and unchristian overlords, or preserving, amid their mountain fastnesses, a sturdy, dangerous and precarious independence. The English poet and traveller in Greece since Byron's time has had quite other things upon which to meditate.

[1] Shelley, *Hellas*, 696–703.

APPENDIX

GEORGE FINLAY'S VIEW OF PHILHELLENISM

In tracing the origins of the philhellenism which finds expression in the poetry of Byron, I have a formidable opponent. For, according to George Finlay, whose account of the existence of the Greek nation from Roman times to his own remains a classic of historical writing, philhellenism had practically no history, or, at least, a very brief one. "For three centuries", he wrote, "the position of the Greek race was one of hopeless degradation. Its connection with the old pagan Hellenes was repudiated by themselves and forgotten by other nations. . . . The modern identification of the Christian Greeks with the pagan Hellenes is the growth of the new series of ideas disseminated by the French Revolution." And later Finlay is still more emphatic:

> Before the commencement of the present century, no modern Greek would have boasted of any ancestral connection with the pagan Hellenes, any more than he would yet think of pretending to a Pelasgic, Dorian, Ionian, or Achaian pedigree.[1]

However, Finlay was wrong; his statement is disproved by numerous quotations throughout my book. The identification of the Christian Greeks with the pagan Hellenes began long before the beginning of the nineteenth century, and was expressed not only throughout the eighteenth century, but also in the seventeenth century, and in an unmistakable form already in the sixteenth century. The truth is this: the notion that the Christian inhabitants of Greece were *not* the descendants of the pagan Hellenes would have seemed scarcely credible before the end of the eighteenth century;[2]

---

[1] *A History of Greece from its Conquest by the Romans to the Present Time, B.C. 164–A.D. 1864* (Oxford, 7 vols., 1877, edited by H. F. Tozer), V, 7, 122.

[2] I can however offer, as an eccentricity, a passage from *A History of Greece, from the Accession of Alexander of Macedon, till its final subjection to the Roman Power* (London, 1782) by John Gast, an Irish cleric: "The present Greeks appear to be a mixed race, of whom few, if any, are of the antient Grecian lineage. Most of them have been transplanted into this country from different parts, and at different periods, by those who were attracted by curiosity, or views of gain." Gast continues, however: "it is worthy of remark, that the Greeks of this day, whether from the influence of climate, or from having fallen into an early imitation of the manners, which on their arrival they found here established, bear in several particulars a striking resemblance to the antient inhabitants" (pp. 708–9). John Gast is generally a rather absurd historian; but it must be acknowledged that he is here perspicacious, or has made a lucky guess.

and I can find very little evidence for the existence of such an opinion. (Whether the modern Greeks are or are not, in fact, the descendants of the ancient Hellenes; and whether either statement really makes sense, are questions which are not to my purpose here; I am concerned with opinion about the Greeks.)

Finlay's point of view has a simple explanation. He had given his all for Greece; and he saw his adopted country firstly under the rule of the Bavarian officials and then under its own politicians, feeding its vanity by linking itself with its remote past. Nowhere in the world does the curse of history weigh so heavily upon a nation as it does upon the Greeks; for what country has such a history of splendours and miseries? Finlay wanted the Greeks to accept themselves as a modern nation, thriftily devoting themselves to the economic improvement and stabilization of their country, and forgetting about the heroes of Marathon and the glories of Periclean Athens. He wrote his great *History*, as he wrote much else, in a somewhat jealous and splenetic mood, both as an apologia and as a tract.

The minute study of Finlay's work which has naturally accompanied my writing the present book has filled me with admiration and respect. He fully merits the eulogy of Richard Garnett (in the *Dictionary of National Biography*) as being "a great historian of the type of Polybius, Procopius, and Machiavelli, a man of affairs, who has qualified himself for treating the public transactions by sharing in them, a soldier, a statesman, and an economist". But Finlay is basically unreliable, not in his facts, but in his mood of relating his facts. He is so anxious to crush any sentimental attitude to the Greeks that he sometimes loses a sense of fair play. He is so consistently anti-sentimental that he becomes exaggeratedly cynical. He is so careful to be unromantic himself that he is tempted to believe that the world has always been, and should always be, unromantic. This is especially true of the volume on the history of Greece during the Ottoman and Venetian domination. He scrupulously examines his sources for details that are humiliating to the Greeks. He carefully brings into his narrative, for example, the fact that, during the Venetian campaign in the Morea, the Hanoverian mercenaries, when short of horses to move their artillery, used Greeks. It is just another prick at the inflated self-esteem, the effervescent vanity, of his Greek readers. Did Finlay really believe he could make any impression on that? Go and catch a falling star. . . . Were it not for their vivacious and incorrigible confidence in their own wits, that tormented nation would have disappeared from the world centuries ago.

Finlay as an historian of the Greek cause is, in one respect, rather
similar to Gibbon as an historian of Christianity. The imaginative
result of their narratives is artistically superb but historically misleading. Finlay's *History* is a work of literature, and can never be
really superseded. But Greece needs interpreters other than Finlay,
as (one might say) Christianity needs interpreters other than Gibbon.

I suspect that the literary intensity of Finlay's Greek history has
given it considerable influence among later writers. At any rate,
I notice that subsequent historians have taken Finlay's point of view
for granted. "In 1820", he wrote, "all questions relating to the East
were then beyond the domain of public opinion, and little was known
in England concerning the conditions of the modern Greeks" (vi, 6).
This, as I believe I have proved, is untrue; but it is, at least, more
restrained in its error than the statements of Finlay's followers.
Here, for example, is J. A. R. Marriott, in his standard work *The
Eastern Question* (1924), on the "startling" Greek revolution:

> For more than four hundred years the Greeks, like the Bulgarians
> and the Serbians, had been all but completely submerged under
> the Ottoman flood. To the outside world they had given no sign
> whatever that they retained the consciousness of national identity,
> still less that they cherished the idea of ever again achieving
> national unity. (p. 9.)

There is sufficient refutation of this notion in the pages of this book.
More truthful (in its way) than the testy philhellenism of the dis-
appointed idealist Finlay, is the bland cynicism of the historian of
Turkey:

> The danger that menaced [the Turkish Empire in 1821] sprang
> from Homer. But for the association with great deeds and noble
> words which the very name of Hellas awakens, no sane man
> assuredly would have meddled in the Greek "War of Indepen-
> dence". The impulse which stirred up the insurrection was not
> so much the sublime passion of freedom as the suggestion of
> Russian agents and that delight in noisy excitement which is the
> heritage of the Greek. Whatever the cause, philanthropists,
> scholars, and enthusiasts, in England and France, fancied that in
> the revolutionary movement, which was partly the effect of the
> ground-swell raised in France a quarter of a century before, they
> could trace the echoes of Thermopylae and Marathon; the songs
> of the klephts were sung in the same tongue—somewhat degraded
> —that Sophocles and Aeschylus had spoken; and a general, natural,

and very creditable feeling spread over Western Europe in favour of the oppressed Greeks.[1]

It is necessary to clear away this historical error because it impedes our view of the English poetry which philhellenism evoked, and gives us a false impression of Byron's kind of originality. Thus (to quote a convenient example), Saintsbury, emphasizing the importance to Byron of his Levantine travels, declared that his genius "required something absolutely new, something of which the average Englishman knew nothing, to awake his spirit".[2] If Byron had written remarkable poetry as a result of visiting the Eskimos, this statement might be justified; but regarding his stay in Greece, it is incorrect. Byron's contemporaries knew better.

[1] Stanley Lane-Poole, *Turkey* (1888), p. 345.
[2] Article on Byron in *Chambers' Encyclopaedia* (1923), ii, 608.

A SELECT BIBLIOGRAPHY OF MODERN WORKS

R. A. AUBIN, *Topographical Poetry in XVIII-century England* (New York, 1936).

J. W. BAGGALLY, *The Klephtic Ballads in Relation to Greek History (1715–1821)* (Oxford, 1936).

HENRY BETTENSON (editor), *Documents of the Christian Church* (Oxford, 1943).

DEMETRIUS BIKÉLAS, "Le Philhellénisme en France", in *Revue d'Histoire Diplomatique*, V (Paris, 1891), pp. 346–65.

G. BLANKEN, *Les Grecs de Cargèse (Corse)* (Leyden, 1951), tom. 1 (no more yet published).

W. A. BORST, *Lord Byron's First Pilgrimage* (Yale Studies in English, No. 109 (New Haven, 1948)).

W. C. BROWN, "The Popularity of English Travel Books about the Near East, 1775–1825", *Philological Quarterly*, XV (1936), pp. 70–80.
"Byron and English Interest in the Near East", *Studies in Philology*, XXXIV (1937), pp. 55–64.
"English Travel Books, 1775–1825", *Philological Quarterly*, XVI (1937), pp. 249–71.

STANLEY CASSON, *Greece and Britain* (1943).

S. C. CHEW, *The Crescent and the Rose. Islam and England during the Renaissance* (New York, 1937).

M. L. CLARKE, *Greek Studies in England, 1700–1830* (Cambridge, 1945).

MICHAEL CONSTANTINIDES, *The Greek Orthodox Church in London* (Oxford, 1933).

LIONEL CUST, *History of the Society of Dilettanti* (1914).

DOUGLAS DAKIN, "The Origins of the Greek Revolution of 1821", in *History* (1952), pp. 228–35.

J. A. DOUGLAS, *The Relations of the Anglican Churches with the Eastern Orthodox* (1921).

THEODORE E. DOWLING and EDWIN W. FLETCHER, *Hellenism in England, A Short History of the Greek People in this Country from the earliest times to the present day* (1915).

MORDECAI EPSTEIN, *The Early History of the Levant Company* (1908).

GEORGE FINLAY, *A History of Greece from its Conquest by the Romans to the Present Time, B.C. 146–A.D. 1864*, 7 vols., ed. H. F. Tozer (Oxford, 1877). This incorporates *The History of Greece under Othoman and Venetian Domination* (Edinburgh, 1856), from which edition I generally quote.

D. M. FOERSTER, *Homer in English Criticism. The Historical Approach in the Eighteenth Century* (Yale Studies in English No. 105, New Haven, 1947).

ADRIAN FORTESCUE, *The Orthodox Eastern Church* (1920).

W. R. HAMILTON, *Historical Notices of the Society of Dilettanti* (1855).

JOSEPH VON HAMMER-PURGSTALL, *Histoire de l'Empire Ottoman* (18 vols., Paris, 1835–43).

GASTON ISAMBERT, *L'Indépendance grecque et l'Europe* (Paris, 1900).

NICOLAS JORGA, *Les Voyageurs Français dans l'Orient Européen*, Conferences faites en Sorbonne (Paris, 1928).

E. J. KIMMEL, *Monumenta Fidei Ecclesiae Orientalis* (Jena, 1850).

COMTE DE LABORDE, *Athènes aux XVe, XVIe, et XVIIe Siècles* (2 vols., Paris, 1854).

STANLEY LANE-POOLE, *Turkey* (1888).

S. A. LARRABEE, *English Bards and Grecian Marbles* (New York, 1943).

HARRY LEVIN, *The Broken Column* (Harvard Undergraduate Essays, Cambridge, Mass., 1931).

JEAN LONGNON, "Quatres siècles de philhellénisme français", in *La Revue de France*, I, No. 6 (June 1, 1921), pp. 512–42.

EMILE MALAKIS, *French Travellers in Greece, 1770–1820: An Early Phase of French Philhellenism* (Philadelphia, 1925).

J. A. R. MARRIOTT, *The Eastern Question* (1924).

JOHN MAVROGORDATO, *Modern Greece* (1931).

ADOLF MICHAELIS, *Ancient Marbles in Great Britain*, translated by C. A. M. Fennell (Cambridge, 1882).

WILLIAM MILLER, *Essays in the Latin Orient* (Cambridge, 1921).
    The Turkish Restoration in Greece (1921).
    The English in Athens before 1821 (1926).

J. M. NEALE, *A History of the Holy Eastern Church* (5 vols., 1850–73).

JOHN PEARSON, *A Biographical Sketch of the Chaplains to the Levant Company* (Cambridge, 1883).

VIRGINIA PENN, "Philhellenism in England (1821–1827)", in *The Slavonic Review*, XIV (1935–6), pp. 363–71, 647–60.

W. G. RICE, "Early English Travellers to Greece and the Levant", in *Essays and Studies in English and Comparative Literature*, University of Michigan, X (1933).

E. F. ROBINSON, *The Early History of Coffee-Houses in England* (1893).

H. G. ROSEDALE, *Queen Elizabeth and the Levant Company. A Diplomatic and Literary Episode of the Establishment of our trade with Turkey* (1904).

PHILIP SCHAFF, *The History of the Creeds* (3 vols., 1878).

A. P. STANLEY, *Lectures on the History of the Eastern Church* (1861) (reprinted in "Everyman's Library", 1907).

B. H. STERN, *The Rise of Romantic Hellenism in English Literature, 1732–1786* (Menasha, 1940).

E. H. SUGDEN, *A Topographical Dictionary to the Works of Shakespeare and his Fellow Dramatists*, Publications of the University of Manchester, No. 168 (Manchester, 1925).

H. V. TEMPERLEY, "The foreign Policy of Canning, 1820–1827" in *The Cambridge History of British Foreign Policy, 1783–1919* (Cambridge, 1923).

M. P. TILLEY, *A Dictionary of the Proverbs in England in the Sixteenth and Seventeenth Centuries* (Ann Arbor, University of Michigan Press, 1950).

ROBERTO WEISS, *Humanism in England during the Fifteenth Century* (Blackwell, Oxford, 1941).

GEORGE WILLIAMS, *The Orthodox Church of the East in the Eighteenth Century, being the Correspondence between the Eastern Patriarchs and the Nonjuring Bishops* (Cambridge (printed), 1868).

A. C. WOOD, *A History of the Levant Company* (1935).

INDEX